# A Nerd Girl's Guide to Cinema

## Movie reviews and musings

## by Kelly Cozy

SMITE
PUBLICATIONS

ISBN: 978-0-9910445-4-2

# CONTENTS

# Thanks and Dedication

A special set of thank-yous to all the usual suspects, but especially to all those who enable my love of oddball movies: Erik Hoard, Joseph Finn, Jeremy Koerner, Albert Muller, Bret Nelson, Steve Ryfle, and Matt Sides. Particular thanks to James Reilly, for taking me on at Horrorview.

Much gratitude to Alan Natale at uxartist.info for the fantastic cover.

Dedicated to the memory of E. Gerry Hoard: mentor, minister, good friend, and partner in movie-watching. I know you've got a good balcony seat at the Cinema Paradisio.

# Foreword by James Reilly, Editor of Horrorview

A long while back, in the early days of Horrorview.com, I received a query from a young woman asking if we'd consider adding her decidedly more feminine perspective to what, at the time, was mainly a boy's club known mostly for its contributors' testosterone-fueled rants and an all-consuming obsession with boobies. While I was perfectly content with our internet equivalent of the *Little Rascals'* He-Man Woman Haters Club, I was also quite taken with this young lady's "voice," as while it was definitely feminine, I also found it comfortably conversational, exceptionally witty, and not at all afraid to get down and dirty when it needed to. I knew she'd fit right in and, for nearly a decade now, Kelly Cozy — aka Suicide Blonde — has been one of Horrorview's most loyal and valued contributors.

I always look forward to new reviews from "The Blonde," as they're not only consistently funny and well-written, but they're also like a mini "date night" with the coolest, geekiest chick you ever met. Kelly's got a way of easing you into her reviews that instantly plops you onto the tattered sofa beside her, sipping a Moscow mule and munching popcorn as the opening credits crawl across the screen. A few minutes in, you're either laughing yourself silly as she comes to the realization that nostalgia's a deceptive bitch (as in her review of *Galaxy of Terror*) or watching with your hands over your eyes as she subjects herself to the all-too-real horrors of a film like Pier Pasolini's thoroughly depraved *Salò*. Often amusing and always insightful, Kelly's reviews have garnered her lot of fans, and I'm one of her biggest (both figuratively and literally).

When Kelly asked me to write the foreword to this collection of some of her favorite reviews as well as a metric butt-load of new stuff written especially for those of you holding this book (or tablet, or smart phone, or whatever form of sorcery you kids use to read the written word these days), I was truly humbled and honored. Then I got a little scared, and maybe even a touch selfish. I mean, what if this book's a massive hit? Hell, it certainly deserves to be, but if it is, will she still find time to write for our little ol' site? Will she still invite us over for Moroccan food despite the fact we live on opposite sides of the country? Then I remind myself that if you love something, you have to set it free. If it doesn't come back, well, at least you'll get a few new page views out of the deal!

In all seriousness, we do love our Blonde, and we're sure you will, too. So sit back and let Kelly take you on a journey through the fun, freaky, and fantastic world of cinema in a way only our resident "Nerd Girl" can.

# Introduction

It's been a long and twisty road for this book. When I was a kid, back in the 1970s, I would read the Sunday entertainment section and be fascinated by the strange movie ads. This fascination took a different turn in the 1980s with the advent of home video. No longer did I stare at the newspaper. Now I stood in the "Horror" or the "Cult classics" section of the local video rental store, gazing at lurid box cover art, wishing I could talk my mother into renting some of these movies, and knowing full well I never could.

About the same time as the video revolution, I became interested in movie reviews. If I couldn't see the movies that intrigued me, at least I could find out what others thought of them. Probably my first exposure to reviews was the show *Sneak Previews*, with Roger Ebert and Gene Siskel giving their now-famous thumbs-up and thumbs-down reviews. It was always enjoyable when they disagreed, not least because it made me realize that intelligent people who respected each others' opinions could disagree, passionately at times.

Other critics whose work I enjoyed included Pauline Kael, whose books were a staple checkout for me at my university library; Joe Bob Briggs, drive-in critic extraordinaire with his cheerful tallies of the breasts, blood, and beasts in each film; and, most of all, Danny Peary, whose *Cult Movies* books opened my eyes to new films.

I didn't write my own reviews with any regularity until the early years of the new millennium. I was taking a hiatus from fiction writing, largely out of the sheer exhaustion brought on by motherhood, when the website Horrorview put out a call for new reviewers. I'd already been reading the site for quite some time and, figuring I had nothing to lose, auditioned with a review of *I Spit On Your Grave*. I still maintain that Jim Reilly, Horrorview's editor, was so astounded to find a woman who not only admitted to watching *I Spit* but had some relatively positive things to say about it, that he hired me out of the sheer novelty factor. My gig with the site has been tremendously enjoyable, and has led to some great friendships.

Shortly after independently publishing my debut novel, *The Day After Yesterday*, I got the idea of doing my own movie review book. A portion of the book consists of reviews that appeared on Horrorview (in slightly different form), and the rest are original to this book.

At first I had planned to cover many of the major geek classics. But on reflection, I realized that if you're interested in this book, you've already seen *Star Wars*, or *The Lord of the Rings*, or *Monty Python and the Holy Grail*, or *The Nightmare Before Christmas*, or *The Princess Bride* ... you get the idea. My goal is to steer you toward some films that are a bit off the beaten path, and while there are plenty of horror, action, and sci-fi films covered here, you'll also find reviews for many other genres: film noir, Western, art-house favorites, romantic comedies, chick flicks, musicals, anime, and even a porn film.

The hardest part of this book was limiting myself to 200 movies. There are so very many films out there, and not nearly the time available to watch them. I'm sure that for months afterward I will be slapping myself upside the head and saying, "I can't believe I forgot to review *The Cockroach That Ate Cincinnati*!" I've included a list at the end of another 200 films you could do much worse than to watch. And if you want to chat about any of the movies, feel free to drop me a line at smitepublications@gmail.com or follow @Kelly_Cozy on Twitter.

I wish you happy reading, and happy watching!

-Kelly Cozy

February 2015

# In Gratitude

Dedicated to these directors, whose films tweaked the psyche of young-and-impressionable me.

Brian De Palma
Bob Fosse
Terry Gilliam
Alfred Hitchcock
David Lynch
Ken Russell
Peter Weir

It's all your fault, gentlemen.

# Alice, Sweet Alice

*Catholic girls*

**Year:** 1976

**Director:** Alfred Sole

**Screenplay:** Alfred Sole and Rosemary Ritvo

**Cast:** Paula Sheppard, Linda Miller, Brooke Shields

As a connoisseur of Catholic horror films, it's refreshing to find one that isn't focused on possession or the Antichrist. Rather, *Alice, Sweet Alice* finds its horrors in the earthly religion that is supposed to foster faith, but in this story ends up doing the very opposite.

In a blue-collar East Coast town at the beginning of the Kennedy presidency, Katherine takes her daughters Alice (Paula Sheppard in a remarkable performance) and Karen (Brooke Shields in her movie debut) to the church rectory. There they meet with handsome Father What-A-Waste, I mean Father Tom. From this opening scene we sense things are not as they should be. For one thing, Katherine seems a bit too familiar with the priest, calling him just plain "Tom." And both Katherine and Father Tom blatantly favor Karen over older sister Alice, whom we also learn has recently been denied Holy Communion. This preferential treatment may not be as unjustified as it seems, for Alice soon proves that she is in fact a hostile child who's constantly in trouble at school, who steals things from her younger sister, and who likes to terrorize people while dressing in her school rain slicker and a semi-translucent mask.

On the day of Karen's first Communion, the girl is strangled to death by a figure in a — you guessed it — rain slicker and semi-translucent mask. Suspicion falls on Alice. The massive familial and societal dysfunction swirling around Alice — her mother vacillates between denial and defensiveness, her violently passive-aggressive aunt all but accuses Alice of her sister's murder, and the men in her life are absent (her father), ineffectual (Father Tom), or predatory (the grotesque landlord, who has to be seen to be believed) — only alienate Alice more and deepen her mental imbalance. And soon more attacks take place...

When it comes to the slasher subgenre, I'm partial to films that break the standard template, and *Alice, Sweet Alice* does just that. Director Alfred Sole makes the most of his clearly low budget, using location shooting and unknown actors to give the film a very realistic feel, while at the same time bringing considerable visual style and some memorably creepy visuals to the film. There are attacks and killings, but they're brutal, ugly affairs, and the victims aren't pretty teens

14

to be leered at beforehand.

What makes *Alice, Sweet Alice* most interesting is its setting, at a very transitional time in Catholic America. The first Catholic President is in the early days of his term, but the reforms of Vatican II have yet to take place: Mass is still said in Latin, women still wear hats or other head coverings in church, and there's a certain distance between the Church and its followers. And yet religion seems to bring no consolation to the characters, whose lives are filled with dysfunction and petty rivalries. It's telling that Alice is repeatedly denied Communion, just as she fails to get help from her family for her obvious emotional troubles.

The acting is for the most part a bit broad, but the one standout is Paula Sheppard as Alice. Sheppard plays Alice as a girl with a flair for the dramatic, who struggles under the restrictive society she's in, and who only knows how to attract attention in a negative way. She does indeed get attention, but little to no understanding, and by the end of the film it's clear how much damage that's done.

The low budget shows its seams, and the screenplay's a bit clunky at times. It's also effective, nasty, and intelligent (and sincere — I bet my next paycheck that Sole, who also cowrote the screenplay, grew up in a setting much like the movie's). But it's definitely worth watching, particularly if you are interested in a different kind of slasher or in the treatment of religion in films.

# All That Jazz

*It's showtime, folks*

**Year:** 1979

**Director:** Bob Fosse

**Screenplay:** Bob Fosse and Robert Alan Arthur

**Cast:** Roy Scheider, Ann Reinking, Jessica Lange

Creativity can be a harsh mistress, an unpleasant truth that's illustrated to dazzling effect in Bob Fosse's semi-autobiographical movie.

Joe Gideon (Roy Scheider in arguably the best performance of his career) is burning the candle at both ends — in fact, if the candle had six ends he'd probably be burning all of those. He's finishing the final edit of a movie he's directed; at the same time he's casting dancers for a new Broadway play. There's also his personal life keeping him busy — the star of his Broadway show is his ex-wife Audrey; he has a steady lover, Katie; he also has a string of casual mistresses and one-night stands. He needs Dexedrine and cigarettes to maintain his frantic pace, and alcohol to calm himself down. This has been going on for years, and now he's getting warning signals both physical (in the form of chest pains) and spiritual (in the form of Jessica Lange as Angelique, a death angel he talks to in his inner monologues).

*All That Jazz* is a schizophrenic film. It juxtaposes the gritty reality of making movies and Broadway shows — the time spent in the editing room, the hassles with money men and the press, the sweaty hours of dance rehearsals in a grubby studio far from the glitz of the stage, the merciless culling of a thousand hopeful young dancers down to a chosen few — with the end result of theatrical spectacle and graceful dancers' bodies in motion.

Likewise, its protagonist is something of a split personality. He's successful in his career but his personal life is a shambles. Work is "all there is" to his life, but creativity doesn't bring him fulfillment — there's too much riding on it, and even at Gideon's level there's rejection. This is sublimely illustrated in one of the film's most famous sequences, the "Take Off With Us" dance number in which an insipid Broadway song is brought to life first in a standard (though very skillfully done and enjoyable) way, then turned into an energetic, erotic dance that leaves dancers (and the audience) breathless. It's clearly inspired by Gideon's own life and the emptiness of his fast-and-loose sex life, but it's summarily rejected by the money men and will never see a stage.

The film becomes even more schizophrenic after Gideon suffers a heart attack that even he can't ignore, and lands in the hospital. While undergoing open heart surgery (footage of a real surgical procedure is used here, in all its gory glory) his mind serves up musical fantasias, primarily of the women in his life urging him to mend his ways and embrace life instead of death. The reality of scalpels and tubes and life-saving equipment is not just contrasted with the dazzlingly-choreographed dance numbers, but incorporated right alongside it.

It's crazy and self-indulgent, but there's real pain and heart at the center of the film, thanks largely to Roy Scheider. It's probably the best role he ever had, and it taps into a vulnerability he was seldom given a chance to show in his characters. Gideon isn't always a good man or even a likable one, but he's passionate about his art and his quest for perfection inspires his dancers and keeps people like ex-wife Audrey loyal to him. Yet it's his desire for perfection that puts him on a collision course with death, as his intake of speed, booze, and (unfiltered!) cigarettes begins to seem like slow-motion suicide as a way to avoid the pain of failure.

There's a quiet moment that often gets lost in the film, but to me it sums up the dilemma of the artist. At one point Gideon confesses to his sympathetic Angel of Death: "When I see a rose, that's perfect. That's perfect! I want to look up to God and say, 'How the hell did you do that? And why the hell can't *I* do that?'"

That's the subtext, but there's plenty of surface. Fosse was known for his sinuous, sensual, at times blatantly sexual choreography, and *All That Jazz* showcases it fully, from the previously mentioned "Take Off With Us" number to its climactic "Bye Bye Life" denouement.

It's schizophrenic, over the top, flashy, and more than a bit morbid. It's also one of the most honest movies I've ever seen about the creative process.

# Altered States

*Going ape*

**Year:** 1980

**Director:** Ken Russell

**Screenplay:** Paddy Chayefsky, based on his novel

**Cast:** William Hurt, Blair Brown, Bob Balaban, Charles Haid

Inspired by reading *Phallic Frenzy: Ken Russell and His Films* (nifty title!), I loaded up my queue with just about all the Russell films available on DVD. First up: *Altered States*. It's a surprisingly restrained film for Russell, and its flaws are, despite Russell's looniness, not attributable to him.

It's the late 1960s and mad scientist manqué Eddie Jessup (William Hurt in his big-screen debut) is conducting experiments with sensory deprivation. His somewhat vague goal is to find some sort of Ultimate Truth™. Or that's what he says to Emily (Blair Brown), an anthropology student who becomes Jessup's lover and later his wife. Jessup's quest for Ultimate Truth™ soon lead him to add hallucinogens to his sensory deprivation experiments and somehow this combination causes him to actually alter his DNA and physical structure, and eventually transmogrify into an ape man and a fetus/amoeba thing. No, really.

Despite having one of cinema's more fractious productions (first-slated director Arthur Penn dropped out of the project, Russell and screenwriter Paddy Chayefsky despised each other, Chayefsky took his name off the credits without even seeing the film), *Altered States* has some undeniable strengths. The movie was Russell's first American film and he shows that when he's not getting carried away with being Ken Russell he can be a strong, effective director. Even the hallucination scenes work within the context of the story and serve to give us some insight into Jessup's mind. They're rife with surreal and at times religious imagery, and there's a curiously tactile quality to the second hallucination scene in particular — Russell uses fireworks to demonstrate the physical and mental discomfort Jessup is experiencing, and the sequence has a strangely haunting coda as the figures of Jessup and Emily are eroded by a sandstorm.

Greatly aiding Russell are the cast, all of whom acquit themselves very well and create sympathy for the characters that isn't generated by the screenplay. Hurt has a physical attractiveness and charm that distract the audience from his character's unlikability. Brown convinces us she loves Jessup even when we see no reason why she should. Adding some humor and common sense to the proceedings are Bob Balaban (who would later go on to direct the completely deranged movie *Parents*) and Charles Haid.

*Altered States'* fatal flaws lie in is screenplay. Written by Paddy Chayefsky from his novel, the screenplay serves up huge chunks of expository dialogue that is never convincing (I hang around guys who design spacecraft and they don't talk like this), along with bogus "science" that asks us to believe a person can alter their physical structure by tripping on 'shrooms. Though forbidden to change even one word of the dialogue without being sued by Chayefsky, Russell and the actors (probably sensing that a reverent treatment of the dialogue would make the movie as exciting as watching Congressional hearings) manage to dodge the clunkiness by having the dialogue be said at breakneck speed, with characters overlapping each others' words or even speaking through mouthfuls of food.

But they can't get around the inherent silliness of the concept, nor can they make us really care about Jessup and his search for Ultimate Truth™. There's a brief attempt to create sympathy for him when he reveals his search was instigated by sorrow over the death of his father, but this is never mentioned again. Hurt is handsome and charismatic in his debut, but even he can't make us care about the selfish, pretentious, monomaniacal character. It's a testimony to Blair Brown's performance that we not only believe she loves Jessup, but never see her as pathetic for doing so.

The special effects of *Altered States* hold up surprisingly well. Save for the "moment of creation" hallucination, which strongly resembles Laser Floyd, the makeup and visual effects are well-executed, even when the underlying concepts are ridiculous. The effects have a strong physicality that couldn't be achieved using modern CGI technology.

*Altered States* is one of the more interesting failures I've seen. As long as you don't think about it too much and just go with the flow, you'll likely enjoy it.

# American History X

*Your racist friend*

**Year:** 1998

**Director:** Tony Kaye

**Screenplay:** David McKenna

**Cast:** Edward Norton, Edward Furlong, Avery Brooks

If you're just not cynical and depressed enough these days, and feel the need to see the uglier side of human nature, you could do worse than to watch *American History X*, a muddled but brutal and at times disturbing look at how hate can destroy people.

Derek Vinyard (Edward Norton's performance is the reason to see this movie) is a neo-Nazi skinhead who's the puppet of a white supremacist (Stacy Keach) and who's idolized by the disaffected white kids in his run-down California beach town. One night Derek kills two black men who were trying to steal his truck, and gets sent to the big house. Several years later, Derek's a free man, and his younger brother Danny (Edward Furlong) is following in Derek's skinhead footsteps. Only it seems that, while in the slams, Derek has seen the error of his ways.

*American History X* is at times a very frustrating film in that it seems perpetually to be walking a tightrope. Tony Kaye's direction is at times effective, but is marred by heavy-handedness and a melodramatic score that has both choirs and "danger music" (thankfully not at the same time). The screenplay can't quite decide what it wants to be: at several times it threatens to become a police drama, and often — particularly when Furlong narrates — it seems like a really messed-up Afterschool Special (one with nudity, profanity, and prison rape).

Likewise the acting veers between brilliance and banality. Norton is the center of the film. He's visually captivating — he packed on 30 pounds of muscle for the role — and he radiates a creepy charisma as the skinhead leader. It's not hard to see why he's so idolized by these losers looking for somewhere to focus their rage and someone to give their lives meaning. It's almost as if Norton plays three different characters over the course of the film: soft-spoken teenage Derek who absorbs his father's casual racism; skinhead Derek who looks elated when he finally has a chance to (he feels justifiably) kill a black man; and enlightened Derek who knows what he's done is wrong but who still sometimes resorts to violence.

Unfortunately, Norton's great performance just makes the other cast members look worse. Edward Furlong isn't as annoying as he was in *Terminator 2* (he could hardly be more annoying) but his character is a cipher, and Furlong doesn't give us any reason to care about him. Avery

Brooks is good as Norton's former and Furlong's current teacher, but isn't given enough to do. And Elliot Gould is just embarrassing as another teacher.

The violence of *American History X* is, save for one instance, not gory but it is disturbing. But more unsettling is the way hate and violence unravel an ordinary American family. There's the semi-notorious "bite the curb" scene, but for some reason the scene where a dinner argument degenerates into violence lingers longer in the memory.

*American History X* succeeds with its portrayal of Derek and his character arc; it fails with what it means to say about racism. With one exception (Derek's father) the hate is extreme — skinheads and gangbangers. It's all too easy to dismiss them as cartoonish and far-fetched. If as much thought had gone into the story as it did into Derek's character, and if Kaye had restrained some of his stylistic flourishes, *American History X* could have been a much more powerful film.

# A*P*E

*Mad monkey kung fu*

**Year:** 1976

**Director:** Paul Leder

**Screenplay:** Paul Leder and Reuben Leder

**Cast:** Rod Arrants, Joanna DeVarona, Lee Nak Hoon

Have you ever watched *King Kong* — the 1933, 1976, or 2005 versions, it doesn't matter which — and thought to yourself: "Gee, this is a pretty good movie. But I wonder what it would be like if it was made by a bunch of nobodies for about twelve bucks; was filmed in a bleak, depressing part of South Korea; had special effects that make *Destroy All Monsters* look like *Avatar*; had gratuitous swearing and attempted rape scenes; and was so poorly paced that 80 minutes felt like two hours. Oh, and it should be in crappy 3-D too."

Well, if you've ever done that, the good news is that you can watch *A*P*E* and get exactly what you're looking for! *A*P*E* (and no, I don't know why it's spelled that way with the asterisks) is a cheap ripoff of *King Kong* released to coincide with the DeLaurentiis remake back in '76. The ads state that the movie is "Not to be confused with *King Kong*" which seems a bit disingenuous considering that's exactly what the film-makers hoped would happen.

I'll say this for *A*P*E*, it starts off with a bang. A model ship bobs over the waters, and then we meet two crew members, who make reference to something in the hold of their ship, and hope that the tranquilizing gas lasts another few days. No sooner have they said that, when a big hairy fist punches its way out of the ship. One of the crew members barely has time to utter a lackadaisical "Oh shit" and the toy ship explodes.

Next we see a giant ape, presumably freed from the ship, standing waist deep in the ocean. We also see a bright, silvery thing zipping through the water, but it's not until the ape starts "fighting" with a shark that we realize what it's supposed to be.

A word on this "shark fight." If you (like me) thought the zombie vs. shark duel in Lucio Fulci's *Zombi* was disappointing, this ape vs. shark duel makes it look a lot better by comparison. Basically the ape has hold of what is obviously a dead shark, no doubt purchased on sale at the fish mart, its mouth all limp and floppy because its jaws have been removed. Anyway, eventually the ape gets tired of wrestling with a dead shark and makes its way to land where he stomps on some buildings.

Meanwhile, at the Seoul airport, movie star Marilyn Baker (Joanna DeVarona) has arrived to start work on a new movie. (One of the stranger aspects of *A\*P\*E* is that Marilyn's movie seems to consist entirely of attempted rape scenes.) When Marilyn isn't making her movie she's snogging her boyfriend Tom (Rod Arrants). Tom is supposed to be a journalist, but during press conferences he never takes a note or has a tape recorder handy.

Eventually, after the ape has terrorized some children who have broken into a closed amusement park, interrupted a martial arts fight, stepped over a toy cow, thrown a snake at (and hit) the camera, and freaked out a hang glider, he sees Marilyn and becomes instantly smitten. The military does what it always does in these situations, and the ape dies, spewing a quart of fake blood as he does so (and bringing to mind unhelpful comparisons to Monty Python's "Scott of the Antarctic" sketch).

It's rare to see a movie so hilariously shoddy on every level. Acting, script, effects — all bottom-of-the-barrel. The film is so cheap that all the screams in this movie, whether they are the cries of the crowds fleeing the ape or Marilyn's shrieks of terror, seem to be recorded on a 15-second loop that constantly replays. Likewise, the movie uses footage over and over, making the whole thing a Kafkaesque experience as you watch the same clip of a Styrofoam boulder come at you five or six times.

The one thing *A\*P\*E* tries to do that's a bit different is the 3-D. The disc, of course, is only 2-D, but in a way that's funnier as you watch all the scenes that were meant to be 3-D highlights — the ape flinging rocks and 55-gallon drums at the camera, soldiers pointing their guns into frame, martial artists shooting flaming arrows at the lens, and in the silliest 3-D moment, a soldier driving his jeep into a two-by-four that breaks his windshield.

The pace flags dramatically in the movie's second half, when we alternate between the military guys arguing, the ape wandering around the city, and Marilyn hiding out in hopes that the ape doesn't find her. And there's a puppet show. Don't ask.

The DVD has nothing beyond scene selections and the transfer is as good as a shoddy effort like this can hope for. I rather like seeing all the scratches and pops in the film — it gives you that "It's 3 a.m. and I'm channel surfing, and dear God what is this thing I'm watching?" feel. It's a perfect film for a drunken party, and one of *Mystery Science Theater 3000*'s great missed opportunities.

# The Arena

*A funny thing happened on the way to the forum*

**Year:** 2001

**Director:** Timur Bekmambetov

**Screenplay:** John William Corrington

**Cast:** Karen McDougal, Lisa Dergen, Viktor Verzhbitsky

Sometimes it just doesn't do to be a completist. Having seen and loved Timur Bekmambetov's *Night Watch*, I thought I'd give his debut feature, *The Arena*, a whirl.

*Night Watch* it ain't. Let's put it this way. You have to start somewhere, and not every director gets it right the first time.

In the waning days of the Roman Empire, at a settlement on the empire's outskirts, governor Timarchus (Viktor Verzhbitsky, chewing the scenery) is bored and cranky. He misses the gladiator fights back in Rome, and the local talent just isn't up to scratch. He sends his lackey to Rome to fetch a few gladiators. The lackey also brings some women for the local brothel, including Jessemina (Karen McDougal, a former *Playboy* Playmate) and Bodicia (Lisa Dergen, another former *Playboy* Playmate). As time goes on, the bitter and unbalanced Timarchus decides to have the brothel women trained as gladiators (gladiatrices?) and fight in the arena.

It sounds like a simple exploitation movie, and that's what it should have been. Unfortunately Bekmambetov and screenwriter John William Corrington decide to give us lots of backstory and some character development. Usually I'm all in favor of this, but McDougal and Dergen are beautiful blank slates, no worse actresses than you'd expect but no better either, who can't bring the necessary emotion to the roles. By contrast, Sandahl Bergman in *Conan the Barbarian*, while not a great actress, had the charisma and physical presence needed to make her character believable. With McDougal and Dergen, the best route would have been to go the straightforward exploitation route, with lots more girlfights and ass-kicking.

But that probably wouldn't have saved *The Arena*, which suffers most from Bekmambetov's overly stylized direction. *Night Watch* was highly stylized, but the style suited the story. In *The Arena*, Bekmambetov not only uses too many flashy tricks, but he uses them at the oddest times. Rarely if ever is the camera stable — often the camera movement is so shaky and wild it's impossible to tell what's going on. Then there are the inappropriate music choices (beautiful choral music during a rape) and strange cinematography (all the scenes in the gladiatorial arena are in sepia). Bekmambetov doesn't seem to know what to do with his actors. Dergen and McDougal are flat and one-note; Verzhbitsky, so chilling in *Night Watch*, is seriously out-of-control. Then there's the scene where the Roman soldiers celebrate something or other by putting on their armor and hopping in unison. Yes, hopping, and it's the most bewildering cinematic scene since the dog started talking in *Summer of Sam*.

There are some good moments. I particularly liked a scene when the fight trainer chooses which women will fight, and as he looks at each, there's the sound of a sword being drawn. There are some interesting visuals. But it's a rare instance when the style and the substance work together.

*The Arena* isn't a good movie, but there's something weirdly endearing about its badness, like poetry written by a teenager. Plus, Bekmambetov did improve as a director — my poetry still stinks.

# The Bad Seed

*The kid ain't right*

**Year:** 1956

**Director:** Mervyn LeRoy

**Screenplay:** John Lee Mahin, based on the play by Maxwell Anderson and the novel by William March

**Cast:** Patty McCormack, Nancy Kelly, Henry Jones

Next time you get bullied into coughing up a baby shower present for a coworker who has been boring you silly with details about her morning sickness, let your evil side run wild and get her the 1956 classic *The Bad Seed.*

The bad seed in question is little Rhoda Penmark (Patty McCormack in an iconic, Oscar-nominated performance), who seems to be most adults' idea of the perfect child. She's pretty, polite, and tidy. Her outward appearance and surface charm hide something very unsettling — Rhoda has no empathy, and no emotional connection to anyone. What she does have is greed — when a boy at her school wins the gold penmanship medal that Rhoda had been coveting, and the boy is later found drowned at the school picnic, Rhoda's mother Christine (Nancy Kelly) begins realizing what her daughter really is.

Adapted from Maxwell Anderson's stage play, which was based on the novel by William March, *The Bad Seed* is very much a mixed bag. The stage play was quite popular, and director Mervyn LeRoy chose to replicate the play as much as he could, even using much of the same cast. The result is not a movie but a filmed play, at times so static it makes the film of *Glengarry Glen Ross* look like a Michael Bay movie. There's even a curtain call at the end. LeRoy gets some of the actors to make the transition from stage to screen — Henry Jones as a creepy caretaker and Eileen Heckart as the drunken mother of the drowned boy are particularly effective. Unfortunately Nancy Kelly as Christine turns in an overly stagy performance of the clutch-the-forehead, "when in trouble or in doubt, run in circles scream and shout" school. Since she has most of the dialogue, her performance is quite wearying by the movie's end.

More successful is Patty McCormack as Rhoda. She never comes across as a "real" kid, but it works because Rhoda **isn't** a real kid. She's a sociopath masquerading as the kind of kid adults think is ideal. It's significant that adults love Rhoda but children detest her, and that the more educated an adult, the less able he or she is to see what Rhoda really is. Only the disreputable caretaker Leroy sees through Rhoda, and even he fatally underestimates her. McCormack's performance doesn't always work — she comes off false when she's arguing with her mother or Leroy. But she's chilling when she's unobserved by others and lets her true feelings — or lack of them — show.

In addition to being stagy, *The Bad Seed* is also marred by a fairly ridiculous ending thanks to the Hays Code, which didn't want to show a criminal getting away unpunished. It's not a movie that's going to frighten most people, but it is a fun curiosity piece. The book is worth a read as well.

# Bad Taste

*I got a chunky bit*

**Year:** 1988

**Director:** Peter Jackson

**Screenplay:** Peter Jackson

**Cast:** Peter Jackson, Pete O'Herne, Mike Minett, Terry Potter

Unfriendly extraterrestrials have landed in New Zealand, and the entire population of a small coastal town has disappeared. The only inhabitants are some curiously zombie-like humanoids, all dressed identically in jeans and blue workshirts, and with a decided taste for eating people — with a spoon!

Derek, Barry, Frank, and Ozzy are promptly summoned to the scene. As the **A**stro **I**nvestigative and **D**efense **S**ervice ("I wish they'd change that name!" laments Ozzy) it's their duty to protect the earth "**and** the moon" against alien forces. Arriving in a purple Ford Capri blasting heavy metal music, and armed with machine guns and a rocket launcher, they get to work without further ado.

The debut film of Peter Jackson (yes, the *Lord of the Rings* Peter Jackson) is both a labor of love and the world's longest gross-out joke. Filmed mostly on weekends over a four-year period with a budget of less than half a million dollars, *Bad Taste* often seems like a glorified student film. The cast are clearly amateurs. The script, such as it is, was largely improvised and includes dialogue about "intergalactic wankers." The film's plot is not so much a story as an excuse for some outrageously gory — but often hilarious — set pieces.

Ah yes, the gore. It's clear that not only did much of the film's small budget go to special effects, but that Jackson knew how to make every penny count. He milks each effect for maximum splattery goodness, with guts spilling, heads rolling, and blood spurting in every conceivable direction.

What keeps this all from simply being a parade of distastefulness is the sheer absurdity of the situation. With the film's premise that aliens are shipping human bits to their intergalactic fast food chain, it makes perfect sense for one bullet to bisect an alien, and for the heroic forces of humanity to be a bunch of nerds and at least one lunatic (Jackson's Derek is clearly unhinged at the beginning of the film, and a tumble off a cliff resulting in a nasty head injury doesn't help his mental state). *Bad Taste* is, in many ways, a grown-up, gory version of a Warner Brothers cartoon.

The film drags a bit in its second half, which consists mostly of a big gun battle between our heroes and the aliens, but whenever the viewer's interest starts to flag, Jackson brings in a bizarre bit of humor — drop-kicking an alien head, Derek's car, the rocket-launcher-meets-sheep incident — to give us a laugh.

You'll look hard for signs that Jackson was the man to direct *Lord of the Rings*, but you won't find many. The clearest signs are Jackson's special effects wizardry, his ability to use his budget to its maximum, and his eye for interesting New Zealand locations. But ultimately *Bad Taste* is, like its follow-up, the even more insane and gross *Meet the Feebles*, a bit juvenile. It's a movie for beer, popcorn, and laughing with your friends — that is, friends who also find the idea of eating brains with a spoon to be hilarious.

# The Beast of Yucca Flats

*Time for go to bed*

**Year:** 1961

**Director:** Coleman Francis

**Screenplay:** Coleman Francis

**Cast:** Tor Johnson, Douglas Mellor, Barbara Francis

I have renewed respect for the *Mystery Science Theater 3000* troupe. Not only did they have to watch *The Beast of Yucca Flats* without wacky commentary (because they had to write the wacky commentary), they had to watch it several times.

There are few examples of cinematic ineptitude as mind-boggling as this movie — it does nothing right, and its only saving grace is a direct result of its ineptitude.

The movie starts with the (very loud) sound of a ticking clock. We see a wan, drab young woman dry herself off after a shower, complete with a quick (and wholly unappealing) glimpse of her breasts. As the woman sits on her bed, she's grabbed by the neck and strangled most unconvincingly by a pair of meaty hands belonging, it's implied, to the titular beast. Said beast also molests the strangled woman in a vague, off-camera way.

This scene is a trifle surreal because the "beast" technically doesn't exist yet. He's Joseph Javorski (Tor Johnson in his last screen role), a Soviet scientist who's defected with some valuable information about the Russian space program. For some reason Javorski meets with U.S. contacts near the Yucca Flats nuclear testing range. But before he can hand over his information, two Soviet agents appear on the scene and a lackadaisical gunfight ensues, followed by an even more lackadaisical car chase. Javorski flees (and by "flees" I mean "slowly lumbers") into the wilderness. Unfortunately, he wanders into Yucca Flats on the day they're testing an A-bomb. I suppose this could happen to anyone.

The A-bomb's radiation (and some yucko pancake makeup) transform Javorski into "the beast." Said beast holes up in a cave, strangles random people, abducts women, and grunts and flails a lot. Eventually local law enforcement sits up and takes notice, and a lengthy manhunt ensues, most of which is spent with the lawmen shooting from an airplane at an innocent man who's trying to find his lost kids. After a bit of rasslin' and some gunfire, Tor keels over and has a bizarre encounter with a bunny rabbit that's supposed to be a statement about something, I think.

I'm not exaggerating when I say that nothing in this movie works. The direction is nonexistent, the acting is beyond nonexistent, the story is ludicrous, the effects more so, and thank God above that the movie is less than an hour long — just on the far side of bearable.

What does work? The narration. There's almost no dialogue in the movie — whether the soundtrack was lost a la *The Creeping Terror* or whether the lack of dialogue was deliberate is unclear. I suspect the latter, because even when characters have dialogue their faces are out of the frame — perhaps director Coleman Francis didn't want to spend the money on synched sound. The movie's loss is our gain, because the narration (provided by Francis himself) is a joy. It's flat and pretentious and weirdly poetical — Francis comes off as Ed Wood's older, grumpier brother.

Some choice samples of this narration include:

"A man runs, someone shoots at him."

"Nothing bothers some people, not even flying saucers."

"Boys from the city. Not yet caught by the whirlwind of Progress. Feed soda pop to the thirsty pigs."

"Always on the prowl. Looking for something or somebody to kill. Quench the killer's thirst."

And my all-time favorite: "Flag on the moon. How did it get there?"

You've got to love narration like that. Watch if you dare.

# Beyond the Door

*Because "Beyond the Window" didn't scan*

**Year:** 1975

**Director:** Ovidio Assonitis and Robert Barrett

**Screenplay:** Ovidio Assonitis, Robert Barrett, and Antonio Troiso

**Cast:** Juliet Mills, Gabriele Lavia, Richard Johnson

I had a horrifying realization the other day. I looked at the list of books I'd read in the past year and out of 48, I didn't finish reading 7. That's probably over 10 percent! (Someone who isn't math-impaired, please confirm this.)

That doesn't mean… no, it couldn't be… I might be actually developing critical standards? *Quelle horreur!* It would explain, however, why watching the Italian Exorcist ripoff *Beyond the Door* left me feeling vaguely (at times not-so-vaguely) bored. For a movie that made enough money to spawn two (totally unrelated) sequels and that shows up with alarming frequency in my horror movie reference books, *Beyond the Door* is a dull, surprisingly shoddy, and at times unintentionally funny movie.

The movie gets extra Pretentious Points for its opening. Over a black screen a deep-voiced narrator says some mumbo-jumbo, implies he's the devil, and dares us not to believe what we're about to see. Then it's candles galore and what appears to be a Black Mass. A white-robed blonde runs away while a black-garbed bearded fellow looks slightly disappointed.

When we next see the blonde, we learn her name is Jessica (Juliet Mills, sister of Hayley "Pollyanna" Mills — ponder that, won't you?). She's married to Robert, a record producer with perpetual bed-head. We also learn that the film-makers couldn't get their titles straight — the opening credits tell us we're watching *The Devil Within Her*, while the end credits insist we've just seen *Beyond the Door*.

Jessica's just learned she's pregnant, and both she and Robert seem rather ambivalent about the news. This is understandable, since the two kids they already have — a hateful, potty-mouthed girl who's obsessed with reading *Love Story* and an insipid little boy who consumes nothing but Campbell's pea soup (with a straw, right out of the can) — are poster children for those "safe haven" programs that let you abandon kids without fear of prosecution.

To make matters worse, Jessica's pregnancy is apparently proceeding at an extremely rapid rate (I say "apparently" because Jessica never looks even remotely pregnant until the end of the film,

28

when it looks like she swallowed a soccer ball). Jessica starts levitating, spinning her head 360 degrees, talking in a too-deep voice, yarking up last week's creamed spinach, and causing the bathroom towels to burst into flame. Ordinarily I'd categorize these as symptoms of severe PMS and prescribe lots of chocolate and bubble baths, but since Jessica's already pregnant that can't be the case.

Her tousled husband frets, her doctor wants to pack Jessica off to an asylum, and eventually the bearded fellow from the Black Mass at the beginning (remember him?) shows up claiming he can help Jessica. But does he really want to? And will anyone care?

*Beyond the Door* does throw in a halfway interesting scene now and then — the levitation effect is rather cool, even if it doesn't have any importance to the story. The possession scenes are nothing that hasn't been done better before or since, though there's a good sequence in which the toys in the children's room gradually begin acting weird. But far too much of the film is occupied with filler, the most egregious example of which is when Robert takes a walk through the city and is hassled by street musicians. No, really. And none of it is helped by the director's very odd use of flashbacks, jump cuts, and freeze frames; or by the incoherent scenes with the bearded guy; or by the characters who are one-dimensional at best and unlikable at worst.

If the admittedly effective trailer terrified you during your childhood years, you may want to give the movie a view. Just don't set your expectations too high, and make sure you have some snacks on hand or maybe a book to read during the boring bits.

# The Big Red One

*War stories*

**Year:** 1980 (theatrical release), 2004 (reconstruction DVD)

**Director:** Samuel Fuller

**Screenplay:** Samuel Fuller

**Cast:** Lee Marvin, Mark Hamill, Robert Carradine

There's never been a war movie quite like *The Big Red One*, probably because there's never been a director so qualified to make such a movie. Director Samuel Fuller started out as a journalist, served in the real Big Red One division, and turned his hand first to photojournalism and then to movies. Despite being his most personal film, and one of his most polished and professional works, *The Big Red One* was cut by 40 minutes on its initial release in 1980. It's been unjustly forgotten over the years, but a painstaking effort by, among others, film critic Richard Schickel, has given us a film close to Fuller's original vision (Fuller died in 1997).

*The Big Red One* opens with a black-and-white prologue set in World War I France. A lone American soldier makes his way across no-man's-land. He's attacked by a battle-maddened horse, and then kills a German soldier only to learn that the armistice was signed a few hours earlier. Jump forward to World War II and that soldier is now a sergeant (Lee Marvin), leading the titular division and in particular four sharpshooters: Griff (Mark Hamill), Vinci (Bobby Di Cicco), Johnson (Kelly Ward), and Fuller's stand-in, the cigar-chewing journalist Zab (Robert Carradine, who also narrates).

The film follows the division as they are sent from place to place — North Africa, France, Belgium. Along the way the four sharpshooters and their sergeant deal with ambushes, capture, the confusion of battle, the lulls in between battles, and the knowledge that at any moment they could be attacked or killed (or watch a comrade die).

*The Big Red One* has been criticized for being episodic, but that quality only enhances the realism of the movie. These men are ordinary soldiers who aren't privy to the military decision-making and have no idea where they will be fighting from one day to the next, or why. Fuller uses the episodic nature of the movie to his advantage, creating setpieces that are funny, horrific, or even surreal (as when the division raids an insane asylum that's being used by the Nazis as a command base).

Fuller also excels at portraying the humanity of the soldiers as well. Griff's lapses into cowardice and the sergeant's lingering guilt over the man he killed after the armistice are particularly well done. Interestingly, Fuller also gives a certain amount of sympathy to the other side in his portrayal of Schroeder, a German officer whose story reflects and provides contrast to the American sergeant's experiences.

The theme of the film, expressed by Zab near the end, is that the only glory in war is surviving. With all respect to Fuller, I'd beg to differ — the glory is surviving while still retaining one's humanity. It's easy to write these soldiers off as cold when we see their gallows humor and what seems like a lighthearted attitude toward death. But Fuller makes it very clear that those attitudes are just protection, and these men are still deeply affected by what they see. This is clearly shown in a haunting, nearly dialogue-free sequence in which the soldiers raid what turns out to be a concentration camp.

Fuller's films are often strange beasts, blending cynicism with sentiment while laboring under budgetary constraints. It's not hard to see why some critics didn't take to his blend of tough-guy dialogue with unabashed sentiment, and the mix doesn't always work (note the bizarre musical interlude in the otherwise terrific *The Naked Kiss*). But despite a bit of melodramatic contrivance,

*The Big Red One* manages to avoid these flaws. It even holds its own against films with far bigger budgets, making up in intimacy what it lacks in scope. An example is the Omaha Beach landing, in which the carnage is demonstrated by the simple effect of the waves washing over a dead soldier, the water becoming a deeper shade of crimson as the attack goes on.

If you've any interest in war movies, or if you simply want to see a well-done portrait of conflict and how it affects its participants, seek out *The Big Red One*.

# The Black Dahlia

*Half the woman she used to be*

**Year:** 2006

**Director:** Brian De Palma

**Screenplay:** Josh Friedman, based on the novel by James Ellroy

**Cast:** Josh Hartnett, Scarlett Johansson, Aaron Eckhart, Hilary Swank

On January 15, 1947, the body of aspiring starlet Elizabeth Short, who came to be known as the Black Dahlia, was found in a South Central Los Angeles empty lot. Short was not simply murdered: she had been beaten; her mouth cut from ear to ear; and her body had been cut in half, the internal organs removed. The killer was never found and the case remains unsolved.

The Black Dahlia murder has wielded a grim fascination for people over the years. Crime novelist James Ellroy put his own spin on the story in his 1987 novel, and now the novel has been adapted into a Brian De Palma film.

*The Black Dahlia* is a strange film, less a murder mystery and more an exploration of how the murder affects those involved in its investigation. LAPD detectives Bucky Bleichert (Josh Hartnett) and Lee Blanchard (Aaron Eckhart) are boxing rivals and good friends, their relationship miraculously uncomplicated despite them both being in various degrees of love with Lee's girlfriend, former prostitute Kay Lake (Scarlett Johansson). Their triangle is upset when Blanchard becomes obsessed with the Dahlia case, and when Kay's abusive former pimp is due to be released from prison. Complicating matters for Bucky is Madeline Linscott (Hilary Swank in full-tilt femme fatale mode), a Dahlia look-alike who may or may not know more than she's telling about the murder.

I want to adore *The Black Dahlia* as I adore another Ellroy adaptation, *L.A. Confidential*, but I can't. *The Black Dahlia* does have a lot going for it. The cinematography is lush and gorgeous, and the sets do a fine job of re-creating 1940s Los Angeles — all the more amazing considering that the movie was shot in Bulgaria. Elizabeth Short's murder is not exploited for cheap thrills. The body is discovered in long shot, and it is more through description than through visuals that we learn what was done to her. De Palma keeps a leash on fancy director tricks, but knows exactly how much flash to use and when: The lengthy tracking shot when the Dahlia's body is discovered is amazing, and the scene when Bucky meets Madeline's horrible family is ghoulish black comedy. The acting is hit-or-miss: Eckhart gives a tightly-wound, intense performance, but unfortunately he's not given enough screen time. Hilary Swank steals the show as a spoiled society girl (at times she sounds like Katharine Hepburn) with a taste for rough trade. And Mia Kirshner plays the Dahlia in screen test footage — Kirshner and Swank are the heart of the movie, its yin and yang of damaged women.

Unfortunately the "miss" parts of the acting are given more screen time than the movie can bear. Hartnett simply seems too young for the role; he lacks the edge necessary for a character who's nicknamed "Mr. Ice" — too often he comes across as "Mr. Cardboard." He's also given the task of providing the movie's noir-narration, and his strained, hesitant voice isn't suited for it. Johansson looks fabulous in 1940s hair and clothes. But her performance is all surface — we learn almost nothing about Kay, nor is it ever clear why Lee and Bucky are both so in love with her (to be fair, this was also a problem in the novel).

Also hampering the movie is Josh Friedman's screenplay. Adapting Ellroy novels is a thankless task, as each book contains enough plot for three books. Friedman's screenplay isn't streamlined enough, and he doesn't give enough distinction to the many minor characters — it's often difficult to know what's going on, particularly in the last third of the movie. Fans of earlier De Palma films should keep their eyes peeled for *Phantom of the Paradise* star Bill Finley in a small but key role.

# Black Sheep

*Wooly bully*

**Year:** 2007

**Director:** Jonathan King

**Screenplay:** Jonathan King

**Cast:** Nathan Meister, Peter Feeney, Danielle Mason

It's hard to think of a more unlikely animal on which to base a horror film than the sheep. Well, perhaps rabbits, but that's been done already (see *Night of the Lepus*). Nevertheless, writer-director Jonathan King has given us *Black Sheep*, a charming tale of mutant predator sheep that wisely plays its subject for laughs and thrills. And while it isn't as successful as it could be at evoking either of those, it's still quite a bit of fun and a refreshing break from the bloated sequels and grim horror fare that's out in theaters now.

Henry and Angus Oldfield are brothers growing up on their father's sheep ranch in New Zealand. One day a prank Angus plays on Henry goes awry, and by coincidence their father dies that same day. We jump forward fifteen years to find Henry (Nathan Meister) a sheep-phobic who can't pass a flock without calling his therapist. Brother Angus (Peter Feeney looks like Bruce Campbell's antipodean cousin) has made the ranch prosper but also has implemented a reckless genetic engineering program. (Ah, genetic engineering gone wrong. Like toxic waste and Indian burial grounds, if you did not exist, the movies would have had to invent you.)

When Henry arrives to sell Angus his share of the farm, two animal rights activists steal a mutant sheep fetus that proceeds to bite one of the activists, and then some of the sheep. The activist starts feeling icky, the sheep start acting wacky, and soon Henry and the other activist, hippie chick Experience (Danielle Mason) have to find a way to stop the mutant sheep before they devour everyone in their path.

*Black Sheep* pulls no punches when it comes to gore — we see the sheep chow down on arms, legs, innards, and other body parts, but the gore isn't offensive. It's excessive in the same way as Peter Jackson's early work (clearly an influence on the makers of *Black Sheep*). Like those movies, the humor is outrageous but never mean-spirited, and works most of the time, though a few jokes do fall flat, especially near the end.

Where the movie falls short is in its characters, which are all two-dimensional at best. The actors are good sports and do as well as they can with the underwritten roles. And while I can't fault *Black Sheep* for its brisk pace — its 87-minute length is refreshing — more time could be spent on developing the relationship between Henry and Angus instead of asking us to take their animosity for granted.

Kudos must go to the special effects team. Weta Workshop did the honors and a fine job they did, mixing gloppy latex for the attack scenes with CGI to create flocks of rampaging sheep. (This last was necessary because sheep are not the most trainable animals, being dumb as a box of rocks.) And the New Zealand locations are drop-dead gorgeous — if the movie doesn't hold your interest, just gaze at the scenery.

As a horror-comedy *Black Sheep* doesn't quite achieve the heights of *Evil Dead 2* or *Slither*, but it's a fun, gory, and surprisingly good-hearted tale.

# The Blob

*I had Jell-o today*

**Year:** 1988

**Director:** Chuck Russell

**Screenplay:** Chuck Russell and Frank Darabont

**Cast:** Donovan Leitch, Shawnee Smith, Kevin Dillon

I'll admit it right now: I've never seen the original 1958 film of *The Blob*, largely because I've never been much enthused about Fifties horror. I've also never gotten the appeal of Steve McQueen (with the exception of *Papillon*). This means it's probably good for me to review the 1988 remake of *The Blob*, because I won't get all screechy about a classic being defiled, which is what I recall the reaction being at the time the remake was in theaters.

A nice opening montage sets the scene of a down-on-its-luck ski town, and introduces us to the lead characters, none of whose names I can recall. There's the Not-So-Dumb Jock (Donovan Leitch, son of the guy who sang "Mellow Yellow"), the Toothy Cheerleader Gal (Shawnee Smith, who would go on to wear a reverse bear trap on her face in *Saw*) and the Rebel Without A Clue (the extremely annoying Kevin Dillon). One fateful night a meteorite crashes in the woods. First on the scene is the town's resident Old Hermit Dude, who examines the meteor by poking at it with a big stick. Faster than you can say "Meteor shit!" the Hermit Dude finds himself with a gelatinous, carnivorous blob on his hand. Hermit Dude stumbles into the road where he's nearly run over by Not-So-Dumb Jock and Toothy Cheerleader Gal — soon joined by Rebel Without A Clue, they take Hermit Dude to the hospital where the blob finds lots of tasty humans to snack on.

I'll give *The Blob* some credit — it's not a total by-the-numbers retread. There are a number of surprising deaths, both in who dies and how (of course, now that I've mentioned this it won't be nearly as surprising for you, and isn't that a cruel irony?). Even scenes that seem like they'll be completely predictable, such as the kitchen sink scene, play out in unexpected ways. The cast is good and believable, and if you're a fan of genre films and character actors you'll find yourself saying, "Wait! It's that guy who was in that thing!" a lot. Familiar faces include Candy Clark (*Man Who Fell to Earth*), Paul McCrane (*Fame, The Shawshank Redemption, Robocop*), and Jack Nance (*Eraserhead, Blue Velvet, Twin Peaks*).

The effects are good as well — especially considering that this was pre-CGI. Unlike its predecessor, which in the clips I've seen seems to just amble about, this blob is fast, smart, and sneaky. It slithers on the ceiling, sends out tentacles, implodes phone booths, swats one poor guy like a fly, and sometimes leaves nasty half-dissolved corpses behind. I recall much hue and cry about the gore back when the film was in theaters, but it won't bother anyone who's seen John Carpenter's *The Thing*.

Sadly, *The Blob* becomes pretty pedestrian in its last third. It doesn't help that the original film has become such a part of our pop culture that even if you haven't seen it, you know they contain the blob by freezing it. That same device is used here, and it's hard not to spend the last third of the movie wondering why they don't find a way to freeze the darn thing. Worse still, the climactic freezing scene is not only very implausible, it's accompanied by twinkly Christmas music that sounds like an *Edward Scissorhands* reject. The effects in the end scenes are shaky as well, with some very obvious blue screen work. And then there's the twisty final scene, which falls totally flat.

In the end, what could have been a superior B movie is only an above-average B movie. I recommend watching it with a couple of alcoholic beverages on hand (though you may want to avoid Jell-o shooters).

# A Boy and His Dog

*Post-apocalyptic dog chow*

**Year:** 1975

**Director:** L. Q. Jones

**Screenplay:** L. Q. Jones, based on the short story by Harlan Ellison

**Cast:** Don Johnson, Susanne Benton, Jason Robards

The other night I decided to kill two birds with one stone — fill in a gap in my knowledge of 1970s-vintage genre films, and see the adaptation of one of my favorite writer's best stories.

Of science fiction author Harlan Ellison's stories, "A Boy and His Dog" is one of the most famous, and rightly so. Set in a postapocalyptic future, the story concerns roving outlaw Vic and telepathic dog Blood. Together they roam the desolate world, working together to survive. Vic helps find food for Blood, and Blood helps Vic avoid and fight other outlaws and mutated "screamers" that can kill with a touch; Blood also finds women for Vic to rape.

Despite the grim scenario, the story has surprising humor and warmth portraying the relationship between Vic and Blood. Each depends on the other for survival. And although the two argue constantly — Blood mocks Vic's lust and ignorance, Vic threatens to leave Blood on his own —

it's clear that their bickering is a cover for a deep affection. (Ellison wrote the story for his own dog, Abhu.) But their relationship is knocked off balance when Vic falls for Quilla June Holmes, a woman from one of the underground cities where civilization carries on as normally as it can.

L. Q. Jones' adaptation of the story is for the most part quite faithful. Vic (a young Don Johnson — yes, that Don Johnson) and Blood (Tim McIntire provides the voice for Tiger the dog) scrape out a living in the wasteland that's Phoenix, Arizona. One night at a makeshift theater, Blood detects Quilla June. When Quilla June, after a night of wild sex with Vic, bops Vic on the head with a flashlight and flees back underground, Vic follows, leaving Blood to wait for him.

The first third of the movie is strongest. The desert is suitably empty, and Jones does a good job portraying the barren, cruel existence. There is no vegetation, all food comes out of cans scrounged up from destroyed buildings, and life is cheap. Nowhere is this more clear than in the scene when Vic finds a woman who's been raped and murdered by a roving gang — his response is not sadness over the woman's fate but a complaint that "she could have been used a few more times." Vic and Blood need each other to survive in such a world, and Johnson and Tiger/McIntire have the chemistry needed to make us believe in their relationship. The dialogue is taken almost verbatim from Ellison's novella, and I could have watched them bicker for hours.

When Jones veers off the path of the novella is also where the movie loses its edge. The movie's Quilla June is a schemer and something of a bitch; the book's was a woman doomed to be a victim. This change, which at first seems positive — changing Quilla June from a passive to an active person — in fact lessens the overall effect of the film, turning a serious tale about love and survival into a ghoulish joke. Also hurting the film is Jones' portrayal of the underground society. For the most part the society mirrors Ellison's — a small-town paradise reminiscent of a town in a Ray Bradbury story. But for some reason Jones puts all the characters in clownish makeup, white faces, pink cheeks, and bright-red lips. It's a bizarre touch that takes us out of the film's reality, and the movie never really recovers.

Despite the flaws and the obvious low budget, the movie is worth renting, particularly for Vic and Blood. I've never been a fan of Johnson's but here he does a good job, giving the amoral Vic a boyish charm that makes him likable. Tiger is a great animal actor, especially considering this was pre-CGI, and McIntire gives Blood the perfect voice — intelligent, cynical, and world-weary.

# Bubba Ho-Tep

*Hail to the King*

**Year:** 2002

**Director:** Don Coscarelli

**Screenplay:** Don Coscarelli, based on the short story by Joe R. Lansdale

**Cast:** Bruce Campbell, Ossie Davis

*Bubba Ho-Tep* is one of cinema's best surprises: a intentionally ridiculous premise that could have been milked solely for cheap laughs is actually a heartfelt meditation on aging and lost opportunities. And there's a mummy that likes to devour souls, preferably sucking them out through a person's anus.

Look, just trust me on this one.

At the Shady Rest Convalescent Home in east Texas, one of the residents is Elvis Presley. Or at least someone claiming to be Elvis Presley. "Elvis" (Bruce Campbell proving beyond a shadow of a doubt that he is indeed a very good actor) claims that years ago he switched identities with an Elvis impersonator named Sebastian Haff. They even had a contract (which unfortunately was lost in a BBQ accident). But then the impersonator died and Elvis fell off a stage, broke his hip, went into a coma, and is now languishing in a rest home and possibly dying of cancer. It turns out that Elvis isn't the only home resident whose identity is in question. There's also a man claiming to be President John Kennedy (Ossie Davis), who says that his brain is in a jar in Washington DC and that the reason he's black is because "they dyed me this color!"

No one believes the two men, but they soon have other matters on their minds when residents are attacked by vicious scarabs and by a mummy who stalks the halls while dressed in cowboy hat and boots, writes bathroom graffiti in hieroglyphics, and devours the souls of the residents. Both Elvis and JFK know they don't have much time left in their lives, so they decide to go out guns blazing, and kill the mummy Elvis names "Bubba Ho-Tep."

There is plenty of silliness in *Bubba Ho-Tep*, of a very welcome kind (I'm particularly fond of the ancient Egyptian insults the mummy hurls at his two would-be nemeses). Yet it's also a melancholy reflection on the toll of old age. After Elvis lashes out at two people who don't believe he's the real Presley, he laments that at his age "everything you do is either worthless or sadly amusing." It's significant that the Shady Rest home isn't a vile, horrible place. No one's abused or neglected. Yet it isn't a pleasant place, either. It's a dumping ground for people no one wants any longer. (We never see any resident get a visitor.) Small wonder that Elvis sees the battle against the mummy not just as a way to make up for the lost opportunities of his life, but as the first really interesting thing that's happened to him in years.

None of this would work were it not for the two lead actors, whose casting and chemistry is vital to the success of the movie. Bruce Campbell is astounding as Elvis/Sebastian, particularly in a flashback scene when Elvis meets with Haff (whose fanboy reaction at meeting The King is comedy gold). Less celebrated but nearly as good is Ossie Davis as JFK, somehow retaining dignity while saying lines like "Cleopatra does the nasty."

If there's a flaw in the film it's that the threat the mummy poses isn't sufficiently realized. We only see him claim one victim, and that person arguably had it coming. But we're still thrilled to see two crazy old guys make a brave stand to protect their souls and the souls of others at the rest home. Like the rest of the film, it's both ludicrous and surprisingly moving.

---

# Burn After Reading

*Absurdity with a body count*

**Year:** 2008

**Director:** The Coen Brothers

**Screenplay:** The Coen Brothers

**Cast:** Frances McDormand, Brad Pitt, George Clooney, Tilda Swinton, John Malkovich

---

Joel and Ethan Coen's follow-up to 2007's grimly majestic *No Country For Old Men* seems like a lark — an excuse for the film-makers to pal around with their favorite actors and let off steam. But funny as *Burn After Reading* is, in a way it's the flip side of *No Country*. In both movies, boneheaded decisions send everyday situations out of control and leave violence and bafflement in their wake.

*Burn After Reading* opens as a nifty parody of government thrillers, as a planet's eye view descends to CIA headquarters. Longtime agent Oswald Cox (John Malkovich, delightfully profane) is being demoted. Enraged, Cox quits and begins writing a tell-all memoir about his agency days. Cox's coldhearted wife Katie (icy Tilda Swinton), however, is highly displeased and begins making plans to divorce Cox and take up with her longtime lover, former U. S. Marshal and current exercise-and-sex addict Harry Pfarrar (adorable George Clooney).

Unfortunately, Cox's memoirs are found by gym employees Linda (Frances McDormand) and dumber-than-he-looks Chad (scene-stealing Brad Pitt). Linda wants money for extensive cosmetic surgery and Chad is just, well, Chad — they decide to extort money from Cox in exchange for the memoir. This does not end well

*Burn After Reading* is more grounded in reality than some of the other Coen comedies such as *The Big Lebowski* or *Raising Arizona*. Its laughs aren't as broad or obvious — more often they're in the subtleties of the situation or of the performances. For example, one of the funniest scenes is when Chad confronts Cox with the blackmail scheme — the laughs come from recognizing that Chad is emulating not how a CIA spook would act, but how he believes (in his dim-bulb way) a spook would act. If it sounds a bit esoteric, it is. But the best laughs in the movie are its least blatant ones.

The performances are all top-notch, as the actors disappear into their characters. Though some of them might be caricatures, they are nonetheless real people, from Malkovich's old-school spook to Clooney's increasingly paranoid good-time guy to McDormand's average woman trying to stave off middle age. The direction is likewise excellent, with the Coens taking their time to set up the situation and almost make the audience believe it's watching a straight thriller until the absurdity begins.

# Caligula

*Vomitorium*

**Year:** 1979

**Director:** It's complicated

**Screenplay:** It's complicated

**Cast:** Malcolm McDowell, Teresa Ann Savoy, Helen Mirren, Peter O'Toole, John Gielgud

I can think of few movies that better exemplify the concept of "train wreck" better than *Caligula*. It's the bastard child of a marriage between high art and trashy porn, using history as an excuse for showing all manner of decadence and nastiness. This isn't necessarily a bad thing, as say what you will about *Caligula* — there's never been another movie quite like it. And there never will be, which is probably for the best.

The opening few minutes are actually rather promising, with titles that say "PAGAN ROME" and then that nifty quote from the Gospels about gaining the world and losing your soul. Then we go right into an outdoor frolic with Caligula (Malcolm McDowell with his trademark slightly-mad charisma) and his sister Drusilla (Teresa Ann Savoy). But this idyll is not to last, as soon Caligula is summoned to visit the ailing emperor Tiberius (Peter O'Toole). Caligula is pretty nervous about this, and who can blame him? Tiberius is holed up at his Capri retreat, surrounded by more naked people than you can shake a stick at, many of them freakish and deformed, others spending all their time doing various odd sexual things. Tiberius himself, aside from being rather insane, also looks to be dying from about six different kinds of venereal disease. What's more, he loathes Caligula, who has to spend the entire visit buttering up to Tiberius and making sure Tiberius doesn't find out about Caligula's affair with Drusilla. (Frankly I'm not sure what Tiberius is so worked up about, as the Caligula/Drusilla relationship is possibly the healthiest one we see in this movie, which isn't saying much.) I have to add that during this segment we get one of the film's most notorious scenes: a soldier who's drunk on the job has his penis tied tightly with a bootlace, then he's force-fed wine and later stabbed in the gut so the wine spills everywhere. This scene manages to be completely gratuitous while at the same time illustrating how easy it is to die a horrible death at the whim of an insane ruler.

It says a lot for general opinion of Caligula that Tiberius's devoted adviser Nerva (John Gielgud in a two-scene cameo) commits suicide rather than live under the rule of a "reptile" (incidentally, Gielgud saying "reptile" is one of the best moments of the film).

Caligula (narrowly) manages to avoid being poisoned or killed in other ways; soon Tiberius dies and Caligula wastes no time prying the imperial ring off Tiberius' finger. Then there's that awkward moment when (surprise!) Tiberius isn't dead. Fortunately Caligula's fix-it man Macro is there to make sure Tiberius is dead for real.

From there we get into Caligula's reign, which soon becomes a cavalcade of insanity, torture, and betrayals, highlights of which include but are not limited to more sister-bonking; marriage to Helen Mirren; a giant moving wall that's also a head-mowing machine (trust me on this); a man's genitals being cut off and fed to dogs; and much, much more. And throughout there are plenty of scenes inserted by producer Bob Guccione in which random people we've never seen before and will never see again commence with lesbian sex scenes or blowjobs.

If you're thinking it all sounds like a colossal mess, you'd be absolutely right. This is apparent from the opening credits, which include: "Adapted from an original screenplay by Gore Vidal" and "edited by the production." There is no director listed; Tinto Brass is credited for "principal photography" and there are "additional scenes directed and photographed by Giancarlo Lui and Bob Guccione" (those additional scenes wouldn't be the random sex ones I mentioned in the previous paragraph, would they?). Given all this, and the scandal, cuts, and even lawsuits that have accompanied the film, it's surprising the movie works as well as it does. Which isn't saying a lot, but there are hints of a good movie hidden deep. This is particularly evident in the movie's first 40 minutes or so, which deal with Caligula's attempts to become emperor and avoid being murdered by his insane uncle or by any one of a dozen backstabbers and plotters. The scenes in Tiberius' grotto of decadence have a hallucinatory quality that's at times fairly disturbing, as it's clear that at any moment we might get treated to some scene of gratuitous violence or weird sexuality (most of which are barely given a glance by the characters, which makes things even more unsettling).

Unfortunately, after Caligula gains power the film degenerates into a parade of violence, perversion, and insanity, which rather than being exciting or interesting, ends up being tiresome and repulsive (the film's two-and-a-half-hours-plus running time doesn't help — granted, this is the uncut version but with a movie like this, if you're going to watch it you might as well see it in all its glory). The rather ramshackle editing doesn't help, and at times it's difficult to tell what's going on, who's betraying whom, and how much time has passed. This isn't to say the movie's without worth. Aside from the sheer novelty factor of it all, there are moments of comic nastiness and the horror of living under such a ruler. As for the acting, Malcolm McDowell proves once again that no matter how bad a movie is, he's always worth watching (it helps that he's at the peak of his good looks), and he throws himself into the role with his usual verve. The rest of the acting is hit-and-miss: Teresa Ann Savoy is pretty as Drusilla but can't call for the level of scheming needed for such a character. Helen Mirren, aside from being able to add "most promiscuous woman in Rome" to her character resume, has surprisingly little to do. John Gielgud exits with dignity intact, and Peter O'Toole trades in dignity for portraying Tiberius as a man so diseased physically and morally that you're relieved when he's no longer on screen.

It's not really a film I can recommend, as it's so flawed and often distasteful. Yet there really is no other film like it. Often it's as tense as any horror film, not because we don't know the outcome — it's obvious things won't have a happy ending for any of the principals — but because throughout there's the sense that anything can happen at any moment. The good moments can't outbalance the flaws, and if you're interested in the history you'd be better off with the *I, Claudius* miniseries. But if you want to see a movie that is both messed-up and a mess, *Caligula* will serve its purpose.

# Cannibal Ferox

*T'aint the meat, it's the humanity*

**Year:** 1981

**Director:** Umberto Lenzi

**Screenplay:** Umberto Lenzi

**Cast:** John Morghen, Lorraine de Selle, Zora Kerova

The problem with being an aficionado of any particular genre is that you have to at least dabble in some of the sub-genres if you want to maintain your street cred. Trust me, I had no desire to watch any of the notorious Italian cannibal movies from the late 1970s and early 1980s, but I did eventually cave in. The good news is that I never have to watch another one*. The bad news is that what has been seen cannot be unseen, and now I have some very ugly images in my head.

*Cannibal Ferox* has a somewhat muddled opening segment in New York City, in which we learn that cops are looking for a notorious drug dealer named Mike. From there we segue to our lead trio, anthropology student Gloria, her brother Rudy, and trashy gal Pat. Gloria is heading down to the Amazon jungles as part of her thesis work, which is to prove that cannibalism doesn't exist among the Amazonian tribes. Now, it's been a while since I was in college and I never went to grad school, but isn't it a bit difficult to prove a negative? Is one road trip to the jungle enough for Gloria to prove that cannibalism never took place, not even once?

I've just put way more thought into Gloria's situation than the screenwriter did, so I'll move on. Our trio ventures into the jungle and promptly wreck their jeep. As they look for a village, Gloria sees a native eating a caterpillar and freaks out (she seems awfully squeamish for someone writing a thesis on cannibalism). They come upon a village that's mostly deserted save for the women and children, and they also encounter Mike, the drug dealer that was sought after in the opening scene. Mike and his buddy have been looking for emeralds. Mike's also been sampling way too much of his cocaine supply, and has been mistreating the natives grievously. For some extra fun, he gets Pat all hopped up on coke and they molest a native girl. Not long after, all the men of the tribe show up, and our intrepid drug dealers and anthropology students learn that meat's back on the menu.

*Cannibal Ferox*, also known by the delightful title *Make Them Die Slowly*, is one of the more notorious of the cannibal subgenre. Lucky me. Not only is it extremely gruesome in its violence — there's eye-gouging, trepanning (look it up), a woman hung up by hooks through her breasts, and not one but two penis amputations — but there is actual violence and death meted out to animals. This isn't like the bull sacrifice in *Apocalypse Now*, which was part of a legitimate religious ceremony. In *Cannibal Ferox*, a turtle is hacked to pieces while still alive in a cheap-shot attempt at blurring the line between fiction and reality, and to give the impression that the violence against humans is real as well. Yet we know that the humans in this movie, no matter how unpleasant their experience may have been, signed on for this willingly and can go home and wash off the fake blood. That turtle isn't so lucky.

This nastiness could be alleviated somewhat, if not excused, if the rest of the film had some redeeming qualities. But it doesn't. It's not even entertaining in a train-wreck way. The characters are monsters or morons, and nothing in the acting or screenplay can make them interesting, let alone sympathetic. By contrast, the Australian nature-horror film *Long Weekend* put two unlikable characters through some hellish paces, but because they were characters rather than caricatures, they kept the audience's interest. Really, the film's only agenda is to ride a trend and say, "I bet you never saw anybody do **this** on screen before!"

*I did end up watching another one, which to my surprise I rather liked. *Massacre in Dinosaur Valley* has no animal cruelty, and is ridiculous and fairly lighthearted rather than the nihilistic wallow of *Cannibal Ferox*.

---

# Carnival of Souls

*Limbo*

**Year:** 1962

**Director:** Herk Harvey

**Screenplay:** John Clifford

**Cast:** Candace Hilligoss, Frances Feist, Sidney Berger

---

I have a deep fascination for abandoned amusement parks. As they fall into disrepair and are reclaimed by nature, their stillness and silence become compelling. If you share this interest — and if you want to see one of the most influential horror films ever made — then be sure to watch *Carnival of Souls*.

Somewhere in the American Midwest, a carful of boys challenge a carful of girls to a drag race. The girls' car goes off a bridge and plunges into a deep, muddy river. Three hours later there is still no sign of the girls' car, but then one of the girls, Mary Henry (Candace Hilligoss) emerges onto the riverbank bedraggled, muddy, and with no memory of how she survived the wreck.

Mary wastes little time in getting on with her life. She's determined to start a new job as an organist at a church in Utah. On her way there, she's spooked by a mysterious, cadaverous man and entranced by the sight of an abandoned amusement pavilion. Once she arrives in town, Mary finds herself under pressure from a doctor to deal with her recent trauma, from a minister to truly believe in the religious music she plays, and from a suitor who thinks she needs to loosen up and have fun. All the while, the cadaverous man keeps haunting Mary, and soon she visits the abandoned pavilion, perhaps to stay there.

*Carnival of Souls* won't captivate audiences with its acting (aside from Hilligoss, the actors are fairly wooden), its story (which must have been a head-bender in 1962 but will be familiar to today's viewers), or its dialogue (which is frequently too on-the-nose). But none of that matters, because the movie's imagery is still startling and haunting, and imitated by moviemakers even today (the ghoul man's underwater appearance was clearly an inspiration for the Dead Marshes scene in *The Lord of the Rings: The Two Tower*s). Also powerful is the movie's use of sound and silence, echoes of which can be seen today in the films of David Lynch.

Doing much of the heavy lifting is the film's setting — specifically the abandoned amusement park that Mary is repeatedly drawn to. Once a family park and dance pavilion on the Great Salt Lake, it's a place of emptiness and ruined beauty, and the scenes there are never less than captivating.

The movie also benefits from the performance of Candace Hilligoss as Mary, which is all the more remarkable given that Mary isn't a terribly sympathetic character. She shows no feelings for the girls (presumably her friends) who did not survive the car wreck, doesn't stop to see her parents on the way to her new job, and is distant emotionally, physically, and spiritually. Part of the mystery of the film is wondering if Mary's state is a result of the accident, or if she was always this way. It's to Hilligoss's credit that she always makes Mary and her plight compelling to watch, even if Mary is distant from others and from the audience.

Once a staple of public-domain TV and video releases, *Carnival of Souls* is now available from Criterion in an extras-packed set. The movie's a must-see for anyone who likes horror films or if they love abandoned amusement pavilions.

# Carrie

*Blood is compulsory*

**Year:** 1976

**Director:** Brian De Palma

**Screenplay:** Lawrence D. Cohen, based on the novel by Stephen King

**Cast:** Sissy Spacek, Piper Laurie, Amy Irving, Nancy Allen, John Travolta, William Katt

I once read an installment of Matt Groening's cartoon strip *Life In Hell*, in which he described "the cruelest group in the universe" as "a roving pack of malicious 11-year-old girls." The cartoon that illustrates this shows a group of evil girls all saying, "Cry, Debbie, cry! Cry, Debbie, cry!" in unison.

I can attest that Mr. Groening is absolutely correct. I will go further and say that all females fall into one of two categories: You were Debbie, or you were one of the evil girls making Debbie cry.

I was Debbie. Yes, I'm still bitter about this, why do you ask?

Fortunately for the Debbies of the world, we have *Carrie,* Brian De Palma's fine adaptation of Stephen King's debut novel, to provide us with identification and catharsis. Which is a fancy way of saying it gives me a much-needed opportunity to bounce on the sofa, fling popcorn into the air, and yell, "You go, Carrie! Burn down that prom! Don't let those bitches get away with it!"

(I may overidentify with this movie a bit. Please bear with me.)

*Carrie* opens with a scene that will feel all-too-familiar to many of us. It's phys ed time and the high school girls are playing volleyball. We soon hear in the chatter of the girls on one team that they should send the ball to Carrie because she's sure to miss it and lose the game. Sure enough, she does, to the disgust and contempt of her team-mates.

That's bad enough, especially for those of us who got picked last for every team. But things get exponentially worse for Carrie in the shower afterward when she gets her period. It's a perfect storm of terror and humiliation: though she's sixteen Carrie's never had a period before, and because of her extremely repressive upbringing, she knows nothing of what's happening. The other girls respond to her fear and her pleas for help by throwing tampons and pads at her, chanting "Plug it up! Plug it up!" all the while. Sympathetic gym teacher Miss Collins intervenes, but something else has happened. At the peak of Carrie's hysteria an overhead lamp shatters.

Carrie's first period has made her a woman, but it's also brought her something else: telekinesis.

Things only get worse for Carrie when she gets to the home she shares with her domineering, religious-fanatic mother (Piper Laurie). Carrie's mother believes that menstruation is literally a curse, brought on by sinful thoughts, and locks her screaming daughter into a prayer closet that has the world's creepiest statue of Saint Sebastian. The worst part is that we know these imprisonments, beatings, and harangues are part of Carrie's everyday life.

One of the girls who taunted Carrie in the locker room, Sue (Amy Irving) feels remorse for her role, and asks her boyfriend Tommy (William Katt) to take Carrie to the prom. Tommy's invitation, along with Carrie's newfound powers, give her new confidence. But chief mean girl Chris (wonderfully bitchy Nancy Allen) and her second-in-command Norma (P. J. Soles) enlist the help of Chris' boyfriend Billy (John Travolta) to humiliate Carrie in front of the entire prom. The consequences will be deadly.

*Carrie* is considered a horror film, yet the events that should make it horror — the climactic scene at the prom when Carrie snaps and unleashes her telekinetic power — feels more like rough justice. The real horrors are in Carrie's life, from the mockery of her peers, which has clearly been going on her whole life, to her mother's abuse, and the indifference of her teachers and school officials. Only Miss Collins and Sue try to help, but their efforts are too little, too late. That's the real horror, and the tragedy.

Everything about the movie works so well. Screenwriter Lawrence D. Cohen has smartly adapted King's novel — the novel's finale, when Carrie lays waste not just to the prom but to most of the town, has been jettisoned, no doubt for budget reasons, but this also serves to make Carrie more sympathetic. De Palma's direction is very much of its time, with gauzy soft focus, scenes speeded up for no reason, spinning camerawork, and most notably, split screen. Yet it works. It's over the top, but we're seeing this story through the eyes of high schoolers, when everything is intense and every emotion is magnified. Many of the scenes work on multiple levels. The famous title sequence, with its slow-motion pan through the girls' locker room (and over the girls' bodies) is of course an excuse to take a look inside the locker room. But it also illustrates the girls' ease with their bodies and their sexuality — by contrast, when we see Carrie she's set apart from the girls, hidden in the shower's mist, alone and furtive. The setup reflects her feeling of separation from the other girls and her separation from her physical self and her sexuality (her years-too-late first menstrual period is not just a trigger for her latent telekinesis, it's also indicative of her sexual repression). Similarly, when Carrie has her first dance and first kiss at the prom, the camera spinning around her and Tommy isn't just De Palma using his bag of tricks — it shows us how Carrie feels.

But the undoubted highlight, and what gives De Palma a lifetime pass, is the marvelous sequence of suspense before Chris plays her hideous joke on Carrie. We know what's coming and we're in agony because we've finally seen Carrie be happy. It's also a scene you love to watch because it's paced perfectly, and because De Palma throws in so many fine details, like the paper streamer that falls from where the buckets of blood lie hidden, to Chris licking her lips just before she pulls the cord.

Which brings us to the actors. Sissy Spacek is a wonder as Carrie, a sensitive girl who only wants to belong and be accepted. From the first scene she makes Carrie believable and sympathetic, and if you're not on her side when she takes vengeance, then there's something wrong with you. Also strong are Amy Irving as Sue, who feels remorse for how Carrie's been treated; Nancy Allen as Chris, whose loathing of Carrie is so vicious that it poses interesting questions about why she is so mean; and P. J. Soles as the bright-eyed, slap-worthy Norma. Often overlooked is William Katt as Tommy — despite a really unfortunate white-boy 'fro (ah, the 1970s!) his character shifts believably from a nice guy who goes along with his girlfriend's whim to help Carrie, to one who seems to truly understand what a special night this is for Carrie and sincerely wants to make her happy. Piper Laurie as Carrie's mother nabbed an Oscar nomination (as did Spacek) but the performance hasn't aged as well as the others; it's still plenty effective. And yes, that's John Travolta as Billy, and though he doesn't do much, that's more the script's doing than anything else.

It's a film that's got a place close to my heart. It's a movie for everyone who was ever made fun of, picked on, or just plain ignored. It's scary and cathartic — which is what good horror should be.

# The Changeling

*The haunted mansion*

**Year:** 1980

**Director:** Peter Medak

**Screenplay:** William Gray and Diana Maddox

**Cast:** George C. Scott, Trish Van Devere, Melvyn Douglas

Would you like a ghost story that is actually creepy? That has characters that you care about? That isn't filled with jittery camera stutter effects and meaningless jump scares? Then dim the lights, get a blanket to hide under, and watch *The Changeling*.

The story opens with George C. Scott as John Russell, a composer on a wintry vacation with his wife and daughter. In tried-and-true "let's ruin Mr. Happy Guy's life" fashion, wife and daughter are killed in a freak road accident, right before Russell's eyes, no less. Several months later,

Russell is doing his best to move on with life, taking a teaching position at a college in Washington state. Wanting a living space where he can also work on his music, he rents a huge, gorgeous mansion with the help of historical society member Claire (Trish Van Devere). But all is not well in the mansion. Doors open and close on their own, and a rhythmic pounding sound reverberates through the house at the same time every morning. Something in the house is trying to get Russell's attention, and when he investigates he'll find buried bones, ugly secrets, and a murdered child whose spirit is decidedly not at rest.

*The Changeling* is one of those movies that I'm afraid will never get the wider recognition it deserves. Overlooked in a glut of horror films during its 1980 release, it's probably too subtle and genteel for today's horror audiences. Which is a shame, because while not without flaws, it's a compelling, creepy film. Director Peter Medak does a nice job with atmosphere and takes his time setting up the situation and the characters. Of particular note is the way the manifestations of the haunting gradually increase in strength as more of the haunting's reasons are uncovered — the implication is that as the truth of the child's murder is revealed, the ghost grows stronger and more able to take whatever justice it can.

Assisting a great deal in the proceedings is George C. Scott as Russell. Some have criticized the casting of Scott, but I can't see the reason for this. Scott's character is, despite his grief, thoroughly grounded in reality and willing to accept the manifestations for what they are and try to understand them. It's clear throughout that the ghost is reaching out to Russell because of his bereavement, and also clear that Russell is attempting to help the child's ghost in part because he was unable to save his own child. Scott also gives the character a nice world-weary attitude in the movie's last quarter, when people who'd rather that buried secrets stay buried interpret Russell's truth-seeking as attempts for extortion.

The spooky scenes range from the simple — a single note struck on a piano — to the more subtle creepiness of Scott discovering that the melody he thought he was composing is, note-for-note, that heard on the dead child's music box. For sheer scares the highlights are a seance in which a medium and her husband use automatic writing to communicate with the ghost, whose "voice" is also later heard on a tape recording, and a horrifying vision of the child's murder. Unfortunately things go a bit over the top at the film's end, but overall that's forgivable.

It's an intelligent, well-crafted, nicely melancholy film that doesn't get the recognition it deserves.

# Chitty Chitty Bang Bang

*Well, it rhymes with "Chitty"*

**Year:** 1968

**Director:** Ken Hughes

**Screenplay:** Ken Hughes and Roald Dahl, based on the novel by Ian Fleming

**Cast:** Dick Van Dyke, Sally Ann Howes, Lionel Jeffries, Benny Hill, Gert Frobe

There are three kinds of movies you saw when you were a kid. Good ones that hold up when you're an adult; bad ones that were enjoyable then but haven't stood the test of time; and movies that even a kid could tell weren't good.

*Chitty Chitty Bang Bang* is an example of that third kind of movie, a mishmash that never comes together in any appealing way. It's too flimsy for an epic, yet is bloated out to a 2-hour-and-20-minute runtime (complete with intermission). The songs (a principal reason for the length of the film) with rare exception are turgid or unmemorable. It's got just enough weirdness to be uncomfortable, yet never embraces and revels in its weirdness the way, for example, *Willy Wonka and the Chocolate Factory* does.

We're in England in the early 20th century, where wacky inventor Caractacus Potts (Dick Van Dyke doing the best he can with what he's been given) lives with his two young children Jemima and Jeremy, and with his deluded military father (Lionel Jeffries). Caractacus has the requisite "meet cute" with Truly Scrumptious (Sally Ann Howes), the daughter of a local candy magnate, when she nearly runs over his hooky-playing children. By this time it's clear even to Caractacus that his inventions won't pay the rent — in fact, he's flat broke. He makes one last invention, turning a broken-down race car that his children have played in at the scrapyard into a miraculous car named Chitty Chitty Bang Bang. However, it seems that some Teutonic foreigners have their eye on this car as well...

I feel the need to point out that the car — the thing that gives the movie its very title — doesn't even show up in the movie until the halfway point. After that we've still got shenanigans involving spies who covet the car, a trip to the kingdom of Vulgaria where children are outlawed, the kidnap and rescue of Potts' children, and much more. Watching the movie in its entirety is like eating a big box of candy all at once: you're left feeling queasy and with the vague knowledge that it had no nutritional value whatsoever.

To be fair, there are some good elements in the film. Dick Van Dyke shines, and he's been mercifully freed of the horrible accent we all remember from *Mary Poppins*. His highlight is the

"Me Old Bamboo" song-and-dance number in which his character is one step behind all the other dancers yet manages to steal the show. The Child Catcher, who rounds up and imprisons any child in Vulgaria, is creepy enough that people who haven't seen the film in decades remember him when they don't remember anything else about it. And there's a nice turn from Benny Hill (yes, you read that correctly) as a toymaker who helps Potts and Truly rescue the children.

Unfortunately, those moments are buried deep. For every "Me Old Bamboo" there are two or three songs that slow the pace to roughly that of molasses in January (and one song in particular, "Lovely Lonely Man," doesn't even seem to have a melody). For every fun moment there are three or four jokes that misfire or a sequence that's just there because someone thought it was cool. There's just too much chaff and not enough wheat to make the film worth watching, except as a nostalgia fix, and there are far better options available for that.

# A Christmas Carol

*God bless us, every one*

**Year:** 1984

**Director:** Clive Donner

**Screenplay:** Roger O. Hirson, based on the novel by Charles Dickens

**Cast:** George C. Scott, Edward Woodward, David Warner, Angela Pleasance

*A Christmas Carol* is one of those stories that has worked its way so deeply into our culture and psyche that even people who haven't read the book know the story. Movie adaptations, stage versions, cartoons, and parodies abound. Like all good stories, there's more to it than meets the eye, which is why it deserves its near-hallowed status.

This 1984 adaptation for TV features George C. Scott as Ebenezer Scrooge, everyone's favorite miserable miser. Scrooge hates Christmas almost as much as he loves money — he refuses to give to holidaytime charities, tells his nephew Fred (Roger Rees, with terrifying hair) that he'd see himself in hell rather than come to Christmas dinner, and very begrudgingly gives his beleagured clerk Bob Cratchit (David Warner) the day off. But that Christmas eve, Scrooge's former business partner Jacob Marley, seven years dead and his spirit bound with chains and condemned to wander forever, shows up to give Scrooge a chance to redeem himself. The agents of his redemption are the spirits of Christmas Past (Angela Pleasance, Donald's lookalike daughter), Christmas Present (Edward Woodward), and Christmas Yet-to-Come (some tall spooky-looking guy).

Like a holiday feast that offers something for every palate, this adaptation of *A Christmas Carol* has something to please nearly everyone. The acting is superlative, particularly George C. Scott as Scrooge. Unlike many stage and screen Scrooges, Scott doesn't immediately see the error of his ways. Witness his gleeful appraisal, "There's a lot of buying!" when Christmas Present shows him revelers purchasing the food for their holiday meals — it's hard to overcome a lifelong habit of avariciousness. His redemption is all the more moving because it does not happen easily.

Scott's performance alone makes the movie worth watching, but all the supporting players are fine as well. It's good to see David Warner play a good guy for a change; he's masterful in the scene when despite his professions that his ailing son Tiny Tim is getting stronger, we can tell that he knows the boy will not survive. Frank Finlay as Jacob Marley conveys the terrible anguish and regret of the damned. Angela Pleasance as the spirit of Christmas Past is ethereal and unrelenting — no matter how much Scrooge wants her to, she won't let him avoid seeing the bad choices he's made. Edward Woodward is jovial as the spirit of Christmas Present, but his best moment is a somewhat sinister one, as he repeats Scrooge's uncaring, "Are there no workhouses? Are there no prisons?" to him. Kudos go to the casting director for finding a Tiny Tim who actually does look like he won't live to see another Christmas.

The screenplay, by Roger Hirson, is remarkably faithful to Dickens' book. The largest change is to give a reason why Scrooge is abandoned at school as a child — Scrooge's mother died giving birth to him, and his father holds him a grudge — that dovetails nicely with Scrooge's rejection of his nephew, son of Scrooge's much-loved sister Fan. The screenplay also makes it clear that Scrooge's miserly actions have consequences — because of his business tactics, the price of bread will go up and the poor will suffer. Scrooge's redemption is not just a matter of his own well-being, it benefits others as well.

Clive Donner's direction makes it clear that the story, despite its holiday trappings, has some fairly horrific elements. The first image is of Jacob Marley's funeral procession, and Marley's appearance is genuinely creepy. For my money the scariest scene is the hellish London underworld, where people live in squalor and sell whatever valuables they can steal off the dead.

The DVD looks fine, especially considering the film was shot for TV in the mid-1980s. Sadly, there are no extras to speak of. Nevertheless, you should watch *A Christmas Carol* if you feel the need for some ghostly holiday viewing.

# The Company of Wolves

*Oh, look! A metaphor!*

**Year:** 1984

**Director:** Neil Jordan

**Screenplay:** Neil Jordan and Angela Carter, based on short stories by Angela Carter

**Cast:** Sarah Patterson, Angela Lansbury, David Warner

The beauty of folk tales is that they can be enjoyed on several levels, and a fine example of this is Neil Jordan's *The Company of Wolves*, which takes the sexual subtext of werewolf myth and of the "Little Red Riding Hood" story in particular, and gives us a dreamy tale of a teen girl's fears and fantasies of crossing into adulthood.

The film opens with a modern framing device, as thirteen-year-old Rosaleen is upstairs asleep with what she claims is a "tummyache" (any woman will tell you that this is code for "menstrual cramps"). Rosaleen's room may be full of toys, but she's gotten into her older sister's makeup and rouged her face and lips. During her nap she dreams that her family lives in a vaguely medieval time, in a forest that is clearly artificial yet bursting to the seams with the forces of nature — scarcely a scene goes by without some bird or animal flitting through the frame. When she isn't attending to her household chores, dream-Rosaleen spends a lot of time with her grandmother (Angela Lansbury), soaking up tales of the beast that hides inside men. The grandmother instructs Rosaleen to never stray from the path in the woods, and never to trust a man whose eyebrows meet in the middle (such men are sure to be wolves in disguise).

But Rosaleen is torn between wanting to stay untouched and safe, and a feeling that a beastly sort of man might not be all that bad to meet. She soon gets her chance when, while clad in her bright red cloak, on her way to her grandmother's house she meets a charming huntsman whose eyebrows do indeed meet.

What is most striking about *The Company of Wolves* is its ambiguity, and its refusal to take sides. The grandmother's warnings are well-meant, yet she tells Rosaleen to fear **all** men. Rosaleen wants to heed the warnings, yet she has seen her parents' healthy, loving relationship and knows that being sexually active doesn't by necessity make one a victim. Like the wolfish huntsman she meets, Rosaleen is caught between two worlds: the everyday one of her village, and the fantastical world of the forest, where stork eggs contain tiny porcelain statues of babies, a woman rejected by her aristocratic suitor can turn her former lover into a wolf, and where the Devil (a one-scene, uncredited cameo by Terence Stamp) rides around in a white luxury car. The movie refuses to label wolfkind as evil; this is most notably demonstrated by a story in which a wounded wolf girl seeks shelter from a priest and is not condemned, but given help and shelter as another of God's creatures.

Director Jordan gives the film a nice fever dream quality, so that we feel that we're watching Rosaleen's subconscious put together a patchwork of various folk tales. The low budget hampers the transformation scenes, particularly the first major one, but the final one (which made it onto the movie's posters) is still effective by virtue of its simplicity.

Helping the movie a great deal are the performances. Sarah Patterson is magnetic as Rosaleen, and it's a shame she was in virtually no other films after this. Angela Lansbury was born to play the grandmother, her voice making a delight of her tales and aphorisms.

It's not terribly linear and those in search of typical horror movie shocks will come away bored, but it's dreamlike and definitely a different beast.

# Conan the Barbarian

*Hear the lamentations of their women*

**Year:** 1982

**Director:** John Milius

**Screenplay:** John Milius and Oliver Stone, based on the stories by Robert E. Howard

**Cast:** Arnold Schwarzenegger, James Earl Jones, Sandahl Bergman, Gerry Lopez

There were so many cheesy knockoffs of *Conan the Barbarian* back in the 1980s that looking at it nowadays, the movie is surprising in many ways. It has real respect for fantasy fiction in general, and the Conan stories of Robert Howard in particular; it never condescends to the material; and though far from perfect, the movie gets enough elements just right so that it works well, and still entertains when its more gaudy imitators (I'm looking at you, *Red Sonja*) are forgotten.

It's in the days of "high adventure" as a narrator tells us, and young Conan lives in a village with his swordsmith father and his mother. A gang of motley raiders arrives, led by Thulsa Doom (James Earl Jones), a fellow with a hypnotic gaze (which he uses to disarm Conan's mother) and a banner with two serpents. Remember that banner, it will be important later on. Most of the villagers, including Conan's parents, are slaughtered, the swords Conan's father was famous for making are taken by Thulsa Doom, and Conan is sold into slavery. Conan is chained to a giant wheel in the middle of nowhere, the purpose of which seems to be to turn Conan into Arnold Schwarzenegger after a few decades.

It works like a charm, and once Conan's buff enough he's given training and turned into a fighter, pitted against others so people can bet on the outcome. For reasons of plot convenience he's set free, where he teams up with thieves Subotai (surfer Gerry Lopez) and Valeria (dancer Sandahl Bergman) to earn a living. They steal a jewel from the temple of a snake cult, whose leader happens to be Thulsa Doom. And when a king (slumming Max von Sydow) whose daughter has joined Doom's cult offers the thieves a vast reward to kidnap his daughter from the cult, Conan sees an opportunity not just for some easy money, but for some long-overdue vengeance.

*Conan the Barbarian's* story isn't terribly original, and none of the actors are going to win any accolades. And yet everything about the movie works, even when it shouldn't. Director John Milius finds just the right tone of seriousness, without letting the proceedings bog down. He also takes his time setting things up, letting us get a feel for this world of magic, brutality, and dubious heroics. He's aided in this by a rousing, epic score by Basil Poledouris, and by his actors — and not just the slumming A-listers of Jones and von Sydow.

It isn't until well into the film that Schwarzenegger gets his first line, but it's a doozy: "Crush your enemies, see them driven before you, and hear the lamentations of their women!" It sums up perfectly the balance of seriousness (the quote is a spin on one of Ghengis Khan's) and silliness. The film was early in Schwarzenegger's career and his accent, while thick, enhances his suitability for the role. Throughout the film, the mishmash of races and accents work to establish this world as a place where different cultures meet and clash. This feeling is best demonstrated in the early scenes, after Conan meets first Subotai and then Valeria, and they team up to steal for a living. None of the three are especially good actors in terms of line readings, but their physicality (Lopez was a champion surfer, Bergman a professional dancer) makes them far more believable inhabitants of this world than if they were master thespians.

Which isn't to say that Jones and von Sydow don't hold their own — far from it. They may be above the material but you wouldn't know it from their performances. Jones in particular seems to relish the chance to play such a villain, using his sonorous voice to make lines like, "Contemplate this on the Tree of Woe," sound like poisoned honey.

It's a thoroughly entertaining affair, unstinting in its brutality and blood, a feast for the eye from its attractive cast to the still-solid special effects. And you get to see James Earl Jones turn into a snake! What more could you ask for!

# The Cook, The Thief, His Wife, And Her Lover

*To serve man*

**Year:** 1989

**Director:** Peter Greenaway

**Screenplay:** Peter Greenaway

**Cast:** Richard Bohringer, Michael Gambon, Helen Mirren, Alan Howard

"…part of him wondered how something could be so ugly and so beautiful and part of him just plain jazzed on it."

The above line, from James Ellroy's novel *L. A. Confidential*, sums up my feelings for *The Cook, The Thief, His Wife, And Her Lover*. It's a film that shows ugliness both moral (the titular Thief) and physical (brutal violence, sexual abuse, rotting meat) and juxtaposes the ugliness with lush cinematography, gorgeous sets, wonderful acting, and beautiful music.

At La Hollandaise restaurant, Richard the cook (dignified Richard Bohringer) and all the restaurant guests and staff suffer the presence of Albert Spica the thief (Michael Gambon's ferocious, vulgar performance will be a shock to those who only know him as Dumbledore from the *Harry Potter* movies). Albert is loud, crude, and violence-prone, but his hold over Richard (financial, it's implied) is such that he is able to do what he wants while on the restaurant premises. This includes abusing other patrons both verbally and physically — in the film's notorious opening sequence, he forces another restaurant owner to eat dog shit.

The person who suffers most at Albert's hands is his wife Georgina (the always fantastic Helen Mirren). Georgina is a kind-hearted, intelligent woman — unlike Albert, she can actually pronounce the French menu items — who's been cowed into terrified submission by years of Albert's abuse. But one evening Georgina spots a man nearby quietly reading a book while enjoying dinner. The two make eye contact, and before the next course is served they are making love in the women's restroom. Their affair is carried on in the restaurant, under Albert's nose, aided and abetted by the cook…until Albert finds out.

Suffice to say that by the end of the film, contrary to the old Klingon proverb, revenge is not a dish best served cold. It should be hot, with a fine wine accompanying it.

*Cook/Thief/Wife/Lover* makes for a strange viewing experience. It is at times an incredibly beautiful film — it's a treat to watch the costumes change color as the characters proceed from outside the restaurant (blue), to the kitchen (green), into the dining room (red), and finally to the bathroom (white). The outfits worn by Albert's entourage (costumes are by Jean-Paul Gaultier) mimic those in the mural that dominates the wall in the restaurant. The lush cinematography makes beauty of unlikely things — Georgina and her lover at one point frolic in a room full of hanging game birds and feathers. The music is equally lovely, though some may wish for less of the boy soprano. Michael Nyman's score, based on a piece written for a funeral, drives the film and perfectly mirrors its excessive and downbeat side, with a hint of black humor.

It's at times a funny film, though director Peter Greenaway never lets us laugh for very long. A scene when Georgina finally stands up to her husband with a blackly comical taunt ("Being infertile makes me a safe bet for a good screw.") gives us an instant to savor her hard-won victory before she's punched in the stomach and brutally manhandled into Albert's car. The film's violence, though not overtly gory, is vicious and painful to watch. When I saw it in the theater, one scene made me turn away, and out of the corner of my eye I saw many others in the audience also turning away. It's also not a film to watch with Grandma, with lots of vulgar language, extended scenes with full-frontal nudity, and some repulsive imagery (the van full of rotten meat is particularly memorable).

None of this would work if it were not for the actors, who are all brilliant. Richard Bohringer's cook is every artist who's had to work an awful day job or suffer an insufferable patron for the sake of his art. Michael Gambon is downright frightening as the thief — Albert knows no boundaries and by the end, even his fellow criminals are disgusted by his behavior. Helen Mirren takes what could have been the one-dimensional character of a straying wife and portrays Georgina as a woman desperate for not just for physical comfort but for safety and peace. Alan Howard as the lover has the most difficult role — his character doesn't even speak for the first third of the film (he's shushed by the silence-cherishing Georgina), and what makes him most attractive to Georgina are his gentleness and bookishness. Yet he makes us understand why Georgina soon falls in love with him, and why she must take a terrible revenge for him. And we can't forget Tim Roth, who would later appear in some of Quentin Tarantino's films, as Mitchell, the most odious of Albert's henchmen.

*Cook/Thief/Wife/Lover* has been called everything from political satire to shameless pornography. I see it as a nice fable of revenge, and just desserts.

# Countess Dracula

*Bathing beauty*

**Year:** 1971

**Director:** Peter Sasdy

**Screenplay:** Jeremy Paul

**Cast:** Ingrid Pitt, Nigel Green, Sandor Eles, Lesley-Anne Down

I know some of you are as burned out on vampires as I am, but don't let the title of *Countess Dracula* put you off. Despite its title, it's not really a vampire story (save on a metaphorical level). In a way it's scarier than traditional vampire tales because it has its roots not just in reality, but in history.

At an unspecified medieval time, in an unnamed European country, Countess Elizabeth (Ingrid Pitt) has recently been widowed. She doesn't seem terribly cut up about the loss of her husband. What she is mourning is the passing of her youthful beauty, especially now that handsome military captain Imre (Sandor Eles) has come to stay at her castle to hear the reading of the count's will.

Growing steadily more bitter and frustrated over Imre's lack of interest in her, Elizabeth soon finds a way to win him, through a most unexpected source. While beating a servant girl for a minor infraction, Elizabeth gets spattered with the girl's blood and discovers that the blood of young women can restore her youth. One dead servant girl later, Elizabeth is young and gorgeous once more, and goes after Imre. Unfortunately she discovers that not only are the de-aging properties of the blood temporary, but when her wrinkles and other signs of aging return, they are increasingly worse. Desperate to regain her youth and Imre's love, Elizabeth sends her castle steward and former lover Captain Dobi (Nigel Green) out to get more young women to slaughter, all the while passing herself off as her own daughter Ilona (Lesley-Anne Down), whom she's had kidnapped and held captive so she won't blow Elizabeth's secret.

You're probably thinking that this won't end well.

If you, like me, have a passing interest in Weird Shit Throughout History, you probably recognize that *Countess Dracula*'s story much resembles that of Elizabeth Bathory, a sixteenth-century Hungarian noblewoman. Depending on whose accounts you read, Bathory tortured and killed (or had her servants kill) anywhere from several dozen to more than 600 victims, all young women (daughters of peasants or lesser gentry). The accounts of using blood as a beauty treatment didn't arise until many years later (Bathory's tortures were more mundane but still horrific, including burning, beating, and starving the women, as well as dousing them with water on subzero nights and leaving them outside to freeze to death), but it's these tales that have given her the nickname of the Blood Countess.

*Countess Dracula* touches on the Bathory legend just enough to give the story a kick. It also benefits from its portrayal of the nobility as predators and the common folk as prey. At the film's start, when Elizabeth and Captain Dobi are leaving the count's funeral, they are accosted by a peasant who begs for an employment opportunity the late count had promised him; their carriage runs him over and neither Elizabeth nor Dobi blink an eye. Likewise, Elizabeth sees a steady stream of young women as her due; Dobi's reluctance to help her comes not out of moral qualms or pity for the women, but because Elizabeth has rejected him in favor of Imre.

The movie has a lot going for it. Typically gorgeous Hammer photography, excellent sets borrowed from *Anne of the Thousand Days*, and an excellent (albeit dubbed) performance by Ingrid Pitt. As vicious as her character is, it's hard not to pity her when she loses her briefly-regained beauty and becomes even more aged and ugly. And though the movie's fairly tame by today's standards, there's still plenty of bared bosoms and red-paint blood to keep things lively, and a memorable scene of Elizabeth giving herself a sponge-bath beauty treatment with blood.

Yet the movie also feels like a missed opportunity. More could have been done with the story's historical background. And more could have been done with the relationship between Elizabeth and her daughter Ilona (who's conveniently been away for years), as Elizabeth is willing to sacrifice her own daughter to gain restored youth and the suitor that by rights would wed her daughter. Instead we get many annoying scenes of the beautiful but deeply stupid Ilona making feeble escape attempts and crying hysterically.

It's worth watching, though, for Pitt's performance and a peek at real-life horrors that are worse than any tale of fanged vampires.

# Creepshow

*Want to see something really scary?*

**Year:** 1982

**Director:** George Romero

**Screenplay:** Stephen King

**Cast:** Hal Holbrook, Leslie Nielsen, Stephen King, Adrienne Barbeau, E. G. Marshall

With one exception, I've never been much of a fan of comics. That exception, oddly enough, is for a set of comics published before I was even thought of, much less born: the E.C. comics of the 1950s. E.C. was most notorious for its horror comics *Tales From the Crypt, The Vault of Horror,* and *The Haunt of Fear*, but they also had titles for science fiction/fantasy, crime, and even war stories.

The E.C. stories often followed a prescribed formula. Nasty person commits a crime or breaks the moral and/or social code in some way, and then receives a hideous comeuppance that's very appropriate for and (at times) totally out of proportion to the misdeed. Oftentimes the writers and artists would use the stories to comment on social issues of the day, from race relations to political paranoia. But more often than not, the tales were an opportunity for readers to witness transgression in a safe fashion because more often than not, the transgression was punished.

The comics are long gone, but their spirit lives on, and one of the prime examples is *Creepshow*. Featuring five stories written by Stephen King (plus a wrap-around segment starring King's son Joe, who's now a published author in his own right under the name Joe Hill), directed by George Romero, featuring a bevy of accomplished actors, and with animation/illustration by E.C. artist Jack Kamen, the film is a good glimpse into the bonkers mindset of the E.C. world.

Story number one is, unfortunately, the weakest of the lot. "Father's Day" tells the story of some stereotypical rich assholes telling the newest member of their family (Ed Harris, looking young and really odd with a relatively full head of hair) about their great-aunt Bedelia (Viveca Lindfors). Years ago, Bedelia was saddled with caring for her hateful invalid father. When Daddy, in a fit of Freudian rage, had Bedelia's lover murdered, Bedelia bashed her father's head in with a marble ashtray — on Father's Day, no less. Years have gone by and Bedelia got away with the crime, but wouldn't you know? Daddy's not going to let a trivial thing like death stop him from getting some revenge.

Story number two kicks things up a notch with "The Lonesome Death of Jordy Verrill" starring Stephen King in his acting debut. Jordy is a dirt farmer who thinks he's scored big time when a meteor lands on his property. Unfortunately the meteor breaks, leaking some glowing blue goo ("meteor shit!") onto the ground and Jordy's fingers. While Jordy imagines taking the meteor to his local university's Department of Meteors and getting the princely sum of $200 for it, the meteor shit is causing some nasty plant life to grow…everywhere.

The first two stories played up the humorous aspect more, but things get more horrific with the third entry, "Something to Tide You Over." Harry (Ted Danson) has been sleeping with the wife of local rich bastard Richard (Leslie Nielsen, surprisingly sinister). Richard's discovered the affair and won't be content with a divorce from his wife. Instead, he forces the couple at gunpoint to be buried up to their necks on the beach below the high tide line. Unfortunately for Richard, he didn't watch the first story and doesn't know that death has never been an impediment if someone really wants revenge.

From the beach we head to the halls of academia for "The Crate." Said crate has been forgotten under a university staircase for many years, and contains something very unpleasant and very hungry. And a henpecked teacher (Hal Holbrook) thinks he would love to introduce the crate's occupant to his vulgar, hateful wife (Adrienne Barbeau).

The last story ends things on a particularly freaky note, especially if you're a roach-phobe like me. "They're Creeping Up on You" tells of Upson Pratt (E. G. Marshall, who was not paid nearly enough) a Howard Hughes-type businessman and germaphobe who's obsessed with ruining peoples' lives and with the roaches that somehow keep getting into his sterile apartment. On the night that Pratt's driven a man to suicide, the power goes out and he's got no way to keep the roaches away.

If you're a fan of the horror genre, it's hard to find a film that's more fun than *Creepshow*. For the most part the stories hit the right balance between humor and horror, nicely juxtaposing the two. The humor is nice and visually witty, whether it's in the teacher's fantasies of revenge on his awful wife or Jordy's imaginings of the Department of Meteors. The horror isn't stinted on either, particularly in the "Tide" and "Creeping" stories (though this could just be my phobias of drowning and roaches). The use of individual stories keeps things brisk (Romero has never had much of a knack for snappy pacing), and Romero makes particularly good use of framing (often using cartoon backgrounds or silhouettes) and color to set the scene and make the tonal shifts work.

The actors all bring the fun, and not a single one condescends to the material. Of particular note are Nielsen, who's amusing and creepy in his sadistic glee as he watches his wife and her lover drown; Marshall, who's like Ebenezer Scrooge without hope of redemption; and Hal Holbrook, a basically decent guy who sees a monster as a heaven-sent opportunity for some peace and quiet. As for King, his debut is better than any of the cameos he'd make over the years (I'm well aware this is damning with faint praise) and he brings a nice slapsticky quality to self-described "lunkhead" Jordy.

It's silly, scary, and just plain fun.

# The Curse of the Cat People

*Dream world*

**Year:** 1944

**Director:** Robert Wise and Gunther V. Fritsch

**Screenplay:** DeWitt Bodeen

**Cast:** Ann Carter, Simone Simon, Kent Smith, Jane Randolph

Usually it's not a good sign when a sequel has little to do with the original film, but I urge everyone to make an exception for *The Curse of the Cat People.*

It's several years after the events of *Cat People.* Ollie and Alice are married and have a daughter, Amy (a lovely performance by Ann Carter). All seems to be well save that Amy is a dreamy girl with an imagination far too big for her, and has trouble making friends. It doesn't help that she senses, at least on a subconscious level, that her parents keep secrets about the past, and that her father in particular frowns on Amy's flights of fancy. One day a mysterious voice in a creepy old house entices Amy, and she's tossed a ring, which she then uses to wish for a friend. Said friend appears in the guise of Irena (Simone Simon), Ollie's first wife, who died at the end of *Cat People.* Ollie gets more and more bent out of shape about his daughter's time spent in a fantasy world, but the real danger comes from the creepy old house, where a mother-and-daughter pair locked in a poisonous, dysfunctional relationship will be the real threat to Amy.

*The Curse of the Cat People* is a lovely little gem, particularly for those of us who in our childhood years had big imaginations and trouble making friends (may I point out that the beauty of being a novelist is that you can spend hours being with your imaginary friends, and even get paid for it!). There's a special quality to the film and the way it treats fantasy that reminds me of Ray Bradbury's fiction. Particularly enjoyable is the way that Amy (and we) watch Irena's presence emerge, becoming more corporeal the more Amy needs her friendship. It can be debated endlessly whether Irena is a ghost or a fantasy (I'm inclined toward the former) but in the end this doesn't matter; what matters is that Irena loves and cherishes Amy in a way even her well-meaning parents don't.

I also appreciate that the movie doesn't shy away from the sad or dangerous parts of fantasy. Ghost or imaginary friend, Irena can only help Amy so much, and Amy will eventually have to let her go. The scene when Irena tells Amy this is a heartbreaking one, especially as it comes right after Amy's been spanked by her father for "lying" about Irena. And there's the creepy old house where Amy has made friends of a sort with the old woman who gave her the ring. The old woman lives with her daughter as a caretaker, yet insists that the daughter's an impostor and that the woman's "real" daughter died as a child. It's never clear if the old woman is delusional or if this is one really dysfunctional relationship; regardless, by film's end the daughter has more or less snapped, and is a danger to Amy.

Throughout, the film has some lovely, haunting imagery. From the sinister house where the mother and daughter live, to Amy happily playing in a windswept garden with her friend, there's a dreamlike quality that's unlike most other films. Probably my favorite image is Irena standing outside in the snow, singing a French Christmas carol that only Amy can hear.

It's not a horror film, really, though it does have its spooky moments. And it's not really a sequel to *Cat People*, strictly speaking. But it's a unique film, with a fairy-tale quality that's unlike anything I've seen.

# Damien: Omen 2

*We need to talk about Damien*

**Year:** 1978

**Director:** Don Taylor

**Screenplay:** Stanley Mann and Michael Hodges

**Cast:** William Holden, Lee Grant, Jonathan Scott-Taylor

*The Omen*'s unimaginatively titled sequel, *Damien: Omen 2*, proves that the rule of diminishing returns applies to the Antichrist as well as to us ordinary mortals. Kind of reassuring, when you think about it.

*Omen 2* starts off just a few days after *The Omen* ended (you'd be lost if you hadn't seen the first movie so I won't summarize; if you're going to watch *Omen 2* be sure you watch *The Omen* first). Bugenhagen, the archeologist who gave Gregory Peck the magic daggers needed to kill Damien, has just found a mural which includes an Identi-Kit portrait of Damien not only at age 5, but at age 12. Very convenient, that, but unfortunately Bugenhagen and some unlucky bastard who accompanied him to gawk at the mural are buried alive in a cave-in.

(Note to aspiring screenwriters — if you're trying to create an atmosphere of dread, it helps if you don't give characters giggle-inducing names like "Bugenhagen.")

Jump forward seven years, and we find everybody's favorite Antichrist Damien Thorn (Jonathan

Scott-Taylor, channeling Draco Malfoy), living with his wealthy uncle Richard (William Holden), aunt Ann (Lee Grant), and cousin Mark (Lucas Donat) in Chicago. Everything is hunky-dory except that Richard's ancient Aunt Marion (Sylvia Sidney) hates Damien and doesn't want Damien and Mark to go to the same military academy together. So far the worst thing we've seen Damien do is try to mooch cigarettes off the chauffeur, but Aunt Marion's suspicions are enough to make her the first of many victims of mysterious deaths. In this case, it's a heart attack induced by an evil raven (who is always accompanied by a peculiar retching sound on the soundtrack).

So Mark and Damien are off to military school, where their new sergeant, Neff, is played by Lance Henriksen, astonishingly baby-faced and smooth-voiced. Neff is the first to drop some hints about Damien's true nature. Similar hints are dropped by Buher (terminally bland Robert Foxworth), a Thorn Corporation employee who yammers about profiting from famine a lot. And some people start figuring out that the boy ain't right, and meeting nasty ends.

In other words, it's a lot like the first movie, only without the novelty of "discovering" that Damien is the son of Satan. The only mysteries are (a) is Damien going to find out he's the Antichrist and (b) what will he do when he finds out. Since the answers are, respectively, yes and nothing much, all that's left to create suspense is to wonder who's going to die, and how yucky will the demise be.

Technically *Damien: Omen 2* is all right. Director Don Taylor's credits are mostly in television and it shows: the cinematography has a flat, muddy look. The score is less bombastic than that of the first movie. The death scenes are more ludicrous or imaginative, depending on your frame of mind, but the effects are good and a couple deaths are genuinely creepy.

But it's the screenplay for *Damien: Omen 2* that kills the film. It's a slapdash affair, enough to make you wonder if they lost the final script and were working from an early draft. Much mention is made of the Whore of Babylon statue, but it's forgotten after the first third or so. Likewise, the film is clearly setting up Neff and Buher as two of the Four Horsemen (War and Famine). But we never get Pestilence or Death; either the concept was abandoned or they were saving those two for the sequel. Even the Retching Raven of Doom gets forgotten after the first half.

Where the film fails most grievously is when Damien learns he is the Antichrist. He flees his dorm and runs to the nearby lake, where he screams, "Why? Why me?" The movie could have taken an interesting route, and shown us Damien fighting against and eventually succumbing to his evil nature. Unfortunately, after that outburst Damien seems pretty much OK with being what and who he is. And who can blame him, really? He can smite people who piss him off, be unharmed by poison gas, and is a total chick magnet at the academy's cotillion. Superman didn't have it that good!

Even the gory deaths are ultimately failures. The decapitation of David Warner in *The Omen* worked not just because it was a shocking effect, but because Warner's character was interesting and had audience sympathy. *Omen 2*'s comparable death scene, the elevator scene, is flashy and gory but happens to a character we've barely met and don't care about, and the impact just isn't the same — which sums up the movie as a whole.

# Day of the Animals

*Those crazy critters*

**Year:** 1977

**Director:** William Girdler

**Screenplay:** William Norton and Eleanor E. Norton

**Cast:** Christopher George, Leslie Nielsen, Lynda Day George

Even though I like "nature kicks ass" movies from the 1970s, I know better than to hold them to very high artistic standards (rather, I regard them as "good baloney" in the words of Stephen King). But while I can usually overlook a movie's flaws if it gives me angry critters noshing on B actors, I can't give *Day of the Animals* much of a break. It's not just bad, it's inexcusably dull.

Steve Buckner (Christopher George) and his Native American buddy Santee (Syrian actor Michael Ansara) fly two helicopters filled with hikers of varying degrees of obnoxiousness high up into the mountains, with the intention of hiking back down to civilization, camping out and living off the land. There's just one small hitch. Seems that ozone depletion is making animals at high altitudes crazy mad at the humans and their aerosol deodorant-loving ways. (Think about that next time you spritz on the Right Guard!)

So while the city folk try to make their way out of the boonies, assorted critters are stalking them and even working together to pick off people. We've got attacks by mountain lions, turkey buzzards, hawks, snakes, bears, wolves, and a rogue pack of German Shepherds.

It all should be fun but it isn't, probably because unlike *Frogs*, which recognized the ludicrousness of the premise and served up its horror with a knowing wink, *Day of the Animals* plays things mostly straight, starting with its oh-so-serious opening credits crawl that says what we're about to see **could** happen **if** ozone depletion continues. I'm as in favor of keeping the ozone layer strong as the next person, but this had me rolling my eyes so hard I bumped my brain.

The acting, with one exception, is lackluster. The exception is Leslie Nielsen, who plays an

64

advertising executive who's the most obnoxious of the hikers. He's an asshat from his first appearance, calling George's character "hotshot" and Ansara's character "Kemosabe." Things get really fun when Nielsen flips his lid, goes *Lord of the Flies*, takes off his shirt, and starts shoving people around, spitting out insults like "bitch" and "cockroach." He kills one hiker, delivers a loony rant to/against/at God, and then tries to rape another hiker. Fortunately, her honor is saved by a chivalrous bear — Nielsen decides bear rassling is more fun than rape and tries to kill the bear, with the expected results. Unfortunately, after this whacked-out scene the movie resumes its dull progression towards improbable deaths and a *deus ex machina* ending.

To be fair, *Day of the Animals* was trying to educate us about ozone depletion. And I did learn a few things from the movie:

- If you can't get your transistor radio to work, try throwing it in the river.
- If you've got painful bone cancer, a strenuous hike through the middle of nowhere will make you feel ever so much better.
- If your wife won't let you rescue her from being attacked by vultures, it's a safe bet that your marriage cannot be saved.
- You can survive an attack by a wolf or mountain lion with nothing more than a few scratches. However, if a German Shepherd attacks you, you're toast.
- Khaki leisure suits and heels are the ideal gear for mountain treks. Top it all off with a Gilligan hat.
- Rats can fly!

# Day Watch (Dnevnoi Dozor)

*Turn off the dark*

**Year:** 2006

**Director:** Timur Bekmambetov

**Screenplay:** Timur Bekmambetov, based on the novel by Sergei Lukyanenko

**Cast:** Konstantin Khabensky, Mariya Poroshina, Vladimir Menshov, Viktor Verzhbitsky

The Russian film *Night Watch* was a stylish, fast-paced look at a world where the forces of Light and Dark are in precarious balance and where witches, magicians, and vampires jostle with ordinary reality. Now we have the sequel, *Day Watch*. Unlike many (most? all?) of the current crop of sequels, *Day Watch* not only improves on its predecessor but continues the story arc in a most satisfying way.

Though most of the film is in Russian with (very stylish!) subtitles, an English-language narrator gives us a quick summary of the events of the *Night Watch* movie, along with the history of the Chalk of Destiny, which can be used to change the future by rewriting the past. We're then plunged into the story proper: minor magician Anton (Konstantin Khabensky) is training new recruit Svetlana (Mariya Poroshina), the "cursed virgin" from *Night Watch*. Anton and Svetlana are falling in love but are unhappy about it, knowing that Svetlana's magical gifts far exceed Anton's and their relationship will never last. Adding to Anton's woes, his estranged son Yegor (Dima Martynov) is destined to be a very powerful Dark magician — in fact, should Svetlana and Yegor ever meet, the balance between Light and Dark will be upset and the result will be war. The prospect of war delights Zavulon (Viktor Verzhbitsky) leader of the Dark forces, while Gesser (Vladimir Menshov), leader of Light, wants to prevent war. To further complicate matters, someone is murdering Dark Others, and Anton is being framed for the crimes. All this, and a search for the Chalk of Destiny too. Whew!

Luckily, director Timur Bekmambetov juggles the film's stories quite deftly, thanks to a solid screenplay co-authored by Bekmambetov, Alexander Talal, and Sergei Lukyanenko (author of the *Night Watch, Day Watch*, and *Dusk Watch* novels). *Day Watch* is slower-paced than *Night Watch*, and allows both the story and the characters room to develop, making for a less frenetic, more satisfying film. However, eye candy fans need not despair: *Day Watch* has a bigger budget than *Night Watch* and not only are the special effects markedly improved, but they are put to better use as well. Bekmambetov can't completely let go of his "oooh, shiny!" instincts, though: there's a completely extraneous scene involving a car that delights the eye without taking too much time away from the story.

The actors, all returning from the previous film, are much better served by the sequel. *Night Watch* was too fast-paced and focused on setpieces to allow the actors much time to explore the characters. *Day Watch* redeems this well: Khabensky and Poroshina have a fine melancholy in their scenes. Khabensky and Galina Tyunina (the sorceress who was earlier trapped in an owl's body) have a strong camaraderie that's tested when they have to switch bodies (it's the funniest part in the movie and has the best acting). Menshov has quiet dignity and Verzhbitsky has not-so-quiet menace.

Not everything works — occasionally the actors (Verzhbitsky in particular) and the film's score don't seem to hit the right note. Yegor's character isn't sufficiently explored; he comes off as a dark-haired Draco Malfoy, all slicked-down hair and pouty glares, and it's never understandable why Anton wants to reforge their relationship. And although I quite liked the ending, which concludes the story arc nicely if this ends up being the last movie, while allowing plenty of room for another sequel if one happens, I'm sure I'll be hearing arguments about the ending for some time.

If you liked *Night Watch*, or if you wanted to like it more than you did, by all means see *Day*

*Watch*. With most of the strengths and few of the weaknesses of the earlier film, it's a rare thing these days — a sequel that's stronger and smarter, and isn't superfluous.

# Daybreakers

***Sparkle-free vampires***

**Year:** 2010

**Director:** The Spierig Brothers

**Screenplay:** The Spierig Brothers

**Cast:** Ethan Hawke, Willem Dafoe, Sam Neill

Just when I was thinking that the concept of the vampire as a frightening monster was going to be done in — not by holy water and wooden stakes but by sparkle and poofy hair and emo-boy posturing — along comes *Daybreakers*, giving vampire movies a much-needed shot in the arm. It's not perfect, but it gets quite a bit right and it's damned refreshing in its way.

In the year 2019, a vampire plague has pretty much taken over the world, and non-vampire humans now account for only 5 percent of the population. This is a problem not just for the humans but for the vampires as well. You see, consumption of human blood isn't a matter of choice for these vampires. If they go too long without it they begin to change from creatures who more or less look human (save for the usual pasty skin, fangs, and yellowish-brown eyes) to a sort of human-bat hybrid, immensely powerful and completely insane. Drinking animal blood isn't an adequate substitute and feeding off other vampires (or for the truly desperate, one's own blood) only make this descent into savagery happen that much quicker.

At a biochemistry lab run by the transparently evil Bromley (Sam Neill, bringing his Damien Thorn smirk out of retirement), researcher Ed Dalton (Ethan Hawke) is working on a human blood substitute. Unfortunately, his trials on vampire subjects have met with what one could charitably call a lack of success. Ed has a vested interest in finding a substitute — he's been subsisting off animal blood and is starting to show signs of deterioration. By chance he runs into a group of humans who say they have information about a possible cure for vampirism; unfortunately Ed's brother Frankie (Michael Dorman) is a soldier charged with hunting down humans so they can be farmed for their blood.

*Daybreakers* has a lot going for it. The central premise is good if a bit implausible and the world where vampires are the majority is presented well. The Spierig Brothers, who both wrote and directed, have obviously put a lot of thought into what a mostly-vampire world would require to function — cars that have special UV shields to enable daytime driving, "subwalks" instead of sidewalks to provide shelter during daylight hours, and "farms" where humans are imprisoned and milked of their blood. Rarely if ever is the vampiric plague presented as a good thing — the transformation of blood-starved vampires into feral bat beasts aside, it's delightfully disturbing to see professional businessmen go into a rage because their coffee has only 5 percent human blood in it, to see "civilized" people go into ecstasy as they lick spilled blood off the floor, and to see a young vampire girl commit suicide by deliberately exposing herself to the sun. (Unfortunately the use of wooden stakes against the vampires doesn't work well — it's never explained how the wood destroys the vampires and it comes off as just silly.)

While the movie is far too reliant on use of weird lighting to set the scene and the mood, overall the visual effects are quite effective. The use of physical effects rather than CGI is much welcomed, especially with the bat creatures and the use of stage blood. The only effects misstep is the vampire eyes — the effect is not all that necessary and it's distracting, particularly when the actors seem to keep their eyes open a bit too often, possibly to show off the effect.

Which brings us to the weaker points of *Daybreakers*. The story is not terribly original, as Ed and the humans work to find a cure for vampirism, all the while dodging soldiers and the evil head of the biochem lab. This could be overlooked if the characters and the actors were more compelling. As written, Ed Dalton simply isn't that interesting, and his portrayal by that Black Hole of Charisma, Ethan Hawke, does the film no favors. Faring better is Willem Dafoe as a human with a Secret That Changes Everything — he comes off poorly at first with a weird accent (and the nickname "Elvis" doesn't help), but in time he's the strongest character in the film. I confess I was disappointed with Sam Neill — it's a pleasure to see him on the big screen once more but sadly he seems to be collecting a paycheck with this one, letting his "I once played the Antichrist" baggage do the heavy lifting for him.

There's enough here to please the fans, particularly if you're really, **really** tired of pretty-boy, do-nothing vampires. The *Daybreakers* vampires are old school, undead ghouls that are scary for a change. They're Nosferatu's great-grandchildren and I got a kick of seeing them on screen.

# The Dead Zone

*The ICE is gonna BREAK!*

**Year:** 1983

**Director:** David Cronenberg

**Screenplay:** Jeffrey Boam, based on the novel by Stephen King

**Cast:** Christopher Walken, Brooke Adams, Martin Sheen

I love Stephen King, but he's always suffered from a perception problem among people who aren't familiar with his work. He's been dismissed as a purveyor of cheap thrills, and while he has indeed provided cheap thrills (and there's nothing wrong with that), he's also created works of great characterization and sympathy for the human condition.

Arriving during a glut of not-always-successful film adaptations of King's work, *The Dead Zone* is often overlooked. Certainly it isn't one of the more well-known films based on King's stories, which is a shame, because it has so much to offer, on so many levels.

Schoolteacher Johnny Smith (Christopher Walken in one of his most nuanced and iconic performances) is an ordinary guy with a good life. He enjoys his job and is deeply in love with his girlfriend Sarah (Brooke Adams). But a car wreck on a rainy night puts an end to all that, and Johnny spends the next five years in a coma. Johnny wakes to find that he's barely able to walk (thanks to his leg muscles atrophying during the coma), his mother has gone off the deep end into religious zealotry, Sarah has moved on and married another man, and last but certainly not least, he now has the ability to touch a person's hand and see their past or even their future.

Johnny's devastated at the upheaval of his life, and his newfound ability seems a curse rather than a blessing. It's clear that the precognitive spells are distressing physically and emotionally, and soon Johnny becomes a recluse, keeping his contact with people to a bare minimum. But when he's asked to help in the search for a killer who's been preying on young women, and when he finds out that a popular politician (Martin Sheen) is a very dangerous man, Johnny does what he can to help, no matter how high the price.

Though lumped in with horror, *The Dead Zone*, isn't really a horror film save for a few moments (the discovery of the Castle Rock killer, for one). Rather, it's a tragic drama — Johnny is a nice guy who in no way deserves the accident that puts him in the coma. His anger and bitterness toward his situation are understandable, and even at his lowest point, when he initially refuses to help find the Castle Rock killer, he's always sympathetic. Credit goes to the characterization by King and screenwriter Jeffrey Boam, but also to Walken for his underrated performance. It's probably one of the actor's most natural performances, and though it has the Walken trademarks and tics, they don't feel like affectations. He makes you feel for this nice, ordinary guy who's been given an extraordinary power and must decide what to do with it.

Walken is ably supported by a fantastic cast. Adams is sweet as a character whose actions could have alienated audience sympathy; Herbert Lom has a fine role as Johnny's doctor and confidant; Anthony Zerbe is an asshole dad who hires Johnny as tutor for his son; and let's not forget Martin Sheen as Greg Stillson, a politician whose easy charm hides his maniacal side.

It's always a bit of a shock to realize this film was directed by David Cronenberg. It's even more surprising to look at his chronology and realize the film is preceded by *Videodrome* and followed by *The Fly* — two of Cronenberg's more, um, visceral and grotesque films. By contrast, *The Dead Zone* is almost genteel. Save for one moment there's almost no blood, and even the scene when Johnny psychically witnesses the Castle Rock killer's latest murder is relatively discreet. Cronenberg's early films were often criticized for being cold, but *The Dead Zone* is full of warmth and sympathy for its characters (it's notable that Cronenberg's next project, *The Fly*, also had a great deal of effective, sympathetic characterization). Cronenberg and Walken work effectively together to make the audience realize just how unpleasant the precognitive spells are for Johnny (legend has it that Cronenberg would fire a gun to get violent flinches from the notoriously gun-phobic Walken).

There's a deep but somehow enjoyable melancholy to the film, which is enhanced by its wintry locale and Michael Kamen's effective score. My advice is to not worry about what genre it's classified as — just sit back and enjoy a moving, interesting story with good characters and some great acting.

# Death Bed: The Bed That Eats

*No, really*

**Year:** 1977

**Director:** George Barry

**Screenplay:** George Barry

**Cast:** Demene Hall, Dave Marsh, Julie Ritter

I'll be frank. I rented *Death Bed: The Bed That Eats* because of its title. It struck me funny. Why the subtitle? Why not just *Death Bed*? And why "the bed that eats"? Why not "the bed that kills"?

The joke's on me, because the subtitle is perfectly appropriate. This bed does indeed eat people. We first see it in action when a young couple visit the abandoned mansion where the bed resides. While the couple commence romantic frolicking, the bed starts bubbling up yellow foam that sucks down their picnic lunch, "eats" it (we see the food dissolving in what looks like a yellow-tinted fish tank), and then spits out apple cores and chicken bones. The bed then discreetly draws the curtains and devours the couple. And this all happens before the credits!

*Death Bed: The Bed That Eats* is one of the more bizarre films I've seen in a long time. Filming started in 1972; the movie was completed in 1977 and played an indie fest here and there, but couldn't get a distributor and remained without an official release until its DVD debut in 2003. This long time on the shelf wouldn't indicate a film of great quality, and *Death Bed* isn't a great film. But there's a lot of imagination behind it and it's nice to see a low-budget '70s-era horror film that doesn't rip off *Texas Chainsaw, The Exorcist,* or *Last House on the Left*.

After the opening segment when our happy couple is devoured by the bed, we meet the narrator. He's an artist who was eaten by the bed; however, because he was dying of tuberculosis, the bed didn't find him tasty and he ended up in a limbo dimension behind one of his paintings on the wall. This painter has been in limbo for 60 years, and he gives us a rather jumbled history of the bed and some of the people it's devoured. Then things liven up with the visit of three young women to the abandoned house where the bed waits, tasty treats for the bed except for one, whom the bed finds frightening for some reason…

As you've no doubt realized, *Death Bed: The Bed That Eats* is a bit out to lunch (pun definitely intended). It's less a horror film than a wonky art film, almost European in its tone and style. There are a few genuinely surreal images (a rose bush sprouting from the skull of a devoured victim, a "book of dead people" that contains reflecting pages). The pace is sluggish (the film could easily have been pared down by half an hour), but what really makes *Death Bed: The Bed That Eats* a strange experience is the shifts in tone. Some of the devouring scenes are comical (there's one involving a swingers' orgy that's truly hilarious), one is serene and almost erotic, another is clearly intended to be horrifying. The film's most gruesome moment, when a person's hands are devoured by the bed, leaving only the bones, is botched when the character's reaction is a bemused "Huh" expression.

The cast are no-names, and while they aren't great, for the most part they're not bad either (the main exception is the guy who gets his hands dissolved — he's awful). One woman is a dead ringer for Linda Lovelace, if that floats your boat.

Overall *Death Bed* has a lot of interesting things going on, but the whole thing just doesn't hold together all that well. (Perhaps it could be shortened and teamed up with other films about

71

carnivorous furniture — a vicious coat tree, or perhaps a rabid bidet?) Still, I have to give it points for originality and effort.

# Death Race 2000

*Drive, he said*

**Year:** 1975

**Director:** Paul Bartel

**Screenplay:** Robert Thom and Charles B. Griffith

**Cast:** David Carradine, Sylvester Stallone, Simone Griffith

It isn't always easy being a nerdgirl. It often happens that people are shocked that I haven't seen some particular genre film. "What? I can't believe **you** haven't seen [insert name of film]!" Over the years I've gotten this about movies ranging from *Harold and Maude* to *Caligula*.

Most recently, friends were astounded that "**You** haven't seen *Death Race 2000*?" So it behooved me to watch the movie.

And I loved every minute of it.

In the not-too-distant future, a fascist American government keeps the populace happy by giving the people what they want. And what they want is a no-holds-barred transcontinental road race in which the winners not only have to drive from New York to Los Angeles and get there first, but rack up points along the way by running over any pedestrians they can. (Young-to-middle-age men get the fewest points, children under 12 the most, prompting one driver's navigator to exclaim, "If they scatter, go for the baby!")

The contestants include the oft-injured and much-reassembled Frankenstein (David Carradine), Italian-American thug Machine Gun Joe Viterbo (a pre-*Rocky* Sylvester Stallone), good ol' gal Calamity Jane (Mary Woronov), and Ilsa-esque Nazi Matilda the Hun (Roberta Collins). Each driver is accompanied by a navigator (remember, this is before GPS) to provide driving directions and sexual favors. Frankenstein's situation is complicated by the fact that his navigator, Annie Smith (Simone Griffith), is the grand-daughter of Thomasina Paine, the leader of a revolutionary group that wants to bring down the government. The group also wants to put a stop to the race, and is willing to do anything — including kill the racers — do to this.

It's lots of souped-up cars, fast driving, sassy banter, and quick flashes of gore. There's also a great deal of satire that is surprisingly relevant today: the death race could be taken from any of today's reality shows; there's an Oprah-esque reporter who interviews the widow of the first pedestrian killed mere hours after the man's death; when the revolutionaries begin their attacks the blame is assigned to the French. It works just as well as it did in 1975 — possibly even better. The only element of the film that is jarringly out-of-date is the fashion (especially the blue eye shadow — yikes!).

The movie is nicely-balanced. The characters and their banter keep the race scenes from becoming tedious. The satire isn't too heavy-handed. The violence is brief but plentiful, and too cartoonish to be disturbing. It's the very definition of a popcorn movie.

# Deception

*Paging Captain Obvious*

**Year:** 2008

**Director:** Mark Langenegger

**Screenplay:** Mark Bomback

**Cast:** Hugh Jackman, Ewan McGregor, Michelle Williams

Sometimes the gods of cinema point and laugh at you. Case in point: I was home sick and did I watch something worthy? Revisit *Seven Samurai* perhaps, or finally get around to watching *The Godfather*? Nope. I watched *Deception*, and only because it starred two of my favorite Imaginary Boyfriends: Hugh Jackman and Ewan McGregor. I have no one to blame but myself, letting lust direct my viewing choices, and *Deception* is a tepid, thrill-less thriller with several twists but no surprises, and not even the considerable charms of Mr. Jackman and Mr. McGregor can do much to alleviate the tedium.

Hired-gun accountant Jonathan (Ewan McGregor, hit with the nerdy stick) spends his days number crunching and watching life go by (lots of unsubtle scenes of him in glass-walled conference rooms bring the point home). One night, dashing corporate lawyer Wyatt (Hugh Jackman, who can file my legal briefs any day) stops by, chats with the lonely accountant, shares a joint with him, and invites him to a tennis game the next day, and later in the week, to an evening at a strip club. Not long after Jonathan confesses that he doesn't get out much and hasn't been with very many women, he and Wyatt accidentally swap phones. Jonathan answers a call on Wyatt's phone and soon finds that he (in place of Wyatt) is a member of a sex club. Callers say, "Are you free tonight?" and liaisons are arranged, with little conversation between the parties and no names exchanged. This delights Jonathan for a while (as well it should — one of his dates is the still-gorgeous Charlotte Rampling) but things change when one of the club members turns out to be a girl who caught his fancy earlier on a subway platform (Michelle Williams).

Soon Jonathan and the girl (known only as "S") start seeing each other outside of the sex club's restrictions, and if you can't discern that there's more to "S" than meets the eye, or that Wyatt's friendship may not be as benevolent as it seems, you've never seen a movie before (heck, you haven't even paid attention to the movie's title).

*Deception* isn't so much a bad movie as it is relentlessly mediocre. The only distinctive things about it are its absurdly overqualified cast, who all do a fine if unremarkable job. Jackman is all charm, even when his evil side is revealed, so that it's clear how he's been able to use his looks and charm to his advantage for so long. McGregor does a good job as the buttoned-down nerd (though he's done no favors by the film's desaturated cinematography, which makes him look like he escaped the TB ward), a man who longs for excitement in life but can't take the steps toward it. Williams is fine but lacks the charisma to be the woman-of-mystery the script wants her to be. And it's a delight to see Charlotte Rampling on the screen.

Everything else about the movie just sits there. It takes up time and gave everyone involved a paycheck, and that's about it.

# Demoniacs

*Quelle horreur!*

**Year:** 1974

**Director:** Jean Rollin

**Screenplay:** Jean Rollin

**Cast:** Joelle Coeur, John Rico, Lieva Lone, Patricia Hermenier

I've not a clue if *Demoniacs* is a good example of French director Jean Rollin's style. As horror it doesn't work, but as a strange little tale with copious nudity, a bit of surrealism, and a dollop of eroticism, it manages to be both dull and fascinating at the same time.

Set in a lonely coastal town, *Demoniacs* opens on a not-too-promising note, with lengthy introductions to four wreckers — modern-day pirates who lure ships onto the rocks and then take the treasure for themselves. We get a lot of character background on these wreckers, almost none of which is relevant to the story, and besides, the only wrecker you'll remember is Tina (Joelle

Coeur), who I'll refer to hereafter as Tits Ahoy because she spends the entire film either topless or entirely nude.

One stormy moonlit night (continuity is not this film's strong suit), Tits Ahoy and her friends, while scavenging treasure from their latest wreck, happen upon two shipwrecked survivors — blonde girls dressed in white, whose names we never learn. Tits Ahoy's friends beat and rape the girls, then leave them for dead. Later, in a local tavern, one of the wreckers sees visions of the girls as bloody ghosts. The girls, not quite as dead as the wreckers had hoped, make their way to the town's haunted ruins, where they find a guy who looks like Rasputin, a woman dressed up like a clown, and a guy who looks a lot like David Copperfield and is, I think, the devil. This latter fellow offers to help the girls take revenge on their tormentors.

*Demoniacs* is not a good movie, strictly speaking. The acting is nothing to speak of, the story is weak, and while Rollin clearly sympathizes with his traumatized blondes, he doesn't give their revenge a satisfying payoff. Yet there's a strange fascination about it — you're never quite where any given scene is going, and there are enough surreal touches and imagery to keep interest from flagging. As a horror film it's a failure — there's little onscreen violence, and the blood looks like orange Kool-Aid. But the plentiful nudity makes up for that, since most of the people involved are quite attractive — Coeur can't act but you certainly won't forget her nude cavorting, nor the way she gets a bit too into the raping and pillaging.

There's plenty about *Demoniacs* that I don't get. Why does the David Copperfield devil's lovemaking technique include interpretive dance? What happened with that guy with the giant glass bottle? How did the tide come in so fast? Why did those monks show up?

And then I remember — it's French!

# Destroy All Monsters

*The monster mash*

**Year:** 1968

**Director:** Ishiro Honda

**Screenplay:** Ishiro Honda and Takeshi Kimura

**Cast:** Akira Kubo, Jun Tazaki, Yukiko Kobayashi

Kids these days don't know how easy they've got it. Back in my day, we didn't have entire networks devoted to cartoons. No, we had just a few hours on Saturday morning, and there was always that moment when you knew that cartoons were over for the day because *Soul Train* was starting up. And back in my day, you couldn't just rent Japanese monster movies whenever you felt like it. Nope, you had to check the local listings to see what was on.

Which made it all the more sweet when you saw that Sunday afternoon at 2 p.m. they were going to show *Destroy All Monsters*. Because it was the best monster movie ever, and everyone knew it. **All** the monsters (the ones that mattered, anyway)! Destroying the world (or major cities, anyway)! Oh yeah! Pour yourself a glass of milk, put some Hershey's chocolate syrup in it, nag your Mom into making some Jiffy Pop, and settle in for some quality TV time.

The problem is, now that *Destroy All Monsters* is available on DVD to watch at one's pleasure, it becomes apparent that childhood expectations and memories of the movie don't quite match up with the qualities of the movie itself. Face it, what we wanted from *Destroy All Monsters* — 45 minutes of monsters arriving in major cities and fucking shit up, followed by 45 minutes of the monsters opening cans of whoop-ass on each other — is not what we get.

So what **do** we get? Well, we find out that all the world's monsters have been relocated to an island (and let me tell you, when I was a kid, finding out there was no such place as Monster Island ranked just below finding out there was no Santa Claus). The monsters are kept in place by special technology we have to take for granted, and have unlimited food (giant-size bowls of Purina Monster Chow, one assumes). There's a scientific institute on the island where scientists can observe Godzilla, Rodan, Mothra (caterpillar form), Manda, Baragon, Gorosaurus, and a few of the B-list monsters doing what monsters do when they aren't trashing cities.

But this idyll is not to last, for soon a mysterious gas renders the scientists and monsters unconscious. Not long after that, the scientists and monsters are under control of a super-intelligent race of aliens. Despite dressing like Diana Ross in the disco years, the aliens soon demonstrate their superiority by sending the monsters to trash various cities around the world. Godzilla attacks New York City, Mothra takes on Beijing, Rodan trashes Moscow, and so on. Unfortunately the attacks only last long enough for the monsters to trash the one model available to represent each city, and then we go into a long monster-free sequence involving some guys going to the aliens' moon base to figure out a way to get control of the monsters. The reason most fans of a certain age don't remember this part of the movie very well is because we were getting more popcorn, or our moms were making us take out the trash or something. Anyway, it all ends in a grand finale with the "good" monsters tag-teaming against everybody's favorite "bad" monster, King Ghidorah. And there's a spaceship that gets blown up, too.

Despite not being quite up to the expectations we all had of it when we were kids, *Destroy All Monsters* is still a lot of fun. Much of the movie's amusement value comes from its flaws; most notably the awkward dialogue in the dubbed English version ("You let the monsters loose! While the chief was gone!" is often quoted at my house when one of the cats gets out), and the lesser-known monsters like Spiga, Manda, and that one guy who looks like a flying squirrel.

It's not the movie we all wanted, but it's still pretty darn good for what it is.

# The Devil's Advocate

*The hell of it all*

**Year:** 1997

**Director:** Taylor Hackford

**Screenplay:** Jonathan Lemkin and Tony Gilroy, based on the novel by Andrew Neiderman

**Cast:** Keanu Reeves, Al Pacino, Charlize Theron

"Good trash" can be hard to define. A good trashy movie should be entertaining, but not complete fluff. It should be stupid, but not insulting. It should be *The Devil's Advocate*.

*The Devil's Advocate* revolves around the idea that lawyers are tools of the devil and use the law to give the devil a greater hold over mankind. I am shocked, shocked to learn this. It's actually a pretty interesting idea, but any serious consideration of it goes out the window when we meet our protagonist, hotshot Florida lawyer Kevin Lomax (Keanu Reeves). I shouldn't be too harsh on Keanu — he tries very hard here, and his accent is better than I would have expected. But he will always be Bill or Ted to me (I can never remember which) and impossible to take seriously as a lawyer who's never once lost a case.

We see Lomax in action during a quite creepy scene where he defends a grade-school teacher who's been accused of molesting one of his students. Lomax knows the man is guilty but overcomes his distaste, discredits the molested girl's testimony, and wins the case. Soon after he's offered a position at a swank Manhattan law firm headed by Al Pacino, whose character (in one of many "get it??" moments) is named John Milton. Lomax takes the job and starts winning big cases. He and his wife Mary Ann (Charlize Theron) move into a posh apartment, hobnob with the rich and famous, and live the high life. Until Mary Ann starts sinking into depression and hallucinations, and Lomax learned his new boss isn't quite what he appears to be.

*The Devil's Advocate* is a subtle film, in the way that an anvil dropped on one's head is subtle, and that's part of its fun. Everything is over-the-top, from the set design of the law offices to the legal grandstanding. Most over-the-top is Pacino, who plays Milton as a lusty, foul-mouthed guy who's all about appeasing his appetites for money, power, winning, women, and so on. At the same time it's a fairly one-note performance, and by the time the final hoo-hah speech comes, you'll be wishing Pacino would shut up for five minutes, and wondering why the Prince of Darkness is such a one-dimensional character.

Charlize Theron does a good job as the wife who's lured by the good life but finds herself lonely, ignored, depressed, and vulnerable to evil (at one point she gets a radically short haircut, which anyone who's seen *Rosemary's Baby* will tell you is never a good sign).

The movie looks gorgeous, and director Taylor Hackford wields his cinematic bag of tricks with great glee. At times he seems to think he's doing a remake of *Koyaanisqatsi,* with inexplicably speeded-up skyscapes, but it all works with the bombastic nature of the movie. If you're in the mood for some fun that's clever and stupid at the same time, you could do lots worse.

## The Devils

*Hell will hold no surprises for you*

**Year:** 1971

**Director:** Ken Russell

**Screenplay:** Ken Russell, based on the play by John Whiting and the book by Aldous Huxley

**Cast:** Oliver Reed, Vanessa Redgrave, Michael Gothard

It's 1634 and the town of Loudun, France, is in a precarious situation. Protected by the city walls and by its strong-willed governor, it's maintained a measure of independence from both the decadent monarchy and the power-hungry Catholic church. It's also been a haven for the persecuted Protestant minority.

But when the plague claims the governor's life, the power of Loudun falls into the hands of the town's head Catholic priest, Father Grandier (Oliver Reed). Grandier is in many ways a just man: he refuses to persecute Protestants and he does his best to maintain the town's freedom.

But Grandier has made many enemies over the years. Never one to take the vow of celibacy seriously, he is in fact quite the ladies' man and his string of mistresses includes the daughter of the town magistrate. When the girl becomes pregnant and Grandier callously dumps her, the magistrate seeks revenge against Grandier. And Grandier has other enemies: his colleague Father Mignon is jealous of Grandier's wanton ways; Baron de Laubardemont, Cardinal Richelieu's right-hand man, has been thwarted by Grandier in his attempt to demolish the city walls and Loudun's independence; the local doctor and chemist resent Grandier's interference in their medical quackery (their "treatment" of plague victims is horrifying).

But the key to Grandier's undoing is a woman he has never even met — the Mother Superior of the town's convent, Sister Jeanne (Vanessa Redgrave). Crazed by sexual repression, Sister Jeanne has been coveting Grandier for years. When she hears that Grandier has fallen in love and "married" one of his parishioners, the devout Madeline de Brou, Sister Jeanne snaps and accuses Grandier of being a sorcerer who has seduced Jeanne and her entire convent into cavorting with devils. This outlandish accusation is just what Grandier's enemies need to bring him down.

*The Devils* is a fascinating if sometimes frustrating film. It's based on an historical event (documented thoroughly in Aldous Huxley's book *The Devils of Loudun*). Though screenwriter and director Ken Russell has taken some liberties with the facts, what makes the film so unsettling is that the events set in motion by Grandier's indiscretions and Jeanne's accusations — blasphemy, torture, and state-sanctioned murder — actually happened.

Of course, because the director is Ken Russell, the events aren't depicted with the sort of reverence or verisimilitude found in typically Hollywood productions. Rather, Russell has melded his own idiosyncrasies with the historical events and for once, makes it work.

The sets, designed by Derek Jarman, are anachronistically modern — full of minimalist white-tiled structures that have none of the comfort of typical homes or churches. The countryside and town are ravaged by plague (a departure from historical fact), making Loudun not the most hospitable place even before the witchcraft accusations begin. It's when Sister Jeanne comes on the scene that the film begins its descent into insanity, with crazed camera angles, vivid hallucination sequences, and Peter Maxwell Davies' jarring score that sounds like Hell's Muzak.

*The Devils* garnered a fair amount of critical vilification as well as extensive trouble with censors, and it's not hard to see why. To its credit, the film takes a surprising amount of time setting up the situation and making it clear just how precarious Grandier's position is, and also that his downfall comes at a time when he's finding some redemption through Madeline's love and becoming a better man of God. It's the second half of the film, when Jeanne makes her accusations, that brought the film so much trouble on its release and still has power to shock and appall. Jeanne is subjected to a sadistic exorcism procedure; her fellow nuns are threatened with execution unless they corroborate Jeanne's story. The nuns then, under the guise of being exorcised, indulge in a frenzy of nude cavorting and blasphemy (the sequence is classic Freudian "return of the repressed," considering that many of these women had no calling to be nuns and were dumped into convents because they were unmarriageable for various reasons). When Grandier comes on the scene, sanity is far from restored. He's put through a mock trial, tortured, and finally burned alive while the city's walls are razed by Laubardemont.

The frenetic imagery won *The Devils* its share of condemnation. But a second reason for the critical praise and antipathy the film still receives is its ambiguity. Russell never tells the viewer how to feel and as a result the viewer is left to sort out: Is the film reveling in its depiction of blasphemy or condemning it? Is it anti-Catholic or pro-faith? How complicit are Grandier and Jeanne in their fates? It's not an easy film to watch, and provides no simple answers.

Praise must go to the actors involved, who manage to keep the movie from turning into a freak show. As Grandier, Oliver Reed turns in his best performance ever. Grandier is a complex, often contradictory man who does his best to protect the town and shelter Protestants from persecution, but who can callously dump his young lover when she becomes pregnant. He's intelligent and driven, yet prone to curious self-destructive tendencies, and has a knack for making enemies. Most fascinating is his relationship with Madeline — at the beginning, it's clear that he's planning just another seduction, but he falls in love, and his newfound devotion to Madeline brings him closer to God as well (so of course, that's when the trap created by his enemies springs closed on him). Reed's most shattering moment is when, after undergoing hideous torture, he's asked if he loves the Church. His reply is: "Not today."

As Sister Jeanne, Vanessa Redgrave uses a twisted body (Sister Jeanne was a hunchback), her angelic face, and mad eyes and laughter to convey the hysteria of a woman who's spent years in the claustrophobic confines of the cloister when she has no religious calling. Her fantasy sequences early in the film, when she imagines herself cured of her affliction and as a seductive Mary Magdalene to Grandier's Christ, make it clear that Jeanne has a Madame Bovary-esque need for attention and self-dramatization. Most appallingly, she actually comes to relish the abuse heaped on her by her exorcisers — for once in her life she's the center of attention.

Other performances are strong as well. With his curly hair and cherubic face, Dudley Sutton makes his cold, ruthless Laubardemont all the more frightening. Murray Melvin is odious as Father Mignon, whose envy of Grandier helps set things in motion (it's he who first gives Jeanne's accusations credibility). Michael Gothard (sporting John Lennon sunglasses and vaguely hippie-ish garb) is way over-the-top as Father Barre, the chief exorcist — he and the other exorcists take a sadistic pleasure in their work, and their facial expressions are the scariest sights in the film. Bringing sadness to the film is Gemma Jones as Madeline, the one wholly sympathetic character in the story.

*The Devils* is a hard movie to watch, and even harder to recommend with its brutal imagery and hysterical tone. Yet it works — it's more frightening than many horror films, and it's fascinating both as a character study and as an exploration of the abuses of political and religious power.

# District B13

*No parkour-ing zone*

**Year:** 2004

**Director:** Pierre Morel

**Screenplay:** Luc Besson and Bibi Naceri

**Cast:** Cyril Raffaelli, David Belle, Dany Verissimo, Bibi Naceri

If you'd have suggested I add a French action movie to the rental queue, I'd have been doubtful. But then I would have remembered fine fare like *Leon/The Professional* and two-thirds of *The Fifth Element* (the portion without Chris Tucker), and seen Luc Besson's name as *District B13*'s co-writer and producer. And I would have said, "Oh, mais oui!"

*District B13* isn't in the league of *Leon/The Professional*, and it hasn't *The Fifth Element*'s straight-faced silliness, but it's an entertaining romp that falls just a bit short of being a perfect popcorn movie.

In the not-too-distant future, crappy neighborhoods are walled off into districts and given only token police and social services. The worst of these is District B13, home to all sorts of criminal elements, including drug and crime lord Taha (co-writer Bibi Naceri). It's also home to possibly the only honest man in the district, Leito (David Belle). In addition to being an upright citizen, Leito is also quite handsome, has lovely abs, and does that "free running" stuff. Unfortunately Leito gets shafted by the cops and tossed in jail, while his extremely feisty sister Lola (Dany Verissimo) is captured by Taha and turned into his junkie slave.

Then there's honest, upright policeman Damien (Cyril Raffaelli). Despite sharing a name with the Antichrist, Damien is dedicated to law and order, and also happens to be a martial arts expert, as he helpfully demonstrates in a big fight scene set in a casino.

It's at this point — roughly halfway through the film — that the actual plot kicks in. A nuclear missile has been stolen and accidentally activated. (Oops! Clumsy!) It's located somewhere in District B13, so Damien has to go looking for it to defuse it, with Leito as his somewhat reluctant accomplice. Oh, and Leito also plans to rescue his sister and get some revenge on Taha.

For its first two thirds, *District B13* is a fun, delightfully brainless actioner. The free running and the martial arts are well-choreographed and exciting to watch, and the actors look great the whole time. Taha is a suitably slimy villain, and a scary guy named "Yeti" shows up to add some fun.

Sadly, the last third fizzles out as the film seems to build toward a final big battle that never arrives, and as Damien takes a moment (well, several moments) to get across the point of the story. I like a little political subtext as much as the next gal, but not when it brings the movie to a halt.

The movie is a good deal of fun, and well worth renting just for the free running scenes, which wonderfully blend action with physical grace.

# Django Unchained

*Necktie. Nickel. Noodle. It's definitely an "N" word.*

**Year:** 2012

**Director:** Quentin Tarantino

**Screenplay:** Quentin Tarantino

**Cast:** Jamie Foxx, Christoph Waltz, Kerry Washington, Leonardo DiCaprio, Samuel L. Jackson

Quentin Tarantino's latest movie is, like so many of his other films, a delightful stew of many film genres: Western, blaxploitation, revenge drama, heroic origin story. It opens in 1858 Texas, with two slave traders transporting half a dozen slaves through the wilderness. The slaves are barefooted and wearing little beyond rags despite the subzero temperatures, and they're shackled together. Out of the night emerges Dr. King Schultz (charming Christoph Waltz) an apparent dentist who's looking to buy a slave from a particular plantation. The slave in question is Django (Jamie Foxx), and when Schultz's offer to buy Django is refused, things get very bloody very quickly.

It turns out that Schultz is actually a bounty hunter, hired by the government to hunt down outlaws and bring them back dead or alive (Schultz prefers dead, as it makes the transportation and collection of the bounty much easier). He's looking for three men known as the Brittle Brothers, who were overseers at the plantation where Django was a slave. Django and his wife Broomhilda von Shaft (Kerry Washington), in love but forbidden by their master to marry, had tried to run away but were caught by the Brittle Brothers, then sold after being whipped and branded. Schultz needs Django's help to catch the brothers, as he doesn't know what they look like. In return, Schultz will set Django free and help him to find and rescue Broomhilda.

The pleasures of *Django Unchained* are many, from the eloquence of Schultz as he talks his way out of various scrapes, to an encounter with a proto-KKK group that's like a lost scene from *Blazing Saddles*, to the bloody revenge on vile slave-owners. There are moments of pure cinematic pleasure as well, particularly when Schultz trains Django in the fine art of bounty hunting while Jim Croce's "I Got a Name" plays on the soundtrack. But the movie doesn't shirk from the horrors of slavery. We see glimpses early on, from the raw ankles of the enslaved men at the film's beginning to the brutal scene of Broomhilda's whipping. But once Schultz and Django arrive at the plantation where Broomhilda is kept, the film takes a turn for the grim. The plantation's owner, Calvin Candie (Leonardo DiCaprio in sleazy lizard mode) is a freak for "Mandingo fights" in which slaves fight each other bare-handed, often to the death. The introduction for Candie is also the introduction for one of these fights, a shockingly violent affair. Things only get worse when the party arrives at Candie's plantation, called Candie Land (a joke that stops being funny once we learn of the notorious reputation the place has among slaves), where runaway slaves are mauled to death by dogs or imprisoned in metal boxes left out in the sun. From there it's a duel of wits for Django and Schultz against not just Candie, but against his head house servant Stephen (almost unrecognizable Samuel L. Jackson), who's in many ways the real power at Candie Land, and who's deeply suspicious and resentful of Django and Schultz.

Through it all Tarantino shows his trademark mastery with actors, getting excellent performances from the entire cast. Foxx turns in a nice, subtle performance, saying little but letting you know what Django's thinking through his eyes and small gestures. Waltz has the more showy part, playing Schultz as a nice-guy version of Hans Landa from *Inglourious Basterds*, a man who's very honorable in his way despite the bloody nature of his profession. Washington hasn't much to do but conveys resilience and inner toughness for her character. I've never been much of a DiCaprio fan, but he's a wonder as Calvin Candie, an idiot who fancies himself a Francophile but can't even pronounce "monsieur" correctly, who holds the power of life and death over people. And then there's Samuel L. Jackson as Stephen, shifting from jovial servility in front of his masters to being a petty tyrant to the other slaves.

Tarantino also displays his usual adeptness with the film's mood and tone, shifting on a dime when needed. He also never loses sight of the horrors of slavery: violence done toward the slaves is brutal, gritty, and realistic (it's sometimes even filmed differently); violence toward the slave-owners is gaudy and occasionally even cartoonish (one demise is something that could easily have happened to Wile E. Coyote).

There are many little details in the story to appreciate, from a Beethoven melody's unexpected effect to a slave not knowing how to talk to a free black man. Like many Tarantino efforts, it will definitely stand up to repeat viewings, when one can feel less tense and take in more of the details.

If the film doesn't reach the level of *Inglourious Basterds*, it's probably because it's something of a lateral move for Tarantino, and some of his tricks are familiar. Like *Basterds, Django Unchained* has its share of build-ups that lead to unexpected resolutions and subterfuges that don't pan out as planned. And though the movie flies by, its pacing seems off in the last quarter. But it's still an immensely satisfying film, hilarious and appalling by turns, and if it doesn't right history's wrongs on the scale that *Basterds* did, the rough justice meted out is very pleasing.

# Dr. Horrible's Sing-Along Blog

*Everyone's a hero*

**Year:** 2008

**Director:** Joss Whedon

**Screenplay:** Joss Whedon, Jed Whedon, Zack Whedon, and Maurissa Tancharoen

**Cast:** Neil Patrick Harris, Nathan Fillion, Felicia Day

Aspiring supervillain Dr. Horrible (Neil Patrick Harris) is having a tough go of things. Unwilling to settle for joining the Henchman's Union, he's just sent in his application to the Evil League of Evil. In the meantime, he's working up the courage to say hello to his dream-girl Penny (Felicia Day), whom he sees every week at the Laundromat. Not helping matters is Dr. Horrible's nemesis, Captain Hammer (Nathan Fillion), a superhero whose physical strength is only exceeded by the size of his ego, who not only beats up Dr. Horrible on a regular basis but soon has his own eye on the fair Penny. Did I mention that the whole thing's a musical? Hijinks and some tuneful moments ensue.

Conceived as a side project during a writer's strike, *Dr. Horrible's Sing-Along Blog* distills the best of Joss Whedon's work on *Buffy the Vampire Slayer, Angel*, and *Firefly* into a 45-minute musical dramedy. No spoilers — suffice to say that the story is Whedon at his best and his worst, which amount to the same thing, really.

The musical format won't be surprising to anyone who watched "Once More With Feeling," the musical episode that was the highlight of *Buffy the Vampire Slayer*'s sixth season. *Dr. Horrible*'s songs, co-written by Whedon with Zack Whedon, Jed Whedon, and Maurissa Tancharoen, are arguably as good as the ones for "Once More With Feeling" and flow so seamlessly with the story that they feel natural (with none of the "I feel a song coming on!" artifice that afflicts many movie musicals).

As silly as much of *Dr. Horrible* is — face it, we're in a parallel world here with villains named Moist and Fake Thomas Jefferson — it packs a remarkable amount of character depth and emotion into its brief running time, as well as some nifty satire on what constitutes real villainy and real heroics. None of it would work were it not for the cast, who all find the right tone and play the absurdity straight-faced. Harris has the biggest and most complex role, making Dr. Horrible completely convincing as both a lovesick nerd and someone who wants to make the world better by tearing it down. As Dr. Horrible's dream girl and the real hero of the story, Felicia Day is sweet and goodhearted without making her character too cloying or unbelievable. And of course there's Nathan Fillion as the moronic and egotistical Captain Hammer, all smarm and swagger.

The most standout DVD extra is "Commentary! The Musical," a (you guessed it) musical commentary featuring the writers and stars. As a commentary goes it's not worth much, rarely addressing what's happening on screen, but extremely enjoyable for the songs and the good-natured ribbing all those involved give each other. Musical highlights are Fillion's soulful "I'm Better Than Neil," Tancharoen's lament explaining why she didn't play Penny ("Nobody's Asian in the Movies"), and even Joss gets a turn.

More relevant commentary happens in the film-maker's commentary, which brings the cast and writers together again to actually discuss what we see on screen, explain the technical difficulties of working on such a tight time frame and low budget. Nearly as funny as the musical commentary, this one's a delight. A set of three brief featurettes discuss the movie, the music, and the reception the fans gave the show and includes footage from the Comic-Con panel (I was there! Way in the back!). Lastly, there are fan video applications to join the Evil League of Evil, some of which are forgettable but a few (notably the ones from Tur-Mohel, Lord Stabbington, Enfant Terrible, and The Reverend) stand out and are amusing.

Great story, great music, great acting, and great extras. Go watch it now. Bad Horse demands it.

# Edison Force

*Power outage*

**Year:** 2005

**Director:** David J. Burke

**Screenplay:** David J. Burke

**Cast:** Morgan Freeman, LL Cool J, Justin Timberlake, Kevin Spacey

A friend told me about this movie and I didn't believe him. But look, you can see for yourself — direct-to-DVD and starring a rapper, a pop singer, and two of my all-time favorite actors. Consider my mind boggled. *Edison Force* was apparently supposed to be Justin Timberlake's big-screen debut but after poor test screenings it was unceremoniously dumped to video. I'm not one who automatically trusts in the wisdom of test audiences, but they were definitely right this time. *Edison Force* is bad, but not in an entertaining way. It's just dull, dull, dull. One of those movies you can safely multitask while watching.

In the shiny-on-the-outside, corrupt-on-the-inside city of Edison, the ultra-tough special police force (acronym is F.R.A.T. — oooh, clever!) is getting out of hand. Not content with cleaning up the streets, they're now funneling money confiscated from crime scenes directly into the political coffers, and executing suspects for trivial matters. This doesn't sit well with new cop Rafe Deed (LL Cool J and his one facial expression), and soon a rookie reporter (Justin Timberlake in "Jimmy Olsen" mode) for the local rag starts putting together a story about the police and political corruption. Antagonizing and encouraging Timberlake is his boss (Morgan Freeman, on autopilot), a former Pulitzer-winning reporter who's disillusioned and drinks a lot. (We know Freeman's character isn't completely disillusioned because he can still groove out to that "Time Has Come Today" song.) Coming to the aid of Freeman and Timberlake is Kevin Spacey, an investigator who wears his shirts buttoned up all the way a la David Lynch and has a horrifying hairpiece (it looks as if a marmoset died on top of his head).

Timberlake isn't as bad as you'd expect, but he's not that good either. He's convincing early on as the rookie journalist, projecting an "I don't know what the hell I'm doing" vibe that I remember well from my own journalism days. Unfortunately he never really loses that vibe, and his attempts to do serious scenes show that he learned his craft at the Elijah Wood School of Wide-Eyed Earnestness. One can't blame Timberlake for the movie, though — the story is unremarkable in every way, and the direction workmanlike at best. I'm not sure if Freeman and Spacey could have saved it, even if they had put in some actual effort.

There are one or two not-bad scenes. A gory gunshot to the head livens things up, and there's a nice brawl between two cops that takes place in an office — the cops end up using staplers and phones to beat each other, and it shouldn't work but does.

But even these scenes can't save matters, and as the movie slogs to its inevitable conclusion, you may find yourself alleviating the tedium by pondering such questions as: Will the actor playing the police force captain ever pick an accent and stick with it? If they had substituted a mannequin for the Cary Elwes character, would anyone have noticed? Does LL Cool J have an expression beyond "surly" in his repertoire? What if that thing on top of Spacey's head is a Tribble? How will they transport it to the Klingon ship before it reproduces? And why did Freeman and Spacey sign on for this movie anyway? Did they need the money for mortgage payments, a new pool, or hookers and blow? (I'm not being judgy, I'm just curious.)

Recommended only if you are home sick with the flu and need to kill time before you can take more Nyquil.

# El Diablo

*The mild bunch*

**Year:** 1990

**Director:** Peter Markle

**Screenplay:** Tommy Lee Wallace, John Carpenter, and Bill Phillips

**Cast:** Anthony Edwards, Louis Gossett Jr., John Glover, Joe Pantoliano

I'm probably going to get lots of stick from cinemaphiles for choosing *El Diablo* as this guide's lone Western entry. Yes, I know I should have chosen *Unforgiven* or *The Wild Bunch* or *Fistful of Dollars*. Heck, I probably should have finally gotten around to watching *The Searchers* or *Red River*. But the purpose of this guide is to steer you to things that are off the beaten path, and what meets that definition better than a little-known made-for-cable movie? The good news is that *El Diablo*, while by no means a classic of the genre, is a thoroughly pleasant comedic Western.

Billy Ray Smith (Anthony Edwards, bumbling and baby-faced) is a schoolteacher in a typical small Western town. He's not very diligent about teaching things like arithmetic, preferring instead to read the thrilling stories of Kid Durango out loud to his class. But Billy Ray soon learns the difference between fiction and reality when a band of outlaws led by the infamous El Diablo (Robert Beltran) come to town, rob the bank, kill a few townspeople, and abduct Nettie, one of Billy Ray's students. A rescue attempt fails when the posse is massacred and the sheriff has his tongue removed (off-screen, thankfully), so Billy Ray takes it on himself to rescue Nettie. The only problem is that Billy Ray is the greenest of greenhorns, and cannot shoot or ride to save his life, let alone anyone else's. By chance Billy Ray meets Van Leek (Louis Gossett Jr.), a hard-bitten outlaw who takes pity on Billy Ray and rounds up a motley crew to venture down into Mexico and rescue Nettie.

As you've no doubt surmised, *El Diablo* is not exactly blazing with originality. What it does have is a likable comic streak (though the humor occasionally gets a bit dark, such as a running gag with Billy Ray's horses), and actors who bring the fun. Edwards and Gossett make a fun team, and several of the team that's recruited for the rescue mission make a good impression as well — most notably John Glover as a con man/minister and Joe Pantoliano as a Kid Durango who's not at all what Billy Ray expects.

The movie's main weakness is its story (and yes, that's John Carpenter sharing screenwriter duties), which starts out strong if unremarkable, and falls apart a bit in its final act, when a couple of minor plot threads are completely forgotten about, and when the writers take a character in a direction that seems fairly unlikely (unless said character has a whopping case of Stockholm Syndrome). But it's an enjoyable film overall, largely because of the humor and the actors.

# Equinox

*Off to a good start*

**Year:** 1970

**Director:** Jack Woods

**Screenplay:** Mark Thomas McGee and Jack Woods

**Cast:** Edward Connell, Barbara Hewitt, Frank Bonner, Jack Woods

When it comes to art, sincerity trumps all. That particularly applies to low-budget film-making. Sincerity and a real desire to make as good a movie as possible are what matters — not whether the budget is tiny or the locations limited or the cast amateurish.

You won't find a much better example of sincere, low-budget film-making than *Equinox*. Originally shot as a student film for less than $7,000, it was expanded into a feature and helped launch the careers of special effects maestros Dave Allen and Dennis Muren.

Mental patient David has spent the last year in a catatonic stupor, after fleeing the local woods with a tale of terror and then being hit by a driverless car. An interview David gave when first arriving at the institution gives the reason. He and friend Jim were asked by David's geology professor, Dr. Waterman, to come to Waterman's mountain cabin; seems the professor had found something important. David and Jim decide to turn the meetup with Dr. Waterman into a picnic; tagging along are Jim's girlfriend Vicki and David's blind date Susan. They find Waterman's cabin in ruins with no sign of the professor; a mysterious, beetle-browed sheriff named "Mr. Asmodeus;" and a castle that appears and disappears without warning. And this is **before** they find a creepy old man in a cave, a mysterious book, and some pretty-darn-cool, Harryhausen-esque monsters. In the movies, picnics in the woods never turn out well.

The plot of *Equinox* won't win prizes for originality, but the movie's rather remarkable for what it manages to achieve on an obviously low budget. It originally started as a student film, and though scenes were reshot and added to bring it up to feature length, even the student film scenes have been crafted with care. The camerawork is good (though a bit too reliant on the fisheye-lens at one point — you'll know it when you see it). The acting is nothing stellar but is also much better than one would expect from beginners.

What really makes *Equinox* stand out from other microbudget films is the effects. A nice blend of mattes, forced perspective, camera tricks, and stop-motion animation, they are crude and products of their time, but remarkably well done. The only misstep is a monster who can best be described as the bastard child of Alley-Oop and the Jolly Green Giant, and that's a problem with the concept, not the execution.

It will be no surprise to anyone that those responsible for the effects in *Equinox* went on to bigger and better things, deservedly so. Dennis Muren would go on to work on most of the *Star Wars* movies, *Terminator 2, The Abyss*, and many others, and would win many Oscars. And Dave Allen would also go on to a long career in the movies, with work on films ranging from *Laserblast* to *Honey, I Shrunk the Kids*.

Whether you've got an interest in movie special effects or simply want proof that a low-budget film doesn't have to be crap, take the time to watch *Equinox*.

# Event Horizon

*My eyes!*

**Year:** 1997

**Director:** Paul W. S. Anderson

**Screenplay:** Philip Eisner

**Cast:** Sam Neill, Laurence Fishburne, Kathleen Quinlan

Probably one of the more frustrating situations I face when watching a movie is when I'm confronted with a good idea that got flubbed in the execution. *Event Horizon* may not be the best example of this phenomenon, but it's in the top ten, I'd guess.

Lovecraftian horror? Check. People confronted by the sins of the past? Check. Toss in some good actors and some decent effects and it should work, right? But unfortunately *Event Horizon* only gets it half right, so you'll spend the movie alternating between "this is really creepy" and "this is really stupid."

It starts well, I'll give it that. Some years in the future, the spaceship Event Horizon is doing a top-secret mission to test its instantaneous travel system, which can transport it across the galaxy in a second. But on its maiden voyage, it vanished. Well, I suppose these things happen. But hey! Seven years later it reappears! Isn't that nice?

A search-and-rescue ship with the usual motley crew is sent out to the Event Horizon to find out what happened and if there are any survivors. Leading the crew is the perpetually cranky Captain Miller (perpetually cranky Laurence Fishburne). Also joining the team is Dr. Weir (Sam Neill), who helped design the Event Horizon, and whose haunted eyes and strange manner hint that what they find on the ship may not be so great.

It's when the crew boards the Event Horizon that the flip-flop between creepy and stupid gets out of control. Every genuinely unsettling bit, like the reveal of a horrifying amount of blood on one of the windows, is negated by the design of the ship's engine, a ridiculous tunnel that not only looks like a meat grinder but is actually referred to as such. Gosh, I don't think anything could go wrong in such a place, do you? And the person who designed such a thing couldn't be crazy as a shithouse rat, could he?

*Event Horizon* tries too hard. It wants to be *Alien*, but what made *Alien* so powerful was that its characters and surroundings were so ordinary. The Nostromo's crew may have been flying through space, but their ship's design was recognizable and fairly practical, and the characters were a bunch of working stiffs just wanting to go home. Whereas the situations and design of Event Horizon, while pleasing to the eye in a pretty-creepy way, would tip off any sensible person that Bad Shit Is Going To Go Down Soon.

This wouldn't matter so much if we had characters worth caring about, but there aren't any save for Kathleen Quinlan's medical technician. Neill does a good job, but it's simply too obvious from the start that he's going to be the one to get bad stuff started (or maybe I can never forget that he once played Damien Thorn). The main problem is that we simply don't know enough about the crew to make them much more than cannon fodder, and their fates mean nothing to us. Sure, it is a gory shock when one character gets opened up along the torso, but even though we've established that the ship uses one's fears and past against you, we never learned anything about this character that made his fate explicable.

Director Paul W. S. Anderson manages to get enough creepiness in so that it's not a total waste of time, but low expectations will help a lot (as will a latent crush on Sam Neill, who brings as much fun as he can to the proceedings).

# Intermission: What's on TV?

A whole book could be written about nerdy television — but I'm afraid it won't be written by yours truly.

I blame my mother. It was the 1970s, and Mom was going through a bit of a crunchy phase. Around the time sugary cereals were banned from the house, Mom also put the kibosh on most TV. I have to say I don't really mind this. I never really got in the TV habit, which has enabled me to get a lot done.

That said, a few shows have filtered through and are powerful enough influences on me to merit inclusion in this book.

## The Electric Company

This was the kid's show I liked best while growing up. It didn't have that vaguely creepy vibe that *Sesame Street* often gave off; instead it had my favorite superhero, LetterMan (faster than a rolling "O", stronger than silent "E"), and Morgan Freeman encouraging kids to read. What more could you ask for?

## The Twilight Zone

This was a mainstay of summer vacation, and of Thanksgivings when local TV would often have a marathon of episodes. The show's quality varied wildly, and some episodes haven't stood the test of time, but when the show was on its game, it was fantastic. At its very best the show was a fusion of surrealism, morality play, and showcase for nifty acting (particularly from character actors). You all know the classics, but some of my favorite lesser-known episodes are character-focused stories: "A Passage for Trumpet," "Nervous Man in a Four-Dollar Room," "The Trouble With Templeton," "Deaths Head Revisited," "A Piano in the House," "In Praise of Pip," "The Masks," and "The Last Night of a Jockey."

## Twin Peaks

David Lynch does a prime-time mystery/soap opera as only he can. When a young prom queen named Laura Palmer is found murdered, the case brings an eccentric FBI agent to the oddball town of Twin Peaks. There's plenty of quirky humor to be found, but also unforgettable characters and a dark undercurrent of secrets (the latter explored more deeply in the spinoff/prequel film *Twin Peaks: Fire Walk With Me*).

## Buffy the Vampire Slayer

For a long time I avoided this show solely because of its name, and because I didn't see how the concept (high school girl does battle with vampires and other monsters) could be anything other than ridiculous. Shows what I knew. Joss Whedon took this admittedly silly premise and made it into a remarkable show about friendship, the toll of heroism, and much more.

## Firefly

Lightning strikes again with Whedon's single-season wonder, a combination of Western and science fiction genres. Though part of its enduring appeal comes from its very brevity and the fact that it never had a chance to wear out its welcome, the joys of its premise, dialogue, and uniformly excellent ensemble cast cannot be denied.

## Breaking Bad

The story of a high school chemistry teacher who, faced with inoperable lung cancer, opts to raise money for his family by cooking crystal meth, is both a nail-biting exercise in suspense and plot twists, and a phenomenal character study. Recommended to writers who want to see how to transform an initially sympathetic character into one of the all-time great evil bastards.

# Excalibur

*The stuff of legends*

**Year:** 1981

**Director:** John Boorman

**Screenplay:** Rospo Pallenberg and John Boorman

**Cast:** Nigel Terry, Helen Mirren, Nicol Williamson

The list of films that are "better than they had any right to be" is surely a long one, and surely *Excalibur*, John Boorman's adaptation of Arthurian legend, is at the top of that list. It's a film that gets one thing wrong for every two things it gets right, and somehow manages to hit the sweet spot between Silly and Serious, and end up being emotionally affecting in the bargain.

All this is apparent from frame one of the film, which opens with titles and explanatory text in a cheesy typeface much like the one Yes used on all their album covers in the 1970s, accompanied by the stone-gorgeous music from Richard Wagner's *Gotterdamerung*. There immediately follows a night-time battle that's notable for its ferocity, and for introducing Uther Pendragon (scenery-chewing Gabriel Byrne) and wizard Merlin (Nicol Williamson, stealing every scene he's in). Uther's just won a battle and feels this makes him worthy to wield "the sword of power" Excalibur. Merlin agrees, though he seems to have doubts.

Said doubts are more than justified at the banquet celebrating the truce between Uther and the duke of Cornwall. The duke makes the spectacularly bad choice of having his wife Igraine dance for the men; Uther decides he must have Igraine even if it means war. Merlin is annoyed but uses his magic to allow Uther to impersonate the duke (and have him killed) and have sex with Igraine. Their child will be Arthur, a king who will heal the land and become the stuff of legends.

From there the myth plays out: a dying Uther thrusts Excalibur into a stone, where it can be retrieved only by the true king; Arthur is raised by Sir Ector and eventually draws the sword, becoming king; his friends become the Knights of the Round Table; Arthur marries Guinevere (Cherie Lunghi); a love triangle forms between Arthur, Guenivere, and Arthur's best friend and favorite knight Lancelot; Arthur's witchy half-sister Morgana (Helen Mirren) stirs up trouble — you know how it goes. Even if you're not familiar with the legends, Boorman somehow makes it all readily understandable even though he provides very little exposition and background.

Perhaps what helps the film is that despite the story being one of legendary/mythical proportions, its characters never cease to be human, with human frailties and strengths that are easily recognizable. These range from Uther's lust for Igraine and Morgana's lust for power to Arthur's sincere desire to be a good king, even when his quest for justice puts his own happiness and his marriage at risk. Throughout Boorman emphasizes duality: magic and religion, pride and humility, basest lust and noblest aspirations. Arthur himself is the essence of duality: a king destined to unite men and provide justice, despite being the product of betrayal and rape.

The film hits the ground running with the opening battle scene and keeps a strong pace for quite a while. Even during the scenes when Arthur first acquires Excalibur and runs away from his responsibilities, only to be lectured by Merlin, the pace doesn't flag. This is primarily due to the strong acting by Williamson, whose voice wraps itself around the often florid dialogue and makes it work, and by Nigel Terry as Arthur. Terry's performance is often, sadly, overlooked: he has to be a legendary figure throughout, and Terry carries the role well from inexperienced (but savvy) youth to world-weary leader of men. Unfortunately the movie hits a bit of a slump with the "love" story between Lancelot and Guinevere; it's never convincing and you'll just want to slap the two of them. Much more entertaining is the banter between Merlin and Morgana: they're both representatives of a faith that's being replaced by Christianity, but while Merlin accepts this and seeks to preserve peace, Morgana rebels against it and stirs up chaos.

There are obvious budgetary limitations at play during the film — one wonders if the opening battle was filmed at night to disguise the fact that there seem to be only two-dozen men involved. But Boorman gives the film a mythic, magical quality (music selections by Wagner and, most famously, Carl Orff's "O Fortuna" from *Carmina Burana* help out a lot) that lets one overlook the seams where the budget shows and the occasionally muddy narrative.

It helps that the acting is uniformly excellent. In addition to Williamson and Terry, we have Helen Mirren as a slinky, sexy Morgana and Paul Geoffrey as a noble Percival. Cherie Lunghi as Guinevere and Nicholas Clay as Lancelot are let down by the characters, who just aren't appealing in any retelling of the myths, but give it their all nonetheless. Keep an eye out for astonishingly young Liam Neeson and Patrick Stewart in the cast as well.

It's flawed and sincere, silly and serious. And that's what makes it so memorable.

# The Exorcist III

*"Legion is my name," he answered*

**Year:** 1990

**Director:** William Peter Blatty

**Screenplay:** William Peter Blatty, based on his novel *Legion*

**Cast:** George C. Scott, Ed Flanders, Brad Dourif, Jason Miller, Nicol Williamson

The perfect is the enemy of the good. I'm a firm believer in this, and not just because it helps me rationalize my fetish for guys with lantern jaws and abnormally large chins. It's true for movies as well, and a fine example is the contrast between *The Exorcist* and *The Exorcist III*.

*The Exorcist* is a film that's pretty darn close to perfect. Tone, cinematography, acting — perfect. It's an excellent adaptation as well. By contrast, *The Exorcist III* has some occasionally silly moments and unrealistic dialogue, a confusing story, and a climactic exorcism scene that's clearly the result of movie studio interference.

And of the two, *The Exorcist III* is the movie I re-watch most often. Because the first film, while superior, is cold. Its human moments — Father Karras' anguish over his mother's illness and death, and Chris MacNeil's desperation about her daughter's strange behavior — are sometimes frozen out by that chilly perfection. *Exorcist III*, while flawed throughout, is a much more human and warm film, and because of that is much more enjoyable to watch than its predecessor.

It's fifteen years to the day after the events of *The Exorcist,* and Detective Kinderman (George C. Scott) and Father Dyer (Ed Flanders) are taking their minds off the loss of their old friend Father Damien Karras (for this film Kinderman's relationship with Karras has been retconned from acquaintance to longtime friendship) by going to see *It's a Wonderful Life*. Kinderman has more than the past on his mind, though. A young boy has been hideously murdered, and the killer's methods are exactly those of the Gemini Killer, a murderer who died in the electric chair on (you guessed it!) the very night Father Karras died defeating the demon possessing Regan MacNeil. You can rest assured this is not a coincidence; nor is it a coincidence that the murdered boy and the next couple victims have a connection to the MacNeil possession. And when a patient on the disturbed ward of the local hospital looks like Father Karras and claims to be the Gemini Killer...well, things get complicated.

It's clear from this description that *Exorcist III* is a bit of a mess. Its plot leans heavily on contrivance, and Kinderman doesn't come off as the best detective (the "headless statue" reveal is a great "gotcha" moment but you wonder how Kinderman overlooked it). Yet it works despite its flaws, creating a peculiar alchemy from its atmosphere, acting, and quirky scenes and dialogue.

It's a striking film in visual terms, and this is evident from its opening moments when the sanctuary of a church is violated by a powerful, demonic wind. During this sequence, a statue of Christ suddenly opens its eyes. It's an image that doesn't recur and doesn't actually mean anything in terms of the film's story, yet it's one of the touches that makes this film memorable. This visual sense is carried throughout, and while it occasionally veers into the ridiculous, the overall result is good. Sometimes it's even both at the same time, such as Kinderman's dream of a way station to heaven. It's striking in its scares as well, most notably the "hallway scene" which even the film's detractors admit is a masterful sequence.

The acting is wonderful throughout. Scott plays Kinderman as a man who uses cynicism and bluster to cover his deep loathing of the crimes he investigates and his lack of faith in God or in anything that can justify the evil in the world. His scenes with Ed Flanders' Father Dyer are a joy to watch; they have the easy camaraderie of old friends and their surface bickering covers deep affection (note the way Kinderman runs most of the way to Dyer's hospital room, only to get into character just outside the door and stroll casually in). It's a shame we can't have a spin-off TV show in which they team up and solve mysteries. The supporting cast is all fine as well, from Brad Dourif's terrifying Gemini Killer to Scott Wilson as a doctor on the verge of a breakdown. Even Jason Miller as Karras and Nicol Williamson as exorcist Father Morning, both of whom were shoehorned into the film at the studio's insistence that there be an actual exorcism in the film, do well.

Blatty, who adapted the story from his novel *Legion*, wisely keeps most of the horrors off-screen. Save for one moment in the tacked-on exorcism scene, there's remarkably little onscreen violence and gore. Though horrific crimes happen, they take place out of sight for the most part and Blatty lets aftermath descriptions and long, appalled silences as hardened investigators contemplate the crimes, clue us in to the awful nature of what they've seen. These scenes never let us forget the human cost of murder, and help us identify with Kinderman as he wonders how a loving God can let such things happen.

It's flawed and serious and silly and spiritual in its own way. It's not the excellent film its predecessor is (please note: I just pretend *Exorcist 2: The Heretic* never happened), but it's unjustly overlooked and worth watching.

# Fair Game

*Mamba Number 5*

**Year:** 1988

**Director:** Mario Orfini

**Screenplay:** Mario Orfini and Lidia Ravera

**Cast:** Gregg Henry, Trudie Styler, Bill Moseley

I'm just not afraid of snakes. I've had snakes for pets and think they are awesome creatures, so if a movie is going to have snakes be objects of fear, it's going to have to sell that concept really well. The "black mamba in the house" thriller *Fair Game* does not do that.

Frankly, I'm not sure even ophidiophobes could find *Fair Game* thrilling, or even interesting. It takes a decent premise and competent actors and gives us a movie that leaves you checking your watch multiple times even though the film's barely 80 minutes long.

A car drives through the desert as cheesy 1980s synth music plays (get used to cheesy 80s music, you'll be hearing a lot of it). The driver arrives at the home of tattooed snake farmer Bill Moseley (all young and baby-faced!) who sells the driver a black mamba. Genre fans take note: This is Moseley's only scene in the film, and though he's good, he doesn't make the rest of this movie worth watching.

Turns out that the driver is a rich electronics whiz who's still angry about being left by his ladyfriend, an oh-so-kooky artistic type. Personally, I think these two are better off being rid of each other. Mr. Creepy (Gregg Henry) is a cold, controlling guy with serious anger issues. Ms. Annoying (Trudie "Mrs. Sting" Styler) is a free spirit who sculpts octopi out of Play-Doh and talks to her pet turtles. Wait, I take that back — they should stay together so they don't inflict themselves on unsuspecting people.

Anyway, Mr. Creepy drops in on Ms. Annoying and after some vague yet long-winded talk about their failed relationship, he leaves, but not before (a) setting the black mamba loose in her apartment and (b) rigging the front door so it can't be opened. Did I mention that in addition to being incredibly huge, Ms. Annoying's house has just the one door, and not a single window. (And she's an artist? Don't they need, I don't know, light to see what they're doing?) Did I mention that Mr. Creepy has injected the mamba with hormones to make it extra-aggressive? Welcome to Plot Convenience Theater, folks!

The movie gets really tedious for a while as Ms. Annoying works on her Play-Doh sculptures, talks to herself, runs a bath, talks to herself, videotapes a "kiss off" message to Mr. Creepy, talks to herself, and eventually discovers there's a mamba in her apartment. Then she cranks up the annoyingness as she tries to elude the mamba, which seems to have acquired the power of teleportation — no matter where she goes in her huge house, the snake is right there! Did I mention that Mr. Creepy is following the antics of Ms. Annoying and the mamba, on this ridiculous video game setup?

If you've ever wanted to see Sting's wife run around in her underwear and throw lit matches at a snake, this is the movie for you.

*Fair Game*'s main problem is that the two main characters are so unappealing it's hard to feel much interest in the situation (the black mamba, on the other hand, just oozes screen charisma and it's a shame the screenplay didn't have the mamba and Moseley team up to solve mysteries — I'd watch that movie). Moreover, it's impossible to fathom what these two people ever saw in each other or how they'd have had the emotional investment that would explain why they're so bitter now. And Ms. Annoying's actions once she discovers the snake are just inexplicable — for example, she's learned from some magazine clippings she just happens to have lying around that the mamba is attracted to adrenaline, so she creates **more** adrenaline by running madly around her house. By then I was rooting for the mamba.

# Fight Club

*Pow! Boff! Smack!*

**Year:** 1999

**Director:** David Fincher

**Screenplay:** Jim Uhls, based on the novel by Chuck Palahniuk

**Cast:** Edward Norton, Brad Pitt, Helena Bonham Carter

*Fight Club* was a box office disappointment in its 1999 release and it's not hard to see why. The source novel, Chuck Palahniuk's debut, was not a mega-bestseller. Two of the three leads were cast against type. The film was difficult to market and the negative criticisms (basically "guys beat each other up a lot") got the most press. Mr. Average Moviegoer may well have been still too squicked and baffled by, respectively, *Se7en* and *The Game* to want to see another David Fincher film. Likewise, the film's violence (not overtly gory but brutal and realistic), nonlinear structure, and willingness to play games with its audience may have turned off viewers.

The film's nameless Narrator (Edward Norton in an Oscar-worthy performance) isn't having such a good time lately. He has a job he despises as a claims reviewer for an auto company whose vehicles regularly have accidents that incinerate the car's passengers. Said job forces him to travel constantly, which doesn't help his crippling insomnia and his total detachment from other people. Refused tranquilizers by his doctor, the Narrator starts going to support groups for people suffering from testicular cancer, brain parasites, tuberculosis, and other diseases. Only there, masquerading as a disease victim, is he able to cry, get some emotional release, and get some sleep.

Unfortunately he soon meets another support group "tourist," Marla (Helena Bonham Carter, leaving those Merchant-Ivory movies way behind). When there's another "faker" in the room, the Narrator can't cry, and his insomnia returns. It's shortly after this, on a return flight from a business trip, that the Narrator meets soap huckster Tyler Durden (Brad Pitt, skanky and charismatic). That same night, when the Narrator comes home to find that his condo has been blown up and all his worldly possessions are so much rubble, he calls Tyler asking for a place to stay. After a few beers in a local dive, Tyler says he'll give the Narrator a place to stay. On one condition.

"I want you to hit me as hard as you can."

The Narrator's and Tyler's parking lot brawls become a regular thing. And soon one of the onlookers asks if he can be next. Thus is born Fight Club.

To say more would risk ruining not just a significant plot twist, but all the little zigzags that the *Fight Club* story takes.

Praise must go first to David Fincher, who opens up the full bag of stylistic tricks — flashbacks, computer animation, sound distortion, odd camera angles, voiceover, breaking of the fourth wall, and so on. But they never feel like tricks. *Fight Club* is an intensely personal film, in that its perspective is solely that of the Narrator's. Every event is seen through his eyes, and filtered through his perspective. We can't always trust the Narrator's version of things; but then, neither can he.

Kudos are also due to screenwriter Jim Uhls (and to *Seven* scribe Andrew Kevin Walker, who did some uncredited work on the screenplay) for not only translating such a difficult novel to the screen, but in doing it so well that Palahniuk himself claims to like the film better than his book — particularly the ending.

I also want to mention the film's score by The Dust Brothers, which is a perfect accompaniment to the film.

Last but certainly not least, praise goes to every member of the cast, all of whom are perfect in their roles. Edward Norton should have been Oscar-nominated for his performance as the Narrator, engaging our interest if not always our sympathy as his life starts getting out of control. Brad Pitt as Tyler skanks up his good looks and radiates a sleazy charisma that makes you nod your head during his primitive philosophizing, and of course we mustn't overlook his lovely, lovely abs! Helena Bonham Carter will be a shock to those who know her only from films like *A Room With a View*, and ends up being the movie's only wholly sympathetic character.

*Fight Club* received a lot of negative press when it was released for its violence. And while there isn't much gore, the film doesn't shy away from the effects that brutal fighting would leave. Rob Bottin's makeup will make you wince, especially when you realize that these battered, bloodied people all have to get up and go to work the next day. Ouch.

*Fight Club* has also been criticized for the primitive philosophizing of Tyler Durden. It's immature. It's supposed to be. The key to this philosophy (indeed, the key to the entire movie) lies in the Narrator's assertion that he is "a thirty-year-old boy." It's the no-substance sloganeering of someone who's grown, but never grown up.

You've probably seen it by now, but if for some reason you still haven't, give it a try.

# The Final Conflict

*It's the end of the world as we know it and I feel underwhelmed*

**Year:** 1981

**Director:** Graham Baker

**Screenplay:** Andrew Birkin

**Cast:** Sam Neill, Lisa Harrow, Rossano Brazzi

"This is the way the world ends/Not with a bang but a whimper."

This was how T. S. Eliot ended his brilliant poem "The Hollow Men," and these words also nicely sum up how the *Omen* series ends.

*The Final Conflict* opens promisingly with a wordless sequence showing a construction crew unearthing the seven daggers that can kill the Antichrist. These daggers go up for auction and find their way into the hands of Father DeCarlo (Rossano Brazzi, in a nicely dignified performance) who enlists the help of six other monks to form a posse to go after the Antichrist.

The Antichrist is, of course, our old fiend, I mean, friend, Damien Thorn (Sam Neill in one of his earliest roles). Damien's all growed up now, and is the head of the ridiculously powerful and wealthy Thorn Corporation. Despite what the incredibly misleading DVD cover would have you believe, Damien is **not** President of the United States, though he is contemplating a Senate run in a couple years. The job he's currently angling for is that of ambassador to England. Then the current ambassador has a very convenient and quite gory shotgun suicide (induced by one of those demonic Rottweilers from the first movie), leaving the post of ambassador open. (P. S. — Damien gets the job.)

Why ambassador to England, you ask? Well, after consulting a totally fictitious book of the Bible, Damien has determined that not only is Christ about to be reborn (which will put a definite crimp in Damien's apocalyptic plans) but will be reborn in England. Father DeCarlo and his monks have figured this out too, and head off to England.

This is where the movie goes downhill. Never mind the fact that in the previous two films it was clearly stated that all seven daggers were needed to kill Damien and in *The Final Conflict*, just one will do (consistency has never been this franchise's strong suit); the real problem is that most of the monks have apparently graduated from the Keystone Kops school of stealth and agility. This wouldn't be so bad, except that the monks meet their ends in ways either hopelessly mundane (mistakenly stabbed, falling off a bridge) to laugh-out-loud ridiculous — Death By Snoopy, indeed.

The movie comes close to redeeming itself with a genuinely creepy sequence in which Damien's followers are given the task of killing all male babies born on a particular night, to eliminate the new Christ child. Though not explicit at all, the sequence is chilling not just because it breaks the cinematic taboo of death and children, but because so many of Damien's followers are children themselves, or people in positions of trust, including a nurse and a priest.

This sequence aside, the whole movie just seems obligatory. Director Graham Baker shows no flair or enthusiasm. The Christ child subplot is resolved so ambiguously as to be almost incoherent (this was the second time I'd seen the film and I still wasn't sure what had happened). *The Final Conflict* lacks *The Omen's* deep seriousness and courage of its convictions, or *Omen 2*'s "Ain't **that** a nasty way to go!" death scenes.

The actors try hard. Sam Neill, despite a terrible haircut and a tendency to smirk too much, gives it his all but can't overcome the lethargy of the film. Rossano Brazzi is to this film what David Warner was to *The Omen* — a voice of calm belief and reason, who knows not only what is going on but how unbelievable it seems to an average person. And Lisa Harrow stands out as Kate, a TV journalist who falls for Damien, then learns some unpleasant truths about him, and must make some hard choices.

*The Final Conflict* has one of the weaker endings I've seen. While it makes sense theologically for ultimate evil to not stand much of a chance against ultimate good, there had to be a more satisfying way to resolve this than the Hallmark card ending the movie gives us.

# The Fisher King

*Holy fools*

**Year:** 1991

**Director:** Terry Gilliam

**Screenplay:** Richard LaGravenese

**Cast:** Jeff Bridges, Robin Williams, Mercedes Ruehl, Amanda Plummer

My two favorite themes in fiction are revenge and redemption. The first is more commonplace, probably because it's easier to dramatize. Redemption is much trickier. I can think of few films that give us a better redemption story than *The Fisher King*.

Howard Stern-esque shock jock Jack Lucas (Jeff Bridges in a beautiful performance) is living what he considers the high life. He's rich, has a beautiful girlfriend, may be getting a starring role in a sitcom, and his radio personality gig lets him be insulting and condescending without consequence. That is, until his careless rant to an unbalanced listener about evil yuppies results in the listener taking a shotgun to a restaurant and killing seven people before turning the gun on himself. Three years later, Jack is a morose, borderline-suicidal alcoholic, unable to hold a job, living off his long-suffering girlfriend Anne (Mercedes Ruehl). One night he's mistaken for a homeless man and nearly set on fire by two thugs, when his life is saved by Parry (Robin Williams). Parry's a homeless man with delusions of being a knight...and three years earlier Parry was a college professor whose wife was the first victim of the Jack's radio listener (her murder sent Parry into catatonia, and when he emerged he was no longer a professor but a homeless wannabe-knight).

Jack soon understands the reason for Parry's insanity, and tries to help him. He finds that simply foisting money on Parry doesn't help (Parry doesn't care about money). It seems that his chance for redemption lies in two tasks: helping Parry woo the woman of his dreams, a mousy, eccentric woman named Lydia (Amanda Plummer); and in securing a cup Parry says is the Holy Grail, in reality a knickknack in a rich man's house.

*The Fisher King* is not only a redemption story, but a fairy tale. Indeed, it's the invisible fairies that only Parry sees that tell him that Jack is "the one." It's a nice touch of ambiguity that this could mean that Jack is the one responsible for Parry's loss and emotional trauma, or it could mean that Jack is indeed the one to help Parry get the grail and the girl and some happiness in his life again. Of course, both may be true. *The Fisher King*'s New York setting is, thanks to Terry Gilliam's off-kilter portrayal, a place where magic is found in the unlikeliest areas. The shining example of this is the justifiably famous Grand Central Station sequence: as Parry follows Lydia, the station becomes a beautiful ballroom and the commuters waltz. But the magic isn't all lovely, as the Red Knight (a genuinely terrifying figure) that haunts and pursues Parry demonstrates.

For all the moments of spectacle, at its heart the movie is a character piece, a story of flawed and damaged people who come together, and all of the actors are more than up to the job. Williams puts his usual manic buoyancy into the character of Parry and not just his cheerful moments but his terror of his past and of the Red Knight as well — but his best moment is a quiet one, as he recounts the myth of the fisher king to Jack. The always underrated Bridges gives a moving, multilayered performance as a man who's trying to find redemption and become a real human being. It's refreshing that Bridges, Gilliam, and screenwriter Richard LaGravenese aren't afraid to let Jack be a real bastard at times; this makes his redemption all the more satisfying. The women don't have as much to do but they make every moment count. Mercedes Ruehl justly won a Best Supporting Actress Oscar for her role as Anne, whose brashness and tough NYC girl persona hide her vulnerability and her deep need for love that makes her sell herself short and put up with Jack's bullshit. And Plummer brings a peculiar beauty to Lydia as only she can, with Lydia's loneliness and fear of rejection just below the surface.

It's a remarkable, moving film that is arguably Gilliam's most mature work, with his flights of fancy given just the right amount of time and his chilliness alleviated by LaGravenese's screenplay. Sadly, the film isn't mentioned much these days, which is a shame. By all means, seek it out.

# Fist of the North Star

*The sound of one jaw dropping*

**Year:** 1986 (Japanese release)/1991 (English release)

**Director:** Toyoo Ashida

**Screenplay:** Susumu Takaku, based on the manga series by Buronson and Tetsuo Hara

**Cast:** John Vickery (voice, English release), Melodee Spivack (voice, English release), Wally Burr (voice, English release)

I'm going to go on the record here as not being especially fond of anime. With rare exception I find the voices grating, the animation not that interesting, and the plots uninvolving or incomprehensible. And I won't even get into some of the weird sexual shit (I'm trying to recall the days of innocence when I had not seen *Urotsukidoji: Legend of the Overfiend*).

But I'm trying to be inclusive in this book and if I'm going to include, for example, a nasty Italian cannibal movie, I should include an anime film as well. I don't think *Fist of the North Star* is particularly good as anime goes, but it's so unabashedly random and over-the-top (not to mention having one of the worst endings I have ever seen) that I'm fond of it in a way.

We open with your traditional post-apocalyptic world, and I'll admit there's a really nice touch during an apocalypse flashback scene when we see the spirits of thousands of dead people departing. We then join our hero Ken and his girlfriend Julia, who are minding their own business traversing the wasteland when they are accosted by Shin, who calls himself Fist of the South Star and declares that Julia is his woman now. Ken fights the good fight but is defeated, and then insult is added to injury when, after Shen makes off with Julia, Ken's brother Jagi, who's been observing the fight, tosses Ken into a chasm where he plummets for what feels like five minutes, bouncing off ledges in true Wile E. Coyote fashion.

Some time later Ken, who did not die after his ass-kicking and plummeting, and who has been getting new powers and eating his Wheaties, shows up just in time to save two annoying kids from marauders. Then he teams up with a fighter named Rei to save Rei's sister and beat up Jagi, and then Ken's other brother Raoh, who's been waging war like mad, arrives to unleash even more whoop-ass.

Most of the non-Miyazaki anime I've seen has a peculiar fever-dream quality to it, especially in terms of pacing and plot. In the given moment it makes sense, but when you try to actually articulate what's happening you realize you have no idea. *Fist of the North Star* is a stellar example of this quality. There is plot to be found in the film — quite a bit of it, actually — but really the film seems to exist as an excuse to put some of the most over-the-top, gory martial arts battles ever seen on the screen. No one simply falls over and dies in this film. They scream, their heads expand like Jiffy Pop and explode, they spray blood in huge arterial fountains, their guts and eyeballs go a-flying, and they get their arms cut off so cleanly they don't even realize it at first. In fact, everything about this film is over the top. Nearly every time a male character enters a scene, the earth crumbles beneath his feet. No one has dialogue in this movie; they proclaim everything while their eyes turn strange colors and their hair blows in the wind. Speaking of the dialogue, one moment it's pompous pseudo-philosophizing, the next moment people are saying things like, "Say your goodbyes, lardass, because you're already dead."

A problem with the film is its sheer repetitiveness. Yes, watching someone rupture and explode after being punched by Ken is amusing at first, but it becomes wearying about an hour in.

Fortunately there is just enough randomness (such as the fellow who can not only turn his body into steel but keeps changing size from scene to scene) to keep things from getting too dull. And then there's the ending. You will hear a loud clang after the ending. This will be the sound of your jaw hitting the floor in sheer disbelief. I'm trying not to oversell this, but 23 years after we first saw this movie, my husband and I still talk about how ridiculous the ending was.

It's not a good movie in any conventional sense, but it is memorable.

# Flesh + Blood

*Ren Faire was never like this*

**Year:** 1985

**Director:** Paul Verhoeven

**Screenplay:** Gerard Soeteman and Paul Verhoeven

**Cast:** Rutger Hauer, Jennifer Jason Leigh, Tom Burlinson

Whenever I get into a funk about the state of the world, I find it's helpful to look at history. Once I've taken a peek into the past and seen how ugly, squalid, and brutal life could be for most people, I'm usually able to put things in perspective.

*Flesh + Blood* won't fit anyone's ideal of high art, and I've no idea how historically accurate it is, but the movie makes it clear that life in 16th century Europe wasn't one big Renaissance Faire.

It's somewhere in Western Europe, the year is 1501. A band of mercenaries led by Martin (Rutger Hauer in his prime!) help a lord recapture his castle. Unfortunately the lord is a bit short of funds, and reneges on his promises of payment to the mercenaries and throws them out into the rain. Fueled by a desire for revenge on the lord, and egged on by their resident religious man, a half-mad "Cardinal," the mercenaries ambush a caravan, injuring the lord and capturing Princess Agnes (Jennifer Jason Leigh, who spends a good chunk of the film naked) who is betrothed to the lord's son, Prince Stephen (the seriously bland Tom Burlinson).

The mercenaries, with Agnes as a perhaps-willing accomplice, take over a small castle. Soon Stephen arrives with soldiers to storm the castle and get Agnes back. To complicate matters, the countryside is being overrun with bubonic plague outbreaks.

For its first two-thirds, *Flesh + Blood* is an entertaining and fairly realistic view of a time that, while no longer the Dark Ages, had its fair share of hardships and brutality. When Stephen and

Agnes profess their love (they've known each other for less than an hour) their first kiss is exchanged under a tree from whose limb hang the grotesquely decayed corpses of two hanged criminals. More interesting is that while Agnes is a princess who's spent her whole life in a convent, and Stephen is a scholar, neither pay the corpses any particular attention or find anything unusual about it. Likewise, in the opening battle, property is destroyed, slaughter is wholesale, women are raped, and it's all commonplace.

The film gets rather silly in its last third, when Stephen and his men build a siege machine that is ridiculously elaborate while also inviting comparisons to the Trojan Rabbit in *Monty Python and the Holy Grail*. More effective and rather disturbing is a look at germ warfare, sixteenth-century style (hint: a plague-infested dog carcass makes for an effective biological weapon, especially if it ends up in the water supply).

Also weakening the film is Tom Burlinson as Stephen. We're meant to empathize with Stephen (as much as we can empathize with anyone in this movie); he's learned and intelligent, he rejects the superstition of the times and protests his father's cruelty. But more often than not he comes off as merely arrogant, and Burlinson lacks charisma of any kind. More than once he reminded me of Tom Cruise in *Legend*. This is not a good thing.

Giving much stronger performances are Rutger Hauer as Martin and Jennifer Jason Leigh as Agnes. Throughout the film Hauer is intelligent and charismatic, to the extent that you often take Martin's side even as you recognize he's a murderer and rapist. Leigh gives probably the most interesting performance, playing a woman who does nothing without calculation, and works every situation to her best advantage.

Which leads us to the most controversial and most interesting part of *Flesh + Blood*: the relationship between Martin and Agnes. When Agnes is captured by the mercenaries, she's raped by Martin. The scene is particularly chilling because Agnes begs the women in the mercenary band to help her. Not only do they not help, they mock her and help hold her down. Agnes then turns the situation as much to her own benefit as she can by pretending to enjoy the rape, and persuading Martin to be the only one to have her sexually. Although Martin never outright promises this, he prevents the others in the group from abusing Agnes.

It's never clear if Agnes comes to have feelings for Martin, or if she is merely submitting to and encouraging his desires to keep him interested in her and prevent him from handing her over to the rest of the mercenaries. It's to the actors' credit and to Verhoeven's that what could have been a reprehensible premise (a woman falling for her rapist) and is not only logical within the context of the film, but an interesting reflection on what was necessary to survive in such a brutal time.

Though not for the squeamish or the easily offended, *Flesh + Blood* is entertaining for anyone interested in the grittier side of history. Huzzah!

# Flesh Gordon

*Star whores*

**Year:** 1974

**Director:** Howard Ziehm and Michael Benveniste

**Screenplay:** Michael Benveniste

**Cast:** Jason Williams, Suzanne Fields, Joseph Hudgins

I'm no expert in the fields of adult cinema, but it seems that the 1970s were a odd time for the genre. In addition to "classic" X features like *Deep Throat* and *Behind the Green Door*, you also had porn versions of *Alice in Wonderland, Hansel and Gretel*, and even *The Erotic Adventures of Pinocchio*.

Joining the ranks of odd porn is *Flesh Gordon*, a parody of the *Flash Gordon* serial that manages to offer lots of skin, sex that falls just short of hardcore, a by-the-numbers sci-fi plot, and some fun surprises along the way.

The world is being bombarded by a ray that causes all under its influence to engage in frantic sex with whoever is nearest. This wouldn't be such a bad thing except when an airliner's entire crew join the passengers in their orgy, causing the plane to crash. Oops. Bailing out of the plane at the last minute are Flesh Gordon (Jason Williams, with unfortunate hair) and Dale Ardor (Suzanne Fields, often naked). The two make their way to the lair of Dr. Flexi Jerkoff (Joseph Hudgins turns in the best performance in the film), and the three board his penis-shaped rocket to the planet Porno. The planet's ruler, evil Emperor Wang (William Hunt, overacting shamelessly) is the one behind the sex ray, using it to make Earth so chaotic he can take over.

As they fight to defeat the evil emperor, Flesh and his friends encounter rapacious robots, Penisaurus monsters (one-eyed, of course), Amazon women, the Robin Hood-esque (and very gay) Prince Precious and his band of merry men. They'll be flushed down a giant toilet, learn how to use the Power Pasties (don't ask), and save Dale from a horny monster who speaks in craaaaaazy beatnik lingo.

If it sounds ridiculous, that's because it is. It's also not especially erotic, nor is it very explicit — I've heard some prints contained hardcore but none of that is in the DVD, despite the promise of 15 minutes of restored footage. The acting is mostly awful, although Hudgins and Hunt seem to be having fun. The humor is sophomoric at best (you'll laugh and groan at the same time).

But the movie's saved by the film-maker's love for science fiction films — a mere porn ripoff wouldn't have gone to the trouble of the fun spaceship models and the stop-motion animated monsters, which are not in the Harryhausen league but definitely add some class to this movie. There's also a strangely innocent tone to a lot of this — a celebratory orgy by Wang's servants consists of naked people doing the Bunny Hop. Must be seen to be believed.

*Flesh Gordon* is more a curiosity piece than an actual movie, but you could do a lot worse if you're looking for some laughs.

# Four Flies on Grey Velvet

*Possible sequel: Five Gnats on Mauve Polyester*

**Year:** 1971

**Director:** Dario Argento

**Screenplay:** Dario Argento

**Cast:** Michael Brandon, Mimsy Farmer

Hey, everybody! I've got good news and bad news! The good news is that *Four Flies on Grey Velvet*, one of Dario Argento's early giallo films, is finally on DVD. The bad news is that the movie isn't very interesting.

Drummer Roberto Tobias (Michael Brandon, looking like he escaped from Emerson, Lake, and Palmer's *Love Beach* album cover) is having a bad day. Not only does his band suck, but he's being stalked by a weird guy in sunglasses. Roberto confronts the man at an abandoned theater, the guy pulls a knife, and in the feeble struggle that ensues Roberto accidentally stabs the man, who then falls into the theater's orchestra pit. Oops, clumsy! Worse still, somebody wearing a creepy doll mask is in the balcony, taking pictures of the whole thing. Well, I suppose that sort of thing could happen to anyone.

Roberto tries to forget the whole thing ever happened, but soon the doll-masked person is sending Roberto taunting letters, slipping photographs of the killing into his record collection, and sneaking around Roberto's house in the dead of night. Roberto's wife Nina (Mimsy Farmer) wants to go to the police but Roberto opts instead to hire a swishy private investigator to look into matters. Meanwhile, Roberto's maid has figured out something's amiss and decides to take up blackmail. And the body count goes up.

This all makes *Four Flies on Grey Velvet* sound much more interesting than it really is. Sadly, the film is done in by a sluggish pace, a dearth of action/suspense scenes, and a plot that's slapdash even by Argento's standards. Things pick up a bit in the film's last quarter when we get a fascinating if ludicrous forensic technique to try to identify a murderer, a lengthy "why I did it" monologue by the killer, and the world's ugliest necklace as a plot point.

But it's hard work getting to that point. The Argento films I've seen have been made or broken by the strength of the protagonists. In his better efforts, such as *Deep Red* and *Suspiria*, the protagonists are interesting, savvy people who do more than just react to what happens around them (it helps that those films starred David Hemmings and Jessica Harper, respectively — actors able to engage audience sympathy). But Argento's weaker films (such as *Opera* and *Inferno*) have all been marred by dull, unsympathetic protagonists, and *Four Flies on Grey Velvet* is no exception. Roberto has no personality and Brandon's sleepwalk of a performance does the character no favors. Worse, Roberto and Nina's relationship, despite being central to the story, is vaguely defined and the actors have so little chemistry they come off as glorified housemates. (Roberto's willingness to jump in the sack with Nina's cousin the moment Nina's out the door doesn't gain him any sympathy from the audience either.)

There are a few tense moments and effective images, but overall it's for Argento completists only.

---

# Freaks

*One of us*

**Year:** 1932

**Director:** Tod Browning

**Screenplay:** Clarence Aaron "Tod" Robbins

**Cast:** Olga Baclanova, Harry Earles, Henry Victor, Leila Hyams

---

Possibly the most controversial of the wave of horror films that started in 1931 with classics like *Frankenstein* and *Dracula, Freaks* is an oddity. Perhaps too flawed to be a true classic, it's been condemned as exploitation, banned, rediscovered, and its worth still debated to this day.

There's trouble brewing under the big top of a traveling circus. Beautiful trapeze artist Cleopatra (Olga Baclanova) is adored by dwarf Hans (Harry Earles). Hans is engaged to Frieda (Daisy Earles) and Cleopatra has eyes for thuggish muscleman Hercules (Henry Victor), but when Cleopatra finds out that Hans is heir to a fortune, she marries Hans and then begins to poison him. And when Hans' fellow "freaks" — dwarfs, microcephalics, people without limbs, and more —

find out, they take a terrible revenge on Cleopatra and Hercules.

Like one of its circus performer characters, *Freaks* is a movie that walks many tightropes, and this is what has given the film its lasting power over the years. This is nowhere more prevalent than in the film's use of real people with real physical anomalies to portray the "freaks." Stephen King once wrote that we can only feel comfortable with horror when we can see the zipper on the back of the monster suit. And while the circus freaks in the movie are not the monsters of the film (that dubious honor goes to the characters of Cleopatra and Hercules), their physical differences are unsettling even to modern audiences. The impact of this was even greater back in the 1930s — as film historian David Skal points out in his insightful commentary, at the time of the film's release many considered those with physical deformities to be "subhuman" — microcephalics (called "pinheads" in the film) were often exhibited in carnivals as "missing links" between apes and men.

The question of whether or not the film exploits the "freaks" is a question that has been asked since the film's release. Certainly they're made to appear horrific in their final scene when they take revenge on Cleopatra and Hercules, but it's also clear that the audience is seeing the freaks through the villains' eyes. Browning wisely refrains from making the movie a "freaks vs. normal people" conflict. Two of the "normal" performers, seal trainer Venus (Leila Hyams) and clown Phroso (Wallace Ford), always treat the freaks as they would any other fellow performer in the circus; Venus offers Frieda a shoulder to cry on and Phroso joins the celebration when the Bearded Lady has a baby. And there's a fun sequence when the circus ringleader visits all the performers and we get to see how they've learned to use their anomalies to make a living: limbless Prince Randian rolls and lights his own cigarette and legless "human torso" Johnny Eck gets around on hands as well as anyone could with legs.

*Freaks* suffered problems with censorship from the very beginning, and the 62-minute running time of this cut is drastically shortened from its original script. Moreover, the original ending has long since been lost, and up to three different endings have been in circulation at one point or another. The film was a box office failure and was later shown under misleading titles like *Forbidden Love* and *Nature's Mistakes*, luring viewers who thought they would see a nudie film. In England the movie was banned for thirty years.

Much as I'm against censorship, it's probably best that we're seeing *Freaks* in a somewhat abbreviated form. The film feels longer than its just-over-an-hour running time. The first 45 minutes are downright sluggish at times, with humor that doesn't quite work and choppy transitions between scenes. Browning's best work was in the silent era, and he shows his discomfort with sound films. He isn't helped by the fact that many of the performers give awkward, stilted line readings (Daisy Earles in particular) and that the accents and sound recording limitations sometimes render dialogue unintelligible.

But the film kicks into overdrive with the wedding banquet. At first humorous, the scene escalates in tension as Cleopatra and Hercules get very drunk, make fun of Hans, and openly display their passion for each other. Hans is humiliated, Frieda leaves, and the freaks pass around a loving cup filled with champagne, singing that they accept Cleopatra as "one of us." Cleopatra reacts with scorn and revulsion, and her fate is sealed.

The DVD offers up a fine set of extras — all of the endings that can be found, a featurette on the film and the performers, and commentary from Skal (whose book *The Monster Show* also covered *Freaks* in detail) that describes cut scenes, the reasons for the intensity of the reaction to the film on its release, and the life and work of Browning and many of the film's performers.

It's not always a comfortable viewing experience, but there will never be a movie like it again.

# Frogs

*Ambiguous amphibians*

**Year:** 1972

**Director:** George McCowan

**Screenplay:** Robert Hutchison and Robert Blees

**Cast:** Ray Milland, Sam Elliott, Joan Van Ark

One of my favorite subgenres of horror is the "Nature Bites Back" film. This was a staple of the 1970s, when people sat up and took notice about pollution, and ecology became a hip topic. The movies all followed the same basic format: Man messes with nature (via littering, pollution, bogus science) and nature's critters fight back by noshing on B-list actors.

*Frogs* is a shining example of the subgenre. It's a silly film that isn't the slightest bit frightening unless you have reptile/amphibian issues, but is entertaining nonetheless.

Freelance photographer Pickett Smith (Sam Elliott, nearly unrecognizable without his mustache) is canoeing along the Florida waterways, snapping photos of local critters. But the further he canoes, the more pollution he sees: beer cans, discarded toys, sewage, and so on. He doesn't see Iron Eyes Cody with a tear in his eye, but perhaps that footage got left on the cutting room floor.

Pickett soon ventures out onto a lake, where a speedboat swamps his canoe and tosses Pickett into the water. The speedboat is driven by Karen Crockett (astonishingly scrawny Joan Van Ark) and her brother Clint (Adam Roarke), who are there for the annual Independence Day family reunion with their grumpy patriarch (Ray Milland) and extended dysfunctional family. Karen and Clint bring Pickett back to the family mansion so he can get some dry clothes.

But it's not all ice cream and lollipops at Casa del Crockett. Papa Crockett is a tradition-bound grouch who gets upset when the grandkids are five minutes late for lunch. The place is overrun with frogs, and Grover the handyman is missing. It turns out Grover has met his end at the hands of the local critters, and soon all the island's wildlife, including snakes, spiders, geckos, snapping turtles, alligators, leeches, and butterflies will be joining forces to knock off the Crocketts.

Like most films of this type, *Frogs* takes a little while to get going, with chitchat that could be called "character development" if the movie had any actual characters, as opposed to critter chow. No matter, because the film's Florida setting is atmospheric and creepy, the people are unlikable enough to make us root for the critters (but not so unlikable that watching them is painful), and the actors mostly keep straight faces. The death scenes are plentiful and ridiculous in a good way, though I'm still puzzling over the Death by Spider Silly String. And of course, there's the baffling Snapping Turtle Incident, in which a full-grown woman somehow gets stuck in ankle-deep mud and is killed off-screen by a snapping turtle.

The most puzzling thing about *Frogs* is, well, the frogs. Despite the film's title and the poster art ("Today the pond! Tomorrow the world!"), the frogs don't actually do much but croak a lot, sit around, hop menacingly (did I just write that?), and jump onto the birthday cake. The implication is that the frogs are the leaders of the critter uprising, which actually makes sense (did I just write that?) seeing as how frogs are among the first creatures in an ecosystem to show the effects of pollution.

*Frogs* isn't without its flaws — aside from the cardboard characters and inherent silliness of the premise, there are bad day-for-night shots, obvious insertion of stock footage, and breathing corpses. But the flaws are somehow endearing.

If you've ever wanted to see lizards use poison gas to kill a man, *Frogs* is your film.

# Galaxy of Terror

*The worms go in, the worms go out*

**Year:** 1981

**Director:** Bruce D. Clark

**Screenplay:** Marc Siegler and B. D. Clark

**Cast:** Edward Albert, Erin Moran, Robert Englund, Sid Haig, Grace Zabriskie, Zalman King

I love Netflix, but I also miss the days of going to the video store. Inevitably I'd make my way to the horror, science fiction, and cult movies sections, look at the lurid cover art and wonder if I'd be able to persuade my mom to let us rent some of these things (more often than not I was unsuccessful). Nowadays I'm finally getting to see some of the movies whose VHS cover art fascinated me so long ago, and while many of these movies have ended up as disappointments, I'm glad to say that *Galaxy of Terror* was a perfectly satisfying B movie.

Transmissions from the spaceship Remus, last known to have landed on the planet Organthus, have abruptly ceased. The vaguely sinister Planet Master, who is probably not a nice guy, immediately sends another spaceship, Quest, on a rescue mission. After a bumpy journey with some delightfully cheesy special effects, the rescue ship arrives to find the Remus in ruins (along with a lot of other ships) and no sign of the Remus' crew. And while there seem to be no inhabitants on Organthus, what the planet does have in an uncanny ability to tap into one's deepest fears, and use those fears to alter reality.

*Galaxy of Terror* is fun to watch for a variety of reasons. Though clearly an *Alien* ripoff (motley spaceship crew sent on dubious rescue mission and hijinks ensue) it uses the stolen premise as a starting point rather than trying to slavishly re-create the source material. The central idea of a force that can tap into the subconscious and use a person's fears against them is strong enough to make up for the weak screenplay. The characters are thinly sketched at best, but the cast is game and for the most part put in good performances — an unexpected delight is seeing lots of familiar genre actors. Robert Englund, Grace Zabriskie, and Sid Haig are all on hand, along with *My Favorite Martian* himself, Ray Walston, future *9 ½ Weeks* director Zalman King, and Erin Moran, best known as Joanie Cunningham from *Happy Days*.

The movie looks great. Though clearly shot on a low budget, the sets are effective and there's some truly striking imagery throughout — particularly the scenes inside the mysterious pyramid found on the planet. If bits of the production design look hauntingly familiar, there's a good reason for that. The production designer and second unit director was a fellow called James

Cameron — he went on to make a few movies you might have heard of.

Also of note are the special effects. These are old-school, practical effects and as such they have an organic quality that makes them all the more effective. There's some nifty (if briefly glimpsed) stop-motion animation, and some startling gore effects that pack a real punch. Probably the only effects misstep is a giant worm — the prop itself is well-made but it lumbers around like the Snuffulufagus from *Sesame Street,* which doesn't exactly terrify.

*Galaxy of Terror's* problem point is its screenplay, which is satisfactory while it's subjecting its characters to nastiness, but weak in all other regards. The ending is particularly nebulous — frankly, I don't have a clue what happened. These quibbles aside, the movie does exactly what it sets out to do — give you an entertaining time. And those of you who may have been avoiding it because of **that** scene (the one with the giant worm that made the movie semi-notorious back in the day) can rest assured that the whole thing is too absurd to be disturbing or even very offensive

If you need a nostalgia fix for the good old days of B-movie ripoffs, look no further than *Galaxy of Terror.*

# The Gates of Hell

*The one with the gut-barfing*

**Year:** 1980

**Director:** Lucio Fulci

**Screenplay:** Lucio Fulci and Dardano Sacchetti

**Cast:** Christopher George, Katriona Macoll

The only thing more difficult than remembering which Italian cannibal movie is which is trying to remember which Italian zombie movie is which. Let's see, now was *The Gates of Hell* the one with the splinter in the eyeball? No, that was *Zombie.* Wait, was it the one when acid ate that lady's face off? No, that was *The Beyond.* Or was it the one where the zombie rat set off the zombie plague? Bother, that was *Hell of the Living Dead.* Oh, now I remember! *The Gates of Hell* is the one where the lady barfs up her entire digestive tract! How **could** I have forgotten?

(The cruel irony is that even though I got all these movies mixed up, the only reason I can do that is because I know way more than a normal person should about Italian zombie movies. Somebody help me!)

For those of you who still want to read on even after that bit about the digestive tract, here goes. In the town of Dunwich, New England (a very Italian-looking New England, I might add), a priest commits suicide in the local graveyard. This sequence is remarkable for several reasons, not the least of which is a priest committing suicide, which would pretty much put him on the Hell Express if I remember my catechism correctly. But it's especially noteworthy because when the priest tosses his hangman's rope over a tree branch, the foley guys have dubbed in the sound of a whip cracking. Then the priest just sort of levitates about six feet in the air so he can put his neck in the noose (I wish I could do that so I wouldn't need a stepladder to get the casserole dish off the top shelf). All this is accompanied by meandering, pseudo-progressive rock music that sounds like a Pink Floyd reject (around the time of *Obscured by Clouds*, perhaps).

The priest's suicide is witnessed by a group of psychics holding a séance. The lead psychic, Mary (Katriona Macoll) is so freaked out by the priest's suicide that she spazzes out and has a fatal heart attack right there! But lucky for Mary, she's not only just mostly dead (still slightly alive), but she hasn't been embalmed and her cemetery employs the world's laziest gravediggers. They just lower her into the grave and figure they'll do the actual burying in the morning. Right about this time reporter Peter (Christopher George), loitering in the cemetery, hears Mary's screams and busts open her casket with a pickaxe. I must point out that while the movie is overall fairly ridiculous, the rescue from the premature burial is genuinely suspenseful, as Peter sends the pickaxe slamming through the casket lid, mere inches from Mary's face.

It turns out that the priest's suicide opened the gates of Hell, and now the dead are roaming around killing people and being gross. It's up to Peter and Mary to put a stop to things, but it won't be easy. Dunwich isn't a fun place to be, what with the zombies who can (a) teleport and (b) rip the back of your skull off and play with your brains. Add in catapulting rats, a rain of maggots, and the local pervert getting a drill put through his skull for reasons I don't recall and which probably weren't important anyway, and you have a zombie movie as only the Italians know how to make them.

You've probably gathered that not much in this movie makes sense. Apologists like to say that this is done deliberately, to reproduce the feel of a nightmare, and so on. I'm of the opinion that director Lucio Fulci (a prolific director who dabbled in all genres but made quite a name for himself with movies like this one, plus *Zombie*, *The Beyond*, and *The House by the Cemetery*) was only interested in plot as a means to get him to the next disgusting setpiece. Combine this lackadaisical approach to story with disregard for logic, one-dimensional characters, enthusiastic if not-terribly-good acting, decent atmosphere (hope you like fog machines), and lots of gore, and you have a movie that's not good in any usual sense of the word, but very entertaining if you're in the right mood. Adding to the fun are things like the aforementioned foley work during the priest's suicide scene, as well as the fact that the rain of maggots is generated by a (clearly visible) snowblower.

*The Gates of Hell* is also quite an educational film. Just a few of the things I learned:

- Do not have a staring contest with a dead priest. It will make your eyes bleed and then you'll vomit up your entire digestive tract. Really.
- The back of the human skull has the consistency and durability of a marshmallow, thereby making it very easy for zombies to rip off the back of your head and play with your brain.
- In most cemeteries, the bodies are only buried an inch or two below the surface, for the zombies' convenience when resurrecting.
- It's standard practice in "New England" to be buried *sans* embalming, with a mirror on the inside of your coffin lid.
- It's purely optional for your movie to have an actual ending.

This big bowl of cinematic spaghetti also goes by the title *City of the Living Dead.*

---

# Glengarry Glen Ross

*Death of a fuckin' salesman*

**Year:** 1992

**Director:** James Foley

**Screenplay:** David Mamet, based on his play

**Cast:** Al Pacino, Jack Lemmon, Alec Baldwin, Ed Harris, Alan Arkin, Kevin Spacey, Jonathan Pryce

---

If you ever doubt Thoreau's assertion that most men lead lives of quiet desperation, just watch *Glengarry Glen Ross* and you'll know how right he is.

That desperation is evident from the first post-credits scene: two men in adjacent phone booths. One, Shelley Levene (Jack Lemmon) is talking to his daughter, who's seriously ill and in the hospital; the other, Dave Moss (Ed Harris) is trying to close a real-estate deal with a client who is clearly not interested. Both men hang up in disgust, and after venting about the weak sales leads they have and after taking out their ire on office manager John Williamson (Kevin Spacey), they go to the real estate sales office they work for.

That's when the desperation goes to a whole new level. A flashy consultant (Alec Baldwin) informs the salesmen that they are fired unless they get better sales numbers, and gives them a savage dressing-down that is full of slurs on their abilities as salesmen and on their masculinity.

The salesman with the highest numbers for the month will get a Cadillac; the one with the second-highest numbers will get a set of steak knives; everyone else is fired. With that, the salesmen — has-been Levene, temperamental Moss, and bumbling George Aaronow (Alan Arkin) — are sent out into the rainy night to save their jobs. Levene tries to wheedle stronger leads out of Williamson, and Moss and Aaronow discuss the situation. Meanwhile, hot-shot salesman Ricky Roma (Al Pacino), who missed the pep talk, schmoozes a drunk, morose businessman. And the next morning, the salesmen arrive at the office to find that the office has been burglarized and the new sales leads — which can help save these men's jobs — have been stolen.

Watching *Glengarry Glen Ross* is an exercise in duality. It's difficult to watch these men go through such doomed, desperate measures to save their jobs: Levene's servile sales tactics that served him well in the past but aren't helping him now; Moss's short-fuse anger at the job, his clients, the bosses, and his fellow salesmen; and Aaronow's self-fulfilling defeatism. The only salesman who seems to be on his game is Roma, but hiding behind his cocky exuberance is the knowledge that the luck will run out and he'll be like Levene, running on fumes and scrambling to make a sale, any kind of sale. Things aren't better on the company end of things, where office manager Williamson not only is responsible for the sales team but is the recipient of endless amounts of verbal abuse from his bitter employees. It's clear in every interaction that Williamson has taken years of contempt and insults from the salesmen, and when he finally gets a chance for payback, it's one of the more depressing and cynical moments put on film.

What sweetens this bitter pill is watching great actors at the top of their game. Every single one brings his character to vivid life, not just through David Mamet's gloriously profane dialogue, but through every movement, from Lemmon's hunched posture to Harris' fidgety time-bomb movements to Baldwin's self-satisfied swagger. In words and actions they convey the central theme of the play, that (as Levene puts it) "a man is his job" and if a man can't do his job, not just his livelihood but his identity as a man is threatened.

James Foley's direction makes good use of locale, so that the film doesn't feel overly stagy as adaptations of plays often do. The constantly pouring rain, combined with the camerawork often saturated in red, gives you the impression that these men are in a kind of hell.

It's a well-made but thoroughly depressing film; however, if you've had a bad day at work, it can help put things in perspective for you.

# Godzilla Vs. Hedorah

*It's garbage day*

**Year:** 1971

**Director:** Yoshimitsu Banno

**Screenplay:** Yoshimitsu Banno and Takeshi Kimura

**Cast:** Akira Yamauchi, Haruo Nakajima, Kengo Nakayama

What the hell did I just watch?

(I ask that question frequently but I never expected to say it about a Godzilla movie. See, I grew up watching Japanese monster movies on the local TV station's "Monster Rally" show every weekend so I fully accept that giant turtles can fly while spinning like one of those ground blooming flowers you get in your fireworks box set, or that international government agencies will immediately defer to the wisdom of short-pantsed boys named Ken. I can take the normal insanity of a Godzilla movie in stride. But this movie is a whole new level of wackadoo.)

I ask again: What the hell did I just watch?

*Godzilla vs. Hedorah* (or as it's known in America, *Godzilla vs. the Smog Monster*) is a truly odd Godzilla film, and that's apparent from the opening credits: As oh-so-trippy psychedelic oil lights flash and the theme song "Kaese! Taiyô wo" plays (it **will** get stuck in your head and there's nothing you can do about it) we watch scenes of sludgy, filth-covered water. In one rather effective shot, and the first of many uneasily creepy moments, the sludge contains a broken mannequin that at first glance resembles a corpse. I hope you like those scenes of the creeping pollution, because you'll see more of them. A lot more.

We meet up with our standard little kid Ken and his scientist Dad, fretful Mom, and hep-cat older brother. Anyway, soon a grizzled old fisherman brings a strange tadpole to scientist Dad to examine, and sooner than you can say, "*Prophecy* totally ripped off this story angle," it's clear that the tadpole is a new kind of monster that's created from and lives off pollution.

Soon the monster, dubbed Hedorah, is giving anyone who touches it an acid burn, sending toxic sludge into a nightclub, and climbing up on top of a factory to suck on the smokestacks and breathe in the fumes. He also starts flying around and spraying sulfuric acid in his wake, causing people to have reactions ranging from coughing fits to dissolving away to a skeleton in mere seconds. Hep-cat brother thinks the answer is to hold a rave on Mount Fuji (no, really) but Ken knows what's really needed is for Godzilla to show up and kick some butt.

118

The plot as described above is only slightly nuttier than many other Godzilla movies. But what puts *Godzilla vs. Hedorah* into its own weird area is its combination of obvious sincerity and batshit lunacy. The latter is demonstrated in many ways.

There's the wildly inconsistent tone, which veers from typical Godzilla kiddie fare to preachy message movie to horror film. There are the baffling artistic decisions: Who can explain the odd little animated sequences that pop up in the film's first two thirds? (They're like Gerald Scarfe's animation segments for *Pink Floyd: The Wall* except that they're not good.) What about that nightclub hallucination sequence, in which hep-cat brother imagines that all the people in the club have fish heads? What's with the bit with all the TVs (including yet another disturbing image, this one of a crying baby up to its neck in sludge), and with the use of Hokusai's *Great Wave off Kanagawa* at the ending (just before blatant bid for a sequel)? And who decided to have the music for the film be so wildly inappropriate? Godzilla in particular gets a bizarre theme that's heavy on the horns and sounds like a drunken burlesque band trying to play a Spaghetti Western tune.

Speaking of Godzilla, this movie isn't the big guy's finest hour. This was into his "big cuddly" phase when he'd show up to bail out mankind's (or at least Japan's) ass from various threats. (Note to self: Get to work on scholarly treatise of Godzilla's character arc from vicious monster to friendly big lizard.) His first smackdown with Hedorah is indecisive; his second takes place mostly on a barren plain, at night, with no buildings to knock over or set fire to. In a departure from established form, the monsters spend relatively little time with fisticuffs and a lot of time staring each other down, doing odd little sidesteps and hand gestures. Oh, and Godzilla demonstrates a newfound talent. He can use his atomic breath as a sort of jet engine and fly through the air. I'm not making any of this up.

I suppose I have to give props to screenwriter and director Yoshimitsu Banno for trying to do something outside the box. It's clear he's very sincere about the film's ecological message, and the movie does look very polished for a Godzilla film. Unfortunately, "different" does not always equal "good" and *Godzilla vs. Hedorah* isn't a good movie.

What really does the movie in is its reliance on gruesome imagery — not bad in itself but sufficiently out of character with other Godzilla films to make the viewing experience uncomfortable. It's too juvenile to be taken seriously and too dark and creepy to be fare for children. Parents: take note of the high onscreen body count and numerous scenes of people being reduced to skeletons by Hedorah's acid.

I've got a soft spot for interesting failures, and *Godzilla vs. Hedorah* definitely qualifies. It's worth a view if you're a fan of the genre, if only to see its nutty peak/nadir.

# Gothic

*Scary stories to tell in the dark*

**Year:** 1986

**Director:** Ken Russell

**Screenplay:** Stephen Volk

**Cast:** Natasha Richardson, Gabriel Byrne, Julian Sands, Miriam Cyr

Certain events in history seem to defy novelists' and moviemakers' attempts to dramatize them. One such event is the fateful evening when Lord Byron, Percy Shelley, Mary Godwin (soon to be Mary Shelley), Mary's half-sister Claire Clairmont, and Byron's physician Dr. John Polidori came up with ideas for supernatural stories, the most famous of which would be Mary Shelley's *Frankenstein.* Such a combination of literary personalities, many of whom where quite controversial in their day, would seem ready for a literary or cinematic adaptation. But it hasn't turned out that way.

Certainly the most gaudy if not the most well-known movie to portray the Byron-Shelley-Godwin-Clairmont-Polidori shindig, *Gothic* is a typical Ken Russell interesting failure, rife with overacting, historical liberties, and perverse sexual and religious imagery. Like most Russell movies, it's not good in the strictest sense, but it's seldom dull and at times gives hints of a much better, more serious movie.

Lord Byron, the rock star of poets, is in exile at his mansion in Switzerland; he's accompanied by his physician (read: sycophant and all-around whipping boy) Dr. John Polidori. Joining Byron for the night are fellow poet Percy Shelley, Shelley's mistress (he's married to another woman) Mary Godwin, and Mary's half-sister Claire, who is Byron's lover. No sooner are all the parties in the door then shenanigans begin: playing hide-and-seek, shagging, quaffing vast amounts of laudanum, and generally acting like overgrown children (the long-suffering expressions of Byron's servants are a particularly nice touch) in a house that contains robotic belly dancers, goats, and jars full of leeches. Things settle down a bit when they take turns reading a book of ghost stories, and this scene is the first sign of a better movie lurking within. As Mary and Claire read, we see them participating in the story not just as narrators but as characters, each projecting their fears into the story.

The party then holds a séance and things start to get very bizarre, as the characters then stumble around the house encountering their personal demons, having arguments, and in the film's best sequence, getting a glimpse into the future, which holds tragedy for all of them. By the next morning, fate is set in motion and Mary Godwin-Shelley will have the inspiration for *Frankenstein.*

The main problem with *Gothic* is that it takes fascinating, tragic figures from history and turns them into insufferable twats. Blame goes to screenwriter Stephen Volk, who thinks poets spend all their time goofing around like overgrown toddlers while spewing faux-philosophical dialogue that would make even the most pretentious undergrad wince. The actors don't help. Gabriel Byrne as Byron alternates between chewing the scenery and letting his dark, surly good looks do the acting for him. Julian Sands as Shelley is a disgrace to his profession, an over-the-top performance even by Ken Russell's standards. Miriam Cyr plays Claire as a woman who seems to revel in the physical and emotional abuse her lover bestows on her, so it's difficult to feel much sympathy for her.

Coming off better are Natasha Richardson as Mary and Timothy Spall as Polidori. It helps that they are the outsiders in the group, unable to join fully in the infantile revelry. (Mary is still mourning her prematurely born baby and lives in fear that her living child will perish. Polidori is guilt-ridden to the point of self-mutilation and suicide by the conflict between his Catholic faith and his homosexuality.) These characters' conflicts and sorrows are understandable and help gain the audience's sympathy, whereas Shelley's ravings come off as the babble of a nitwit who's had too much laudanum, and Byron seems like a sociopath.

*Gothic* isn't a scary movie per se, though there's a nice jump scene when Mary has a dream that mirrors the famous painting *Nightmare* by Henry Fuseli. The movie's most affecting moment is not one of fear but one of sorrow, as Mary sees the future and realizes that it holds little but madness, grief, and death for all the parties (Russell holds true to history in this scene). This leads to a perhaps unintentionally chilling scene of the morning after, when the revelers enjoy the peaceful day unaware of what the future holds. It's in these scenes that the film has its power, not in the poetical ravings or ooga-booga opium fantasies.

# Grindhouse

*At the late night double feature picture show*

**Year:** 2007

**Director:** Robert Rodriguez (feature and trailer), Quentin Tarantino (feature), Edgar Wright (trailer), Eli Roth (trailer), Rob Zombie (trailer)

**Screenplay:** Robert Rodriguez, Quentin Tarantino, Edgar Wright, Eli Roth, Rob Zombie

**Cast:** Rose McGowan, Freddy Rodriguez, Kurt Russell, Rosario Dawson, Zoe Bell

*Grindhouse* isn't just one movie — it's two movies in one. The first is Robert Rodriguez's mutant zombiethon *Planet Terror*, and the second is Quentin Tarantino's talk-and-adrenaline-fuelled *Death Proof*. In fact, *Grindhouse* is more than a double feature, it's a time machine, taking us back to not so much a golden age of trash cinema — can trash cinema **have** a golden age? — but to a time when going to the movies was not the obligation or chore it so often is, but fun in every way.

Grindhouse opens with the first of four "trailers" for movies that I damn well hope get made: *Machete* is a bloody Mexploitation romp starring the always scary and ever-welcome Danny Trejo. Then it's on to the first feature: *Planet Terror* opens with a fetching go-go dance by the luscious Rose McGowan, then sets the stage for the story proper. A cliché military base next to a cliché small town harbors nasty biochemical weapons that get into the atmosphere and turn most of the populace into oozing cannibal zombies. Doing battle with the zombies are a group of uninfected townspeople including McGowan, her former boyfriend Wray (Freddy Rodriguez), a tough-guy sheriff (Michael Biehn), and two unhappily married doctors (Josh Brolin and Marley Shelton).

*Planet Terror* hits the ground running and never once lets up, piling up a cinematic hot fudge sundae of explosions, gore, guts, bullets, conspiracy, a jar of pickled testicles, and a subplot involving Osama bin Laden.

But there's more to come. *Planet Terror* is followed by three more trailers: Rob Zombie's self-explanatory *Werewolf Women of the SS*, Edgar Wright's Eurotrash haunted house chiller *Don't*, and Eli Roth's holiday massacre *Thanksgiving*. If at least one of these (I vote for *Don't*) doesn't get made into a feature, I'm going to be very annoyed.

But there's even more! Next up is Quentin Tarantino's homage to fast-car features, *Death Proof*. Unlike *Planet Terror*, *Death Proof* takes a while to get going (and in doing so is much more true to the way grindhouse movies really were — most of them have some really slow bits in between all the fun stuff). *Death Proof* follows a group of pretty (and pretty shallow and nasty) young women as they talk, hang out, and have a few drinks at a local bar. Also at the bar is Stuntman Mike (Kurt Russell, stealing the movie), a former movie stuntman who flirts with the women and offers one of them a ride home in his ominous-looking car — an offer she'll very soon wish she'd refused. A second group of women that includes two stuntwomen then catches Stuntman Mike's eye, and the result is a white-knuckle ride for characters and audience members alike.

To say more about the movies or the trailers would be to give away the surprises of *Grindhouse*, and I would not deprive anyone of those. Suffice to say that both *Planet Terror* and *Death Proof* do fine jobs recreating the B- and C-list movies of yesteryear, from the scratched-up prints and clunky camerawork to missing reels that leave out scenes to hilarious effect. Everything works in both movies — every actor hits the right note, with special mention going to McGowan, Rodriguez, and Russell, and kudos to Rosario Dawson and stuntwoman Zoe Bell (Uma Thurman's double in *Kill Bill*) in *Death Proof*, for bringing some warmth and humanity to the goings-on.

# Gymkata

*Hikeeba!*

**Year:** 1985

**Director:** Robert Clouse

**Screenplay:** Charles Robert Carner, based on the novel *The Terrible Game* by Dan Tyler Moore

**Cast:** Kurt Thomas, Richard Norton, Tetchie Agbayani

If you look in the "Well, it **seemed** like a good idea at the time" database (and if there isn't one of those, there certainly ought to be), you'll find *Gymkata* quickly enough.

Set the Wayback Machine for 1984, Mr. Peabody. The U.S. men's gymnastics team has just won gold medals at the Los Angeles Olympics and everyone's pretty happy about it. And someone got the idea that gymnast Kurt Thomas could ride his athletic abilities into a second career as an action movie star.

The very next year gave us *Gymkata*, and the rest is history.

*Gymkata* opens with what feels like ten minutes of Thomas doing his gymnast thing over the opening credits. Two things are noteworthy about this sequence: it's the only time Thomas ever seems comfortable in front of the camera, and (much to my surprise) this movie is **not** a Golan-

Globus production but actually released by a major studio. Reflect on that second fact from time to time over the next 90 minutes.

Interspersed with Kurt's flipping-and-spinning are scenes of some dude apparently being pursued through the wilderness, and who, while crossing a rope bridge over a huge chasm, gets shot with an arrow by some vaguely medieval-looking guys. Before the audience can do more than say, "Huh?" Kurt finishes gymnasticating and immediately gets taken aside by a Shadowy Government Dude.

Turns out that the U.S. government wants to put a satellite thingy for the "Star Wars" Strategic Defense Initiative in the backwater country of Parmistan (pronounced "par-MEE-stan" if you please). But for some reason (i.e., the movie needs a plot) the government can't just ask or negotiate. A U.S. citizen needs to participate in "The Game" — an annual event held in Parmistan in which participants must run an obstacle course and along the way get attacked. They even have to fight their way through a town that's populated entirely by criminally insane people. Oh yeah! The survivor/winner gets to ask the Parmistan government for one favor that **must** be granted. Kurt's mission, should he choose to accept it, is to win "The Game" and ask the Parmistan government to let the U.S. put the satellite thingy in their country.

Incidentally, I still can't decide how I feel about the title of this annual event. I like "The Game" for its simplicity, but can't help wondering if something livelier would have worked better. Maybe something like "Race Toward Your Almost Certain Doom, Charlie Brown!"

I digress. So Kurt goes through one of those complicated training montages (almost none of what he does in this montage has any relevance to later events). Then he meets some shady guys, gets it on with the Parmistan king's improbably hot (not to mention improbably Asian) daughter, rescues the improbably hot daughter when she gets kidnapped, and spends what feels like half an hour running about the alleys of whatever city they're in. Oh, and he also defeats some bad guys using gymnastics.

No, really. In this alleyway there's a pipe going between two buildings that's exactly the same height and has the same weight support capabilities as those bars we saw Kurt twirling on during the opening credits. What are the chances of that happening? Anyway, Kurt does his spinny thing and clocks the bad guys who conveniently walk into range of his feet.

Then it's off to Parmistan where we learn the king is a doofus and his right-hand man is the same guy who shot that other dude with an arrow during the "Huh?" sequence of the opening credits. *Quelle surprise!* Kurt joins in "The Game" and I won't give away the ending, but the only thing missing is a "U.S.A.! U.S.A.!" chant over the climactic freeze frame.

*Gymkata* is one of those movies that gets almost nothing right, so it's hard to narrow down the list of things it gets wrong.

But I'll start with Kurt Thomas. Or actually, with the idea of Kurt Thomas as an action movie star. What the moviemakers didn't take into consideration is that in order to do all that awesome flipping and spinning stuff, gymnasts have to be lithe, tiny, young guys — not brawny action dudes. Thomas has boyish good looks and undeniable physical grace and speed, but when he tries to spout tough action hero dialogue he's about as bad-ass as a seven-year-old. His flat line readings and single facial expression don't help either.

Another problem is the aforementioned use of gymnastics as a martial art. It just doesn't work. First of all, the whole "gymnastics combined with karate" concept is so ridiculous even the narrator for the movie's trailer doesn't buy it. Second of all, to execute said concept the moviemakers need to give Thomas lots of open space for his flips, the aforementioned convenient pipe, and, in the scene that may make you doubt your sanity, a pommel horse in the middle of town. That's right. They made a feeble attempt to disguise it as... um... something that's not a pommel horse? Don't ask me, I just review these things.

But it's all a good kind of wrong, and *Gymkata* is the best movie *Mystery Science Theater 3000* never riffed on. There's so much bad movie gold. I could go on and on but I must single out two things. First, Kurt's wardrobe, which is always some combination/variation of red, white, and blue. U.S.A.! (Unfortunately the wardrobe includes a sweater that had me debating "Is it gay or is it just Eighties?" every time it was on screen.)

Second, I have to give a shout-out to director Robert Clouse, best known for directing *Enter the Dragon*. With *Gymkata* he's made a movie that combines 1970s kitsch with 1980s cheese. I particularly love the overly loud sound effects — a simple punch to the jaw sounds like someone dropped a ham off a three-story building. They don't make 'em like this any more.

## Halloween III: Season of the Witch

*Mischief managed*

**Year:** 1982

**Director:** Tommy Lee Wallace

**Screenplay:** Tommy Lee Wallace

**Cast:** Tom Atkins, Stacey Nelkin, Dan O'Herlihy

It's hard to think of a better example of a movie franchise's "red-headed stepchild" than

*Halloween III: Season of the Witch.* A flop with both critics and fans, it also killed any further movies in the franchise until 1988's *Halloween 4: The Return of Michael Myers,* a full 5 years later. This isn't hard to fathom — the makers took a radical approach in trying to use the *Halloween* name to go in a completely different direction, and anything called *Halloween* that wasn't the unstoppable Shape/Michael character was doomed to failure. (It didn't help that the premise of *Season of the Witch* is more than a bit ridiculous, not that that's entirely a bad thing.)

The good news is that while *Halloween III: Season of the Witch* is not without flaws, it's both silly and creepy at the same time, and in the end is quite entertaining in its own way.

The movie opens with a man running desperately through the night. He's clutching an orange pumpkin mask, and his pursuers are strangely impassive men in suits (kudos to cinematographer Dean Cundey for making all the imagery in this film, but especially of these pursuers, far more ominous and effective than it has any right to be). The man eventually makes his way to a hospital, still clutching the mask and babbling that something or someone has to be stopped. Unfortunately one of the pursuers comes to the hospital, kills the man, and then goes outside and sets himself on fire. Now that's how you start a movie!

Lucky for us, on duty that night is perpetually grumpy doctor Dan (Tom Atkins). Dan's curiosity is piqued when he finds out that the man who immolated himself in the hospital parking lot left behind not a charred corpse or even bones, but a bunch of clockwork gears. Soon he teams up with the daughter of the man who was murdered at the hospital; they determine there's a connection to the pumpkin mask the man was carrying. This mask, along with two other designs (skull and witch, if you must know) made by the Silver Shamrock company, are **the** hot item for Halloween! Kids all over the country are buying them! There's a huge national ad campaign about them, with relentlessly catchy jingle. This all becomes fairly troubling when our amateur sleuths visit Santa Mira, the home of Silver Shamrock, and make some unsettling discoveries.

I won't spoil the surprises, but let's just say that the silly/creepy dynamic continues right up to the movie's closing frames.

In addition to its fine blend of silly and creepy, *Halloween III* also manages to be incredibly dated and remarkably prescient at the same time. The dated elements include a time when there were just three major TV networks (trust me, this is relevant to the plot) and the Silver Shamrock masks, which would have maybe sold like hotcakes in the 1950s but in the 1980s? Not so much. There's something quaint about the idea that kids would wear these generic masks regardless of their costumes.

And yet that detail about the popularity of the masks is one of the things that makes the film so prescient. It was around this time that the news reports were full of parents beating each other up at stores because they **had** to get Cabbage Patch Dolls for their kids, and things haven't changed much since then. Think of any manufactured consumer frenzy over the years from Beanie Babies to Elmo dolls; think of the people you see lined up outside for a new iPhone. And those products don't have a jingle half as catchy as the Silver Shamrock one!

There's plenty of subtext if you're looking for it, but let's face it. The real appeal of this movie is in its goofy cheap thrills. These include but are not limited to: Tom Atkins all rumpled and hungover-looking, a scenery-chewing Dan O'Herlihy as the creator of the masks, bugs and snakes galore, a really unconvincing decapitation, evil robot henchmen, and one of the best ignoring-the-plot-hole moments I have ever seen. Throw in a creepy electronic score along with the aforementioned cinematography to kick it up a notch, and you've got one damn fun evening of entertainment.

# The Hand

*How's that grab you?*

**Year:** 1981

**Director:** Oliver Stone

**Screenplay:** Oliver Stone, based on the novel by Marc Brandell

**Cast:** Michael Caine, Michael Caine's terrifying hair, Michael Caine's vengeful severed hand

Watching *The Hand* was a double whammy of nostalgia for me. It was one of the first R-rated movies I saw, and it was probably the first time I understood that a movie didn't have to actually be good in order to be entertaining.

Michael Caine, in full-tilt go-for-the-money mode, plays a cartoonist whose life's work is a Conan-esque strip called Mandro. (Lots of people trash Caine's acting in this movie, but I think he gets points just for saying "Mandro" with a straight face.) Unfortunately, Caine loses his hand in an auto accident — learning the hard way that all those warnings not to stick your arm out the car window weren't just bullshit.

Caine's loss of his drawing hand tanks his career and more or less puts the kibosh on his already shaky marriage. Most unsettlingly, his hand never is recovered, and as Caine's inner rage grows, his severed hand starts scuttling about, frightening the cat, and eventually throttling people who've pissed Caine off.

What makes *The Hand* either mind-crushingly dull or giggle-inducing (depending on your mood) is the way everyone takes the proceedings so seriously. The bulk of the credit for this oh-so-serious tone goes to Oliver Stone (yes, that Oliver Stone) who wrote the screenplay and directed. I've never been able to discern a sense of humor in Stone's work and *The Hand* is no exception. It doesn't help that there isn't a single likable character — Caine's wife and a student he has a fling with are cheaters, and every other character screws Caine over somehow or is a brainless yokel. Caine himself is never particularly sympathetic, and when he's attacked by his own severed hand it seems entirely appropriate.

Despite Stone's refusal to mine the situation for comedy gold, there are quite a few laughs to be found in *The Hand*. There are the POV shots of the hand (apparently severed hands breathe heavily — who knew?), the numerous is-it-real-or-is-it-a-delusion scenes, the actors gamely thrashing about while being throttled, the faux-artsy cinematography changes from color to black-and-white, and last but certainly not least, Caine's hair. It starts out nice and smooth at the beginning of the film, and as Caine goes batshit so does his hair, and in the last scene he looks like Gene Wilder after electroshock therapy.

Speaking of Caine, he gets a lot of flak for his performance in *The Hand*. And while it's not what you'd call subtle, or even good, it's still quite enjoyable to watch him walk the line between putting in a halfway serious performance and reveling in the inherent ridiculousness of the premise.

I can sense all the readers out there thinking, "Yes, that's all well and good, but tell us — who would win in a fight? Caine's hand or Bruce Campbell's hand from *Evil Dead 2*?" It's a tough decision. Caine's hand does have freakish strength going for it, not to mention its ability to cover great time and distance. But Campbell's hand has the Necronomicon on its side, not to mention that cool dagger. Campbell's hand also has personality, and personality goes a long way. Caine's hand is just a thug.

# Hell of the Living Dead

*The zombie stomp*

**Year:** 1980

**Director:** Bruno Mattei

**Screenplay:** Claudio Fragasso and J. M. Cunilles

**Cast:** Margit Evelyn Newton, Gaby Renom, Franco Garofolo, Jose Gras

Is it really all **that** hard to make a halfway-effective zombie movie? It shouldn't be. There isn't any elaborate mythology to set up. The "shoot-em-in-the-head" idea is so well known it needs no explanation. All you need is a bunch of people willing to slap on some crusty makeup and stagger around, a screenplay that puts some cannon fodder in the vicinity of the undead, and *voila!* Let the brain-eating and gut-munching commence!

Well, apparently director Bruno Mattei found making a half-decent zombie movie to be an insurmountable task because *Hell of the Living Dead* (also known as *Virus*, its Italian title) is easily one the lamer Italian zombie movies you'll see.

The fun begins at a power plant. I mean, a secret installation in New Guinea run by the Hope Center (it just looks like a power plant). (**Note:** Secret installations are never up to any good, particularly when they're run by a group with an "Everything's fine! Really!" name like Hope Center.) All seems to be going well (at least according to the panels of blinky, buttony widgets that are shown for about five solid minutes). Then two guys find a dead rat in what is supposed to be the installation's most sterile area. In a matter of ten seconds the dead rat reanimates, attacks the man holding it, chews through his radiation suit and kills him. As his partner watches, the zombie rat victim flails about in his death throes and hits a lever that sends a greenish gas all through the place. And this, ladies and gentlemen, is how **all** of New Guinea falls victim to a zombie plague. Yep, one guy hits a switch. And did I mention that the project responsible for the zombie plague gas is called "Sweet Death"? Just thought I'd bring that up.

Meanwhile, in what seems to be a completely different film, the most unprofessional special ops team ever is taking out a terrorist group that's holding the American consulate hostage. If you're not paying close attention to a throwaway line of dialogue (and you'd most certainly be forgiven if that's the case), you miss that the terrorists are demanding the closure of all the Hope Centers. Seems those terrorists know something we don't. Maybe they could help stop the zombie plague! Wait, nope, they're dead. Never mind. Let's follow our special ops team to New Guinea.

On arriving, our crack force has limited supplies, no transportation, and only a vague sense of what they're supposed to be doing there. After commandeering a jeep they soon run into our other characters, a shrewish journalist (Margit Evelyn Newton) and her Yanni-ish photographer (Gaby Renom). The muckracking duo are riding around with a bitter married couple and their zombie-bitten kid. This scenario plays out pretty much as you'd expect, with the added bonus of seeing what it would be like to watch Yanni vomit.

Soon the journalists and special ops team are making their way lackadaisically across New Guinea to get to the secret installation (remember it?). This is when *Hell of the Living Dead* achieves its true purpose. Not because of zombie attacks, which we've already seen. And not even because of some completely gratuitous nudity (courtesy of the journalist lady stripping and slapping on body paint in her attempt to go native). But it can be summed up in two words. **STOCK FOOTAGE!**

Yes! Because what every zombie movie needs is to have its running time expanded by a third with completely irrelevant footage of wildlife and indigenous people. During a scene of driving through the forest, one of the characters will look out the window and then we'll get a jump cut to what seems to be *National Geographic* footage of animals, many of which (elephants!?) aren't even found in New Guinea. I can't complain too much, though, because these animals (particularly the fruit bats and what I think is a kangaroo rat) are way more likable and fun to watch than the human characters. Unfortunately, the use of New Guinean natives is used in a similarly shoddy and but far more exploitative fashion, with traditional dance and funeral rituals passed off as fallout from the zombie plague.

It all ends just as you'd imagine it would, with what's supposed to be a dramatic and downbeat ending. Frankly, I was so delighted to see the demise of the unlikable characters (not to mention the end credits) that I was all smiles and laughter.

Aside from a few bits of effective makeup, there really is nothing to save this movie beyond unintentional hilarity (and the awesome fruit bats and kangaroo rat). During the last half, when boredom begins to set in, try amusing yourself by counting the number of times you start to question the inane happenings. Or by speculating if the zombies hypnotize their victims into merely standing there gawping and leaving themselves vulnerable to becoming zombie chow (it certainly would explain a lot). Or by wondering if director Bruno Mattei paid anyone for the mondo and stock footage he appropriated, let alone Goblin's score for *Dawn of the Dead*, which seems to have been lifted note-for-note.

If nothing else, this movie makes things like Lucio Fulci's *Zombi* look a lot better by comparison. And maybe, just maybe, that's enough.

# Henry and June

*Spy in the house of love*

**Year:** 1990

**Director:** Philip Kaufman

**Screenplay:** Philip Kaufman and Rose Kaufman, based on the book by Anaïs Nin

**Cast:** Maria de Medeiros, Fred Ward, Uma Thurman

Philip Kaufman's adaptation of Anaïs Nin's account of her relationship with Henry Miller is like a long afternoon at a tapas restaurant: a meandering delight for the senses.

It's the early 1930s in Paris, and Nin (Maria de Medeiros looks so much like Nin that it's scary) lives a comfortable existence with her doting banker husband Hugo (Richard E. Grant), but Nin isn't looking for comfort. She's in search of something or someone that will make her feel alive. And though she's kept a diary since childhood, and has just written a bold defense of the writing of D. H. Lawrence, she's in search of something to help her writing reach the next level.

This something arrives in the form of American writer Henry Miller (Fred Ward), who's arrived in Paris to work on *Tropic of Cancer*. At first Miller seems to be Nin's opposite: she's well-educated, beautiful, and cultured; he's a bit on the boorish side, a primitive who hangs out with bums and whores, and who can't even pronounce Nin's first name correctly. Yet they prove to be soul mates who inspire each other in life pursuits and in writing, and soon become lovers. Around this time it's clear that both are also in thrall to Miller's wife June (Uma Thurman).

*Henry and June* is probably one of the more faithful adaptations I've ever seen in terms of replicating the tone and character of the writer's voice. Nin's work (what I've read of it) is less prose than poem, with little plot and much sensory impressions and character portraits. This is much the case with *Henry and June*. What would be the main plot in a more traditional film — will Miller be able to get his book published? — is almost an afterthought in the film. The screenplay (a collaboration by director Philip Kaufman and his wife Rose Kaufman) is more interested in the writers' inspiration and process, which is all for the best as we get welcome digressions like the Student Artists' Ball, a street fair and bacchanalia with costumes, body paint, and casual nudity.

The actors are, for the most part, excellent, giving the audience an anchor in this slightly phantasmagorical, bohemian world. Ward and de Medeiros are note-perfect, gradually letting us see past the initial impressions to Nin's earthier side and Miller's more sensitive aspects. Less successful is Uma Thurman as June. Though undeniably sensual (even when she's fully dressed she looks like she's half-naked), she's a liar and a manipulator, and her beauty aside, it's hard to see why Miller and Nin are both so enthralled with her (she's an ungrateful muse as well, dismissing Miller's *Tropic of Cancer* and Nin's *House of Incest*). Coming off surprisingly well is Richard E. Grant with the thankless role of Nin's husband Hugo. Though Hugo's a banker, he dabbles in the arts, but not enough to make him the soul mate Nin needs; it's clear he cherishes Nin (and she to a lesser extent loves him) and somehow manages to escape coming off as a contemptible cuckold (one wonders if he knows of Nin's affair with Miller and is all right with it as long as it isn't thrown in his face). And yes, that's a young Kevin Spacey as a publishing lawyer who's always claiming writers are stealing their best ideas from him.

One of the pleasures of the film is its 1930s Paris setting. Despite the Great Depression ("the crash" is referred to on a couple occasions), this time and place is almost idyllic, the perfect place to be a struggling artist. Summing up the mood perfectly is a moment when a skittish Nin walks past a thuggish-looking pickpocket, only to see him reveal himself as a street magician when he transforms a wallet into a live dove. The only intrusions of the real world are a disturbing radio broadcast from Germany, with crowds cheering for Hitler.

It's a slow, almost lazily-paced film, more about impressions and anecdotes than an actual plot, but this seems perfect for a Nin adaptation.

---

# Hercules and the Captive Women

*I like them big and stupid*

**Year:** 1961

**Director:** Vittorio Cottafavi

**Screenplay:** Vittorio Cottafavi, Sandro Continenza, Duccio Tessari

**Cast:** Reg Park, Fay Spain

---

I'm usually something of a purist when it comes to the arts. I watch movies in widescreen, and with subtitles instead of dubbing. I don't use "shuffle" if I'm listening to an album. And when I'm reading a book series I start with the first book. I don't usually advocate multitasking while watching movies, but I'm going to make an exception here for peplum films in general and *Hercules and the Captive Women* in particular. These movies are perfect for "background watching" because you can fold laundry or do the bills while guys in itty-bitty skirts are yammering on about something or other, and resume watching once Hercules or some other big meathead starts throwing rocks or fighting monsters.

*Hercules and the Captive Women* opens with Herc hanging out in Thebes with his friend Androcles the Theban king. One day when Herc and Androcles are riding around, the screen goes red-filtered and an extremely vague yet threatening prophecy is made. Androcles does what any sensible ruler would do and abandons his throne, hires a bunch of mercenaries, and sets out for a place from which no person has returned to do battle with the vague whatever threatening Thebes. He really wants Herc to tag along, but Herc has promised to stay home this time and spend time with his nagging wife and his wussy son Hylas. Again showing rational leadership, Androcles gets Hylas to roofie Herc and puts him on board the ship. Even after the roofies wear off Herc spends the voyage (in fact, a good third of the film) snoozing, only waking up when the mercenaries mutiny, and again when the ship wrecks.

Just about the time you've run out of laundry to fold, the movie kicks it up a notch. After having a goofy vision of a captured Androcles, Herc washes up on a shore where he sees a woman imprisoned in stone, and when he tries to free her a shape-shifting monster shows up. Herc fights the monster, defeats it, and learns that the woman is the daughter of the queen of Atlantis, who regularly sacrifices people to a god with the unfortunate name of Uranus (one of the highlights of the film is dialogue full of lines like, "Today is dedicated to Uranus!" which are bound to make your inner twelve-year-old happy).

From here things follow the tried-and-true formula of having the evil queen take a fancy to Herc and try to bewitch him, while Herc tries to do some sleuthing and rescue Androcles. Hylas and an annoying midget sidekick team up with the queen's daughter, and it all ends with the utter destruction of Atlantis and its thousands of inhabitants, which I suppose is a good thing? At any rate, Herc, Hylas, Androcles, midget, and queen's daughter seem pretty much OK with it. And it ends the vaguely-defined threat against Thebes, I think.

You'll forgive me for being a bit fuzzy on details but I was folding laundry while I watched this movie.

What I've always liked about Hercules movies and others of its ilk is that they never pretend to be anything other than what they are: an excuse for a ridiculously bulked-up guy to wander around the Italian countryside and through cheesy palace sets fighting swordsmen and throwing rocks at monsters. There's no pretense at being faithful to the myths. It's always clear no one has any interest in creating a coherent story beyond throwing in a couple of exposition scenes.

As Hercules movies go, *Captive Women* is a mixed bag, which means it's par for the course. Reg Park isn't terribly interesting as Hercules, and he's not helped by the fact that Herc spends a good chunk of the film lazing around. Fay Spain is the standard vampy evil queen. What the movie does have going for it are some interesting bits that include the "being swallowed up by stone" prison the queen's daughter is in, bleeding rocks, the shape-shifting monster that Herc fights, a mini-army of identical weird blond guys, and the destruction of Atlantis, which has the always-reliable stock footage of volcanoes erupting thrown in.

It's just dull enough to let you do a few light chores while you watch it, and just interesting enough to enjoy when the action livens up. And really, that's all one should expect from Hercules movies.

# High Anxiety

*Do you like Hitchcock?*

**Year:** 1977

**Director:** Mel Brooks

**Screenplay:** Mel Brooks, Ron Clark, Barry Levinson, and Rudy DeLuca

**Cast:** Mel Brooks, Cloris Leachman, Harvey Korman, Madeline Kahn

The fine art of the parody film seems to have been lost these days, as film-makers opt for merely tossing a bunch of pop culture references at the screen in hopes of gaining a cheap laugh and a few bucks.

Which makes it a shame that Mel Brooks' parody of/homage to the movies of Alfred Hitchcock seems to be forgotten when the subject of Brooks' 1970s heyday comes up. While *High Anxiety* isn't in a league with *Young Frankenstein* (what is?) it's a funny romp that will not only make you laugh but encourage you to revisit some of Hitchcock's work.

Noted psychiatrist Dr. Richard H. Thorndyke (Brooks) has just arrived in Los Angeles to take over as head of The Psycho-Neurotic Institute for the Very, Very Nervous. Thorndyke's flight in wasn't fun — he suffers from an extreme form of acrophobia called vertigo. I mean, called high anxiety. And he isn't reassured when his incompetent chauffeur Brophy hints that Thorndyke's predecessor at the Institute may have been murdered. Nor do his new colleagues at the Institute, the smarmy Dr. Montague (Harvey Korman) and the pointy-bosomed, gargoyle-faced, gravel-voiced Nurse Diesel (Cloris Leachman steals every scene) put him at ease. Before long there are more deaths, a mysterious blonde (Madeline Kahn) whose father is a patient at the Institute, and the truth behind Thorndyke's attacks of high anxiety.

There's a lot to enjoy in *High Anxiety*. It offers up a bounty of references to Hitchcock's films, from the obvious parodies of *Psycho* and *The Birds* to more subtle nods to *North by Northwest, Frenzy, Suspicion*, and *Dial M for Murder*. (I suggest watching a **lot** of Hitchcock (which you should do anyway) before watching *High Anxiety* — you'll get a lot more out of it.) At the same time, it piles on cheerfully juvenile humor (if the pooping pigeons don't appeal to your inner twelve-year-old, nothing will) and "meta" jokes that (literally) break the fourth wall. The pacing is slack and the plot serves as nothing more than a way to get the characters from set piece to set piece, but the whole thing is so good-natured one can't complain.

By this time Brooks and his favorite actors had made a number of films together, and the cast all work well. Brooks is a good lead as the put-upon Dr. Thorndyke (however, one wonders what

Gene Wilder could have done with the role), though Madeline Kahn simply isn't given enough to do. Stealing every scene, though, is Cloris Leachman as the evil Nurse Diesel. Everything she does is hilarious, and her line reading of the simple phrase "It sucks" will have you in giggles.

If you want a loving homage to Hitchcock, you can't go wrong with a little *High Anxiety*.

# The Hills Have Eyes

*Bad road trip*

**Year:** 2006

**Director:** Alexandre Aja

**Screenplay:** Alexandre Aja and Gregory Levasseur

**Cast:** Kathleen Quinlan, Ted Levine, Vinessa Shaw

I have mixed feelings about the proliferation of remakes. On the one hand, there's nothing wrong with taking a bad or average movie and remaking it as a good one (this is rare but it does happen). On the other hand, it gets boring seeing the same titles over and over again. What happened to originality?

I saw the original *The Hills Have Eyes* only recently, and while I wasn't terribly impressed, I could see why it made such a splash at the time. It was gritty, harsh, and had a nasty, brutal edge to it. Mutant hillbillies decimated an all-American family and were even planning to eat a baby. That made drive-in audiences sit up and take notice back in 1977.

Alexandre Aja's remake tries hard to make today's audiences sit up and take notice. He tries a bit too hard, especially in the movie's last third, but in many ways this remake is an improvement on the original.

The movie opens with a group of men in radiation suits testing the desert with Geiger counters, getting very scary readings, only to be made hash of by some local inhabitants. A creepy montage combines nuclear testing footage with pictures of people — many of them children — with genetic deformities caused by radiation.

We then meet a family en route to San Diego. Ex-cop dad (Ted Levine), long-suffering wife (Kathleen Quinlan), their three kids, eldest daughter's husband and baby daughter, and two German Shepherds. The local gas station proprietor, who's just received a batch of valuables (and one unsettling souvenir) from an unseen girl named Ruby, tells the all-American family to take the dirt road shortcut and they'll get to the main highway faster.

The dirt road is booby-trapped with spike strips, the car is totaled, and soon the entire family finds itself under assault by the local mutants, who are looking for food and valuables to steal, women to rape, and people to kill and/or eat.

Anyone who saw Aja's debut movie *High Tension* knows he's no slouch at creating tense atmosphere. His version of *The Hills Have Eyes* is most notable for his use of the desert locale to emphasize the isolation of the characters, something the original film never quite used successfully. (Side note: At the screening for this movie, Wes Craven told me that they'd gone to the location of the original film, in Victorville, California, only to find that the area was too populated and built up to use. The new *Hills Have Eyes* was filmed in Morocco.) Even if the all-American family does survive the mutants, it's not clear how in hell they'll escape the desert, which literally is as far as the eye can see. The characters have been made rather more likable and considerably less stupid, and the acting is strong all-around, with special mention going to Aaron Stanford as the wimpy husband who gets in touch with his homicidal side.

Aja has also fleshed out the lives of the local mutants. In one eerie scene, we see an automobile graveyard of past victims. And the mutants' home, instead of a cave, is a model town built for nuclear testing.

What the new *Hills Have Eyes* also offers is mutants and gore. The mutant family in Craven's film looked, for the most part, like skankier-than-usual hippies. The ones in Aja's film are true mutants, with misshapen faces, deformed hands, and worse. The early glimpses of them are particularly unsettling. Likewise, the new *Hills* has much more gore, including a nasty shotgun suicide, splattery gunshot wounds, and flesh wounds galore.

Unfortunately, while Craven's movie's third act was too short (featuring one of cinema's more abrupt endings), Aja's third act is too long. It's a repetitious sequence of drooling, deformed faces, stabbings and axe-choppings. Some of it is truly gratuitous — if travelers to prey upon are so infrequent, where did all those fresh body parts come from? By the end, I think all but the most ardent gorehounds would trade some grue and splatter for some genuine scares.

# I Spit On Your Grave

*No means no*

**Year:** 1978

**Director:** Meir Zarchi

**Screenplay:** Meir Zarchi

**Cast:** Camille Keaton, Eron Tabor, Richard Pace

For a long time, *I Spit On Your Grave* was on my list of Movies I Will Never Watch, Thank You Very Much. If there's one thing that years of watching weird, warped movies has taught me, it's to listen to that inner voice that asks, "Do you **really** want these images in your head?" The film has been so notorious for so long that I knew (or thought I knew) everything that went on in it, and didn't feel the need to experience it for myself.

But then there arrived a DVD with commentary by film critic extraordinaire Joe Bob Briggs, and I've long been a fan of Mr. Briggs' reviews. Figuring I could always turn the player off if things got too unbearable, I went ahead and gave it a shot.

Let's just sum up what *I Spit On Your Grave* isn't. It isn't very good. It also is not the sadistic glorification of rape it's been described as.

The film's plot is straightforward, to say the least. New York City writer Jennifer (Camille Keaton in a brave performance) has rented a riverside cabin in the countryside to work on her novel. En route to the cabin she catches the eye of local guys Johnny, Stanley, Andy, and Matthew. Mentally-challenged Matthew is also the delivery boy for the market, and finds out the location of Jennifer's cabin when he brings her groceries. One day when Jennifer is sunning herself in a canoe, the men buzz her in a motorboat, then drag her to shore and hold her down with the intention of helping Matthew to lose his virginity. Matthew chickens out, so Johnny rapes her. They let Jennifer go, only to assault her twice more — once in the woods as she makes her way back to the cabin, and again at the cabin where, to add insult to injury, they also make fun of her novel-in-progress and tear up the manuscript. They leave, but then make the colossal mistake (from their perspective) of sending Matthew in to kill Jennifer. He dabs some of her blood on a knife and tells his friends he killed her.

Jennifer recovers, tapes her manuscript back together, and goes to church to ask forgiveness for what she's about to do. Which is to take revenge, pure and simple.

And that's it. There's no subplot, and very little in the way of characterization. The lack of a subplot actually works in the film's favor, as it makes the film solely about Jennifer and the monstrous crime perpetrated against her. There's no police, no courtroom scene.

However, the lack of characterization is a much more grievous flaw, particularly where Jennifer is concerned. We know almost nothing about her at the beginning of the film, and not much more at the end. We may be happy that her quest for revenge is successful, but there's no indication whether her revenge is helpful to her psychologically. Similarly, the men who assault Jennifer are so cartoonishly sexist and loathsome it's as if director and screenwriter Meir Zarchi was going out of his way to make sure they had no redeeming qualities, lest the moral waters of the film be muddied.

Surprisingly, considering the reputation of the film, its portrayal of rape is the least problematical thing about it. The movie is on Jennifer's side from frame one, and the rationalizations offered by the rapists that she brought it on herself are clearly pathetic. Ringleader Johnny claims Jennifer asked for it by wearing a bikini — remind me never to go the beach with this man. Similarly, while there is full nudity during the rapes, the depiction is never eroticized, and often the camera angles show Jennifer's point of view, endeavoring to have the viewer see this from her perspective, and show what an ugly, invasive act this is. Jennifer is always shown as doing her best to fight off the attack, though since she's outnumbered four to one and weighs about 98 pounds soaking wet, there's not much she can do. (In his commentary, Briggs points out that even Charles Bronson got his ass kicked when he was outnumbered.) At the third assault she asks one of the rapists if she can please him another way (presumably a handjob or blowjob), but at this point the poor woman is just trying to get out of this situation alive. Later, she tells two of her rapists she enjoyed it, but that's just to distract them long enough to take revenge. Anyone who thinks the film glorifies or eroticizes rape is just not paying attention.

The film is better made on a technical level than one would expect. The lack of a musical soundtrack gives the whole thing a queasy semi-documentary feel, and there's the occasional striking image.

I want to believe that the film-makers' intentions were good, but the film has too difficult of a tightrope to walk in being an exploitation film without being exploitative. Better movie-makers could have pulled it off. As it is, the movie is terribly flawed and very difficult to watch. So while I feel compelled to defend it from accusations that it glorifies rape, at the same time I can't recommend it to anyone but die-hard horror genre fans who have most likely already seen it anyway.

# Ice Castles

*Melodrama! On ice!*

**Year:** 1978

**Director:** Donald Wrye

**Screenplay:** Donald Wrye and Gary L. Baim

**Cast:** Lynn-Holly Johnson, Robby Benson, Colleen Dewhurst, Tom Skerritt

I must have watched this movie a good half-dozen times back when I was a kid; you must remember that we had fewer TV channels in those days, and cable stations would usually pick a few movies each month and run them over and over again. *Ice Castles* doesn't hold up well, but at the same time I can see why I liked it back in the day.

Talented young skater Lexie (talented young skater Lynn-Holly Johnson in her movie debut) yearns to do more than just skate on her local rink. Unfortunately, at age sixteen she's too old for much of the Olympic-bound competitions, she has no formal training, and her overprotective father doesn't want her to compete lest she lose. But she's soon off to the next regional competition, because there's no movie if she doesn't go.

Lexie does very well, but inexplicably gets low scores. Not to worry, though, because an ambitious skating coach sees Lexie's potential and takes Lexie under her wing. This of course means Lexie has to leave her hometown, her dad, and her boyfriend Nick (Robby Benson). As part of Lexie's push to hit the big time, the coach has her sportscaster friend/fuck-buddy (their relationship is nebulous) film every part of Lexie's training and groom her into a "small-town girl makes it big" persona. Soon Lexie is playing kissy-face with the reporter (ewww), having tearful confrontations with Nick, and worst of all, having her skate routines choreographed to "A Fifth of Beethoven" (if you don't know what I'm referring to, you can be grateful you were not a child of the 1970s). Then the Melodrama-Meter goes through the roof when Lexie has a bad fall, gets a head injury, and is now blind. Will she find the inner strength to skate again?

It's melodrama, to be sure, but at times it's fairly entertaining. The skating scenes are a pleasure to watch. They're also genuinely suspenseful: It's established early on just how vicious the competitions can be (trigger warning: lots of catty mean girls in the competitions), and that one slip-up can ruin not just a competition but a career (adding to the suspense is the first competition in the film with the inexplicably low scores — what was that about?). Johnson is reasonably charming, and old pros Colleen Dewhurst and Tom Skerritt are on hand to help with the acting.

Two things really harm the film and make it a bit of a chore to watch. First, the plot holes. Why does everyone, absolutely everyone, drop Lexie like a hot potato right after her accident? Why wasn't the media all over her tragic story? Speaking of media, what was up with the reporter making out with Lexie when she's sixteen and he's in his late twenties at the very least? What was the whole backstory with Lexie's mom? A little attention paid to these plot problems would have helped immensely. But maybe not enough, because we've still got problem number two: Nick. He's supposed to be Lexie's true love, and even helps coach her after her injury, but let's be honest — the man's a loser. He quits medical school (for reasons that are never explained) and then quits his hockey team. This aside, he's got a nasty passive-aggressive streak, and Benson can't make us care one iota about his character. It doesn't help that Benson and Johnson have little to no chemistry.

But I've got a soft spot for melodrama, and damn if that final skate routine to "Looking Through The Eyes Of Love" doesn't get to me. If this was a guilty pleasure of yours back in the day, you could do worse than to wait for it to turn up on cable.

---

# In the Mouth of Madness

*Final draft*

**Year:** 1994

**Director:** John Carpenter

**Screenplay:** Michael De Luca

**Cast:** Sam Neill, Julie Carmen, Jurgen Prochnow

---

John Carpenter's *In the Mouth of Madness* opens with what I can only describe as book porn. We see a montage of the book printing process: page upon page of print still warm from the press, thrust into the tight yet welcoming embrace of the book covers, the finished books stacked higher and higher until the inevitable peak...

Where was I? Sorry, I get a bit excited by publishing.

Anyway, said books are copies of *The Hobb's End Horror*, written by one Sutter Cane, an immensely popular author. The downside of Cane's work is that it seems to have a negative effect on some of his readers, ranging from hallucinations and delusions to murderous axe-wielding sprees. Now Cane has gone missing, his publisher is extremely anxious to obtain his new manuscript, and the book-buying public will start rioting if the already-delayed book doesn't meet its street date. Enter insurance investigator John Trent (the always-welcome Sam Neill), who along with Cane's editor Linda Styles (Julie Carmen) start searching for Cane. Trent soon finds that the apparently fictional town of Hobb's End does exist, and that's where he and Styles find

Cane (Jurgen Prochnow and his Jiffy-Pop hair). They'll soon wish they hadn't.

It's clear from the outset that *In the Mouth of Madness* won't give us a happy ending. Its opening has a straightjacketed, violently struggling Trent proclaiming that he's not insane, then spending his time in the rubber room covering the walls (and himself) with drawings of crosses while asking a visiting psychiatrist (David Warner, with nothing to do), "It's really going to hell out there, isn't it?" Our misgivings deepen when we meet pre-insanity Trent, a cynical pragmatist if ever there was one. For most of the film's time he searches for a rational explanation for the irrational situations he finds himself in: from the quaint but eerily deserted town of Hobb's End to the Lovecraftian horrors that Cane's writing is calling forth. But finally he realizes what's really happening, unknowing that all the while his pragmatism has not protected him but just made him more of a tool for Cane.

The problem with *In the Mouth of Madness* is one that was shared by an earlier Carpenter film, *Prince of Darkness* — its execution doesn't always serve its ambition as well as it could. Neill makes a fine protagonist, but he's hampered by co-star Carmen, who puts in a fairly terrible performance. Thankfully Jurgen Prochnow as Cane shows up to inject some well-spoken menace into the proceedings, completely selling the notion that Cane's writings have tapped into some unspeakable horrors, and he's thrilled to bits about it. There's a marvelous bit when the walls of reality are revealed to be made of pages from a book, and Trent stares down at what lies in the abyss. Unfortunately the film flubs the effect by having said horrors be a bunch of rubbery monsters. (There's a reason that H. P. Lovecraft — whose influence lies heavy on the film — usually cut away before he had to actually describe some being of apocalyptic evil.) Thankfully, there's enough reality mind games ("My favorite color is blue.") and plot twists to bring it to a satisfyingly "meta" ending.

Probably the thing I enjoy most about the movie is its notion that books have the power to bring about something as huge as the end of the world. It's a refreshing idea, particularly in this day and age, when books often seem to be something to base movies on.

# The Incredible Hulk

*I am Jack's green inner rage*

**Year:** 2008

**Director:** Louis Leterrier

**Screenplay:** Zak Penn

**Cast:** Edward Norton, Liv Tyler, William Hurt, Tim Roth

A reboot of the franchise after Ang Lee's poorly received 2003 effort, *The Incredible Hulk* manages to be an entertaining film — or three-quarters of an entertaining film, but I'll get to that in a moment — that's also remarkably disposable. Rather like a comic book.

Wisely glossing over the origin story that anyone interested in this movie knows already, *The Incredible Hulk* finds rogue scientist Bruce Banner (Edward Norton looking very cute) hiding out in Brazil, making ends meet by working in a soft drink bottling plant, trying to find a cure for his Hulkiness, and working on relaxation techniques that will control his heart rate so he doesn't Hulk out. These early scenes are a showcase of effective storytelling, as we find out through visuals rather than lumps of expository dialogue how Banner got turned into the Hulk, when his last Hulk-out was, and so on.

Unfortunately an accident at the bottling plant causes a drop or two of Banner's blood to end up in some poor bastard's soda pop, which leads to Banner being traced to his hideout. On his tail are General Ross (William Hurt) and bad-ass military man Emil Blonsky (scene-stealing Tim Roth). Hullkiness ensues in the slums of Rio, and Banner is forced to flee north in search of a possible cure and also to see his estranged girlfriend Betty (Liv Tyler).

Everything works surprisingly well for most of the movie. There's a fair amount of humor (particularly the tribute to the "You wouldn't like me when I'm angry" line). The acting is good, with top honors going to Roth, who hasn't been in enough movies lately. Norton's so good at helping us see the angry man inside his unremarkable exterior that he makes the Hulk-out scenes credible. Tyler manages to convey both beauty and brains but unfortunately isn't given much to do beyond Standard Girlfriend Duty (cry, administer hugs, do the hero's shopping). The most unexpected acting treat comes from Tim Blake Nelson as a somewhat loopy scientist.

The effects hold up well. The few bits I've seen from Ang Lee's film made the Hulk look too bright and bouncy. This Hulk gives the impression of mass, though I still think an approach like the TV show might work best — round up some huge guy from WWE and paint him green. This might prevent the film's big failing — the climactic fight between Hulk and Abomination.

It's at this point that the film loses all interest. It's a foregone conclusion who will win so there's no emotional involvement for the audience. The shortcomings of the effects are showcased rather than glossed over — it's like watching the Battle of the Gumbys. And the fighters are so close to being invulnerable that there is no suspense. By contrast, the fight between Iron Man and Iron Monger had suspense, because inside those bad-ass metal suits were fragile humans who could easily be turned into pulp if the fight didn't go their way.

It's pleasant entertainment, even if very little of it lingers in the mind afterward.

# Ironclad

*Getting medieval on your ass*

**Year:** 2011

**Director:** Jonathan English

**Screenplay:** Jonathan English, Erick Kastel, and Stephen McDool

**Cast:** James Purefoy, Paul Giamatti, Brian Cox, Kate Mara

What did moviemakers do before *The Seven Samurai* was made? Surely that film didn't invent the "hastily assembled bunch of fighters has to defend a place against impossible odds" scenario, but it feels like it did. It's inspired countless imitators, of which *Ironclad* is the latest.

It's England in the year 1215, and King John (Paul Giamatti) has been such a lousy king that his barons have rebelled and forced him to sign the Magna Carta, in which he promises to be not such a lousy king. As you can imagine, the king isn't real thrilled about this and he's decided to teach the barons a lesson by systematically taking over their castles and slaughtering the inhabitants, aided and abetted by a group of Danish mercenaries (led by Vladimir Kulich, aka "the guy who was Buliwyf in *The 13th Warrior*"). John's next target is Rochester castle, which will give him control of all of southern England.

Luckily, the Duke of Albany (Brian Cox) has other ideas. He teams up with a disillusioned Templar Knight (James Purefoy) and a ragtag bunch of fighters to hold the castle until French allies arrive to help out the rebellion against John. Then follows a lot of fighting and sieges, but not as much drama or excitement as you'd think.

*Ironclad* has a lot going for it. The cast alone makes it worth a rental. Purefoy does a great deal with a character that's thinly sketched to say the least (more on that in a moment), conveying with few words the toll that years of fighting has taken on his soul. Cox is charismatic and the screen lights up whenever he's on it. Giamatti seems miscast at first, but in the film's second half he gets in touch with his inner despot and portrays John as a sociopathic little man who will do anything to maintain absolute power. And though he only gets three scenes, Charles Dance is on hand to lend some dignity and authority to matters as the Archbishop of Canterbury, who's willing to risk all to keep the rebellion going.

Not all the cast works, though. Derek Jacobi is a bit hammy as the lord of Rochester castle, and Kate Mara as his unhappy, sexually frustrated wife is just terrible. Mara has a nice medieval look to her, but her character is poorly conceived — she's supposed to be Purefoy's soul mate, but comes off as petulant instead — and unlike most of the cast, Mara isn't a strong enough actor to make the role work.

Which leads us to the major flaw of *Ironclad* — the characterization is so thin as to be transparent. The actors have to let their talent and charisma do the heavy lifting, because the screenplay does them no favors. Particularly ill-served are the ragtags that Albany recruits — I never remembered their names. They were "the archer dude" and "the guy who's kind of an asshole" and "the bearded stocky guy who looks like that other bearded stocky guy" and "the guy who looks like Frodo Baggins." When the stakes are this high for the characters, you should be able to care about them. But sympathy for the characters ranks far below that generated by the actors.

What *Ironclad* does have is nasty battles, and a lot of them. The movie has a gritty, gloomy feel to it, and makes it clear that medieval life in general, and warfare in particular, were no picnic. I appreciated the attention to detail (i.e., when preparing for the siege, the Templar makes sure to find out where the castle's water supply comes from and how at risk it is). Director Jonathan English is a little too fond of the spinny-shaky cam, but the action looks good and (to my amateur's eyes) reasonably authentic. It's also very gory, with limbs and hands a-flying and several memorable scenes of people being cloven in twain.

Yet here's something lifeless about the whole affair. A stronger screenplay and better characterization would have made this a classic, but as it stands *Ironclad* is merely serviceable.

# The Island of Dr. Moreau

*House of pain*

**Year:** 1996

**Director:** John Frankenheimer

**Screenplay:** Richard Stanley and Ron Hutchinson, based on the novel by H. G. Wells

**Cast:** Marlon Brando, Val Kilmer, David Thewlis

I'm not going to bother coming up with a witty intro (you, in the back, shouting "That's never stopped you before!" — you may shut up now) because not only was this movie bad, it actually made me angry. Given how much cinema of dubious quality I watch, for a movie to make me angry is a rare event indeed.

This adaptation of H. G. Wells' novel (which I have not read, sadly), *The Island of Dr. Moreau* starts not-too-promisingly with an opening credits montage of eyes, critter-cam effects, and microscopic views of cells and parameciums and amoebas and things. It's scary! And there's, you know, science and stuff!

Our protagonist — he doesn't do anything that would have us call him a hero — is Edward Douglas (David Thewlis, clearly gritting his teeth and waiting until the director calls it a wrap). He's stranded in the middle of the Java Sea with two other survivors of a plane crash. The two other survivors kill each other over the last remaining canteen, leaving Douglas alone. Soon after, he's picked up by a boat. It's never clear who the people on the boat are — suppliers, pirates? What matters is that a fellow named Montgomery (Val Kilmer, looking stoned to the gills) is on board.

We soon find out that Montgomery is the right-hand man of Dr. Moreau (Marlon Brando), a Nobel Prize-winning geneticist who's been thought dead for years but in reality is on his own private island, genetically modifying animals into humans, with varying levels of success. Montgomery keeps the man-critters doped up, and when that isn't enough to keep them in line, Moreau gives them electrical shocks via an implant. Damn, they'll give those Nobel Prizes to anybody, won't they?

Even if you hadn't read the book or seen other adaptations, you'd know that the man-critters get fed up and rebel. What you might not guess is that Moreau would be played as a cross between Hannibal Lecter, Truman Capote, and the Pillsbury Dough-Boy. You might not guess that Moreau would gad about in caftans and white pancake makeup, and at one point wears an ice bucket on his head. Nor would you guess that Montgomery not only dresses up like Moreau but talks like him too, and says the line, "I want to go to dog heaven," with feeling.

It sounds campy as hell, and it is. Yet is somehow manages to be remarkably boring as well. Part of this is because of the script — the only flourishes that lift this film out of the utterly predictable are the wackaloon antics of Brando and Kilmer. The script also doesn't give us anyone to be interested in, let alone care about. Thewlis' character is the obvious choice, but all we ever learn about him is that he was on some sort of U.N. mission when his plane crashed. That's it. I kept waiting for some further relevance — that he was a radical PETA activist come to avenge fluffy bunnies, or something — but he's a complete cipher who exists only to look outraged at the man-critters, yell "Damn" when Montgomery busts the radio, and loll his head in an odd fashion (I'm still not sure what that was about).

John Frankenheimer's direction does the movie no favors — as anyone who saw the turgid icky bear movie *Prophecy* knows, Frankenheimer can't direct horror. (The exception is the final sequence of his 1966 film *Seconds*, which is truly horrifying.) Not only is the film not scary, but it's poorly paced. The middle third in particular is more of a random collection of scenes than a dramatic arc. And of course, Frankenheimer throws in some sledgehammer-subtle "who are the **real** animals?" social commentary, including a montage of Third World people all cranky and pissed off.

The acting is everything you've heard about and then some. Brando's bizarre appearance aside, his acting isn't atrocious — it's just impossible to tell if he intended to play Moreau as a goofy eccentric or if he saw the whole movie as a colossal joke. Thewlis seems to be just biding his time until the closing credits. Kilmer turns in a train wreck of a performance — his Montgomery is a stoned and batshit-crazy blowhard, and Kilmer seems to have really, really gotten into character, if you know what I mean and I think you do. The only actor to survive the film with dignity intact is Ron Perlman as the Sayer of the Law.

Working in the movie's favor are Stan Winston's creature makeup effects, which are remarkable. Unfortunately the effect is dulled when it's juxtaposed with a laughably fake slaughtered rabbit — my kid's plushie toy bunny is more realistic.

So why was I angry? Because everyone involved should have known better. I can forgive incompetence in a debut film or a low-budget effort, but there's too much experience and money behind this film for it to have been this bad. There's also an extremely unpleasant scene involving the dwarf man who dresses like Moreau and was the inspiration for Mini-Me. At one point, and for no reason beyond exploitation, this person is shown naked. It seems to be a cheap shock tactic worthy of a 1930s freak show, not a major motion picture.

I need to go watch *Ronin* now — a **good** Frankenheimer film — to help me forget about this one.

# Jacob's Ladder

*Inferno*

**Year:** 1990

**Director:** Adrian Lyne

**Screenplay:** Bruce Joel Rubin

**Cast:** Tim Robbins, Elizabeth Peña, Danny Aiello

Jacob Singer is a haunted man. He suffers from flashbacks to his days as a soldier in Vietnam, and to one battle in particular. He's still grieving for his son, who died in an accident. His marriage has foundered and his new lover doesn't give him the consolation he truly needs. And now he's seeing strange figures on the streets and subway, people with distorted features who seem to know who he is. When Jacob starts looking for answers, he finds that he's not the only one from his Vietnam troop who's been seeing strange things.

*Jacob's Ladder* is one of my favorite underrated films. Though its central mystery won't be too mysterious these days (its key twist having been done with more finesse by other films I won't name), the movie draws its strengths from so many other avenues that one can forgive a narrative that doesn't always stand up to scrutiny.

The heart of the film is Tim Robbins' performance as Jacob. It's astounding in its raw emotion, and Robbins conveys Jacob's good heart (demonstrated in his love for his family, even his estranged wife, and his loyalty to his fellow soldiers) and deep sorrow. As this is, in part, a horror film, much of the film's unsettling power comes from Jacob's reactions to his increasingly disturbing visions. Robbins' portrayal of terror and trauma are so convincing that he's always sympathetic, never a figure of weakness or a target for ridicule. It's a performance that should have gotten Robbins a nomination of some kind, yet sadly it's consigned to be forgotten in Genre Hell. The rest of the cast is excellent as well, with acting honors also going to Danny Aiello as Jacob's empathetic chiropractor, and Elizabeth Peña as his sensual, mysterious lover Jezzie.

Adrian Lyne is a pleasant surprise as director, eschewing the glossy trash of *Flashdance* and *9 1/2 Weeks* that made his name. The film's set in 1970s New York, and Lyne gives the film an appropriately grim, dour feel. But Lyne's direction truly shines in the vision sequences, in particular a hallucinatory party scene, and a hospital sequence that's easily one of the scariest things I've seen on film. Moreover, he never lets the sequences overwhelm the story or characters, which makes them more effective than a bigger, flashier cavalcade of eye candy could be.

The weak point (which is not all that weak — just not as strong as the rest of the movie) is Bruce Joel Rubin's screenplay. Spoilers prevent me from going into too much detail, but suffice to say that not all the plot threads intersect quite the way they should, with a crucial/key point about the reason for Jacob's visions becoming almost an afterthought.

That aside, it's a frightening, intelligent, and above all, deeply affecting movie, and one that needs to be rediscovered by today's audiences.

# Jaws

*You're gonna need a bigger boat*

**Year:** 1975

**Director:** Steven Spielberg

**Screenplay:** Peter Benchley and Carl Gottlieb, based on the novel by Peter Benchley

**Cast:** Roy Scheider, Richard Dreyfuss, Robert Shaw

I try not to throw around the words "masterpiece" or "perfection" too often, but I really have to use them when I talk about *Jaws*. Everything about it just works so well. The terror it instills in the audience. The three-act dramatic structure. The performances, especially by the three leads. John Williams' famous score. I could go on and on. And it's still being ripped off and paid homage to more than thirty years after its release.

*Jaws* is one of those movies that is so embedded in the American culture that even people who haven't seen it know the basics, but here goes. A great white shark decides to make the New England island of Amity his lunch buffet, his first victim being an unlucky skinny-dipper. Water-phobic sheriff Brody (Roy Scheider in an underrated performance), a New York City émigré who's still settling into his role as Amity's leading lawman, wants to close the beaches but the mayor (odious Murray Hamilton), who's thinking only of the dollars the summer tourists bring in, won't have it. More deaths happen, and it's up to Brody along with ichthyologist Hooper (hyper Richard Dreyfuss) and fisherman/shark hunter Quint (Robert Shaw) head out to sea to kill the shark.

It's hard to pinpoint what makes *Jaws* so effective after all these years. Certainly there's the unease all of us have, consciously or not, at being in the ocean where we are (literally) out of our element. The ocean is big, its motion is out of our control, and most of the time you can't see what's around you. There really is no way to know what's swimming just beyond you or beneath you. And it's not easy to escape it, as the scene of panicked beach-goers fleeing the water demonstrates: people flounder, get knocked over, and no matter how fast they move they're no match for the predator that's after them.

That's a major factor, but what really makes *Jaws* work is how **real** it feels. If the movie was made today, the beaches of Amity would be packed with pretty hardbodies. But the beaches of *Jaws* are full of ordinary people. Families, people of every age and variety, from the partiers in the opening scene to the wannabe landscape painter who sees the shark in the estuary. They're people just like us and we identify with them.

Of the shark-hunting trio, it's Brody we meet first, and though he's the least entertaining of the three, he's the one we relate to. He's a man who's decent — even honorable. He's left crime-ridden New York City behind and, despite his deep fear of the water (notice during the second shark attack scene, he runs down to the water but doesn't get his feet wet) has moved to an island to give his wife and children a better life. He's "not an Islander" and is still finding his way among the town's petty politics; it's not his fault that the beaches aren't closed and more deaths occur, but as a lawman he feels responsible. And when his own son has a narrow escape from the shark it's his duty not just as a lawman but as a father to help find and kill the shark. Always an underrated actor, Scheider gives an excellent performance, particularly when the action moves to Quint's boat and he is completely (and literally of course) in over his head, relegated to "chum duty" because he doesn't know which rope to pull. Probably his best acting moment is during a night-time attack by the shark when Brody draws his handgun and wears a look of fear as he realizes that the weapon that may have served him in the past will do no good.

Fear and bravery are two themes that come up often during the movie's third act, from Brody's last stand against the shark to Hooper's descent into the shark cage. Throughout the shark hunt scenes we've seen Hooper's boyish enthusiasm over the shark become increasingly manic in response to the "arrr, I don't need a city boy on me ship" taunts from Quint. (It's interesting that Quint never taunts Brody but rather treats him with a sort of benign pity.) But all of Hooper's bluster goes away when he's ready to go into the shark cage, and is unable to spit into his mask because the fear reaction has dried up his saliva. Likewise, all of Quint's "here's to swimmin' with bow-legged women" banter goes away, first when he gives his haunting monologue about the *USS Indianapolis*, then when he realizes that of the hundreds of sharks he's hunted, this one may be his match.

Today's blockbusters are so big, so loud, so focused on the next big thrill that they've forgotten how to tell stories and get audience members involved. *Jaws* could be made again. Yes, the shark would look better. But the soul of the movie — ordinary people against the terrors the deep can hold — would be lost. If you need your faith in the power of cinema restored, watch *Jaws* again.

# Joe Versus The Volcano

*The journey, not the destination*

**Year:** 1990

**Director:** John Patrick Shanley

**Screenplay:** John Patrick Shanley

**Cast:** Tom Hanks, Meg Ryan, Lloyd Bridges

Some movies are just destined to not be big commercial hits. Sometimes it's because they're just plain bad, or boring. But sometimes it's because they're a bit too oddball to fit into any of the comfortable boxes people like their entertainment to arrive in. These movies may not have earned lots of money, but the world is a much better place because they were made. Case in point: *Joe Versus the Volcano,* a movie that should be found in the dictionary next to the word "quirky."

Ordinary guy Joe Banks (Tom Hanks) works in a medical supply factory so hellish in its design it looks like something from *Eraserhead.* Joe's a hypochondriac, and at one of his many doctor appointments he's informed that he's got a terminal illness — a "brain cloud." The next day Joe's approached by eccentric billionaire Graynamore (Lloyd Bridges), who offers him an interesting proposition. There's an island in the South Pacific called Waponi-Wu, and on this island is a rare mineral that Graynamore needs. The Waponi people will only give it to him if he can provide a person to sacrifice himself in the island's volcano. Graynamore knows that Joe's got just months to live, so why not go out in a blaze of self-sacrificial glory? With Graynamore paying for all incidental expenses? With nothing left to lose, Joe accepts the offer.

On his way to Waponi-Wu Joe will get a makeover, acquire the best set of luggage ever (write it down, that's plot material), and meet three women who will be important in his life. Mousy coworker Dede, brittle flibbertigibbet Angelica, and ship captain Patricia (all played by Meg Ryan). There will be shipwrecks, a South Pacific tribe fond of orange soda, and yes, the titular encounter with the volcano. (There's also a duck that keeps appearing in random scenes, but I don't know what that's about.)

You've no doubt guessed that *Joe Versus the Volcano* has little, if anything, to do with realism. It's probably best classified as "magical realism," for everything is taken up just a notch higher than it should be. It's not quite magical enough for a fairy tale, and it's not quite a satire either. Really, it's about a desperately unhappy man who's essentially on a suicide mission, and who on the way not only falls in love but has one of cinema's best and most unlikely spiritual epiphanies.

150

The whole thing is pure whimsy without being cloying.

Helping anchor the movie and keep it from being the cinematic equivalent of a bushel of cotton candy is Tom Hanks, whose innate everyman qualities let us identify with morose, hypochondriacal Joe and with searching-for-something Joe and with in-love-with-life-again Joe. Hanks never winks at the whimsical happenings on screen, but takes them in stride and as he does, so does the audience. Meg Ryan is Hanks' equal, and in three roles no less. Anyone who ever doubted Ryan's talent as an actress would do well to watch this movie, as she perfectly portrays three very different women. My favorite of the three characters is probably mousy Dede (I keep wondering what happened to Dede after the events of the movie), but the most quotable is the superficial-yet-unhappy Patricia, whose line, "I have no response to that" gets said around Casa del Cozy with alarming frequency. Unfortunately the movie spends the most time with the third woman, and she's the least interesting of them.

It's a movie that's quite surprising because of all the little things it throws at you along the way: Ossie Davis's chauffeur and sartorial adviser, Carol Kane's two-line cameo role, Dan Hedaya's unforgettable turn as Hanks' horrible boss at the medical supply company, Abe Vigoda as the Waponi chief, the lightning bolt/zigzag motif, the eccentric ship's crew, and so much more. There's a lot of silliness, of course, but there are also moments and images that will stay with you a long time.

# Julie and Julia

*Bon appetit*

**Year:** 2009

**Director:** Nora Ephron

**Screenplay:** Nora Ephron, based on *My Life in France* by Julia Child and *Julie and Julia* by Julie Powell

**Cast:** Meryl Streep, Amy Adams, Stanley Tucci

Anyone who knows me also knows that there are few things I enjoy in life more than cooking, particularly for friends and family. Thanksgiving, Christmas, you name it, I'll have people over and cook for them. I also love to read cookbooks. The ones with lots of pictures are nice, but in the end I prefer cookbooks that tell me why a cooking technique works, or what to do if you don't necessarily have unlimited time and access to ingredients. For like-minded souls, I always recommend Julia Child's *Mastering the Art of French Cooking*. For all its intimidating size it's an easy read and Child never condescends to her readers (for example, she offers tips on how to make canned or frozen peas taste good).

So I am happy to report that *Julie and Julia,* (an adaptation of Child's *My Life in France,* and Julie Powell's *Julie and Julia* book that chronicled her year of making every recipe in *Mastering the Art*) while not an entirely successful film, is a great look at Child's life, and also has plenty of food porn to make up for the movie's flaws.

The movie is partly a biography of Child (a sublime Meryl Streep perfectly captures Child's distinctive voice and mannerisms). It covers her arrival in France with government worker husband Paul; her search for a way to occupy her time; her interest in cooking that leads her to become one of the only female students at a prestigious cooking school; and her joining forces with two other female cooks to write her cookbook (the first of many). These scenes alternate with those of blogger Powell (Amy Adams saves the role through her innate adorability) who, feeling like she hasn't accomplished anything with her life, decides to cook all of the recipes in *Mastering* over the course of a year, and blog about the experience.

If that seems fairly lopsided, it is. And that's the key flaw of *Julie and Julia.* On the one hand, we have a remarkable woman whose *joie de vivre* is infectious, who influenced thousands of people through her work, who changed the way people cook, who set the example for every cooking show with her iconic *The French Chef,* and who faced considerable challenges because of the roles and expectations placed on women at that time. On the other hand, we have a woman who cooks and writes about that, primarily because her bitchy friends are all more materially successful than she is and because her mother tells her she isn't accomplishing anything with her life. It doesn't help that Powell's story (I haven't read her blog or book and have no idea how much the movie reflects real life) takes place not long after 9/11, and Powell's day job is helping people who are suffering the physical and emotional damage related to that event. If Powell's cooking project had been a dream she'd long had, or came from a place of "eat, drink, and be merry, for who knows what will happen tomorrow" it would be much more understandable (and interesting). Instead, she comes off as shallow and petty, and often it seems that she's trying to ride Child's coat-tails. It's to Amy Adams' credit that Powell's character is even remotely likable; any bond the audience feels for Powell is due to Adams' charisma and the beautiful, beautiful food.

Ah yes, the food porn. There is plenty of it, from Child's first encounter with sole *meunière* and the chocolate pie Powell whips up for herself and her husband, to the *boeuf bourguignon* that helped get Child her book deal and the duck *en croute* that Powell serves up. I can't recall any film I've seen in the theater that got quite the same vocal response from its audience as this movie did — every time food appeared, there was a sound somewhere between a sigh and a moan. It truly is a wonder what this film does for food, and that's all the more welcome in these days when meals are being reduced to matters of convenience and calories. Be honest with me — would you rather have a kale smoothie or the *boeuf bourguignon*?

One thing I appreciate is that the movie doesn't shy away from the fact that learning to cook well involves work — I especially liked the mountain of chopped onions we see when Child is refining her techniques (oh, and now I really want some of the French onion soup from *Mastering*; I've made it and it's just divine). But it also shows the satisfaction not just in consuming food but in the preparation; it's an enjoyable labor that brings sustenance and pleasure to everyone.

It's well worth watching for the biographical sections on Child and for the food. Be prepared to be very hungry afterward, though.

# Kill the Irishman

*Something something lucky charms*

**Year:** 2011

**Director:** Jonathan Hensleigh

**Screenplay:** Jonathan Hensleigh and Jeremy Walters, based on the book by Rick Porrello

**Cast:** Ray Stevenson, Val Kilmer, Christopher Walken, Vincent D'Onofrio

I freely admit I was kind of excited to see *Kill the Irishman* after seeing its trailer. A story about an Irish gangster going up against Italian mafia very much appealed to me, as I'm of both Irish and Italian heritage. (I usually tend to emphasize the Italian side of my ancestry, mostly because the Italians are better cooks — really, which would you rather eat: spaghetti carbonara or corned beef and cabbage?) I could be entertained and feel conflicted at the same time, much as I do when I watch Godzilla fight King Ghidorah.

Well, perhaps I should have just watched a classic *kaiju* instead. The novelty of Celtic vs. Mediterranean in the criminal underworld is nearly the only novelty that *Kill the Irishman* has going for it, and that is not enough to save it from a lackluster plot and by-the-numbers direction.

Danny Greene (Ray Stevenson) is a dock worker in 1970s Cleveland. Working conditions aren't great, to say the least, and this gives Greene the opportunity to assume leadership of the longshoreman's union through a combination of guile and physical force. Greene's idealism, such as it is, soon gets buried under the prospect of easy money and corruption, and before long he's busted. He soon gets out by promising to work for the local mafia interests and report on those to the Feds. For a while things are going well, until he tells Christopher Walken to fuck off (that's **never** a good idea) and ends up with a sizable price on his head, prompting a gang war between the Italian mob and Greene's band of upstart Irish criminals.

Greene's story isn't an uninteresting one, but the movie doesn't do it justice. It crams simply too much into the film's running time, skipping over events at breakneck speed. Along the way, plot elements (such as Greene reporting on organized crime activity to the Feds) get dropped, while characters show up with no introduction or explanation of their importance to the story. The most egregious example is Val Kilmer's character, a police detective who knew Greene when they were schoolkids and has inexplicable affection for Greene — aside from providing here-and-there narration, the character is irrelevant to the story.

Moreover, the film wants us to see Greene's character as a tarnished-yet-noble sort. (By the end you'll be very sick of sad Irish music playing during Greene's scenes.) Yet the Greene the filmmakers want us to see doesn't jibe with what we're given via the screenplay. Greene seems to start out his journey for idealistic reasons, but it isn't long before he's hand-in-glove with the mafia and lining his own pockets. Similarly, the action that earns him the enmity of the mafia and puts the bounty on his head isn't one of honor or idealism. Stevenson's performance is good, but not quite up to the task of making Greene into a modern-day Robin Hood — he's got good physical charisma, particularly in the movie's early scenes, but once the 1970s kick in and Greene is a big wheel in local organized crime, he loses his appeal and comes off as an asshole (the pornstache he sports in these scenes doesn't help matters). Also not helping is director Hensleigh, who has clearly studied lots of gangster movies (in particular, *Goodfellas*) but hasn't figured out how to do more than merely imitate.

The movie is pleasant enough entertainment. The Cleveland setting makes a nice change from the usual New York locales, and the late 1960s-early/mid-1970s aesthetic is well done. The supporting cast is ridiculously overqualified and often underused. Walken's role isn't large but it is pivotal, and Vincent D'Onofrio shines as Greene's partner in crime. Also on hand are Robert Davi as a hit man, Paul Sorvino as a mafia don, and Linda Cardinelli as Greene's not-so-long-suffering wife.

# King Kong

*Beauty and the beast*

**Year:** 2005

**Director:** Peter Jackson

**Screenplay:** Peter Jackson, Fran Walsh, and Philippa Boyens

**Cast:** Naomi Watts, Jack Black, Adrien Brody, Andy Serkis

The original *King Kong* is one of those movies that's become embedded in the public consciousness so that even those who haven't seen it know about it. It's been often imitated (and even remade back in 1976) but never duplicated. So it took Peter Jackson considerable guts, as well as the good will he earned as director of the *Lord of the Rings* movies, to take on such a beloved icon and put his own spin on it.

The results, while not quite perfect, are visually stunning and genuinely moving.

The story is the same, with a few embellishments along the way. Ann Darrow (Naomi Watts, perfect in the role) is a struggling vaudeville actress who's already gone weeks without a paycheck and is subsisting off soup kitchen fare when the theater closes and she's without a job. Desperately in search of a leading actress for his new safari film is Carl Denham (Jack Black), who's got possession of a map to a mysterious island he thinks would be the ideal location for his movie. Along for the ride is Jack Driscoll (Adrien Brody), the screenwriter for Denham's movie, who soon starts to have feelings for Ann.

The film-makers and the ship's salty crew arrive at the aptly named Skull Island, and that's when the film really kicks in. The human inhabitants of Skull Island (scary by themselves) waste no time in offering up Ann in a ritual sacrifice. The film and ship crew arrive just in time to see a huge gorilla carry Ann away, and set off in pursuit.

Skull Island is a terrifying place that makes Jurassic Park look like Disneyland. Poor Ann is carried off by Kong, and soon discovers the bones of the previous women who've been sacrificed to Kong. When it's clear she can't escape, the resourceful Ann makes friends with Kong — in one delightful scene she uses vaudeville tricks like backflips and juggling to entertain the ape. Later, of course, she does try to escape, only to encounter ravenous dinosaurs.

Meanwhile, the menfolk are having a worse time. Chased and eaten by dinosaurs, attacked by Kong, and in a truly scary scene, trapped in a pit of nasty giant insects. By the time the men finally rescue Ann, she's made a bond with Kong, whose refusal to let Ann leave, combined with

Denham's desire to exploit "The Eighth Wonder of the World" lead to a tragic finale in New York City.

Jackson's film is part tribute, part embellishment, and part showcase. His love for the original shines through, not only in the faithful re-creation of the story and its characters, but in the humanity he gives Kong. Jackson's Kong is not a monster — he's heroic, gentlemanly in his own way, and appreciates a beautiful sunset. His love for Ann is the greatest thing about him, yet it's his doom, and by the end of the movie he knows this too.

Special effects have improved a great deal since the 1930s, to say the least, and Jackson, true to form, uses everything that's available to him. Kong is a wonderful creation — you forget you're watching computer animation — from the realistic gorilla walk and bellow to the sadness in his eyes. The finale, atop the Empire State Building, is breathtaking, as Jackson uses height to both terrify the audience (my palms were sweaty) and demonstrate the loneliness and futility of Kong's last stand.

And Jackson has put his own stamp on the story. Particularly in the first half, there's much of his trademark goofy humor (and a nice in-joke for fans of *Dead Alive/Braindead*), but fortunately it's not laid on too thick. There is also Jackson's tendency to stretch out his action scenes a bit too long.

A minor but annoying flaw is the buildup without payoff for one of the crew members, Jimmy (Jamie Bell). In the end, he's simply forgotten, as if Jackson was so anxious to get Kong and Ann back to New York City that he forgot about poor Jimmy.

A more serious flaw is Jack Black as Carl Denham. We're asked to believe that Denham gets people to travel to an uncharted island to be in his movie when he has no money to offer anyone and is not a particularly successful film-maker. He has only surface charm, and even that is very thin. There's nothing to explain the loyalty of his assistant Preston (Colin Hanks). Black could have done better if the role had been rewritten somewhat, but as it stands he simply doesn't have the charisma necessary to make us believe that anyone would tag along with him to Skull Island.

But in the end, what we remember is Kong and Ann. Naomi Watts gives a wonderful performance — beautiful but not too glamorous (she's loveliest when she's bedraggled and muddy after fleeing dinosaurs), innocent but not stupid. She understands Kong and knows how wrong it is to take him away from his island home. There's a scene of the two of them in Central Park, sliding on the ice while Christmas trees twinkle in the background, that makes it clear this movie is, at its heart, a love story.

Dino De Laurentiis, when making his ill-advised *King Kong* remake in 1976, famously remarked that "Nobody cry when Jaws die. When the monkey die, everybody gonna cry." I don't know how many cried at Dino's film, but there are sure to be tears at the end of Jackson's.

# King of New York

*Walken in the park*

**Year:** 1990

**Director:** Abel Ferrara

**Screenplay:** Nicholas St. John

**Cast:** Christopher Walken, Laurence Fishburne, Victor Argo, David Caruso, Wesley Snipes

The best thing about the arts is that they let you hang out with shady characters at no risk to yourself. If such a scenario is up your alley, then you'll want to check out *King of New York*, a low-budget crime drama with one of Christopher Walken's better performances.

Walken is Frank White, a drug lord who'd just been released from prison. His gang are starting his re-entry into the life with a bang, eliminating rivals and letting the drug world know that White's back. It's no surprise that White is looking to re-establish himself as one of the drug scene's top players, but what is surprising is that he's using some of his earnings to save a hospital in a low-income section of town; he even says he might run for mayor! But a group of local cops, infuriated by White's flouting of laws and his increasing popularity in the city, hatch a plan to get rid of him by illegal rather than legal means. Suffice to say, this does not end well for anyone.

What's refreshing about *King of New York* is its refusal to portray any single character as wholly good or wholly evil. White is a perfect example: he casually murders his rivals, yet helps get funding for a hospital serving the poor, yet conducts drug deals right in the hospital (within earshot of little kids, no less), yet truthfully says, "I never killed anybody that didn't deserve it." Likewise, the cops pitted against him are sworn to uphold the law, yet circumvent the law in an effort to take down White.

The movie also refuses to explain its characters' motives. Is White really trying to help the poor and downtrodden? Or are his philanthropic efforts just a way to gain recognition from the world outside the drug trade? How much of the cops' resentment against White is because of his law breaking, and how much is because of his success in winning over the public? Director Abel Ferrara and screenwriter Nicholas St. John wisely don't weigh in on this, preferring to let the audience decide.

Despite an obvious low budget, the movie always looks fantastic, and its central action set piece (a nightclub ambush that turns into a chase and shootout in rainy night-time streets) is truly riveting. The acting is across-the-board good. The movie's known for Walken, and he turns in a cold, almost vampiric performance (several times he says things about being "back from the dead" or "my feelings are dead") that gives White just enough surface charm to make his Robin Hood moments believable. He's aided by a fine supporting cast full of "hey, it's that guy!" actors, most notably Wesley Snipes, David Caruso, and Steve Buscemi.

It's not a perfect film, as the timeline is vague and there's a lot of hand-waving for the legal means that keep White out of jail; there are also a couple of less-than-good performances (especially Janet Julian as White's lawyer and lover). But it's grim, gritty, and exciting, and essential viewing for Walken fans.

# Kingdom of the Spiders

*Eight-legged geeks*

**Year:** 1977

**Director:** John "Bud" Cardos

**Screenplay:** Richard Robinson and Alan Caillou

**Cast:** William Shatner, Tiffany Bolling, Woody Strode

Because I am considerate, I'm going to provide two versions of my review.

**Short version:** William Shatner. Hundreds and hundreds of real, live tarantulas. Go watch it, you know you want to.

**Long version:** I've mentioned my love for the "nature kicks ass" subgenre of horror films. Which makes it all the more amazing that not only had I not seen *Kingdom of the Spiders*, but I hadn't even heard it talked about much. (It didn't help that I always got it mixed up with *The Giant Spider Invasion*.) And if you're a fan of these kinds of movies, you really can't go wrong with *Kingdom of the Spiders*. It may not be, strictly speaking, a good film, but it delivers everything it promises (Spiders! Shatner!) and then some.

A Southwestern small town is getting ready for its annual fair, and rancher Colby (Woody Strode) is looking forward to his calf winning a big prize. Unfortunately the calf is attacked by a point-of-view camera angle. (This calf, along with some horses later in the movie, gives a great performance — I'm serious, it looks genuinely terrified.) Colby finds the calf unconscious and foaming at the mouth, and decides this is a job for William Shatner.

Shatner plays "Rack," the local veterinarian. We know Rack is awesome because he is named Rack, because he has a great toupee that doesn't budge even when he's roping steers, wears tight jeans and cool Western wear, and is played by William Shatner. Rack takes some samples from the now-expired calf and sends them off to a lab in Phoenix. The very next day entomologist Diane (Tiffany Bolling) shows up to put some hamfisted feminist subtext into the story and inform Rack that the calf died from spider venom.

Rack scoffs, but stops scoffing when Colby and his wife say, "Yeah, we've got spiders, there's this freaking ginormous spider hill in our field, come and see." Just one of these hills can hold thousands of spiders. And wouldn't you know it? That's not the only hill. There must be another twenty of them just on Colby's ranch alone! And because their natural prey has been eradicated by overuse of DDT and other pesticides, these spiders are pissed off and very hungry.

*Kingdom of the Spiders* is one of those movies that can never be remade, because the technical limitations of the time are what make it so effective. Those spiders — hundreds of them — are not CGI or props. They are real. Think of that when you watch the many scenes of spiders crawling on the characters. I'm not the least bit arachnophobic and even I was getting crawly toward the end. The same praise goes for the camerawork, particularly the "spider-cam" shots — they're effective, not least because the animals being menaced really do look afraid.

The movie also puts some care into its presentation of small-town life, and into the characters. I particularly appreciated it when Bolling's entomologist character finds a tarantula in her hotel room and instead of shrieking, she calmly picks it up, lets it walk on her hands, and then puts it outside. That said, there is still cheese in this movie — plenty of it. 1970s fashions! Outdated discussions of feminism! Awful country-ish ballads on the soundtrack!

I learned many things from *Kingdom of the Spiders*:

- Spiders can teleport. No, really. One moment they're on the ground, the next moment they're up on your shoulder giving you a hickey.
- If you must get past a passel of spiders, don't do anything that could actually hurt them. Don't step on them but just sort of dance awkwardly around them (not even Shatner can make this look good). And if you grab a weapon, make sure it's something really ineffectual like a feather duster.
- Two bites from a tarantula can kill you in seconds, unless you are William Shatner, in which case the more spider bites you receive, the more awesome you are.
- A pistol is not an effective weapon against spiders. And if you see a spider on your hand, do not try to shoot the spider off your hand. I shouldn't have to explain why this is a bad idea.

See? It's entertaining **and** educational!

# KISS Meets the Phantom of the Park

*Rock and roll all night*

**Year:** 1978

**Director:** Gordon Hessler

**Screenplay:** Jan Michael Sherman and Don Buday

**Cast:** Peter Criss, Paul Stanley, Gene Simmons, Ace Frehley, Anthony Zerbe

Has there ever been a band that offered more sizzle and less steak than KISS? Anyone who was a kid in the 1970s can tell you how notorious KISS was. Remember the rumor that KISS was an acronym for Knights In Satan's Service? And yet I never heard their music on the radio — or so I thought. It so happens I **had** heard the music, but I never equated that fairly bland power rock with those guys in their scary makeup, the flames at the concerts, and Gene Simmons' tongue. Now if only KISS had combined their look with a more powerful sound — maybe something like Motorhead's "Orgasmatron" — then we'd have something to be freaked out by.

I missed KISS's TV movie debut because my mother was in her crunchy granola phase and TV was more or less banned from the house. She probably wouldn't have let me watch it, anyway. The good news is that bootleg copies of the film are plentiful and cheap. The visuals aren't pristine, but you can just pretend that it's 1978 and the reception on your TV's rabbit-ears antenna isn't the best.

The movie is worth watching for its opening credits alone, which are some sort of peak/nadir of glorious 1970s cheese. KISS lip-synch to "Rock and Roll All Night" while superimposed over an amusement park (Magic Mountain in Valencia, CA). The highlight may well be when Gene Simmons appears to be King Kong-sized and stands next to the Colossus rollercoaster, ogling some ladies. Frankly, if the entire movie had been a montage of KISS and rollercoasters, that wouldn't have been so bad. Unfortunately, the movie-makers felt the need to give us a story.

And what a story it is. An amusement park is planning to host a KISS concert, and everyone's looking forward to it. Everyone, that is, except Abner Devereaux (Anthony Zerbe), an eccentric inventor whose specialty is the amazingly lifelike robots (clearly people pretending to be robots) that are part of the park's entertainment. When Abner protests the upcoming KISS performance, he gets the pink slip; deciding the only thing to do is enact a complicated revenge scheme against KISS, he sets about turning some local teenage hoodlums into his robots/minions. He also turns a nice-guy park employee into a robot/minion. The nice-guy's distraught girlfriend Melissa does what any sensible person would do — asks KISS to help her find out what's going on.

Because KISS is no mere rock band, oh no! The band members also have magical powers like laser eyes and fire breathing, thanks to their special talismans (which look a lot like cookie-cutters). Moved by Melissa's plight, they take time out from sitting by the pool in their full costume and makeup regalia to help her out. They even take a pause from the "action" to sing "Beth" to her. Isn't that sweet?

At one point Abner tries to defame the real KISS by creating a robot KISS and having them perform. Despite the fact that the fake KISS looks and sounds exactly like the real one, the fans can tell the difference and riot. We are then treated to the decidedly surreal sight of the KISS members fighting against their evil counterparts.

At this point, you might be saying to yourself, "This sounds like a really bad episode of *Scooby-Doo.*" If so, there's a reason for that — the producers of this movie were none other than Hanna-Barbera. Yes, the same Hanna-Barbera that brought you countless Saturday morning cartoons. This goes a long way toward explaining the juvenile, silly qualities of the film. I have to wonder how many people saw this and suddenly realized this fearsome menace from the rock and roll world were just a bunch of guys playing dress-up.

The whole thing is a complete embarrassment for everyone involved, except possibly Gene Simmons, because no matter what, he's Gene Fucking Simmons. The other band members muddle through while looking faintly embarrassed (as well they should). But it's a fantastic time capsule, particularly if you're from Southern California (you'll get to see Magic Mountain when the Revolution and Colossus coasters were new, and back when the park was a place you'd actually want to visit). If nothing else, be sure to watch the opening credits, and savor all the cheese.

# L. A. Confidential

*Men behaving badly*

**Year:** 1997

**Director:** Curtis Hanson

**Screenplay:** Curtis Hanson and Brian Helgeland, based on the novel by James Ellroy

**Cast:** Kevin Spacey, Russell Crowe, Guy Pearce

Someday I'd like to sit down with the Academy of Motion Picture Arts and Sciences and ask what the hell they were thinking when they handed out certain Oscars. And being the voice of reason that I am, surely I could persuade them to revise some awards and give that statue of the naked golden guy to the movies that deserve it.

(Of course I'd also love to end world hunger, invent a clean, renewable energy source, and be able to eat all the Reese's peanut butter cups I want without gaining weight. And a pony, I'd like that too.)

One of the awards I'd like the Academy to reconsider is the Oscar for Best Picture of 1997. This award went to *Titanic*. I liked *Titanic* fine at the time, but it hasn't aged well, and I've never had the urge to watch it again. The movie that should have received the Oscar? *L. A. Confidential.*

Based on the brutal, epic novel by James Ellroy, *L.A. Confidential* is set in 1953 and focuses on three very different Los Angeles policemen. Bud White (Russell Crowe, looking great in a wifebeater T-shirt) is violence-prone and somewhat thuggish but has a soft spot for damsels in distress. Jack Vincennes (Kevin Spacey, looking great in some very snappy clothes) is a narcotics detective who is the technical advisor on the "Badge of Honor" TV show (a thinly disguised "Dragnet") and who gets additional fame and monetary kickbacks from a tabloid magazine by busting movie stars for dope. Ed Exley (Guy Pearce, looking great in glasses) is a young detective precariously balancing his desire for justice against his considerable ambition.

The three are brought together first by a police brutality scandal, then by a multiple slaying at a diner. The diner massacre seems to be an open-and-shut case but soon is revealed as something much bigger, leading to a web of police and political corruption that includes organized crime, heroin, prostitution, blackmail. Oh yes, and violence and murder as well — every character we meet in the movie's first 15 minutes will be beaten up, shot, dead, or some combination of those, by the time the end credits roll.

To say more would spoil the many surprises of *L.A. Confidential* — suffice to say that nothing is quite what it seems. What lifts the story above the usual "evil hiding behind the good" scenario is that good is often found hiding in the unlikeliest places. Badly behaving, amoral men can find the will to work for justice instead of serving their own ambitions and needs (though the price they pay can be high).

Director Curtis Hanson and his co-screenwriter Brian Helgeland have done a remarkable job of capturing Los Angeles in the 1950s — if your concept of the 1950s is based off "Happy Days" and "Leave it to Beaver," think again. Jerry Goldsmith's score is note-perfect, as is the selection of songs from the time that grace the soundtrack.

Hanson and Helgeland's adaptation of Ellroy's novel is one of the best book-to-film translations I've seen. It was no easy task condensing a 500-page book that spans seven years and has enough plot for three books into a two-hour movie, but Hanson and Helgeland succeeded admirably, focusing on the main plot and condensing characters. The result is that you can enjoy both book and movie on their own terms, or in conjunction with each other (which I heartily recommend you do).

One thing that really makes *L. A. Confidential* a joy to watch is the acting. Spacey, Crowe, and Pearce are all magnificent, telling you more with their eyes and their body language than a lesser actor could do in pages of dialogue. The supporting cast is also good: Danny DeVito as an unscrupulous tabloid reporter, Kim Basinger as a Veronica Lake look-alike prostitute, David Strathairn as a decadent businessman (and Basinger's pimp), and James Cromwell as police chief Dudley Smith. Those of you who only know Cromwell from the movie about the talking pig are in for a real treat.

Go ahead and treat yourself to some fine crime drama. Off the record, on the QT and very…hush hush.

# Lair of the White Worm

*You don't have to be Freud to figure that one out*

**Year:** 1988

**Director:** Ken Russell

**Screenplay:** Ken Russell, based on the novel by Bram Stoker

**Cast:** Hugh Grant, Amanda Donohoe, Catherine Oxenberg

I've got a soft spot for batshit-crazy moviemakers. David Lynch and Terry Gilliam are shining examples. As is their predecessor, Ken Russell, whose output includes: straightforward but somehow still excessive literary adaptations like *Women in Love* and *The Rainbow*; wacked-out biographies like *Valentino* and *The Music Lovers*; and wild wallows in imagery (and often heavy-handed symbolism) like *The Devils, Tommy*, and this movie — *Lair of the White Worm*.

Based (I've no idea how faithfully) on a novel by Bram Stoker that I haven't read and haven't heard anything good about, *Lair of the White Worm* isn't a good movie, nor is it particularly frightening, but it is a comical, ghoulish, and entertaining exercise in absurdity.

Somewhere in England, paleontologist Angus Flint (Peter Capaldi) unearths a vaguely reptilian skull while digging on the site of an ancient convent. Despite the fact that Flint's excavation is a whopping two feet deep, the skull is incredibly ancient, and doesn't match up with any known species living or extinct. The find happens on the day Lord D'ampton (Hugh Grant, not stammering at all for a change) hosts his annual party where he re-enacts the myth of his ancestor slaying a fearsome, giant worm that terrorized the area a thousand years ago. Not at all coincidentally, local noblewoman Lady Sylvia Marsh (Amanda Donohoe, the main reason to see the movie) arrives back from vacation. Lady Sylvia is an interesting sort who gads around in fetishistic clothes like thigh-high leather boots and tricorne hats (no idea why, but it is easy on the eyes!) and is very prone to double-entendres involving snakes.

The movie kicks into high gear with its first official wacky moment: young innocent Eve (Catherine Oxenberg is a beautiful blank slate) has a hallucination that involves nuns being attacked and raped by Roman soldiers while a giant white serpent twines around a crucified Christ and bites Christ's arm off. Oh, and Lady Sylvia is in the vision too. Did I mention that Eve and her sister Mary (nope, no loaded names here!) are orphans, their parents having mysteriously vanished when they were near Lady Sylvia's property? Just a coincidence, I'm sure.

As with all the Russell films I've seen, it's impossible to tell if the director's often outlandish style and imagery are meant to evoke laughter or if he's just on a different wavelength than the rest of us. *Lair of the White Worm* hits a note wrong for every note it hits right, and the result is not a melody but a jangle. A prime example is Grant's dream sequence, involving snake imagery, a flight on a Lear jet with the female cast as catfighting stewardesses, and some ludicrous phallic symbolism. It somehow works, except when it doesn't.

The same can be said for the cast. It's Donohoe's show all the way, and her Lady Sylvia should be an icon for females in the horror genre: intelligent, beautiful, and supremely confident. But we know even before she gets dolled up in fangs, blue body paint, snake eyes, and a really scary strap-on that she's not at all human. Donohoe brings a serpentine quality to her walk, and she even sleeps in a basket. In the best, most subtle touch, she flicks her tongue before she kisses a man. Grant is surprisingly good, free of the annoying mannerisms he's well known for. His character is heroic but strangely remote, with a detached "well isn't that the damnedest thing!" air even when he's being attacked by vampire snake-women.

Less successful are the other cast members. Oxenberg and Sammi Davis (who plays Mary) exist to need rescuing. Capaldi is more or less forgettable, and his character is absurdly well-prepared for the climactic showdown, bringing both a mongoose and a grenade along. Yeah.

It's an outlandish romp that somehow doesn't have the cult reputation it deserves.

# Laserblast

*Kapow!*

**Year:** 1978

**Director:** Michael Rae

**Screenplay:** Franne Schacht and Frank Ray Perilli

**Cast:** Kim Milford, Cheryl "Rainbeaux" Smith, Gianni Russo

The big downside of rarely drinking alcohol is that you have to accept everything on its own terms. You can't have the excuse of "I don't know, I was pretty drunk at the time" to fall back on.

Usually I'm OK with this. But heavy drinking might have helped out when I watched *Laserblast*. I'd seen this on *Mystery Science Theater 3000*, where it was a laugh riot, and thought I'd see the movie straight up. Unfortunately, what was amusing with Mike and the 'bots and might have been endearingly bad when seen through booze-colored glasses, ended up being rather dull and pathetic.

The movie opens on a relatively promising note. A green-faced guy staggers through the desert, only to be zapped by a laser and reduced to a black silhouette on the ground, leaving behind a pendant and a giant laser weapon. The shooters, two aliens who look like lumpy dinosaurs and who speak in the "Meh! Mah!" dialect familiar to anyone who saw *Mars Attacks*, congratulate themselves on their accuracy, but then get spooked by a passing Cessna and hop into their spaceship, leaving behind the pendant and the weapon to be found by some unlucky bastard.

Our unlucky bastard is the vaguely reptilian Billy (Kim Milford). Billy's life sucks, not to put too fine a point on it. In the very first scene, Billy's mother goes gadding off to Acapulco, presumably leaving Billy to fend for himself and live off ramen noodles. (Adding a whole new level to the patheticness of Billy's existence, he appears to be checking out his mom's ass in this scene. Eww.) Billy also has a very lame van, with silly Bigfoot decals on the side; enraged by its décor, the van betrays him by refusing to start when Billy challenges local stud Chuck (Mike Bobenko) and Chuck's bitch, um, I mean, sycophant, Froggy (Eddie Deezen). I'm sorry, but when a character played by Eddie Deezen can successfully mock you, it may be time to begin reassessing your life. Billy is also hassled by the cops and by his girlfriend's wacko grandfather (Keenan Wynn in a glorified cameo). The only bright spot in Billy's existence is his girlfriend Kathy (Cheryl "Rainbeaux" Smith), which unfortunately means we get to watch the two of them suck face a lot. Eww. Billy also spends almost the entire movie with his shirt off or open. Eww.

Fortunately, after the opening wallow in the misery that is Billy's existence, Billy discovers the pendant and the laser weapon. This scene is unintentionally hilarious; when Billy first finds the weapon he makes "Pa-pa-pow!" sounds. Really. Soon he discovers that if he fires the weapon while wearing the pendant, he can blow up stuff real good. Unfortunately, the pendant gives him an ooky sore on his chest. Eww. He also starts turning into a green-faced ghoul. Nothing ever works out well for Billy, does it?

So Billy spends the rest of the movie laserblasting those who've done him wrong, and it soon becomes clear that the movie's *raison d'etre* is to blow up stuff real good. Which is fine, except that a plot would be nice, as well as some characters we can be interested in instead of merely having contempt for. Vague attempts at a plot are made, resulting in another glorified cameo, this time by Roddy McDowall as a doctor who examines the ooky sore on Billy's chest. And there's a government guy named Mr. Craig (Gianni Russo) who adds absolutely nothing to the movie.

*Laserblast* is like something the AV geeks at high school might have put together. However, I'm not in high school any more and *Laserblast* ends up being dull, with occasional ventures into sad and lame. The plot is nonexistent. The characters are pitiable at best and obnoxious at worst — it's clear we're supposed to rally behind Billy, but director Michael Rae is no Brian De Palma, and Billy is no Carrie White.

The only bright spots are the things blowing up real good, although there are some head-scratchers here — the pinball machine? The *Star Wars* billboard? And why doesn't anyone notice all these explosions? Also of note are the stop-motion aliens, created by Dave Allen, who worked on many genre movies ranging from *Flesh Gordon* to *Ghostbusters 2*. The aliens made me smile every time I saw them. Also provoking a giggle was a stoned van driver who gives Billy a lift and has a nonsensical, profoundly stupid speech.

Learn from my example, dear readers. If you must watch *Laserblast*, do so with a bunch of good friends. Jack Daniels, Johnny Walker, Sam Adams… you get the idea.

# The Last Wave

*Deluge*

**Year:** 1977

**Director:** Peter Weir

**Screenplay:** Peter Weir, Tony Morphett, and Petru Popescu

**Cast:** Richard Chamberlain, David Gulpilil

There are some movies I can point to without question as being responsible for my mind being what it is today. Movies that tweaked my psyche when it was still young and impressionable. *The Last Wave* is one of those movies. I vividly recall seeing it on cable when I was 8 or 9 — specifically a scene with a rain of frogs, and of its haunting final sequence. It stayed with me for days.

For some time I was reluctant to watch *The Last Wave* as an adult, fearing that the movie would not hold up to my fond recollections of it. You can hardly blame me — it wouldn't have been the first time nostalgia has lied to me. The good news is that *The Last Wave* is as good as I remember it being: enigmatic, dreamlike, and more relevant today than it was at the time of its release.

The film opens at a remote school in the Australian outback, where everything is sunny, hot, and dusty. Though the sky is cloudless, thunder rumbles, and then a fierce rainstorm strikes, with the rain soon turning to hail — not just a few bits of it but fist-size hailstones that cause injury. The outback isn't the only place with freaky weather, we learn, as we jump to Sydney where the city is suffering through an unprecedented number of rainstorms. The rain is having a particular effect on lawyer David (Richard Chamberlain), who finds himself plagued by nightmares and visions of rains and floods. His life soon gets more complicated when he takes on the case of a group of Aborigines believed to have murdered one of their friends. David thinks the murder was in fact a tribal killing to prevent the man from revealing secrets, and his beliefs seem to be confirmed by suspect Chris (David Gulpilil), who's been appearing in David's dreams/visions and knows much more than he's telling about the weather disturbances and what they mean. Let's just say that buying oceanfront property in Sydney may not be a sound financial move.

What makes *The Last Wave* effective is the feeling of impending dread that suffuses it from frame one. It's also an astonishingly tactile film, with water, water everywhere. Frequent rainstorms, an overflowing bath, characters idly touching water from faucets, the haunting images of a drowned city, and its shoreline denouement. You feel clammy by the end of the movie. It's not a film that provides answers — many of its questions are left unresolved — but the viewer doesn't feel cheated because the film is about the failure of people to understand the signs of the end. Whether it's David's failure to understand his visions, Chris' failure to understand David's willingness to help, the society's failure to understand the impact of its mistreatment of the Aboriginal people and of its misuse of the environment — all these failures may (or may not) result in the outcome, which is so inevitable by film's end that it hardly matters whether what we're seeing is really happening or is one of David's visions.

As always, director Peter Weir gets good performances from his cast. Richard Chamberlain's gaunt beauty gives him an ethereal, haunted look that works well for David, who's just now realizing his role in the spiritual world. David Gulpilil is good as Chris, a spokesman for the Aboriginal spirit world and for the physical world, dreamtime and harsh "reality." Kudos also go to the film's cinematography, which makes a mere change in weather something ominous to behold, and to its somewhat dated but still highly appropriate, eerie electronic score.

It's a quiet film that many will call boring, and it's not something you watch without paying full attention. But it's rewarding, and haunting, and most likely you'll have some images from it stay with you for a while. And you'll be very nervous the next time it rains.

# The Legacy

*Inherit the bland*

**Year:** 1979

**Director:** Richard Marquand

**Screenplay:** Jimmy Sangster, Patrick Tilley, and Paul Wheeler

**Cast:** Katherine Ross, Sam Elliott, Roger Daltrey

I have **got** to stop listening to the lying voice of nostalgia. See, I thought this movie was pretty cool when I was 13 or so. How could it not be? It had spooky cats! That cute guy from The Who! Creative death scenes!

What the lying voice of nostalgia failed to mention was that the movie was boring, had awful disco music, the creative death scenes were mostly laughable, and it had one of the most lackadaisical endings ever. And did I mention boring?

Anyway, *The Legacy* opens with California architect Maggie Walsh (Katherine Ross) and Pete (Sam Elliott) her business partner? Fiancé? Man-whore? It's not really clear. Doesn't matter. Maggie gets a job offer in England (the account number on the advance check is 129-666 — oooh, how sinister!) and after some fuss over who will look after their plants while they're away, the happy couple jaunts across the pond.

You can tell the movie's a product of the seventies by the music accompanying the "loving couple frolics about Merrie Englande" montage — disco tune by Kiki Dee! This is why punk rock was inevitable.

I digress. Maggie and Pete are on a motorcycle ride when they get run off the road by upper-class twit Jason Mountolive, who invites them back to the manor for tea while their bike is fixed. Maggie and Pete take him up on the offer only to find that the bike can't be fixed any time soon and they have to stay overnight. Fair enough, but then a helicopter arrives with a full complement of Eurotrash, who all sport ugly rings and give ominous looks every time Jason Mountolive's name is mentioned. It turns out that there's a vague sort of black magic/Satanic pact involved with Mr. Mountolive, to which the posse of Eurotrash all owe their worldly success.

Only, it turns out Mr. Mountolive isn't as chipper as we saw him in his introductory scene. Turns out he's a hideously withered old man who's about to croak and is ready to pick his heir from his houseguests…and his first choice seems to be Maggie. Soon the Eurotrash all start perishing in unlikely and not-nearly-as-entertaining-as-you'd-hope ways and a Big Secret about Maggie emerges. Ho hum.

There are a few bright spots in *The Legacy*, mostly of the unintentional variety. As "Clive," one of the Eurotrash brigade, Roger Daltrey proves that as an actor he's a pretty good rock star (a cutie pie, though). *Rocky Horror* fans will spot Charles "The Criminologist" Gray, sporting a weird accent. The first death scene, involving a pool whose surface inconveniently turns solid, is creepy and well-executed — the others, though, are fairly laughable (especially one character's patently phony demise by fire). And yes, there are spooky cats (none of them black, for a change). There's also a nice shot of Sam Elliott's butt, if that tickles your fancy (he's not my usual type, but he'll do).

The story, which might have made a nice *Night Gallery* episode, is unforgivably padded (especially the "escape" sequence which seems to take up half the running time). The flat cinematography and the utterly pedestrian direction by Richard "I directed *Return of the Jedi*! No, really!" Marquand drain whatever liveliness the story might have had.

# Long Weekend

*Crime against nature*

**Year:** 1978

**Director:** Colin Eggleston

**Screenplay:** Everett De Roche

**Cast:** John Hargreaves, Briony Behets

What is it about Australia? Many of the Australian films I've seen have a strange, otherworldly vibe to them, and a fine example is *Long Weekend*, a "nature strikes back" film unlike any other you may have seen.

A long holiday weekend is about to start, and young marrieds Peter (John Hargreaves) and

Marcia (Briony Behets) are heading off for a camping trip. They could use some relaxation — the couple's every conversation is rife with bitter silences and angry remarks, with many hints to recent troubles in their relationship. If this weren't a sufficient tip-off that the marriage is in trouble, Peter brings home a new rifle for the trip, and proceeds to put Marcia in its sights. Subtle, isn't he?

Not as readily apparent, but of far more consequence, is Peter and Marcia's disregard for nature. The transgressions start out mildly, from Marcia refusing to find a dog-sitter for Peter's dog, to Peter tossing a cigarette butt out their van's window, where we see it set grass afire. The couple should have been tipped off that things weren't going to go well by the fact that their beach destination's closest landmark is an abattoir, that the locals don't seem to have heard of it, and that their first night's journey is blocked by a seemingly impenetrable maze of forest.

The next morning, however, finds them at their destination, where they set up camp. The surroundings are gorgeous — lush vegetation and a lovely beach — but Peter and Marcia don't appreciate their surroundings. The bickering escalates into outright hostility as buried resentments and ugly truths emerge. Their mistreatment of the habitat increases — Peter shoots his rifle randomly and hacks at a tree with an axe, Marcia douses ants with bug spray and smashes an eagle's egg. And then nature starts taking its revenge. Subtly at first, as a frozen chicken thaws and rots in minutes, then more menacingly, as animals attack and the night is full of strange cries.

*Long Weekend* isn't a flashy film full of cheap thrills and jump scares. It's atmospheric and lets its horrors unfold slowly. At times it has almost a documentary feel, with its lush nature photography and the way it lets the couple's drama play out in what feels like real time. The eerie score works to establish the atmosphere of steadily increasing dread. What makes the film effective is that while it's clearly on nature's side, it's not without some sympathy for its unlikable protagonists, particularly in the night-time scenes when they're haunted by some unknown creature's cries (Marcia thinks the cries sound like a baby, a conjecture that takes on greater resonance as the couples' backstory unfolds).

Hargreaves and Behets make their characters real and if not sympathetic, certainly recognizable. The actors have both the ease and the discomfort that come from a longtime relationship that's in its death throes, and it's never pleasant to watch, but it is compelling.

If you want some unsettling, atmospheric horror with that special something that only the Australians seem to bring to the party, give *Long Weekend* a view. Not a good movie for date night, though.

# Lord of the Rings

*We hates it*

**Year:** 1978

**Director:** Ralph Bakshi

**Screenplay:** Chris Conkling and Peter S. Beagle, based on *The Fellowship of the Ring* and *The Two Towers* by J. R. R. Tolkien

**Cast:** Christopher Guard (voice), William Squire (voice), John Hurt (voice), Anthony Daniels (voice)

People of a certain age looked to Peter Jackson's adaptation of *The Lord of the Rings* with a mixture of hope and trepidation. The former because we really wanted a good adaptation, and the latter because, despite all our best efforts, we still remembered Ralph Bakshi's 1978 attempt.

At first glance, animation would seem to be an ideal way to adapt the story. The beauty of animation is its power to show almost anything, and surely this would be the best way to bring Middle Earth and Tolkien's characters to the screen, wouldn't it? Unfortunately, the project was doomed, possibly from the start (I would love a documentary about the making of this film that explores what went wrong and why).

The major problems of the film include the animation. Not the idea of animation itself, mind you, but director Ralph Bakshi's style and his artistic decisions. Elsewhere in this book (my review of *Wizards*, to be precise) you'll see that I'm not a fan of Bakshi's style. While his ideas can be interesting, or at least entertainingly off-kilter, and while he has the occasional arresting image to offer, that's not enough to sustain a film, particularly one with the epic scope and length of *Lord of the Rings*. Things get off to an unpromising start when the backstory of the Rings of Power is told — but not in animation. Instead it's a crimson-hued shadow-puppet show, and the Sauron puppet bears a distracting resemblance to the Knights Who Say "Ni." I am not making this up. The dubious choices go on from there, including but not limited to: rotoscoping that gives the characters a clumsy, jittery feel (it doesn't help that the hobbit characters were clearly rotoscoped from dwarf actors); strange psychedelic bits any time magic is involved, particularly the "ghost ringwraiths in the sky" bit; entire battle sequences using live-action actors with a bit of tinting and animation; the decision to have most male characters wear short skirts out of some 1960s Hercules movie; and some very silly characterization, such as Gimli the tall dwarf, Aragorn the Native American, Boromir the Viking, and Gollum the Grinch — and let's not forget special guest star Beavis as Legolas. The facial expressions for all characters are very distracting, with lots of inappropriate smiling, and many of the actors seem to have been instructed to never remain still for more than a minute. Characters are constantly gesticulating, twirling about, dancing, bugging their eyes out, and twitching.

The problems continue with the story. I believe the film was intended to be the first half of a two-parter, so I won't dock points for ending the film around the 2/3 mark of *The Two Towers*. But the film tries to cram so much into its running time that crucial plot elements are glossed over and the dialogue at times makes no sense to anyone unacquainted with the books. Unless you already know the story, you won't get what's going on (and if you do know the story, you're busy griping about everything from Gandalf the Gray really being Gandalf the Periwinkle Blue to Aragorn waving around a broken sword without explaining why it's so important).

There are also a shocking number of continuity errors and editing gaffes. Characters' hair colors and even their names change from scene to scene, and characters constantly refer to things that were never mentioned.

Even the voice acting is a mixed bag at best. Coming away with their dignity intact are John Hurt as the voice of Aragorn and Norman Bird as Bilbo. I can't say the same for the rest of the cast, though a good part of the blame goes to the animators and the screenplay.

As dreadfully flawed as this movie is, I wager that many people of my age saw it more than once and might even have a certain amount of nostalgia for it. Heck, my sister and I owned the tie-in board game, and oh how I wish I had that game now — some nerd would pay bucks for it, I'm sure. Because for the longest time, this and the Rankin-Bass adaptation of *The Hobbit* (which wasn't any great shakes either but looks much better by comparison) were all we had for film adaptations. You can imagine that many of us let out sighs of relief when the Peter Jackson films came along — they may not have been perfect, but at least they kept Saruman's name consistent and didn't make Samwise look developmentally delayed.

The scary thing is, it could have been much worse — Bakshi's original plan was to have Led Zeppelin songs play throughout the film. Think about that, won't you?

# Lost Highway

*Fugue state*

**Year:** 1997

**Director:** David Lynch

**Screenplay:** David Lynch and Barry Gifford

**Cast:** Bill Pullman, Patricia Arquette, Balthazar Getty

*Lost Highway* is, arguably, the forgotten David Lynch film. I'll come back to possible reasons why it's a second-tier film for Lynch, but for now suffice to say that second-tier or not, it will undoubtedly please the director's fans and is a satisfying mind-fuck.

Fred Madison (Bill Pullman shedding his nice-guy rom-com image) is a jazz saxophonist who's married to Renee (brunette Patricia Arquette). It's hard to say which is more claustrophobic — their beautiful but sterile house, or a marriage that consists of stilted conversation, awkward silences, and unsatisfactory sex. Fred adds suspicions of infidelity to his list of marital problems, and soon afterward the couple receive a videotape. The tape is simply a brief film of their house's exterior. But subsequent tapes show footage of the inside of the house, and of Fred and Renee asleep in their bed.

Unsettling as that is, things get worse. At a party hosted by a person who might be Renee's lover, Fred encounters the Mystery Man (played with sublime creepiness by Robert Blake), who informs Fred that they've met, and that he is not only speaking to Fred at the party but that he's in Fred's house at that very moment. A phone call seems to confirm this. Fred receives another videotape, this one showing that Renee's been brutally murdered. Fred's convicted of the crime and sentenced to death, and while awaiting his appointment with the electric chair starts suffering severe headaches. After a particularly nasty night for Fred, his guards open his cell to find not Fred but Pete Dayton (Balthazar Getty) a nice young auto mechanic with no memory of what he's doing in Fred's cell. The baffled police let Pete go, and he returns to his everyday life. And then things get weird.

In many ways *Lost Highway* is a dry run for *Mulholland Drive*, with its Moebius-strip narrative and recurring and/or doppelganger characters. Yet it lacks the emotional heart of *Mulholland Drive* and fails to give the audience a character it can identify with. Though Pullman puts in a good, quietly tortured performance, we never learn enough about him to sympathize with his eventual plight. Pete is a more obvious choice for a sympathetic character, but before he can win over the audience he makes the boneheaded move of falling for Alice (blonde Patricia Arquette), the girlfriend of gangster Mr. Eddie (delightfully profane Robert Loggia). The real problem with the movie is Arquette, who isn't a strong enough actress to handle the two roles she's assigned, nor is she charismatic enough to make us understand why men would be driven to kill for her.

*Lost Highway* also lacks the odd transcendence of other Lynch films. Despite their grim subject matter, most Lynch films grant their characters moments of grace and even redemption. There's no such moment in *Lost Highway*, which will no doubt please the "it's better because it's darker" crowd but may be one reason the film is somewhat forgotten. It's the most pessimistic of Lynch's movies.

That aside, *Lost Highway* looks and sounds gorgeous. No director uses silence, sound, and shadow quite the way Lynch does, and he makes even an ordinary hallway seem threatening. The score by Angelo Badalamenti, with contributions by Trent Reznor, is effective as always (though like Lynch, Badalamenti seems to be doing a test run for *Mulholland Drive*). However, some of the overly trendy song choices grate.

Fans will be pleased to see what they've come to expect from Lynch: haunting imagery (the scene of a house that explodes in reverse and slow motion is the one that lingers in the mind longest), oddball supporting characters (look for small roles by Gary Busey, Richard Pryor, and Henry Rollins), and a story that's familiar yet plays out in unexpected ways. But perhaps that's what keeps the film from being great — it's Lynch doing what we expect of him.

# Macbeth

*Full of sound and fury*

**Year:** 1972

**Director:** Roman Polanski

**Screenplay:** Roman Polanski and Kenneth Tynan, based on the play by William Shakespeare

**Cast:** Jon Finch, Francesca Annis

The more memorable adaptations of Shakespeare that I've seen are ones that translate the play to the cinematic medium without smothering the play's themes and content in attempts to "modernize" the work. Roman Polanski's adaptation of *Macbeth* succeeds admirably, and will be an interesting jolt to viewers who find the Bard incomprehensible or who think Shakespeare is all people standing around in tights saying funny lines.

The film opens on a dreary beach at low tide: three ragged women dig a hole in the sand and bury a severed arm whose hand still clutches a dagger, and a length of rope fashioned into a hangman's noose. It's so far removed from a stage setting that it's a bit jarring to hear the witches recite the familiar lines ("When shall we three meet again / In thunder, lightning, or in rain") but by the time Macbeth, fresh from glory on the battlefield, and his friend Banquo meet up with the witches, the viewer's accustomed to hearing Shakespeare's lines in the unfamiliar setting.

Events follow those of the play (and if you haven't read it yet, do so immediately — it's a timeless story of power-lust, madness, and revenge). The witches predict that Macbeth (Jon Finch), currently Thane of Cawdor, will also be Thane of Glamis and afterward, king. His friend Banquo is prophesied to not be king himself, but to sire a line of kings. Macbeth initially dismisses the witches' claims, but when King Duncan rewards Macbeth for his battlefield deeds by making him Thane of Glamis, Macbeth sees the predictions as legitimate, and wonders just how he'll become king. Macbeth's vague notions of seizing power become a murderous plan thanks to the initiative of his ambitious, coldhearted wife (Francesca Annis). When King Duncan and his entourage stay at Macbeth's castle, the two murder the king, frame the king's guards for the deed, and cast such suspicion on the king's sons Malcolm and Donalbain that the sons flee abroad. Macbeth becomes king but he's troubled by the witches' prophecy that his line will die out and Banquo's descendants will reign in his stead, and by the defection of lords unhappy with Macbeth's rule, including Macduff, the Thane of Fife. Soon Macbeth becomes more and more ruthless in his attempts to secure his claim, while his wife steadily grows unhinged by her guilt.

What makes this adaptation work is that, aside from the unfamiliar cadences of the language (which we soon grow accustomed to), this doesn't feel like a play. The score by the Third Ear Band is unusual but suits the film well. Monologues are kept to a minimum, with the soliloquies being rendered as voice-overs, a device that works more often than not. (Occasionally one is reminded of David Lynch's *Dune* in which the characters had voice-over exposition while the actors made thinking faces). The castles feel unglamorous and very real, and the outdoor settings on bleak beaches and cold moors not only make the play feel less stagy but emphasize the harsh society.

It's a cold film, not just in the outdoor settings but in its unflinching brutality. Brief though they are, the opening battlefield scenes show the war as a dirty, violent business. In the play Duncan's murder is offstage but it's shown in the film, as is the fact that blood can be difficult to get off one's hands (literally and metaphorically). Probably the most infamous sequence is the attack on Macduff's castle and the murder of his family. The fact that this film was Polanski's first after the murder of Sharon Tate and her unborn child gives the sequence a queasy, disturbing resonance.

The film isn't perfect. The voice-overs grate at times, and the "is this a dagger I see before me" sequence is visualized with psychedelic lighting that ruins the mood. But for the most part the film succeeds, though its violence and nudity don't make it ideal for a high school English class.

# Intermission: Movies I Won't Watch

It may be hard to believe after reading some of my reviews, but I do have standards. I also have a short list of movies I will most likely never watch.

## Magic

Yes, I was one of those wussy little kids who were terrified by the famous commercial.

## Cannibal Holocaust

It's bad enough that I've seen *Cannibal Ferox*, with its disgusting and wholly unnecessary scenes of real animal killings. That film was quite enough, thanks, and I've read enough reviews of *Cannibal Holocaust* to know that whatever redeeming artistic qualities that film has won't be enough to make up for the offensive material.

## Joe's Apartment

I'm roach-phobic. It took me years to work up the guts to watch the "Creeping Up On You" segment from *Creepshow*. I can't handle a whole movie rife with roaches.

## The Last House on the Left and Irreversible

I'm not a huge fan of the rape/revenge subgenre, and if I'm going to watch one, I'd rather watch *I Spit on Your Grave* (now there's a phrase I never thought I'd say) as it actually puts the revenge in the hands of the woman who was assaulted, rather than delegating that to spouses or family members.

## Men Behind the Sun

I stumbled across some images from this film and it took me weeks to recover. I'm actually glad I learned about the film, as its subject matter (medical and other experimentation carried out on prisoners of war by the Japanese during World War II) was unknown to me, and is a part of history that shouldn't be forgotten. I just can't bring myself to watch a movie about it.

## The Human Centipede

Hey, I watched *Salò*. I don't need any more cinematic coprophagia.

## A Serbian Film

If you read the Wikipedia entry and still want to watch it, there's something **really** wrong with you.

# Mad Monster Party

*Spooky shindig*

**Year:** 1967

**Director:** Jules Bass

**Screenplay:** Len Korobkin and Harvey Kurtzman

**Cast:** Boris Karloff (voice), Gale Garnett (voice), Allen Swift (voice), Phyllis Diller (voice)

It may seem hard to believe, but there was a time when kids weren't able to nag their parents into buying DVDs so the kids could watch their favorite movies whenever they wanted to. Yes, back in ye olden days, we had to make an effort to watch movies. If we didn't get taken to the matinee we had to wait for them to show up on TV (which had only 13 channels, and that's if you were lucky) and then watch them. And if you were late or the TV went on the fritz, tough luck.

This wasn't all bad. One reason I haven't bought *The Wizard of Oz* on DVD is because it just doesn't seem right to have it always available for viewing. It used to be a **big event** when *The Wizard of Oz* made its annual appearance on TV — I remember marking the occasion with popcorn and an Orange Crush, waiting for the show to begin. Similarly, if you didn't have folks willing to dump you at the local matinee for an afternoon, the best way to catch many kids' movies was on local TV. That was my first exposure to *Mad Monster Party*, seeing it on the Channel 5 Family Film Festival.

*Mad Monster Party* is now on DVD, which means it's time to see the film in its entirety without commercial interruptions or being dragged away from the TV to go take out the trash. It's also time to see how the movie holds up without being viewed through nostalgia-colored lenses.

Made by Rankin-Bass, the same awesome folks who brought us *Rudolph the Red-nosed Reindeer, The Year Without a Santa Claus, Santa Claus is Coming to Town* and more, *Mad Monster Party* attempts to do for classic movie monsters what they earlier did for Christmas-themed characters, and to break out of the TV time constraints. And for the most part, it was a successful effort.

On his Caribbean island, Dr. Baron von Frankenstein (voice by Boris Karloff) has just created an anti-matter solution, just a few drops of which can destroy anything. Pleased with his success, he sends out party invitations to the most famous monsters: Dracula, the Wolf Man, the Mummy, Dr. Jekyll and Mr. Hyde, the Hunchback of Notre Dame, and the Invisible Man. Also on hand are the Baron's monster creation, the monster's supremely annoying wife (voiced by the supremely annoying Phyllis Diller), a group of zombies that include a Peter Lorre type, and the Baron's secretary, the astonishingly buxom redhead Francesca (voice by Gale Garnett) who probably made many young boys feel funny back in the day. And Felix Flankin will be there too.

"Who?" asks Francesca (and the audience). Well, Felix is a nebbishy, allergy-prone pharmacy clerk who is blind without his glasses and talks like Jimmy Stewart. He's also the Baron's nephew and when the Baron confides to Francesca that he plans to retire and leave all his secrets to Felix, Francesca and many of the monsters start trying to get rid of Felix. That's easier said than done, though. And things get even more complicated when the dreaded monster "It" (no, not the Stephen King *It*) decides to crash the party.

*Mad Monster Party* is something you rarely find these days — a family film. It's suitable for even the youngest viewers, yet won't insult adults' intelligence either. The humor, while heavy on the puns (many courtesy of an uncredited Forry Ackerman), is good for a few chuckles. My favorite moment is when two characters are fleeing danger — one can't go on, and asks the other character to not just leave them behind but leave them with something to read — don't want to be bored while waiting for one's imminent death! And there's an astonishing amount of detail not just in the excellent stop-motion animation but in the sets and backgrounds.

Like many of the Rankin-Bass holiday specials, *Mad Monster Party* includes songs, and most of them are catchy enough so you don't mind if they get stuck in your head. In fact, "Do the Mummy" by Little Tibia and the Fibias (Beatles-esque moptop skeletons) is worthy of inclusion on any Halloween music mix. "One Step Ahead" and "Our Time to Shine" are also good. Unfortunately two songs grate — "You're Different" is "sung" by Diller and besides being annoying does nothing but pad the film's running time. Likewise "Never Was A Love Like Ours" stops the film dead at a point when its pace is beginning to flag.

Which leads me to my main criticism of the film — its pacing. *Mad Monster Party* is extremely episodic, as if Rankin and Bass were still working with TV commercial breaks in mind, and the pace drags in the last half hour. The "Never Was a Love Like Ours" song will have kids squirming and adults looking at their watches; fortunately the mystery monster It shows up to give the movie a raucous and surprisingly poignant ending.

Flaws aside, *Mad Monster Party* is pleasantly ghoulish fun for the whole family.

# Mandingo

*Race relations*

**Year:** 1975

**Director:** Richard Fleischer

**Screenplay:** Norman Wexler, based on the novel by Kyle Onstott

**Cast:** James Mason, Perry King, Susan George, Ken Norton, Brenda Sykes

Most bad movie fans of a certain age have at least heard of *Mandingo*. In its day it was so notorious that the *Kentucky Fried Movie's* "Catholic High School Girls In Trouble" fake trailer declared it was "more offensive than *Mandingo*!" Elements of the film were clearly an inspiration to Quentin Tarantino for *Django Unchained*. And now for those of us with more curiosity than sense comes a DVD release for *Mandingo*.

Based on a novel by Kyle Onstott, the movie opens on the Falconhurst plantation, somewhere in the deep South, some time before the Civil War. Falconhurst is owned by the Maxwell father and son. Dad (a slumming James Mason, his accent all over the place) spends his time nagging his son to get married and have a legitimate heir, and complaining about his rheumatism. He soon finds a way to alleviate the rheumatism when his doctor prescribes using slave children as footstools so the rheumatism can "drain out" of Dad and into the children. Yes, five minutes past the credits and you're already appalled.

Son Hammond (Perry King), meanwhile, isn't keen on getting married as he's too busy having sex with every female slave he's attracted to. After all, it's "master's duty to pleasure the wenches first time." Isn't that thoughtful? Besides, his top priority in life is to get a "Mandingo" slave to compete in bare-knuckle, to-the-death fighting competitions.

Luckily for Hammond, in one trip to New Orleans he ends up with: a wife, when his cousin Blanche (Susan George) agrees to marry him; a new bedmate slave named Ellen (Brenda Sykes); and a Mandingo fighter named Mede (Ken Norton and his one facial expression). Hammond is smitten with Ellen and thrilled at having Mede to train. As for Blanche? Well, the wedding night's a bust when it's apparent she's not a virgin.

Hammond divides his time between his tender-on-the-surface-creepy-in-the-subtext relationship with Ellen and his efforts to make Mede a top fighter. Blanche, ignored and increasingly neurotic and frustrated, drowns her sorrows in sherry and seethes with resentment against Ellen. It's a recipe for disaster that's fully realized when Blanche blackmails Mede into an affair, and nine months later there's that awkward moment when the baby's not white.

179

*Mandingo* isn't nearly as shocking as it was back in the day, but it's just as distasteful. Though not graphic by today's standards, it shows a world in which every person is vile or foolish, with casual acceptance of rape, incest, sadism, infanticide, torture, and murder. The subject matter of slavery and its caustic effect on the society that supports it has potential, but *Mandingo* squanders the opportunity. It's too grim and nasty to be campy, and too inept to take seriously. The subject matter is exploitative, but the film doesn't ask you to leer at the cheap thrills; instead, the camera just sort of sits there and records the happenings in that depressing, dingy way peculiar to 1970s movies.

The only times *Mandingo* is effective is when it strays into horror-film territory. The decaying, decrepit mansion of Falconhurst (notice there are no decorations on the walls and furniture is a bare minimum — it's as if everything has been sold off) is, thanks to the occasional effective bit of camerawork and Maurice Jarre's odd but appropriate score, the ancestor of every creepy Southern house seen in horror movies. And in their own ways, Blanche, Ellen, and Mede are as trapped as any bunch of unlucky kids who strayed into the wrong cabin in the woods. Unfortunately, the three are too cartoonishly neurotic (in Blanche's case) or naive to the point of stupidity (Ellen and Mede) to engender much sympathy.

It's a curiosity piece for aficionados of bad cinema, but you'll probably want to shower after the movie.

# Marathon Man

*Run, run, run, as fast as you can*

**Year:** 1976

**Director:** John Schlesinger

**Screenplay:** William Goldman, based on his novel

**Cast:** Dustin Hoffman, Laurence Olivier, Roy Scheider

In 2008 we lost Roy Scheider, always a tremendously underrated actor. One of his memorable roles is in *Marathon Man* — a taut, intelligent little thriller that's all but forgotten today save for its notorious torture-by-dentistry scene. It's too bad the film is so overlooked, because it's got an intelligent plot, strong performances, and nifty plot twists.

The movie begins with two seemingly unrelated stories. Thomas "Babe" Levy (Dustin Hoffman) is a history grad student who trains for marathon running when he's not in class. Despite the daily taunts he gets from the local kids and a lodging furnished in Squalor Contemporary, Babe's life is looking up — he's gotten into a coveted seminar and has just landed an improbably hot Swiss girlfriend. The other story concerns Scylla (Roy Scheider), an agent for a government agency known only as "Division," who is getting uneasy about the recent murders and disappearances of fellow agents. Uneasiness becomes paranoia when Scylla survives two assassination attempts and realizes the common thread is a former Nazi named Szell (Sir Laurence Olivier).

The storylines converge when Szell leaves his South American haunts and when Scylla is revealed to be Babe's brother. Soon afterward, Babe finds himself in a nightmarish situation where he can trust no one.

I won't reveal any more of the story, which was expertly adapted by William Goldman from his own novel. Suffice to say that there are some surprises in store for characters and audience alike.

What makes *Marathon Man* so suspenseful is the all-pervading paranoia the three major characters feel. Few movies show the effects of fear on men, let alone on intelligent, resourceful men. Babe is the character the audience most identifies with, and his paranoia is the clearest — when he gets pulled into his brother's world he's at a disadvantage because he knows nothing of what's happening and can't give the information people seek, even under torture. Scylla is established early on as an experienced agent, so when he understands the old rules don't apply any longer, the audience knows this is serious business. Even Szell, the fearsomely intelligent, arrogant Nazi, is not immune — there's a scene in NYC's diamond district when Szell realizes too late that any Jew of a certain age might know his true identity.

What *Marathon Man* is most remembered for today is its infamous dental torture scene. The sequence (actually broken into two separate scenes) is remarkable in that it's far briefer than I'd remembered, and that virtually nothing is shown but much is implied. Olivier's repetition of "Is it safe?" is far more chilling than standard evil villain posturing.

What lifts the film above standard thriller fare is Goldman's screenplay, which takes the time to set up the story elements and doesn't dumb itself down. It requires the audience to pay attention and put the puzzle pieces together without big hunks of exposition. Bringing intelligence and class to the proceedings are the cast — all excellent. Hoffman, though by his own admission too old for the role, is a perfect combination of intelligence and naiveté. He also has a remarkable scene when he's trapped in his apartment's tiny bathroom and completely vulnerable to the attackers he can hear on the other side of the door. Olivier is amazing as Szell the Nazi, perfectly capturing the character's unbridled arrogance and cruelty. And Scheider does what he did so well in his 1970s heyday — he brings intelligence and humanity to what could have been a standard tough-guy role.

By all means, give the movie a view. Just don't do so before your next root canal.

# Marnie

***Can this marriage be saved?***

**Year:** 1964

**Director:** Alfred Hitchcock

**Screenplay:** Jay Presson Allen, from the novel by Winston Graham

**Cast:** Tippi Hedren, Sean Connery

I'm about to commit heresy, so get those thumbscrews handy!

Alfred Hitchcock was a great director, but not all his movies were great. *Torn Curtain* was a good example of a not-so-great Hitchcock film: All anyone remembers from is it is one lengthy murder scene.

Sadly, *Marnie* is another Hitchcock film with little to recommend it. It's a curiosity in that it's not a "whodunit" but a "whydunit" — but the "why" is not interesting enough to save the film.

*Marnie* opens with a businessman demanding that the police find his secretary, who seems to have cleaned out the contents of his safe. Observing this is one of the man's clients, wealthy young publisher Mark Rutland (Sean Connery, trying hard to subdue his accent).

In the very next scene we learn the identity of the thief — it's Marnie Edgar (Tippi Hedren, previously in Hitchcock's *The Birds*). Marnie's a compulsive thief who uses a variety of disguises and aliases to rob her wealthy employers. She gives the money to her grumpy mother, who rebuffs Marnie's generosity and love, preferring to lavish attention on little Snotleigh who lives next door. It's clear from Marnie's conversation with her mother that there's a Big Buried Secret in their past, and other none-too-subtle hints abound (Marnie is terrified of thunderstorms and anything blood-red, and is repulsed when a man shows any physical attraction to her). Unfortunately for Marnie, her next target is Mark, who soon discovers her thievery but instead of calling the cops, becomes fascinated by and attracted to Marnie, and blackmails her into marrying him. Needless to say, the honeymoon's a bust, and faster than you can say "Paging Dr. Freud!" Mark is trying to help Marnie uncover that Big Buried Secret and discover why she's so messed up.

I wanted to like *Marnie*, and initially was intrigued by the idea of the mystery being the criminal's motivation rather than identity. But the movie is done in by a glacial pace, dime-store psychology, and lead characters who are neither likable nor interesting. Connery comes off worse

— he seems to be trying so hard to sublimate his accent that his acting suffers for it. Plus, his character is creepy, and not in a good way. His interest in Marnie and what makes her tick never once seems rooted in concern for her well-being, and becomes squirm-inducing when what he intends to be a seduction on their honeymoon ends up a rape (for which we never see him apologize). Even though he never forces himself on her sexually afterward, his amateur psychology often seems to be doing her more harm than good.

Hedren fares better, though she's ill-served by the screenplay. Marnie is so undone by thunderstorms and red-colored things that it's difficult to believe she's functioned as well as she has for so long. Hedren acquits herself well during the movie's one suspenseful scene, when she robs Mark's safe while a cleaning woman works nearby. But there isn't anything to Marnie besides her trauma and its aftermath — once that's resolved, she's just a blank slate.

The movie's essential only for Hitchcock completists.

# Massacre in Dinosaur Valley

*Land of the lost*

**Year:** 1985

**Director:** Michele Massimo Tarantini

**Screenplay:** Michele Massimo Tarantini

**Cast:** Michael Sopkiw, Susane Carvall, Milton Morris

Being a fan of weird movies can occasionally make it a tad difficult to engage in everyday workplace conversations around the water cooler.

"Joe, what did you do this weekend?"

"I watched the big football game. Go [insert name of team here]! Woohoo!"

"That's dandy! Kelly, what did you do this weekend?"

"I watched *Massacre in Dinosaur Valley*."

(Awkward silence follows....)

What these benighted souls don't realize is that while *Massacre in Dinosaur Valley* isn't, strictly speaking, a good movie, it's way better than football. I ask you — does football have boatloads of gratuitous nudity, leeches, plane crashes, spear-throwing, machete hacking, quicksand, piranha attacks, cannibalism, people getting hit in the ass by poison darts, and did I mention gratuitous nudity?

Not that it matters, but here's the plot of *Massacre in Dinosaur Valley*. In sunny Brazil, we meet our mayhem fodder, I mean, characters. Drunken French Pilot is taking Disgruntled 'Nam Vet, the vet's Shrewish Ex-Wife, a Dorky Photographer, and Two Hot Underwear Models on a flight to the next big city. Along for the ride are a Kindly Paleontologist, his Hot Daughter, and an archeologist named Kevin. I mention Kevin by name because he's the only character whose name I can remember, and because he's played by the rather tasty Michael Sopkiw, who's like a blond Bruce Campbell with less talent and an even bigger chin. After some shenanigans that include Kevin getting the crap beaten out of him by some locals, scoring with one of the Hot Underwear Models, and not-so-inadvertently seeing the Professor's Hot Daughter naked in the shower, the plane takes off with the intention of detouring in Dinosaur Valley so Professor, Hot Daughter, and Kevin can go look for fossils. Did I mention that Dinosaur Valley is supposed to be cursed and is home to cannibal tribes?

Anyway, the plane crash-lands unconvincingly in Dinosaur Valley. Professor, Drunken French Pilot, and one of the Hot Underwear Models are killed in the crash. Disgruntled 'Nam Vet puts himself in charge and attempts to lead the motley crew to civilization before the cannibal tribe catches them. Did I mention that in addition to cannibal tribes, Dinosaur Valley is also home to some particularly nasty slave traders?

*Massacre in Dinosaur Valley* is exploitation trash to be sure — the sort of movie in which the flight from pursuing cannibals takes a pause so the party's leader can leer at boobs — but there's something almost lighthearted about it that makes the movie far more enjoyable than similar films (such as *Cannibal Ferox*, a movie I actually regret watching). There's no animal cruelty — though there is a cockfight early on, in his commentary Sopkiw points out that the roosters' feet were bandaged so there was no harm done. The ickiest scenes are actually in the slavers' camp, when the surviving women suffer the unwelcome advances of the camp leader and his lesbian assistant. But the shirtless, tight-jeaned Kevin comes to the rescue and happy Brazilian samba music rolls over the credits. My only complaint is that there were no actual dinosaurs in Dinosaur Valley. If only they'd snuck in some footage from *The Valley of Gwangi* and had Kevin kill a dinosaur with his bare hands, I'd have been in exploitation paradise.

Not a bad choice if you want some old-school exploitation cinema without the cruelty and nihilism of other Italian cannibal/zombie films.

# Master of the Flying Guillotine

*Everybody was kung fu fighting*

**Year:** 1976

**Director:** Yu Wang

**Screenplay:** Yu Wang

**Cast:** Yu Wang, Kang Chin, Lung Wang

I have no idea why I am bothering to even write this review, because if you're a certain kind of person, you'll look at the title *Master of the Flying Guillotine* and say, "Oh hell yes, I must see this!" If you are not that kind of person, you aren't reading this review anyway.

But I do have standards to maintain, so here goes. A blind kung fu master who sports some of the freakiest eyebrows I've ever seen is all annoyed because two of his henchmen were recently killed by a one-armed kung fu master. (There's mention of some political reasons behind this but those hardly matter so I won't go into them.) Blind kung fu master gets out his flying guillotine and starts practicing on some handy statues, then on a live chicken. Animal lovers take note — this movie did **not** get one of those "no animals were harmed" certifications. Once he's finished showing off — I mean, giving his flying guillotine a test drive — he blows up his own house just because, and sets off to find the one-armed kung fu master.

A word about the flying guillotine. It has to be seen to be believed, and manages to be totally ridiculous and fairly awesome at the same time. Kind of like the rest of the movie, now that I think of it.

Turns out the one-armed kung fu master is a teacher at a kung fu school, where we have the obligatory training scenes and the master showing off with some nigh-impossible feats of kung fu. Then everyone heads over to the big kung fu tournament, and this is where the movie hits its apex of awesomeness. Realizing that no one watches these things for the plot, the film-makers give us a lengthy tournament scene pitting fighters against each other. What's more, the fights showcase not just traditional kung fu but Thai boxing and other martial arts specialties. Possibly the highlight of this scene is an Indian guru/fighter who can make his arms ten feet long when it suits him. It's not the most convincing special effect you've ever seen, but it is memorable.

The tournament's going great when blind kung fu guy lets loose with the flying guillotine and decapitates the wrong one-armed man. Oops, clumsy! If you've guessed that there will be a lengthy showdown between blind guy and one-armed guy, you'd be right — but you may not guess that there's a pink-tinged flashback, a scene that gives new meaning to the term "give him a hotfoot" and a big fight in a coffin workshop.

What makes the movie so enjoyable is that there is almost no plot to get in the way of the fun. Once you take it for granted that blind guy must kill one-armed guy and doesn't mind if he gets a few of the wrong one-armed guys along the way, it's all good. From then on it's fights aplenty. Add to this some bad dubbing, cheesy special effects, and a score that keeps it all moving (even if parts seem to have been lifted wholesale from Kraftwerk's *Autobahn* album), and you've got a splendid bit of entertainment.

Once thought to be lost entirely, *Master of the Flying Guillotine* is available on DVD in several editions. You can choose from the English dub or Mandarin, and while the film will never look fantastic, the fades, scratches, and other signs of wear and tear only add to the experience. You could be in a crappy theater in 1977, catching this at the two-dollar matinee. And isn't that a lovely thing?

# Matango

*Fungus among us*

**Year:** 1963

**Director:** Ishiro Honda

**Screenplay:** Takeshi Kimura

**Cast:** Akira Kubo, Kumi Mizuno, Hiroshi Koizumi

Fun fact about me: I'm squeamish about mold and mushrooms. Not all the time. I like mushrooms just fine when they are neatly packaged at the grocery store (I make a wicked good shiitake pasta). But I always get a bit skeeved out when I see mushrooms popping up on my lawn. Similar thing with mold. I love blue cheese, but if a teeny green spot appears on bread, into the trash goes the whole loaf.

I have many virtues. Consistency is not one of them.

These issues surrounding spores, molds, and fungi may help explain why it's taken me so long to get around to watching *Matango* — addicts of late-night TV may know it by another name: *Attack of the Mushroom People*. I've seen the movie derided in a number of places, so I was surprised to find it's a fairly serious, claustrophobic story that's marred by some effects silliness in its last quarter.

The movie opens with a man, presumably the lone survivor of some tragic event, telling us about his experiences. He keeps his back turned to the camera the whole time, which doesn't bode well. Then it's one of cinema's more jarring transitions as we go into the credits sequence, which has cheerful music over scenes of a yacht full of happy people sailing over the bounding main. Our characters are a wealthy businessman and his pals: a professor of psychology, the professor's mousy girlfriend, a mystery novelist, and a sultry singer most of the men fancy. There's also a two-person crew (one of whom wears his sunglasses **all** the time, so he's obviously a hep cat).

Faster than you can say, "the weather started getting rough, the tiny ship was tossed," a storm does indeed arise and takes out the sails and the power. The boat ends up on an island that is truly deserted — aside from inedible vegetation, the island has no life on it — no animals, birds, or fish are to be seen. What the island does have is mushrooms, and lots of them. It also has a shipwreck that's covered in some icky-looking mold. But beggars can't be choosers, so our castaways clean up some rooms and set up quarters in the abandoned ship. Tensions arise as the group squabble among themselves and start seeing strange apparitions. When the meager supplies of food run low, despite the vague warnings found in the wrecked ship's log about not eating the island's mushrooms, those fungi start to look pretty damn tasty, consequences be damned.

Though marred by some silliness late in the game (a six-foot-tall ambulatory mushroom probably sounded good on paper but on screen it's ridiculous), *Matango* is a rather effective film. Director Ishiro Honda uses the island setting well: at first glance it looks fairly hospitable, but the lack of food, constant fog, absence of animal life, and evidence of many past shipwrecks give the impression that the place may actually be malevolent. The actors look sweaty and desperate, and even in the dubbed version effectively portray how the situation breaks down friendships and societal standards — and not even true love may save the day.

*Matango* isn't a fast-paced movie. There are lots of scenes involving the various characters skulking around the island, desperately looking for seaweed or turtle eggs to eat. And several scenes (particularly the first time the strange humanoid figures appear on the ship) end without any real resolution. But it's a moody, effective film that even in its English-language dub is serious rather than silly, and not deserving of the derision it's often received.

# Meet the Feebles

*Muppets from hell*

**Year:** 1989

**Director:** Peter Jackson

**Screenplay:** Peter Jackson, Fran Walsh, Stephen Sinclair, and Danny Mulheron

**Cast:** Donna Akersten (voice), Stuart Devenie (voice), Brian Sergent (voice)

One of cinema's more mind-boggling moments took place when Peter Jackson won the Best Director award for *Lord of the Rings: The Return of the King*. In his acceptance speech Jackson thanked those who had been with him from the early days of "*Bad Taste* and *Meet the Feebles*."

It was hard to say which was more startling — that two fairly obscure and insanely gory films should get such international recognition, or that unsuspecting people who loved the *Rings* movies might stumble on *Meet the Feebles* and rent it.

And have the shock of their lives.

*Meet the Feebles*, Jackson's second film, can best be described as *The Muppet Show* with sex, drugs, and violence. The Feebles Variety Hour is a popular TV show in which all the cast are puppets of varying species (there are no humans in the film at all). We see a quick introduction of the show and its performers, then head backstage to get a more intimate (in every sense of the word) look at the actors and their complicated lives.

Star and songstress Heidi the Hippo is fighting both her food addiction and the break-up of her relationship with the show's producer, Bletch the Walrus. Bletch has a lot going on — in addition to an affair with Samantha the Cat, he's also financing porn films and orchestrating a big drug deal. Harry the Rabbit is in the throes of terminal VD and being pursued by a (literally) shit-eating fly tabloid reporter. Wynyard the knife-throwing frog is a heroin-addicted Vietnam vet (whose *Deer Hunter*-inspired flashback is the film's highlight). Sebastian the Fox, director of the show, is trying to put on a special live performance and yearns for a chance to perform a song he's written about the joys of sodomy. Sid the Elephant is fighting a paternity suit from Sandy the Chicken. In the midst of the filth and chaos are innocents Robert the Hedgehog and Lucille the Poodle, striving to find true love even as Lucille is lusted after by porn film director Trevor the Rat.

Jackson includes something to offend every sensibility, and doesn't leave a thing to the imagination as we watch cute puppets have sex, do drugs, get sick, and eventually try to kill each other. It's hard to decide if the use of puppets makes the film easier to take — you're torn between, "Well, at least it's only puppets doing these things" and "Look at the awful things these cute puppets are doing." The end result is both hilarious and appalling. At times you don't know whether to wail in disgust or scream with laughter — the best solution is to do both.

As he did with *Bad Taste*, Jackson makes every cent of the low budget work. The characters are a mix of hand-operated puppets (a la Kermit the Frog) and full-body costumes, and very well done if not quite in Jim Henson's league. The songs are good as well, with my particular favorites being "One Leg Missing" and the ode to sodomy. *Feebles* is also an improvement over *Bad Taste* in terms of story, with a greater variety of characters and storylines to follow (and no twenty-minute gun battles, although there is a machine-gun rampage). The Vietnam flashback scene is particularly well-done.

But ultimately *Meet the Feebles* is limited by its very excess. There are so many characters and storylines, and the pace so rapid, that it can take more than one viewing to sort it out (and many viewers simply may not be up to a second viewing). So much violence and filth is paraded out that the effect is numbing after a while. Like its predecessor, *Meet the Feebles* feels like a bit of juvenilia that Jackson had to get out of his system before he could make more mature films (of which *Dead Alive* is the first — violent as it is, it's definitely the work of a more grown-up director).

*Meet the Feebles* is like no other movie I've seen — it's not for the faint of heart or weak of stomach, but at times it's also one of the funniest films around.

The most noteworthy thing about the DVD is its case, with the proud proclamation "From the director of *Lord of the Rings*." Can't wait to see those preteen girls with a crush on Orlando Bloom watch a diseased rabbit barf up thirty gallons of vomit.

# Mega Shark Vs. Giant Octopus

*The title says it all*

**Year:** 2009

**Director:** Jack Perez

**Screenplay:** Jack Perez

**Cast:** Deborah Gibson, Lorenzo Lamas, Vic Chao, Sean Lawlor

Hey, remember when that trailer for *Mega Shark Vs. Giant Octopus* was all over the internet?

Remember how awesome that trailer was?

Well, hang on to that memory because the *Mega Shark Vs. Giant Octopus* trailer is ten times more interesting than the movie itself. *Quelle surprise.*

*Mega Shark Vs. Giant Octopus* (or *MSVGO* as I'm going to call it for brevity's sake) opens as nefarious government and/or scientific types (it's not really made clear and to be honest it doesn't really matter) are doing illegal sonar experiments. Witnessing this is ocean-y scientific gal Emma (Deborah Gibson, a long way from singing "Shake Your Love"), who's watching stock footage of whales as she unconvincingly steers a submersible craft. The sonar makes the whales go nuts (as with much of this movie's plot, you have to take this on faith) and they bust open a glacier wherein are frozen our titular beasties, who apparently were too preoccupied with mortal combat to notice that it was getting a mite chilly. The thawed, cranky beasties swim off in search of mayhem to wreak.

And do they ever! Remember that scene from the trailer with the shark leaping out of the water to attack the plane? Well, you see that. And you see the octopus swat a plane from the sky (why these underwater creatures would have such a grudge against aircraft is not explained). You don't see much else, though, so you have to take it on faith that the creatures' path of destruction has cost thousands of lives.

Soon Emma teams up with her old teacher, Paternal Irish Guy (Sean Lawlor), and with a Japanese Scientist (Vic Chao) who's investigating the octopus's wrecking of an oil derrick. Their "what to do?" session is interrupted by Lorenzo Lamas and his Steven Seagal ponytail. Lamas is a terminally douchey government honcho who puts Emma, Paternal Irish Guy, and Japanese Scientist into a Heavily Guarded Secret Lab™ to figure out how to stop the shark and the octopus. An impromptu frolic in a broom closet gives Emma and Japanese Scientist the idea to use pheromones to attract the presumably horny creatures to a place where they can be easily caught and killed. That plan will go smoothly, I'm sure.

*MSVGO* is the sort of movie that you don't have to pause while you get some popcorn or go to the bathroom, because you can tell that it's going to be 20 minutes or so before the shark or the octopus make an appearance. The rest of the time is, shall we say, padded with lots of establishing shots of the ocean, seabirds in flight, people staring pensively out to sea, and so on. The film-makers have tried to make these shots ominous by doing little jump-cuts and flashing lights, but that just made me wonder if my medication needed adjusting.

So yes, 90% of the movie's awesomeness is in the trailer. The rest of the movie is composed of stock footage, padding, recycling the sets, and so on. Yet the whole thing is so honest about its awfulness that it's impossible to get mad at the movie. Plus, it at least tries to break with clichés: it was nice to see the nerdy Asian guy get lucky, and I thought for sure we were going to have one character perish in a scene of noble self-sacrifice. I'm particularly glad we were spared that last, since that also spared us having to watch Deborah Gibson try to do a "NOOOOOOO!" scene.

Speaking of the acting, it's not as bad as you'd expect. Everyone except Gibson seems to be aware of what a ridiculous thing they're doing and maintains good humor throughout. Lamas is quite fun in his unapologetic assholishness (he insults the entire cast in his first five minutes onscreen). Gibson, on the other hand, seems to think a collection of smiles, frowns, and facial twitches constitutes "acting." Plus she reminds me of this annoying college roommate I had who acted all judgmental about the books and movies I liked and also used to borrow things and take **ages** to return them. Yes, I do like to hold on to grudges, why do you ask?

You could watch *MSVGO* if it happens to show up on cable, and you probably won't regret it all that much. Or you could just watch the trailer again, see most of the awesome bits, and be done with it in much less time.

# Miami Connection

*Words fail me*

**Year:** 1987

**Director:** Y. K. Kim and Woo-Sang Park

**Screenplay:** Woo-Sang Park and Richard Diamond

**Cast:** Y. K. Kim, Vincent Hirsch, Maurice Smith

There's a special kind of bad movie. It doesn't show up very often, because it's the perfect blend of ineptitude and sincerity. It's this mix that makes movies like *Plan 9 From Outer Space* and *The Room* so magical. And now *Miami Connection* joins the list.

It's 1987 (and if the blue-soaked night-time cinematography doesn't clue you in to the movie's timeframe, the hilariously dated fashions will) and a cocaine deal in Miami goes wrong when it's ambushed by ninjas. Yes, ninjas, who kill everyone, steal the cocaine, then flee the scene on their motorcycles.

We then move to Orlando (yes, the home of Disney World), where we meet the band Dragon Sound, who play in a neon-festooned club and wow the crowd with their synth-rock songs like "Friends" and "Face the Ninja." As if Dragon Sound weren't already awesome enough, they are all taekwondo black belts, and even share the same house. For reasons I am still unclear on, Dragon Sound run afoul of the local cocaine lord, a rival band, and the motorcycle ninjas, which leads to lots of bloody fights.

Now, I realize that I've made *Miami Connection* sound no more ridiculous than many films from the Eighties, but there's something special going on with this film. There's the amateurish acting, which ranges from the wooden to the over-the-top; the fact that it's impossible to understand the dialogue of lead actor Y. K. Kim half the time; the many scenes of the Dragon Sound band members standing around shirtless (standing around shirtless is to this movie what tossing the football around is to *The Room*); the weirdly improvised dialogue; the surprisingly gory fights, which include arterial spray and decapitation; the strange subplot involving a band member's search for his long-lost father (the monologue that accompanies this search must be heard to be believed); the late-breaking plot development regarding two characters being brothers; the really awkward training montage; the dated-beyond-belief-and-then-some costumes and facial hair (I kept waiting for that one guy's beard to just devour his face entirely); the editing that leaves scenes actually unfinished at times; the tin-eared dialogue; the plethora of characters that makes it difficult to know who's connected to who; the — you know, I can't keep up with this list.

What makes *Miami Connection* so delightful is actually not that gargantuan list of missteps, hilarious though they are. It's the utter sincerity of it all. It's abundantly clear that everyone involved is trying their damndest to make this movie work, and their lack of success only makes their efforts endearing. Much of the credit for this movie has to go to Y. K. Kim who not only stars as taekwondo leader Mark but also wrote the story and co-directed. It's clear that Kim wanted to showcase taekwondo (and I'd bet my next paycheck the Dragon Sound members are students of Kim's) and promote the film's message that brotherhood is awesome, that families can be created rather than born into, and that taekwondo can bring about world peace. Worthy messages all, though they're buried in a silly film (and the world peace bit is somewhat disingenuous after we've seen the body count go through the roof).

I'll just let you experience the whole thing for yourself. But trust me. If you're a bad movie aficionado, you really can't go wrong.

Once languishing in obscurity, *Miami Connection* is now available on Blu-Ray. The transfer is dodgy and full of dings and dents, but that only adds to the movie's charm.

# Mortal Kombat

*Flawless victory!*

**Year:** 1995

**Director:** Paul W. S. Anderson

**Screenplay:** Kevin Droney

**Cast:** Christopher Lambert, Robin Shou, Cary Hiroyuki-Tagawa

The list of good movies based on video games is a short one. So short, in fact, that *Mortal Kombat* might be at the top of the list by default. Of course "good" is used advisedly, as it's by no means a great movie, and it's often very silly, but damn if it isn't entertaining as hell.

I have no idea how much of the movie derives from the actual game, because the last arcade game I played with any regularity was Centipede. That said, *Mortal Kombat* deftly handles its opening exposition, introducing our three main characters. There's Liu Kang (Robin Shou), a martial arts champion who's destined for greatness but has run away from his destiny after his brother was killed by the evil Shang Tsung (Cary Hiroyuki-Tagawa). There's Johnny Cage (Linden Ashby) who's a martial arts movie star plagued by accusations that he's a faker. And Sonya Blade (Bridgette Wilson), some sort of special ops soldier out for vengeance against thuggish Kano, who killed her partner. The trio are lured to an island by Shang Tsung, to participate in Mortal Kombat, a tournament that will decide the fate of the universe; along the way they all get pep talks from lightning demigod Rayden (Christopher Lambert, looking ridiculous).

The fun really starts once the group gets to the island, where they meet a sexy princess who may or may not be on the good guys' side, a four-armed martial arts champion, and fighters with fun powers like freezing everything they touch. There'll be lots of fights, and learning important lessons like facing one's fears and learning to trust your friends.

Pretty much everything about *Mortal Kombat* is entertaining, from its opening techno music that'll make you want to shake your booty, to the fighting sequences, to the fun sets and CGI that's fake-looking (but in an otherworldly way so that you don't mind). The acting is just fine all-around, from Shou's earnestness to the bicker-their-way-to-romance banter of Ashby and Wilson, and Hiroyuki-Tagawa's sneering evilness. Stealing every scene through the sheer silliness of his casting is Christopher Lambert as Rayden, dispensing his fortune-cookie wisdom while talking like Ren from *Ren and Stimpy* (his ridiculous wig and affectless, Tommy Wiseau-esque laugh just add to the fun).

Really, it's just a perfect popcorn movie. And sometimes that's all you need.

# The Naked Kiss

*The oldest profession*

**Year:** 1964

**Director:** Samuel Fuller

**Screenplay:** Samuel Fuller

**Cast:** Constance Towers, Anthony Eisley, Michael Dante

*The Naked Kiss* opens with the sound of frantic jazz, and the sight of a woman savagely beating a drunken man with her handbag. The man pleads for mercy but the woman gives none, not even when, in the struggle, it's revealed that her hair is a wig and she is completely bald. Finally the man's on the floor, semi-conscious; the woman gets his wallet and though he's got several hundred dollars on him, she only takes what she's owed: a mere $75. Then she dons her wig, touches up her makeup, and leaves. Now that's bad-ass!

This remarkable woman is Kelly (Constance Towers, who was also in director Samuel Fuller's other bonkers melodrama, *Shock Corridor*). She's a prostitute, and the man she beat so savagely was her pimp, who'd had her shaved bald to punish her for helping some of his girls find a way out of prostitution. On the run from her pimp's hired thugs, Kelly travels from town to town, pretending to be a champagne saleswoman but really still plying her trade as a hooker. She arrives in the small town of Grantville where her first customer is policeman Griff (Anthony Eisley). Griff immediately knows that Kelly isn't really selling champagne, but that doesn't stop him from sleeping with her, and then the next morning ordering her to go to the brothel in the next town over. But Kelly decides to go straight and rents a room in Grantville, where she soon becomes a splendid nurse at the town's hospital for handicapped children. Before long she's engaged to handsome Grant (Michael Dante), the town's wealthiest, most respected citizen. Kelly seems headed straight toward a fairy-tale ending ... or is she?

Even the movie's biggest fans will most likely admit that *The Naked Kiss* is a flawed film. It's melodramatic as hell, the editing is choppy, and when characters aren't quoting Byron or Baudelaire, they're spouting tough-guy dialogue that makes everyone sound as if they just stepped out of a World War II film. And don't get me started on the musical number (you'll know it when it happens, trust me). But there are great things in the film, too, from striking imagery to issues of sexuality and social hypocrisy that were well ahead of their time when the film was made. There's also just enough sleaze to keep things lively, particularly at the brothel where madam Candy calls her girls "bon-bons."

What makes the film work is Samuel Fuller's cockeyed sincerity. A hard-boiled reporter and decorated soldier before he turned to film-making, Fuller combines a curious sentimentality with cynicism. The two don't always blend well, but Fuller has a third quality, that of sincerity, that engages the audience despite his lack of directorial polish. He's well assisted in *The Naked Kiss* by his leading lady, Constance Towers, who's in turn well-served by Fuller's characterization of Kelly. She's a character about whom we're told little, but about whom we can infer much. She regrets being a prostitute but doesn't try to go straight for many years; she jeopardizes herself by fighting to keep her friend Buff out of the clutches of madam Candy (there's a great scene when she savagely beats Candy and shoves money into her mouth). Because she's an outsider, she befriends other outsiders, from the handicapped children at the hospital to the dotty old spinster she rents a room from. She's well-read but self-taught, for she can quote Goethe but doesn't pronounce his name correctly. She's delighted by Grant's affection for her and his acceptance of her past, so much so that she's willing to let certain misgivings slide... until Grant reveals a dark part of his nature.

It's cheesy, clunky, and a little ridiculous. It's also sincere and bold film-making by a man who made the movies he wanted to make, the way he wanted to make them.

# The Naked Prey

*Watch out for snakes*

**Year:** 1966

**Director:** Cornel Wilde

**Screenplay:** Clint Johnston and Don Peters

**Cast:** Cornel Wilde, Ken Gampu

In this age of movies that are overstuffed, overproduced, and overlong, it's refreshing to see a film like *The Naked Prey* — simple to the point of minimalism, yet remarkably effective.

It's some time in the 19th century and in an unnamed African country, a guide (director and star Cornel Wilde) is leading a safari on an ivory hunt. During the trek, the safari party meets up with a group of local tribesmen. When one of the hunters disregards the guide's advice and insults the tribesmen, the tribe attacks the safari, killing many members and taking others prisoner.

Most of the captured safari party is subjected to fates of varying cruelty — these scenes aren't gory by today's standards but the unpleasantness and humiliation will have most viewers wincing. However, the tribe respects the guide because he knows the language and customs, so they give him a more merciful, honorable fate. He's stripped of all clothes and weapons, given a head start, and then will be hunted down by the tribe.

But the guide proves himself to be fit and savvy, with plenty of ingenuity. What was supposed to be a quick killing becomes a long chase as the guide tries to make it back to his settlement, and the tribesmen try to hunt him down.

That's the entire plot of *The Naked Prey* — for much of its running time it's one man on the run from a group of others, with both hunter and hunted using their skills and brains, and both running afoul of the brutal heat, attacks from snakes and other animals, elusive food (the guide has to eat a raw snake to survive), and attacks by slave traders. There are long stretches with no dialogue, and we never learn which country the story is set in, the guide's name (he's listed as "man" in the credits) or anyone else's name for that matter. But the beauty of the story and Wilde's direction is that we don't need any of these things to enjoy the movie. The clever (though short — 9 pages!) screenplay deftly sketches in the relevant details. We learn early on that this is the last safari the guide will work on, and after this he's retiring to his farm. His contempt for the boorish hunters he works for is clear, and the contempt becomes disgust when the hunters needlessly slaughter elephants and invite the guide to join them in the slave trading business. Credit goes to all the actors, most of whom were amateurs, but especially to Ken Gampu as the lead hunter of the tribesmen. Gampu takes what could have been a stereotypical "evil savage" role and makes it clear that the hunters' insult of him is a deeply humiliating moment, and that he respects the guide not just for his knowledge of local language and custom but for his survival skills as well. Wilde turns in a very good performance as well. In his fifties when the movie was made, he has a better physique than many men half his age and makes it plausible that he could survive in such harsh conditions. Yet Wilde's character never sacrifices his humanity to survive, taking time during his escape to help a young child orphaned by slave raiders' attack on a village.

Wilde's direction is clever, making good use of what looks like documentary footage (note to the squeamish: those are real elephants being killed in the hunt scene). His best moments are when he juxtaposes images of harsh landscapes and thorny bushes with the physically vulnerable characters. At times the comparison of the human struggle with nature's struggles becomes a bit heavy-handed, but overall the directorial touches work better than any amount of exposition ever could.

Criterion has put together a marvelous release with a gorgeous widescreen transfer of the film. The best extra is an insightful commentary by film scholar Stephen Prince, which is particularly enlightening in pointing out how the film both uses and subverts the clichés of colonial and

Western films. Other extras include a trailer, and an account by a North American trapper whose escape from a Native American tribe was the inspiration for *The Naked Prey* (the account is read by Paul Giamatti).

---

# National Lampoon's Animal House

*School daze*

**Year:** 1978

**Director:** John Landis

**Screenplay:** Harold Ramis, Douglas Kenney, and Chris Miller

**Cast:** John Belushi, Tim Matheson, Peter Greene

---

Comedy has always been my least favorite genre of film. Sci-fi, horror, fantasy, or action films may be bad, but there's usually some eye candy or things blowing up to alleviate the tedium. When comedy doesn't work, the movie just sits there like a dead fish, and is as about as entertaining to watch.

Which is why I approached a rewatch of *National Lampoon's Animal House* with some trepidation. I hadn't seen the film since my college days, and had no idea how it would hold up, or if it would still be funny outside of a packed movie theater at midnight.

So I'm happy to report that *Animal House* holds up, and does so very well. Not only is it still funny, but time has been very kind to it. It may not have the edge it once did, but that works in its favor, especially in the current climate of gross-out, mean-spirited comedies.

It's 1962 and the Greek rush season has just started at Faber College. Things aren't going well for Larry (Tom Hulce) and Kent (Stephen Furst) — at the snooty Omega house they're nicknamed (cruelly if accurately) "a wimp and a blimp" and shunted off to a corner with other aspiring members who are foreign, handicapped, or otherwise undesirable. Larry wants to give up, but Kent insists they head to the Delta house; his brother was a member a few years ago and Kent feels he's sure to get in because of this.

Despite an unintentionally rude welcome when they're urinated on by Delta wild man Bluto Blutarski (John Belushi in probably his most famous role), Larry and Kent feel right at home in the Delta house. It's an anarchic den of alcohol, pranks, and total disregard for decorum and academia, presided over by well-meaning house president Hoover (James Widdoes), ladies' man and rush chairman Otter (Tim Matheson), and Otter's second-in-command Boone (Peter Greene).

Larry and Kent are welcomed into the frat, but danger looms on the horizon in the form of Dean Vernon Wormer (John Vernon), who's obsessed with getting rid of the Deltas and enlists the help of smarmy Omegas Greg Marmalard (James Daughton) and Doug Neidermeyer (Mark Metcalf).

Animal House is often called a "slobs vs. snobs" comedy, but really it's much more of a "free spirits vs. conformists" film. The Deltas are the fraternity row version of the island of misfit toys, with members from all walks of life (it's not racially mixed, but bear in mind that the movie's set in 1962). You have wild men Bluto and D-Day (Bruce McGill) rubbing shoulders with mostly respectable Hoover and Otter, and everything in between. (Though it's worth noting that Otter, who could seemingly fit in well at the Omega house with his good looks and smooth manner, isn't nearly as suave as he thinks he is, and his inherent misfit qualities are well-demonstrated during his hilarious tryst with Dean Wormer's wife.) There are no rules at the Delta house save to live life by your own creed, whereas the Omega house (and one assumes, the rest of the campus) is fixated on looks and social status. The Deltas break the rules but no (intentional) harm comes from their tomfoolery, which makes their eventual victories later in life (as the movie tells us what fates await the main characters) all the more sweet.

But it's also just a really funny movie, full of sex jokes and drunken shenanigans, the most hilarious shoulder-angel vs. shoulder-devil scene ever, a dead horse, a toga party, and a really awkward time at an all-black roadside bar. It's not for the easily offended thanks to its frequent nudity and vulgarity, but it's plenty of fun, without the "humiliation humor" so popular today in comedies. Watch it, and while you do, grab a brew, don't cost nothin'.

# The Negotiator

*Let's make a deal*

**Year:** 1998

**Director:** F. Gary Gray

**Screenplay:** James DeMonaco and Kevin Fox

**Cast:** Samuel L. Jackson, Kevin Spacey, David Morse, J. T. Walsh

Well, heck. I'd been meaning to watch this for quite a while now, mostly because it had two of my favorite actors — Samuel L. Jackson and Kevin Spacey. Don't get me wrong, I've suffered through *Kiss of Death* and *Edison Force* and know that the presence of Jackson or Spacey isn't a 100 percent guarantee of quality, but I figured that the pairing would be at least be fun — sort of the cinematic equivalent of a Reese's peanut butter cup.

Sadly, *The Negotiator* is not a bad movie, just blah on nearly every level. I wanted a Reese's peanut butter cup and got toast. Heck.

In Chicago, Lieutenant Danny Roman (Jackson) is a well-respected hostage negotiator. But Roman has been informed by a friend in the police department that scandal is afoot with embezzlement from the pension fund. Soon Roman's friend is killed and Roman is being set up for the killing and for the embezzlement. Faced with losing everything, Roman takes hostages in the Internal Affairs department. Convinced that he can trust no one in his own precinct, Roman calls for a negotiator from another precinct, Lieutenant Chris Sabian (Spacey). Sabian has to help keep the situation under control and help Roman prove his innocence.

It should be exciting. It should be tense. There should be lots of sharp dialogue. But *The Negotiator* just sort of ambles along, wasting the potential of its lead actors.

The direction by F. Gary Gray is surprisingly lifeless, taking far too long to set up the situation. Gray and screenwriters David DeMonaco and Kevin Fox make three fatal errors: they make it clear from the start that Roman is innocent, depriving the situation of ambiguity and tension; the central mystery is both totally predictable and unnecessarily muddled, so by the end you're not sure who did what but you don't care either; and they give the characters of Roman and Sabian almost no screen time or interaction together.

This last flaw is what kills the movie — Jackson and Spacey are powerful enough actors to be able to sustain interest even if all they did was talk to each other for 90 minutes — I'd so watch that. But Jackson's character seems strangely removed from the proceedings after the movie's first third or so. Spacey fares a bit better, although he isn't introduced until 45 minutes into the movie (he gets a clever intro as it appears his character is in a hostage negotiation when really he's mediating a spat between his wife and his daughter). But mostly his character is stuck with telling the police not to do stupid things and then yelling at them when they do stupid things. Neither actor gets a role they can really do justice to. Acting honors actually go to a baby-faced Paul Giamatti, in a minor role as a weasely informant who ends up being one of the hostages.

*The Negotiator* isn't a bad movie, but in the end it's so unmemorable you're left wondering why it was even made. Too bad.

# Night of the Lepus

*It must be bunnies!*

**Year:** 1972

**Director:** William F. Claxton

**Screenplay:** Don Holliday and Gene R. Kearney, based on the novel *The Year of the Angry Rabbit* by Russell Braddon

**Cast:** Janet Leigh, Stuart Whitman, Rory Calhoun, DeForest Kelley

Horror books and movies are, of course, based on peoples' fears. There are the universal fears we all share: death, taxes, and clowns. And the fears and phobias of my friends and family include (but are not limited to): cockroaches, eyeball injury, flaming death, moths, frogs, stinging insects, fish, tidal waves, worms, midgets, ventriloquist dummies, and enclosed spaces.

I've never met anyone who was afraid of rabbits. It seems an unlikely source of fear, but there must be **someone** with leporiphobia. And that someone must have been a friend of a bigwig at MGM studios back in the early 1970s. It's the only thing that can explain *Night of the Lepus*, a film about killer rabbits. No, not like in *Monty Python and the Holy Grail*. These are giant rabbits! That roar! And drool!

Allegedly based on the novel *The Year of the Angry Rabbit* by Russell Braddon (find a copy and send it to me, and I'll buy you an ice cream cone!), *Night of the Lepus* opens with stock footage of rabbits running rampant in Australia and a newscaster to provide helpful exposition. Then we meet a rancher (Rory Calhoun) whose ranch has been nearly destroyed by hordes of bunnies. He doesn't want to poison the lil critters, so he enlists the help of married scientists Janet Leigh and Stuart Whitman to find another way to exterminate the bunnies. The scientists are a rather odd couple — they dress in the height of 1970s fashion (Leigh's pants must be seen to be believed), tool around in an RV camper, and let their little daughter hang around while they conduct what are essentially biological warfare experiments. One day, daughter swaps a bunny that's just received a dose of some experimental serum with a control group bunny (the parentals are in the same room and don't notice a thing). Naturally the experimental bunny gets loose, finds a bunch of girl bunnies, loves them very, very much, and faster than you can say "Flopsy, Mopsy, Cottontail, and Peter," giant bunnies are roaming the countryside killing everything in their path.

Scary? No. Hilarious? Yes. For the first 15 minutes or so. Unfortunately, *Night of the Lepus* has nothing more to offer than its wackaloon concept of giant carnivorous rabbits. Before long the same footage of rabbits running in slow motion around miniature buildings and cars is repeated again and again. To liven things up, on occasion a bunny will leap and then there's an awkward jump cut to an extra wearing a suit made of carpet remnants wrestling with a gamely screaming cast member. There's a surprising amount of gore for a PG movie, but it's all very unconvincing bright red paint.

Not helping matters is the film's utterly straightforward tone. Despite all the obvious opportunities for it, there's not a trace of campy humor. (Not even a character named Warren!) Nor is the film a portentous so-serious-it's-funny movie like *Prophecy*. *Night of the Lepus* plods resolutely from one scene to the next. The actors all keep straight faces and have that glazed "focus on the paycheck" look in their eyes. Things perk up at the finale, when an electrified railroad track that an ordinary-size rabbit could easily jump over is used to fry the giant hopalongs. But ultimately *Night of the Lepus* is a dull affair — like many bad movies, it's more fun to read about than actually watch.

*Star Trek* fans beware: DeForest Kelley is in the movie, but he doesn't do much of anything except wear a cheesy mustache and a really ugly orange sweater.

# Night Watch (Nochnoi Dozor)

*Upsetting the balance*

**Year:** 2004

**Director:** Timur Bekmambetov

**Screenplay:** Timur Bekmambetov and Laeta Kalogridis, based on the novel by Sergei Lukyanenko

**Cast:** Konstantin Khabensky, Vladimir Menshov, Maria Poroshina

The word "fantasy" conjures up many familiar images: magic, wizards, swords, and so on. But the Russian film *Night Watch*, the first in a trilogy based on novels by fantasy writer Sergei Lukyanenko, takes the idea of fantasy into a far different realm — that of modern-day Russia. The result is a movie that combines world-changing magic with everyday reality for a marvelous, unique experience.

Thousands of years ago, the armies of Light and Darkness met on a bridge and battled. But the battle was so evenly matched, there could be no winner. So the leader of Light, Geser (Vladimir Menshov) and the leader of Darkness, Zavulon (Victor Verzhbitsky) formed a truce. Each side formed a team of watchmen to make sure the other side did not break the truce and upset the balance of Light and Darkness.

Jump to modern-day Russia, where ordinary man Anton (Konstantin Khabensky) consults a witch. Anton's wife has left him for another man and he wants her back. The witch assures Anton her spells will bring his wife back, but at a cost — his wife is pregnant and the spell will cause her to lose the child. Anton, told by the witch that the child is not his, agrees.

But before the witch can complete the spell, members of the Night Watch, the forces of Light who keep a watch on Dark forces, stop the spell. Anton is pulled into a twilight realm called The Gloom, where the Light and Dark forces fight, away from human sight. It is then that Anton realizes that he is an Other, a person with special gifts, who can choose to be on the side of Light or Dark.

Anton chooses Light, and works for the Night Watch as a vampire hunter and occasional seer. While trying to prevent a vampire from calling a young victim to her, Anton sees a woman who is the center of a vortex of bad luck — those she touches falls ill and die, and soon her presence means Moscow is threatened by tornadoes and plane crashes. Anton has to help save the young victim of the vampire, and prevent the vortex from destroying the city and upsetting the balance between Light and Dark.

*Night Watch* is a complicated film, and not just because it's the first in a trilogy and has to set up the trilogy's mythology (something it does with surprising ease). Nothing is simple in the world of *Night Watch* — the forces of Darkness must be kept in balance, not defeated. The Night Watch do good work, but often use human bait. Though Light and Darkness are opposed to each other, everything is shades of grey.

It's a complex, divided film visually as well. Witches, sorceresses, and shape-shifters dwell in a society that is itself divided; luxurious apartments for the haves, grimy apartments and crowded subways for the have-nots. The Russian setting makes the film, in a way, an even more otherworldly experience than the *Narnia* or *Lord of the Rings* movies.

Much of the success of *Night Watch* lies in its production design and special effects. Though the film only cost $4 million to make, the effects are often dazzling, with some terrific *Matrix*-esque sequences where time slows down. In one showcase scene, we see a rivet fall off an airplane and follow the rivet's plunge through the air, down into a person's apartment. It's glorious eye candy that also serves the story and the creation of the *Night Watch* world. Even the subtitles (the film is in Russian save for an English voice-over at the prologue and epilogue) work into the film's unique design, moving and even changing color.

My one criticism of *Night Watch* is its fast pace. The movie offers a lot of new ideas and a complicated story, and needs to give the audience time to catch its breath and absorb what it's just seen. It's a movie you need to pay attention to, or you'll be lost.

# Nightmare Alley

*I do not find the hanged man*

**Year:** 1947

**Director:** Edmund Goulding

**Screenplay:** Jules Furthman, based on the novel by William Lindsay Gresham

**Cast:** Tyrone Power, Joan Blondell, Colleen Gray, Helen Walker

The scene is a two-bit carnival, some time during the Depression. The man with the Cheshire Cat grin is Stanton Carlisle (Tyrone Power), and he's grinning because he feels superior to the chumps and rubes who come to the carny every day and are hoodwinked by the games of chance or who believe what the fake fortune teller Zeena (Joan Blondell) tells them. Carlisle is also grinning because he knows that Zeena has a word code that she and her husband Pete (who was once a great mentalist but is now a hopeless drunk) used long ago to achieve fame and fortune; he knows that Zeena is vulnerable to his charms and hopes to seduce her and get the code from her.

But there's fear behind Carlisle's smile. He feels superior to the crowd but is fascinated by the carnival geek, an alcoholic so far gone he's happy to bite the heads off live chickens for the princely sum of a bottle of hooch a day. Carlisle wonders how a man can get so low…and perhaps knows that one day he'll find out.

Carlisle gets the code, and also the carnival's Electric Girl, Molly (Colleen Gray). After being forced into a shotgun marriage by the other carnys when he seduces Molly, Carlisle heads to Chicago where he and Molly become a sensation with their "mind reading" act. But it isn't enough for Carlisle, who soon joins forces with unscrupulous psychologist Lilith (Helen Walker) to get information on her clients. One client in particular, a wealthy man who wants to communicate with the spirit of his dead lover, stands to be Carlisle's biggest "chump."

Widely regarded as one of the grimmest film noirs, *Nightmare Alley* has long been out of circulation due to legal battles. Despite a studio-imposed, (relatively) happy ending, the film is brave for its time. With the exception of good-hearted Molly, every character is a liar; the "best" characters are just honest about their lies. Tyrone Power, the studio's leading romantic actor, was eager for a chance to play a character outside his usual good-guy hero persona and took the role of a self-professed scoundrel who feels nothing but contempt for his fellow man and is willing to use people's deepest fears and miseries against them if it will turn him a profit. And though the film's content is much more subdued than that of the source novel (William Lindsay Gresham's sleazy but smart book, one of my favorites, is well worth seeking out), it still includes geeks, alcoholism, the occult, premarital sex, psychiatry, spiritualism, and a discussion about the nature of blasphemy. Not your typical 1940s Hollywood fare.

The film is a must for anyone who's a fan of film noir. Director Edmund Goulding uses stark black-and-white cinematography and unusual angles to create a mood of foreboding. Of particular note is the scene when Carlisle and Zeena talk before her fortune telling act. Carlisle's face is in shadow, separated from his body by a sharp angle of black. It's almost like watching a headless man.

Just as effective as the look of the film are its actors. Despite being too old for the role, Power gives a strong performance as Carlisle, being both despicable and charming. Blondell is also good as Zeena, a woman who's vowed to stand by her man but is vulnerable to a smooth-talking hottie like Carlisle. Gray is lovely and sweet as Molly; her standout scene is when she threatens to leave Carlisle, telling him his posing as a spiritualist is blasphemy. But the standout female performance is from Helen Walker as Dr. Lilith Ritter; her final scene, when she ruins Carlisle's life, is chilling.

Gresham's book, while certainly not great literature, is pulp fiction of a higher order. The film of *Nightmare Alley* is one of the better adaptations I've seen. Some of the characters have been changed, but those changes are either do not detract from the story (Lilith is more evil in the book, and she is also Carlisle's lover), or are improvements (Molly is more devoted to Carlisle in the book, but she is also quite stupid). My complaints lie with the tacked-on ending imposed by the studio, and that the last third of the film, when Carlisle becomes a fake spiritualist putting the wealthy elite in touch with their dead loved ones, is too rushed.

# The Ninth Configuration

*Kafka talking to a bedbug*

**Year:** 1980

**Director:** William Peter Blatty

**Screenplay:** William Peter Blatty, based on his novel *Twinkle Twinkle "Killer" Kane*

**Cast:** Stacy Keach, Scott Wilson, Ed Flanders, Jason Miller

When critics and fans talk about the film of *The Exorcist*, they rarely bring up what writer William Peter Blatty considered one of the core themes of the book: Father Karras' renewal of his lost faith through witnessing the possession of Regan MacNeil and the exorcism of the demon. Sadly, this theme is overshadowed by all the spinning heads, pea soup regurgitation, and unauthorized use of crucifixes.

This theme of lost and regained faith is better addressed in *The Ninth Configuration*. An abandoned castle in Northern California has been turned into an asylum for U.S. soldiers who, during their service in Vietnam, began exhibiting strange and often colorful behavior. The inmates also include an astronaut, Captain Cutshaw, who aborted a moon mission at the last minute, screaming, "There's nothing up there!" But the inmates' rather idyllic isolation and lunacy will be challenged when a new psychiatrist, Colonel Kane, arrives to take charge. I will say no more to avoid giving away the story; suffice to say that in the world of *The Ninth Configuration*, nothing is quite what it appears to be.

The film originally started life as a novel Blatty wrote in the 1960s called *Twinkle Twinkle "Killer" Kane.* After the success of *The Exorcist*, Blatty had the inspiration and the clout to rewrite the novel as *The Ninth Configuration*, turning the work from a one-joke satire to a more serious (though often hilarious) story about faith, man's capacity for violence, redemption, the nature of evil, the existence of God, and the difficulties of adapting the works of Shakespeare for dogs.

As strange as such a summary seems, it encapsulates fairly well the nature of *The Ninth Configuration*. Part comedy, part drama, part mystery — it's perhaps the ultimate cult film.

Blatty wisely lets the story unfold slowly, giving the viewer time to put the pieces of this rather odd puzzle together. At times the film seems almost like a stage play; there are long dialogue and monologue sequences. At other times, Blatty uses the techniques of cinema rather than the theater to tell the story: the detailed architecture of the castle; dream, fantasy, and flashback sequences. There is an almost unbearable scene in a bar where the tension builds and builds…and builds some more. The inevitable violence is a short, sharp, shock. Not all of Blatty's tricks work. The low budget shows its seams at times, and at least one fantasy sequence was cut because of test audience giggles (the scene, in which crucified angels discuss the asylum's inmates, is available on the DVD). But those are rare, and forgivable, instances.

Where the strength of *The Ninth Configuration* truly lies is in its actors. The film is an actor's dream, with so much give-and-take, so many good lines and monologues, that it's nearly impossible to pick a favorite line (although mine is probably "Robert Browning had the clap, and he caught it from Charlotte and Emily Bronte. He caught it from **both** of them."). And the actors are a director's (and movie-watcher's dream). You may not recognize the names, but you'll know the faces: Ed Flanders (who would be in Blatty's *Exorcist 3/Legion*), Jason Miller (also in *The Exorcist* and *Exorcist 3/Legion*), Joe Spinell (of *Maniac* and *Taxi Driver* fame), Robert Loggia (also in *Lost Highway*), Neville Brand (World War II hero and actor in many films), and many more. All are superb.

But best of all are Stacy Keach as Kane and Scott Wilson as Cutshaw, which is all the more amazing considering that both were last-minute replacements for the actors originally slated for their roles (Nicol Williamson and Michael Moriarty, respectively). Keach does a balancing act as Kane, shifting easily from calm and compassion to almost demonic rage, making his inner struggles clear without overacting. Wilson plays Cutshaw as the sad happy man; his Groucho Marx antics and funny rants never hide the pain in his soul, the pain that is never assuaged until the film's amazing final scene.

*The Ninth Configuration* has had one of cinema's rockier roads. Numerous cuts of varying lengths have circulated at one time or another. Blatty himself withdrew the film from circulation three times, when it was edited poorly or advertised misleadingly. Given this, I'm so delighted to have the film appear on DVD that I'd happily settle for a bare-bones release.

Fortunately, Warner Brothers has put together an excellent release. The extras are quite fine — an insightful, informative commentary by Blatty and film scholar Mark Kermode; a featurette that is fun but doesn't hold up to repeat viewings; a number of deleted scenes, including explanations of why they were cut; and cast biographies and filmographies (which could use an update).

*The Ninth Configuration* is not a film for those looking for spinning heads and other cheap thrills. Some would call it confusing, others call it boring. I call it one of the more moving films I've ever seen. If you're looking for something that's both different and rewarding, give it a view.

# No Country for Old Men

*Badlands*

**Year:** 2007

**Director:** The Coen Brothers

**Screenplay:** The Coen Brothers, based on the novel by Cormac McCarthy

**Cast:** Javier Bardem, Josh Brolin, Tommy Lee Jones

The Coen Brothers' latest film takes what could have been a clichéd good-guys-versus-bad-guys shoot 'em up and gives us not just a tale of white-knuckle suspense, but a meditation on fate, death, and the loss not of innocence but of idealism.

While out hunting in the Texas badlands, local boy Llewellyn Moss (Josh Brolin) comes across the aftermath of a drug deal gone bad: bodies of humans and dogs, abandoned trucks, bags of Mexican heroin, and most crucially, $2 million in cash. He also finds one survivor, a badly wounded man who begs Moss for water. Moss takes the money and leaves the man, only to return later with water when his conscience gets the better of him. But when Moss returns to the scene, others are there as well, and Moss soon finds himself fleeing from remorseless hired killer Anton Chigurh (hypnotically creepy Javier Bardem) who will not be dissuaded from retrieving the money and killing Moss. A step behind both men is aging sheriff Ed Tom Bell (played with dignity and world-weary sorrow by Tommy Lee Jones), who strives to save Moss while being astonished at the cruelty Chigurh is capable of.

A good deal of the story's resonance comes from the source novel. Pulitzer Prize-winner Cormac McCarthy has often explored the themes of fate and the consequences of men's choices for good or evil. (It's no surprise that Moss's undoing stems not from his theft of the money but from his good impulse to bring water to a dying man.) But credit must also go to the Coens, whose adaptation of the novel is both faithful to the book and works on its own as a film. Moreover, every detail of the film feels right — the trailers and hotel rooms feel lived-in, and you can almost smell the fried potatoes at the diner.

Every character feels real as well — especially those that could have been caricatures. All three of the main characters are complex and the actors do the characters justice. Brolin plays Moss as a fundamentally decent man given an opportunity too good to pass up, yet who's ultimately betrayed by his own resourcefulness and stubbornness. Bardem is a wonder, playing Chigurh as a man of strange principle who will mete out life or death on the results of a coin toss, and who seems to take both a perverse pleasure in and a businesslike attitude toward his work — he's more of a force of evil than a person, yet Bardem makes him believable. Jones has the least flashy role but it's at the heart of the movie — he's a third-generation lawman who has seen his share of evil and knows that any day could be the one he faces his own death, yet he's utterly shaken by what he sees during the movie's events. The supporting cast all shine as well, including Kelly MacDonald as Moss's wife, and Woody Harrelson as a hired gun who knows Chigurh and is brought in to get to Moss before Chigurh does.

I've read many complaints about the ending of *No Country For Old Men*, but I can't agree with them. It doesn't adhere to Hollywood convention, nor does it leave us with a sense of closure. Rather like real life. We're left, as Jones' character is, trying to make sense of the world and the evil that men do.

# Nude for Satan

*I have no response to this*

**Year:** 1974

**Director:** Luigi Batzella

**Screenplay:** Luigi Batzella

**Cast:** Rita Calderoni, Stelio Candelli, James Harris

Don't you just love the internet? It makes it ever-so-easy to buy things. In particular, it makes it easy to buy things on impulse. Which is how a certain man (let's call him "Mr. Cozy") went online, saw a DVD with an eye-catching title, and clicked "Proceed to checkout." The film: *Nude For Satan.*

*Nude For Satan* has something of a checkered history. Apparently it made its debut in Italy in '74, had a dismal reception, and has been languishing in a film vault ever since. Now Redemption Films has made *Nude For Satan* available to fans of Italian horror and to insomniac husbands with tendencies to impulse-buy.

You're probably guessing that the title *Nude For Satan* is far more interesting than the film itself, and you'd be exactly right. The film does start nicely, with gawdawful 1970s synth music that sounds like an Emerson Lake and Palmer reject, then in slow motion, a woman goes running through the woods wearing a gauzy white nightgown, which is completely open down the front so you get to see her running totally naked. Full frontal nudity in the first three minutes!

Then we cut to William Benson (Stelio Candelli, dubbed to sound like Marcello Mastroianni after a three-day drinking binge) driving in his Volkswagen Beetle. By the way, *Nude For Satan* also has one of the worst opening credit scenes ever. The Beetle comes to a stop, then the credits roll over a freeze frame of the headlights. Ouch. Where did I leave that Visine?

Benson swerves to avoid a ghostly apparition. When he spins out and comes to a stop, the apparition has disappeared. Then another car spins out, presumably avoiding the same apparition, and Susan (Rita Calderoni, frequently naked) crashes her car. William is a doctor, but he manhandles the unconscious Susan out of the car and carries her to his car (no spine board for her!). Then his car won't start so he goes to find help, just happening to knock on the door of a gloomy old castle.

William enters the castle. Opening doors, he finds a creepy old guy with a knife in his neck, and some people having sex. Then he finds a woman who seems to be the double of Susan, but who keeps calling him "Peter" and treating him like her long-lost love. Soon Susan, apparently recovered from the car wreck, shows up at the castle and meets a fancily dressed gentleman who can appear wherever he chooses, and also has the power to make Susan's clothes magically disappear. It's never stated, but Mr. Fancy Dresser is Satan, I guess. The dapper demon offers Susan a bed for the night, which she ludicrously accepts. Assorted hijinks, including but not limited to gratuitous lesbian encounters, whippings, black magic rites, a dream sequence involving psychedelic candles and yards of billowing chiffon, the single phoniest giant spider I have ever seen, some of the flimsiest underwear I have ever seen, a mysterious medallion, and more things that should be interesting but manage to be quite boring, ensue.

The film slows to a crawl when William's evil double shows up and bores us all silly with some monologue about time having no meaning and the "darker selves," which might help straighten out the plot if the dubbing weren't so awful. An attempt is made to liven things up with a nude Satanic orgy. I'm no expert on nude Satanic orgies, but this seems to be a rather dull one.

The performances are unremarkable. Calderoni is naked frequently, so if that's your cup of tea (it's not mine) go ahead and enjoy. The special effects are laughable, the cinematography is nice but nothing to write home about. The music sounds like bad 1970s progressive rock, heavy on the synths. *Nude For Satan* isn't "so bad it's good." It's one of the dullest films I've ever seen. So why does *Nude For Satan* stay in my DVD collection?

Because of the title. You've got to admit it's an eye-catcher.

# The Omen

*What to expect when you're expecting the Antichrist*

**Year:** 1976

**Director:** Richard Donner

**Screenplay:** David Seltzer

**Cast:** Gregory Peck, Lee Remick, David Warner, Harvey Stephens

I'm sure that at one time the name "Damien" was a respectable name. Maybe not the most popular name, but a fine name nonetheless. Then along came *The Omen*, and "Damien" became about as favored a name as "Judas" or "Lucifer."

I can't say I'm surprised. Little Damien Thorn has been adopted by Ambassador Robert Thorn (Gregory Peck, probably wondering how he went from playing Atticus Finch to this) and his wife

Cathy (Lee Remick) after their baby was allegedly stillborn. Despite the fact that the Thorns know nothing about Damien's parentage (Cathy doesn't even know Damien isn't her son), everything seems fine until Damien's fifth birthday, when his nanny hangs herself in front of Damien and all the other kids. That wouldn't be so bad, except that there's also a big scary Rottweiler hanging around, Damien has a spooky new nanny, Damien has a massive freak-out when he gets near a church, and a wild-eyed priest who claims to know about Damien's true parentage ends up shish-kabobbed. Of course, there's a perfectly legitimate reason for all this, and it's that Damien is the Antichrist, the son of Satan.

Tremendously popular and influential in 1976, *The Omen* doesn't really hold up today. You don't even need a passing interest in the horror genre to be well aware that Damien is the Antichrist, so consequently all the characters in *The Omen* who painstakingly realize Damien's true nature come off as incredibly dense. The sole exception is David Warner as a photographer who has noticed some odd distortions in photos of the nanny and the priest, and who does the most and best investigative work as to Damien's origins. Warner's character isn't figuring out anything the viewer doesn't already know, but he still makes it work.

One of the keys to *The Omen's* success back in the day, and why it doesn't hold up today, is its tone. *The Omen* is a Very Serious Movie. And while I'm no fan of wink-at-the-camera, oh-so-ironic horror films, *The Omen* is proof that it's possible to go too far in the other direction. It's almost as if the film-makers want you to believe all this is actually going on, and push the buttons so hard that the closing quote from Revelations (one of the only verbatim Biblical quotes in the entire movie, I do believe) is more giggle-inducing than the dread-inspiring shocker it wants to be.

It doesn't help that no character with a hint about Damien's true nature can simply come out and say so. Instead, they beat around the bush and waste precious time being bug-eyed and babbling. Again, the exception is Warner, who comes off as intelligent and rational, but willing to believe in the fantastic nature of what's happening, and not just because he's seen one of those spooky distortions in a photograph of himself.

Which brings us to what does still work in *The Omen*; the death scene set-pieces. For a movie famous for its gory death scenes, there is surprisingly little blood, even in the celebrated decapitation scene. The two most effective death scenes, the aforementioned decapitation and the nanny hanging, work because of their timing. You know what's going to happen, but they happen sooner than you expect, before you have time to prepare yourself. Plus, the nanny looks so damned happy to be hanging herself ("Damien, I love you! It's all for you!") that the scene is all the more disturbing. Also effective is the dog attack scene, in which the dogs are genuinely scary (most dog attacks in cinema look like the dog just wants that Milk-Bone in the actor's pocket).

David Seltzer's screenplay is clever on the surface but stupid underneath. Would Ambassador

Thorn really not even look at his stillborn child? Why would it take five years for Damien to start showing signs of Satanic-ness? If the mere sight of a cross is so affecting to Damien, how come the spike that impales the priest comes off a church? And so on.

*The Omen* is fun if you (like me) are a big fan of Catholic horror. Jerry Goldsmith's score is wonderfully overwrought, sounding at times like *Carmina Burana* on steroids, and keeps things moving along. And while Harvey Stephens as Damien is mostly there to look evilly cherubic or cherubically evil, his last scene, smiling directly at the camera, is one of the film's few genuinely spooky moments.

---

# The Painted Veil

*China, my China*

**Year:** 2006

**Director:** John Curran

**Screenplay:** Ronald Nyswaner, based on the novel by W. Somerset Maugham

**Cast:** Naomi Watts, Edward Norton, Toby Jones, Diana Rigg

---

Sometimes you just want to curl up by a fire with a mug of tea and a novel — something that is low on plot but high on characterization. Movies that offer a similar experience don't come along frequently, but for those of you on the lookout for an old-fashioned story of love and redemption, there's *The Painted Veil.*

Set in colonial China in the 1920s, the movie opens with a couple sitting on a lonely country road amidst their luggage, in the rain. They sit far apart from each other and don't speak; they might be strangers. In fact, they're a husband and wife, and in leisurely flashbacks we learn their story. Two years earlier, carefree social butterfly Kitty (Naomi Watts) met taciturn bacteriologist Walter (Edward Norton) at a party. He was instantly infatuated; she barely took notice of him. He soon proposed marriage; she was going to decline but impulsively accepted, mostly to get away from her shrewish mother. They soon proved a mismatch in every way: she liked gossip, parties, games, and sex with the lights on; he didn't talk much, was focused on his work, and preferred sex with the lights off. Soon enough Kitty fell for smooth-talking diplomat Charlie and the two had an affair. An enraged Walter then gave Kitty an ultimatum: he could divorce her and name Charlie as her lover, thereby ruining her in society, or she could accompany him to a remote village where he's volunteered to help out with a cholera epidemic. Kitty saw going to the village as little more than a death sentence, but when Charlie reneged on his promises to divorce his wife and marry Kitty, she had little choice but to go along with Walter.

The couple arrives in the village to find their house's previous occupants (a missionary and his family) dead of cholera, few of the creature comforts they are used to, hostile villagers with a growing resentment of colonials, and of course they have to deal with their own failed marriage. Walter loses himself in his work while Kitty reaches out first to her English neighbor Waddington (Toby Jones) and then to the convent of French nuns and its Mother Superior (Diana Rigg). Slowly, hesitantly, Walter and Kitty both start reaching past their own limitations and seeing each other in a new light.

What is most refreshing about *The Painted Veil* is that its two main characters are equally flawed and sympathetic at the same time. We understand why they've made the choices they have, and how they slowly dismantle their illusions and assumptions about each other. The cruel irony, of course, is that the cholera epidemic is what makes this possible (at times it seems like the world's most passive-aggressive murder-suicide pact, which may well have been Walter's original intention), and then makes it impossible.

With such a subtle, character-driven film, the acting has to be up to snuff. Thankfully, everyone involved brings their A-game. Watts is note-perfect as Kitty, never making the character nobler than she really is, but at the same time revealing that there's depths to Kitty that she never suspected were within herself. Despite a slightly shaky English accent, Norton is nearly Watts' equal (though he has the much less showy role). Toby Jones is a delight in every scene as Waddington, looking like a louche garden gnome. Delightful in her own way is Diana Rigg as the Mother Superior. These two characters exert a profane and sacred influence over the relationship between Walter and Kitty.

The adaptation of W. Somerset Maugham's novel is well done, considering that the novel had even less plot than the movie does. The decision to add a subplot about political unrest doesn't work as well as it should; whereas a more significant alteration (in the resolution of the relationship between Kitty and Charlie) is more successful, if a bit "Hollywood."

It's a quiet film that takes its time exploring its characters and their journey. As such it's a rare treat, and a welcome one.

# Pennies from Heaven

*Schadenfreude: The Musical!*

**Year:** 1981

**Director:** Herbert Ross

**Screenplay:** Dennis Potter

**Cast:** Steve Martin, Bernadette Peters, Jessica Harper, Christopher Walken

I've never been able to get into musicals. The whole framework of them just throws me off. I know this isn't logical, given most of the things I can take in stride during a movie. Giant monsters attacking cities? I'm fine with that. Ghosts and things from outer space and other dimensions? Bring 'em on. But people randomly bursting into song? No, thank you.

There are exceptions, of course. I adore *Singin' In The Rain,* primarily for its early-Hollywood setting, and for its wit, energy, and clever satirical touches (not to mention that Gene Kelly was a stone-gorgeous thing back in the day). There's also the nontraditional fantasia of *All That Jazz,* covered elsewhere in this book. And last but not least, the shiny-on-the-outside, grim-on-the-inside *Pennies From Heaven.*

The movie tips its hand as to which side of its dual nature it favors in the opening credits. Gorgeous heavenly shots of sun-drenched clouds give way to gloom and torrential rain. In 1934 Chicago, in the throes of the Great Depression, Arthur Parker (Steve Martin) is feeling stifled in both his occupation and in his marriage. He's a sheet music salesman, a profession that gives him a hand-to-mouth living thanks to the economic conditions and his unpromising sales territory. And his frigid, repressed wife Joan (Jessica Harper) will give him neither the money to start his dream business of a record store, nor more than the most grudging amount or variety of sex. It's in the opening moments that we also see the central conceit of the film: as Arthur gazes forlornly at his wife, he begins to lip-synch the song, "I'll Never Have to Dream Again." It's jarring to see a serious Arthur mouth along to a song sung by a woman, but the device makes sense and becomes familiar shortly thereafter, when Arthur, rejected by the bank for a loan, fantasizes a Busby Berkeley-style number in which he and the bank manager sing while bank workers dance and chorus girls shower Arthur with money.

Arthur isn't the only one using fantasies of music to alleviate his grim reality. On a business trip he meets schoolteacher Eileen (Bernadette Peters), and she soon proves to be his match in both sexuality and in hopes that life will turn out as happily as it does in the songs. But the lovers' dreams can't compete against the harsh reality of the Depression, and soon Arthur finds himself loathed by his wife, with a failed business on his hands and the law after him for a crime he didn't commit; and Eileen is securing a back-alley abortion and turning to prostitution. There's no happily ever after.

*Pennies From Heaven* is an hour and forty-five minutes of emotional whiplash, as the characters (primarily Arthur and Eileen, but secondary characters get their turns as well) repeatedly fantasize gorgeous musical numbers to cope with their reality. There's emotional whiplash in the characters themselves; Arthur would seem to gain our sympathy at first, saddled as he is with a going-nowhere job and an ill-suited wife. Yet every time he gains the audience's sympathy he almost immediately proves himself a bastard, whether it's treating a homeless accordion player with snide contempt, refusing to recognize just how humiliating Joan finds it to submit to him sexually, or lying to Eileen and dumping her when she gets pregnant. It's a brave performance by Martin, not least because at the time he was known exclusively for his comedy (*Pennies From Heaven* was only his second film role, his first being *The Jerk*). For the most part it's a successful performance, aside from a "hick" accent that is intermittent and unconvincing. Martin throws himself into the dance numbers with agility and verve, and it's shocking to find out that before this role, he had never danced professionally (then again, Martin was always a great physical comedian, so perhaps his dance skills aren't that surprising after all). The rest of the cast is splendid: Bernadette Peters mixes porcelain-doll beauty with a wanton side, making Eileen the only sympathetic character in the movie. Taking on the thankless role of Joan is Jessica Harper; her standout scenes are when, in an effort to save her marriage, she submits herself to what she considers a horribly perverse fantasy of her husband's, and then lets a song show just how much hatred and resentment have built up inside her. And stealing the show with his single scene as a tap-dancing, strip-teasing pimp is Christopher Walken, whose dance to "Let's Misbehave" is worth renting the movie for.

The movie always looks fantastic, too, from its gorgeous dance numbers to the haunting, minimalist scene when Arthur meets his fate. One highlight is a re-creation of Edward Hopper's famous painting *Nighthawks*, a shot held just long enough for you to get the reference without wearing out its welcome. The movie's flaws lie primarily in its pacing. Adapted by Dennis Potter from his six-hour British miniseries, the story feels choppy throughout, especially in its last third, when parts seem to have been cut. Yet the movie is never less than interesting, and always enjoyable as long as you like your musicals with a heavy helping of *schadenfreude*.

# Performance

*Who am I this time?*

**Year:** 1970

**Director:** Donald Cammell and Nicolas Roeg

**Screenplay:** Donald Cammell

**Cast:** James Fox, Mick Jagger

Remember those times in college when everyone in the room was drunk or stoned except for you? And they'd be prattling on about stuff they thought was **so** profound and shit, while you sat there and thought, "Man, these people are boring."

Well, that's pretty much what *Performance* is like. Ta da! End of review. Boy, that one was easy!

Wait, my work ethic just kicked in and told me that I have to write a real review. Oh, hell. Here goes.

Chas (James Fox) is an enforcer for a London crime lord. It's his job to put the fear of God into people who need to get in line with what the crime lord wants. Chas loves his job. Oh, does he love his job. He loves his job so much that the other gangsters are getting creeped out and his boss thinks Chas needs to be reined in. Maybe it was the time Chas doused a man's car with sulfuric acid and then forcibly shaved the man's head. That might have tipped people off to the fact that Chas's elevator doesn't go all the way to the top.

Chas is taught a lesson when gangsters trash his obsessively neat apartment and then strip, beat, and whip him. The physical punishment is meted out by an old friend/rival of Chas's (the details of what led to such bad blood between them are left tantalizingly vague). Chas manages to turn the tables and kills his rival. Now the gangsters are after Chas, who needs a place to hide while he gets the wherewithal to flee the country.

Where Chas ends up is at the basement flat of a somewhat decrepit mansion owned by Turner (Mick Jagger, better than you'd think), a retired rock star who's lost his muse and now lives in druggy paradise with two lovers (Anita Pallenberg and Michele Breton). Soon Chas is seduced by the hedonistic life of Turner and Turner becomes fascinated by Chas's violent life.

It's at this point that the film, which has been somewhat interesting, becomes a real slog as we watch stoned, annoying people have dull conversations and while the directors use lots of obvious imagery in an attempt to be profound (you will be very tired of mirrors and doors by the time the movie ends). The characters of Chas and Turner aren't altogether uninteresting, and Fox (in particular) and Jagger do their best with the roles, but they simply aren't given enough to do. Each gets a standout scene, though. Chas's moment is the aforementioned assault on his apartment and his person. Turner's is what amounts to a music video plopped into the last third of the film, featuring Jagger in a gangster's suit and slicked-back hair singing the terrific song "Memo from Turner." These two sequences lift the film out of its torpor but aren't enough to save it. There's really no reason to care if Chas gets away or if Turner gets his groove back, and the ending, which offers some out-of-left-field violence and a twist that M. Night Shymalan might steal one day, renders the whole thing pointless.

Though it works more as a curiosity piece than an entertaining film, *Performance* isn't a total loss. James Fox puts in an excellent performance; he comes across as a thinner, more straight-laced Daniel Craig, and there's real ferocity in his violent acts in the film's first half. Mick Jagger is better than one would assume, particularly once you get past the "Hey, that's Mick Jagger" reaction and see that he is not just playing himself. (Allegedly the characterization was based on Brian Jones, but Jagger's Turner often reminded me of another doomed musician, Pink Floyd's Syd Barrett.) And the movie always looks great, as it should since the cinematographer was co-director Nicolas Roeg who would go on to movies like *The Man Who Fell to Earth* and *Walkabout*.

Unfortunately the movie's done in by overly pretentious direction and editing, a story that is erudite and nonsensical at the same time, and the supremely annoying female characters.

# Phantom of the Paradise

*After many a summer dies the swan*

**Year:** 1974

**Director:** Brian De Palma

**Screenplay:** Brian De Palma

**Cast:** Paul Williams, William Finley, Jessica Harper

I first saw *Phantom of the Paradise* when I was 8 or 9 years old, and while I'm certain a lot of it went over my head at the time, I also recognized that something cool and unusual was going on. I credit films like *Phantom* and *The Last Wave* with shaping my cinematic tastes.

*Phantom of the Paradise* updates the *Phantom of the Opera* story to the 1970s glitter rock scene. Winslow Leach (William Finley) is a backup pianist for a band called the Juicy Fruits. Winslow has been working on a rock cantata of Faust, which catches the ear of record company impresario Swan (songwriter Paul Williams) who is looking for a special sound to open his new rock concert hall, The Paradise. Swan hoodwinks Winslow into giving Swan his score, steals the music and the credit, and has cops plant heroin on Winslow. Winslow gets sent to Sing Sing, and when he finds out that the Juicy Fruits have released *Faust* as their own work, gets enraged enough to bust out of the big house and vandalize Swan's record studio. In the process he gets his face mangled and burned in a record press (from back when they made vinyl records…anyone else remember vinyl?). So injured that even his voice is destroyed, Winslow dons a black leather outfit, cape, and the Coolest Mask Ever, to become the Phantom of the Paradise. His two goals are to destroy Swan, and to make sure the beautiful songstress Phoenix (Jessica Harper in her debut) sings his cantata.

*Phantom of the Paradise* was probably destined to be both a commercial flop and a beloved cult film. For every one thing it does wrong it does two things right, in its own unique way. DePalma's direction is highly stylized, using distorted lenses and angles, speeded-up sequences, and split-screen. The result is that while clearly set during the early 1970s, the film does not feel badly dated; it seems to exist in its own little bizarro world. The only aspect that doesn't hold up is the glam/goth band The Undead — they were probably shocking in 1974 but are positively tame in our post-GWAR world.

Music — those who create it, those who perform it, and those who profit from it — is the key driver behind *Phantom*. Winslow and Phoenix share a love for the cantata, not a traditional romantic love. Phoenix offers her voice to Swan for the chance to sing. Swan robs Winslow not just of his music but his ability to sing. Paul Williams was, in his day, one of the top songwriters. His *Phantom* songs are pop but they are intelligent and catchy, and they not only tell the *Faust* story but comment on the events in *Phantom* themselves.

The acting is strong all-around. Finley is more appealing in Phantom gear than he is as the nerdy composer, but no matter how destructive and homicidal he becomes, he never loses the audience's sympathy. Paul Williams makes for a surprisingly creepy villain with his beady eyes and peculiar way of speaking without using the sides of his mouth; he's like an evil doll. Harper has the same porcelain-doll beauty and strength she would later show in *Suspiria*; small wonder that Winslow not only wants to have Phoenix sing his cantata, but to keep her from being corrupted. Gerrit Graham is also amusing as a gay glam-rock idol named Beef.

*Phantom* is entertaining and often intelligent, particularly in its depiction of the rock scene and "giving the people what they want." It's far from perfect, though. Winslow and Phoenix's relationship isn't made strong enough to support the story that follows from it. The ending of the movie is chaotic and badly rushed, almost giving the impression that a reel has gone missing. And there must be some kind of record set for continuity problems, particularly in the costumes

(Watch Swan's suit change from tan to black and back again! Watch the Phantom's cape change from silver to red lining!).

In a better world, *Phantom of the Paradise* would have the cult that the far less deserving *Rocky Horror Picture Show* has.

# Phase IV

*The ants go marching two by two*

**Year:** 1974

**Director:** Saul Bass

**Screenplay:** Mayo Simon

**Cast:** Nigel Davenport, Michael Murphy, Lynne Frederick

It's always refreshing to find a movie that tries to do something different instead of relying on the clichés of the day. And while it's not entirely successful, *Phase IV* manages to bridge the gap between science fiction and revenge-of-nature horror, with a bit of post-*2001: A Space Odyssey* surrealism.

A (vaguely described) outer space event briefly has humankind worried, but once the event's over with all seems normal. While most of humanity has gone back to its regular business, Dr. Hobbs (Nigel Davenport) is troubled by unusual behavior among ants. It seems that in certain areas, the ants are leaving off their usual interspecies warfare and cooperating — preying on their predators (and on livestock), creating crop circles, and building strange tower-like structures in the desert.

Hobbs recruits James (Michael Murphy), a young scientist who's had luck deciphering the language of dolphins, and they set up a lab in a geodesic dome in the desert, to see if they can figure out what the ants are up to and what it means for mankind. As Hobbs and James make their way to the dome we see signs that the ant problem isn't as trivial as one would think — an abandoned housing development (the timbers weakened and eaten away by holes bored by the ants), dead livestock (with those unsettling bore holes in their flesh), and more of those odd towers.

Matters begin to escalate when Hobbs provokes the ants into coming closer to the research lab — by blowing up the towers with grenades. Subtle, isn't he? The ants come after the lab, and also attack a local farm. The farm family escapes only to get caught in a biotoxin that Hobbs sprays on the ants, and the only survivor is the family's daughter Kendra (Lynne Frederick, looking like a

Breck Girl). Not only does Kendra's presence complicate the situation, but Hobbs is beginning to show signs of Mad Scientist Syndrome. And the ants have learned how to adapt to the biotoxin and are staging a new, different kind of assault.

*Phase IV* won't please those looking for drive-in jollies or a down-and-dirty creature feature. It's very deliberate both in its pace and in its story. It requires the viewer to pay attention, particularly during the many scenes of the ants in their tunnels, when it becomes clear that the ants are far more intelligent than any of the humans give them credit for. Yet the film lingers in the memory despite the gaps in the story or the sometimes inadequate acting.

Some nice ambiguity is provided by director Saul Bass and writer Mayo Simon's refusal to explain many things. Does the ants' behavior have anything to do with the outer space event? What do the towers and their statue-like shape (reminiscent somehow of the Easter Island statues) mean? Are the ants in control or being controlled? *Phase IV* explains very little, yet is never frustrating.

That's not to say the film is without flaws. The movie lacks a compelling human character — Hobbs is a hubristic jerk from the start and James is fairly bland. The acting is hit-and-miss. The movie is also very much of its time, with a *2001*-inspired ending that is both cool and unsatisfying at the same time. But if you're in the right mood, *Phase IV* is entertaining and a refreshing change of pace.

# Pink Floyd: The Wall

*I'm an asshole and it's everyone's fault but mine*

**Year:** 1982

**Director:** Alan Parker

**Screenplay:** Roger Waters, based on the album by Pink Floyd

**Cast:** Bob Geldof, Eleanor David, Jenny Wright, Bob Hoskins

This is gonna be a tough one.

You see, once upon a time there was an 11-year-old girl who heard this cool "We don't need no education" song on the radio every day on the way home from basketball practice. She got the album with that song on it for her 12th birthday and was never the same after that (Roger Waters, you have so much to answer for!). She ended up with every Pink Floyd album ever made, not to mention most of the solo albums, bought all sorts of band-related paraphernalia, wallpapered her room with Pink Floyd posters, kept a scrapbook with clippings of the band, and bored all her friends and family silly with talk about the music (note: this was in those ancient days before the Internet was invented, so she had no forums or chat rooms to help vent her fandom). And you'd better believe that she went to see the movie of *The Wall* when it was in theaters (and was willing to suffer the embarrassment of being taken to it by her dad, since she wasn't yet old enough to see an R-rated movie).

That girl is more or less grown up now. She's rather less enthusiastic in her fandom these days (the late-1980s ugliness of the band's breakup/reformation, he-said/he-said accusations, and asshatish behavior didn't help). But now here she is to review the movie that she once watched at least once a month, that she once considered one of the Best Movies Ever. Let's see how time and maturity have tempered that assessment, shall we?

First off, *Pink Floyd: The Wall* is a very odd film, and it probably couldn't get made today. It's basically a 90-minute music video, telling its story in a fragmented, occasionally surreal style. We meet rock star Pink (Bob Geldof before he was a knight or a saint) sitting catatonic in his hotel room. What brought him to this sorry state? Glad you asked! Pink has built an emotional wall to insulate himself from the hurtful, hateful world. His father died in World War II when Pink was still an infant, his mother overcompensated for dad's loss by smothering Pink with her attention and overprotectiveness, his schooldays were full of rote learning and corporal punishment, he became a rock star but the tours and drug use took their toll on his already-shaky marriage and his wife left him for another man. So, in addition to developing a very bad case of "It's all about *me*," Pink has shut himself off emotionally. Unfortunately, sitting there all comfortably numb behind his wall means that the darker, fascistic side of his personality now has free reign.

*The Wall* is foremost a triumph of style over substance. It's technically very well done and moves along at a nice clip — kudos go to director Alan Parker, who did probably the best job anyone could have with such an odd project. And of course the music is excellent. Purists will scream about the editing of several songs, though it's forgivable save for the butchery of "Waiting for the Worms." And though a couple songs have been cut, most notably "Hey You," the movie includes the extended "What Shall We Do Now," the elegiac "When the Tigers Broke Free," and re-recorded and improved versions of some songs (most notably "Mother") so I've no complaints. (The missing footage for "Hey You" is included as an extra.) The cinematography succeeds in making some ugly sights look very nice. And praise must go to animator Gerald Scarfe, a longtime collaborator of the band's, for his surrealistic animated sequences that give us a clue as to what goes on in Pink's head. "Goodbye Blue Sky" with its cowering, gas-masked figures, fascist eagle of destruction, and desolate battlefields/graveyards is probably the best marriage of rock music and visuals since the "Eleanor Rigby" sequence in *Yellow Submarine*.

The acting is surprisingly good, considering that aside from incoherent screams there's about 15 lines of actual dialogue in the whole movie. Geldof acquits himself fairly well considering that he'd never acted before (in fact, he despised Pink Floyd's music and only took the gig because he wanted to promote his band The Boomtown Rats) and plays not so much a character as life's whipping boy. (He's especially good in the scene when Pink finds out his wife's taken up with another guy.) Bob Hoskins has a small but memorable role as Pink's manager (his big line before "Comfortably Numb" always is good for a laugh). Everyone else gets the job done, but top acting honors probably go to Kevin McKeon as the adolescent Pink, who manages to gain the audience's empathy, if only for a little while.

Which brings us to the major problem with *The Wall* (please ignore the protests of my inner fangirl). As candy for the eyes and ears, it's great, if not to all tastes with its often brutal violence, copious nudity, and even more copious blood. But while it's possible to identify with Pink — who hasn't had to shut down emotionally to get through bad patches? — it's difficult to empathize with him and impossible to like him or to care much about his situation. Even more problematical is that Pink Floyd's Roger Waters (who wrote most of the album and the movie's screenplay) clearly wants the movie to be a cathartic experience, and he doesn't succeed. All the viewer takes away is that life sucks, shutting yourself off from it sucks more, and if you stop shutting yourself off you will … uh, well, it's not really made clear. What's missing is a scene of Pink finally emerging from behind his wall, and saying, "Now what?"

Which is unfortunate, because aside from a few people who are so compartmentalized that nothing phases them for long, we've all been hurt and we've all wanted to make the pain go away. But we build walls because we don't know what else to do, and by the end of the movie we're no wiser as to what we **should** do.

That aside, if you don't look too deep *The Wall* can be a fun experience, particularly if you view it as *Yellow Submarine's* evil twin.

# Piranha 3D

*Welcome to Lake Chum*

**Year:** 2010

**Director:** Alexandre Aja

**Screenplay:** Pete Goldfinger and Josh Stolberg

**Cast:** Elisabeth Shue, Jerry O'Connell, Ving Rhames

Disclaimer: Although the term "douchebag" is generally accepted as referring to a person of the male gender, for the purposes of this review it will apply to both men and women.

I'm not entirely certain that *Piranha 3D* is a good movie, strictly speaking. It's dumb, but in a very clever way — it never pretends to be anything other than what it is: a vehicle to get as much blood, boobs, and beasts in your face (3D!!!) as possible. And for that you've got to love it.

All is well at the desert oasis of Lake Victoria (actually Lake Havasu in Arizona). Until an earthquake opens a fissure in the lake's bottom and out come a bunch of nasty piranha. They're hungry and pissed, as one local fisherman learns.

The piranhas are actually the second horde of monstrous creatures to invade the lake. It's Spring Break and the place is jammed with horny, obnoxious, drunk college students. So far the local sheriff (Elisabeth Shue playing the one character in the film who is not terminally stupid) and her deputy (Ving Rhames, whose bad-assery makes up for his character's stupidity) are keeping things in check. But the sheriff's son, who's supposed to be babysitting his younger siblings, is instead hanging around with sleazy horndog Derrick (Jerry O'Connell, not playing that "Girls Gone Wild" fellow at all, no sir) on the *S. S. Tits Ahoy*. Soon all the sheriff's kids are in peril, Derrick's douchebaggery has reached epic proportions (putting even more people in danger), and the piranha have arrived at Spring Break Central just in time for the Wet T-Shirt Contest.

Which brings us to the film's gory highlight: DOUCHEBAG SMORGASBORD!!! IN 3D!!!

Finally, finally, someone realized that while CGI does many things well, it simply cannot simulate gory violence. It doesn't look organic enough, and CGI blood ends up looking like those oil droplet knickknacks you used to see a lot in the 1970s. The effects during the douchebag smorgasbord scene are practical, plentiful, and effective. At times they're **too** effective, and the film's tone, which has been cheerfully stupid up to this point, veers into the grotesque. (How this thing got away with an R is beyond me.) Fortunately there's still a rescue-the-kids sequence that brings the film back on balance.

*Piranha 3D* could have been a disaster. Luckily for us, director Alexandre Aja is quite skilled, and (as anyone who saw *High Tension* or his *The Hills Have Eyes* remake can attest) is unconcerned with things such as good taste. Aja knows exactly what the audience wants to see — piranhas eating douchebags, and lots of it. He gives us that. Aja also knows that American cinema has had a dearth of screen nudity in recent years, and he gives us boobs, more boobs, and yet still more boobs (in 3D!!!). Also a naked underwater ballet to class things up.

Aja also has a fine cast that all hit exactly the right note. Shue is good as the beleaguered lawwoman (and the intelligent eye of Hurricane Stupid). Rhames isn't on screen nearly enough. Christopher Lloyd steals his two scenes as a local marine expert who identifies the Piranhasaurus Rex. O'Connell makes his sleazebag character someone you want to see die from his first appearance. And yes, that's Eli Roth as the Wet T-shirt Contest MC.

As for the 3D, I'll confess that I am not on board with the whole 3D trend. The glasses give me a headache and just because a movie **can** be done with 3D effects doesn't mean it **should** be. *Piranha* is an exception, though, because it understands that for this film, the aesthetics don't matter — it's about putting boobs, blood, body parts, and other things in your face. I don't really know enough about 3D to say how well the effects were done, but I did appreciate them sort of as a gore-and-nudity update of the paddle-ball gag in *House of Wax* (the Vincent Price one, not the Paris Hilton one, you philistines).

If the prospect of seeing lots of stupid people dying in horrible ways (and lots of boobs) makes you sit up and take notice, by all means see *Piranha 3D*.

---

# Poseidon

### *A-A-A-G-LUG-G-G-G-G*

**Year:** 2006

**Director:** Wolfgang Petersen

**Screenplay:** Mark Protosevich, based on the novel *The Poseidon Adventure* by Paul Gallico

**Cast:** Josh Lucas, Kurt Russell, Richard Dreyfuss

---

Wolfgang Petersen's war film *Das Boot* is not just one of the best war movies ever made, it's also the best submarine movie ever, and is so gripping and emotionally devastating that I cannot rewatch it very often.

So it's all the more painful to see him directing the maelstrom of mediocrity that is *Poseidon*.

A remake of the 1977 disaster epic (and based on Paul Gallico's novel), *Poseidon* follows the same setup as its predecessor. An absurdly luxurious cruise ship is capsized by a rogue wave, and a motley crew of survivors decide to escape by climbing to the bottom of the capsized ship.

I'm fairly certain that most of the survivors have names, but I'll be damned if I can remember them. So we watch Obvious Hero (Kurt Russell), Stealth Hero (Josh Lucas) lead the way accompanied by Obvious Hero's daughter Dewy-Eyed Maiden, her 100% personality-free boyfriend/fiancée Whatsisface, as well as a Sad Gay Man (Richard Dreyfuss), Screechy Single Mom, Single Mom's Spawn, a Token Latina, a Doomed Busboy, and Leisure Suit Larry. I'm not being facetious — those descriptions sum up everything we learn about the characters, most of this served up in unwieldy chunks of expository dialogue.

This is the fatal flaw of *Poseidon* — we don't look to a disaster movie for in-depth character study, but without characters to be interested in or care about, there's no reason to see this movie as anything but an exercise in stunt work and CGI. It's clear that the movie was severely edited to remove nearly everything but the setup and the action set pieces. For example, unless you're looking at the bottom of the screen when Sad Gay Man sees the rogue wave approaching, you don't realize that he's been ready to jump overboard in a suicide bid (talk about being careful about what you wish for!). Similarly, in between set pieces a character will drop a bit of dialogue about themself but these incidents are so brief and unconnected that the result is awkward and confusing rather than enlightening. The rest of the dialogue is variations on "The water's rising!" "This is the only way out!" "I won't leave you!" and the ever-popular "Nooooo!"

The special effects are impressive, and have come a long way since the original film. The capsizing is very well realized, but strangely uninvolving. Everyone remembers the unlucky bastard who fell into the stained-glass ceiling in the original film; there's no such iconic image in this remake.

The movie progresses from set piece to set piece, and for the most part ends up being as involving as watching a video game. Watching the cast slog through water and dodge debris, you don't worry about the characters so much as you feel sorry for the actors. This even holds true for the movie's one harrowing sequence, a brutally realistic drowning that's almost physically painful to watch. Its power comes not from the character's fate as the realization of what the actor went through for the sequence (whatever he was paid for this movie, it wasn't enough).

It's all capped off by a *Deus ex Machina*-heavy ending that had me rolling my eyes. The only surprise was that one of the dead characters didn't miraculously pop up alive at the end. ("How did you survive being underwater for so long?" "Wasn't easy!")

# Possession

*I told you that bitch was crazy*

**Year:** 1981

**Director:** Andrzej Zulawski

**Screenplay:** Andrzej Zulawski

**Cast:** Isabelle Adjani, Sam Neill, Heinz Bennent

If there isn't a subgenre for art-house horror films, there by-God should be. This subgenre includes Peter Greenaway's *The Cook, The Thief, His Wife, and Her Lover* (also known as "The most pretentious episode of *Tales from the Crypt* ever"), many David Lynch films, Terry Gilliam's *Tideland*, and arguably Stanley Kubrick's adaptation of *The Shining*.

But at the top of the heap is Andrzej Zulawski's *Possession*. It's an art-house horror that tackles marital strife, mental breakdowns, female sexuality, the Cold War, espionage, philosophy, the existence of God, and sex with squid monsters. And maybe World War III. If you're saying, "That sounds like a colossal mess," you'd be correct. But it's not something you're ever going to forget, either.

It's Berlin during the height of the Cold War (and should you find yourself failing to remember just where this film is set, Zulawski's many, many shots of the Berlin Wall will jog your memory). Mark (a very young and pretty Sam Neill) has just returned home from a year away on an unspecified job, possibly behind the Iron Curtain. His homecoming is a bit of a bust, though. His wife Anna (beautiful, batshit Isabelle Adjani) tells him that she doesn't want to see him anymore, doesn't want him to see their child Bob, and that she has taken a lover during his time away. Mark tries to find out from Anna what's gone wrong and how they can put things back together, but Anna isn't forthcoming and every conversation ends with the couple trashing restaurant tables, screaming at or hitting each other, or cutting themselves with electric knives. For a while Mark goes fetal and is so deranged he can't even speak, but when Anna's lover Heinrich (Heinz Bennent) calls, wanting to know where Anna is, Mark snaps out of his funk.

I'm going to digress for a moment about Heinrich. He spends every scene with his shirt open all the way and likes to spout a lot of philosophy (the dubious coherence of which is not helped by his thick accent). He's apparently bisexual, getting way too familiar with Mark at their first meeting, and a martial artist, handily kicking the stuffing out of Mark. And at one point he does some odd posing as if he's doing ballet moves. I'm not making this up.

225

It's clear that Anna's not with Mark, nor with Heinrich, nor is she taking very good care of her child. So what's she up to? Mark hires the least subtle private detective ever, who learns that Anna spends her days in a beautiful-yet-creepy apartment where she's shacked up with some sort of fungus-tentacle creature. Anna spends a good deal of her time having sex with this creature. It may well have knocked her up at one point — in what's probably the film's most notorious scene, Anna has an extended screaming fit in an empty subway tunnel that culminates in what looks like a miscarriage of … your guess is as good as mine. At any rate, the detective discovers the creature, and Anna kills him and turns him into fungus-tentacle-creature chow.

All this and I haven't mentioned the schoolteacher who's Anna's idealized double, a man with pink socks who's a plot point of some kind, the screenplay suddenly remembering Mark's espionage job, and the always-fun "severed head in the refrigerator" gag. Good times!

*Possession* is one of those movies that really can't be classified as "good" or "bad." There's a lot to admire: I particularly like the chilly cinematography that gives Mark and Anna a drained, bloodless look, as if their emotional turmoil is sucking the life out of them. At the same time, this turmoil is so over-the-top that it's hard to take seriously. This isn't the fault of the actors. Neill gives the best performance in the movie, particularly in the beginning as he's reeling with shock over the unexpected ruin of his marriage. He's still interesting later in the film, particularly in his nasty relationship with Heinrich, but his character has ceased to act like a normal human being.

Speaking of not acting like a normal human being, Adjani's performance must be mentioned. Like Neill, she's ill-served by the screenplay, which never once gives a hint if she was ever normal or what her husband and lover ever saw in her. That said, it's certainly unforgettable, as Anna (who for some unknown reason always wears the same indigo-blue dress) has hysterical fits and screams with wild abandon. Yet while it's an amazing performance in an "I wonder how long she spent in the loony bin afterward" way, it's never affecting to watch, save for one scene when Anna stares up at a statue of Christ and makes strange keening sounds. She seems to be begging for something, but we never learn what because the moment's gone and in the next scene she's twitching and screaming and smashing her groceries and herself against a wall.

As a result, the only human moments — and consequently, the only disturbing ones — are those with the two dysfunctional parents and their young child. The scenes when Mark is with Bob are all the more upsetting because we know how fragile Mark's sanity is, and that the collapse of Mark and Anna's relationship will have awful effects on the child.

It's obvious that Zulawski had things he wanted to say, but the movie is so obscure, and yet so obvious (note the presence of the Berlin Wall and the division between Mark and Anna) that nothing coheres. Zulawski hasn't David Lynch's gift of making the surreal somehow comprehensible — I've never walked out of a Lynch film feeling that I didn't get it. I have no idea what's going in much of *Possession*, and yet the whole thing is well-done and insane enough that it's weirdly captivating at times. If you like interesting failures, it might be your cup of tea.

# Prophecy

*Unbearable*

**Year:** 1979

**Director:** John Frankenheimer

**Screenplay:** David Seltzer

**Cast:** Robert Foxworth, Talia Shire, Armand Assante

I'm not sure which is worse — seeing a movie you loved as a child and realizing it's bad, or seeing a movie that scared you when you were a child and finding it not at all frightening. Probably the latter. The former just makes you disappointed, the latter makes you feel like a doofus ("I was scared of **this**?!").

Hey, I was young and foolish then. And I'm old and foolish now, so I've given *Prophecy* a second view and found that it's the dreaded Serious Horror Movie — poorly paced, with obvious scares, and saddled with a flimsy story and characters that can't support the weight that John Frankenheimer wants to bring to the film. (All flaws that would mark Frankenheimer's later foray into the genre, the misbegotten *Island of Dr. Moreau*.)

We open with oh-so-ominous music playing while several men with mining helmets, flashlights, and search dogs comb the woods for … something? Someone? It's not made clear, nor is it explained why they are searching at night. Don't such things usually happen during the day when you can, I don't know, actually **see** things? Anyway, one of the search dogs gets very frightened or enthusiastic about something (again, it's not made clear which) and runs right off a cliff! Wile E. Coyote would be proud! The searchers descend the cliff to rescue the dog and end up being massacred by some unseen thing.

What follows is one of the most bizarre things I've seen in quite some time — a lingering, loving pan over the gory remains of the search team and their dogs, accompanied by lovely classical music. This goes on for a couple minutes, and then we dissolve to cellist Maggie (Talia Shire) as she plays with an orchestra.

You know, I'm beginning to think that whole *auteur* theory may be a bunch of malarkey.

Maggie is married to a public health doctor named Robert (Robert Foxworth, sporting a really unfortunate white man's afro). Robert is cranky because he works in the ghetto and sees things like babies that have been mauled by rats, and nothing he does makes a difference. He's always going on about how awful the world is and how he never, ever wants to bring a child into it. However, he seems to have left all the family planning up to his wife, and you guessed it — Maggie is pregnant and hasn't broken the big news to Robert yet.

Then an old chum of Robert's offers him a chance to go to Maine — seems there's a big dispute between the Evil Industrial Paper Mill and the In-Harmony-With Nature Noble Savages. (Yes, the conflict is that subtle.) The chum thinks Robert could help (with what, it's not made clear) and Robert, happy for a chance to escape the big city, takes the assignment. Maggie tags along, thinking the trip will make it easier for her to tell Robert she's knocked up.

Robert and Maggie soon find out that the conflict is worse than they'd thought; they witness a standoff between Evil Paper Mill Employees and Noble Savages that turns into an axe vs. chainsaw duel that is far duller than it ought to be. Also, it turns out the Noble Savages are being blamed for the deaths of the search team at the beginning of the movie, the disappearances of the people the team was looking for, and anything bad that happens. The police soon blame Noble Savage John Hawks (very sexy Armand Assante) but the local chief says the killings are the work of Katahdin, a deity that is part of all living things, and has come to protect his people.

Now, about this Katahdin. Yes, that's what the creature on the poster is supposed to be. Creepy, isn't it? Borrowing a bit from every living thing — that's pretty neato. I wish we could see that, but what we get instead is a gloopy, half inside-out bear that we never see clearly because it would look even more fake than it does. Granted, Katahdin is very cranky (you would be too if you looked like a big puppet covered in Astroglide) and he smites a fair number of people, but the smitings are so telegraphed and poorly executed (take special note of the sleeping bag demise — it's nearly worth the price of a rental) that the whole thing becomes laughable.

The plot congeals as we learn that the Evil Paper Mill has been releasing mercury into the local environment, which accounts for the raccoon attacks (don't ask), oversized minnows and tadpoles, the high rate of miscarriage and stillbirth among the local populace, and Katahdin the Astroglide Bear. It all ends with one of horror cinema's lamer "gotcha!" moments and the disheartening knowledge that you've wasted 90 minutes of your time.

Performances range from weak to acceptable. Foxworth is supposed to be a passionate and dedicated man of medicine but comes off as a passive-aggressive control freak. He also has a big "hikeeba" moment at the end when he's battling the bear that's giggle-inducing. Shire is very convincing as a woman in her first trimester because she seems to be really tired all the time. Assante has almost nothing to do except spout some Noble Savage philosophy but he looks good doing it so I don't mind.

I feel a bit bad about coming down harshly about this movie, but it's just so disappointing. That poster gives you a hint of what Katahdin could have been, and while he wouldn't have saved the movie, he wouldn't have been as silly as the monster we do get.

---

# Psychomania

*Born to be mild*

**Year:** 1973

**Director:** Don Sharp

**Screenplay:** Julian Zimet and Arnaud d'Usseau

**Cast:** Nicky Henson, Beryl Reid, George Sanders

---

Even bad movies can serve a good purpose in life. If you're home sick, lying on the couch and looking for something to occupy your mind while you wait for the meds to kick in — something that's not too demanding of your intellect yet not so boring that you nod off — you could do a lot worse than to watch *Psychomania.*

*Psychomania* instantly dates itself with credits in that font used on the *Fragile* album by Yes. It then presents us with a slow-mo sequence of motorcyclists driving around the misty English countryside, accompanied by trippy music that's heavy on the reverb. Said motorcyclists are a gang called The Living Dead, and when they get tired with driving loops around the local countryside they indulge in heinous activities like driving through town and knocking packages out of shoppers' arms. Really.

The Living Dead's leader, Tom (Nicky Henson), is bad and we know this because he has a perpetual smirk and Brian Jones hair, and constantly talks about killing himself so he can "cross over." Tom's girlfriend Abby is the "nice" one of the gang and we know this when she tells Tom she can't join him in a suicide pact because she has to help her Mum with the shopping the next day. After a graveyard make-out session during which Tom takes a break from snogging with Abby to capture a frog (no, that's not a euphemism), Tom heads home to chat with his widowed mother and her butler (played respectively by Beryl Reid and George Sanders, both looking faintly embarrassed). Vague conversation and even vaguer hallucinations reveal that Tom's family are some sort of occultists who have figured out how to return from the dead. Turns out it's very simple: You just have to really, **really** believe that you can come back! Wow! Who knew? Oh, and there's a frog amulet involved somehow. (Don't ask me why. I think my meds were kicking in about this time.)

Tom thinks this is just dandy and proceeds to drive his motorcycle off a bridge. The Living Dead bury him up on the misty moor — bury him seated on his motorcycle. Which is cool, but they ruin the scene with a sickly hippie ballad called "Riding Free" that makes Emerson, Lake, and Palmer's "Lucky Man" sound like Blue Cheer's version of "Summertime Blues." Mercifully the song ends and not long thereafter Tom reanimates and drives out of his grave on the motorcycle, looking none the worse for wear, his Brian Jones hair barely mussed. There follows a confusing sequence in which we watch Tom act like an asshole, ostensibly because he's undead, but since he was an asshole before he died it's hard to tell what difference being resurrected makes.

The gang all think this is just dandy, and start killing themselves in various ways. What makes this sequence a trifle surreal is that the key to resurrection apparently lies in believing you'll come back and not chickening out — yet the bikers tend to choose methods (such as drowning or jumping out of planes *sans* parachute) that give them plenty of time for second thoughts.

Anyway, it all goes well for everyone except Abby, whose attempt at overdosing is foiled by her Mum and a police inspector played by one of the guys from *All Creatures Great and Small* (hey, I watched a lot of public television as a kid). Abby decides she doesn't want to die, Mr. All Creatures Great and Small decides to use Abby to catch the rest of the gang, and Tom's mother and butler suddenly decide this resurrecting business is evil and must be stopped.

It's an odd little movie, just different enough to keep one mildly interested. If the makers had put as much thought into the characters (particularly Abby) and into the ramifications of being resurrected (which aside from physical invulnerability seem limited to "makes you somewhat more of a douche than you were when you were alive") as they did into the occasionally clever camerawork and the pretty good motorcycle stunts, it could have been an enjoyably surreal ride.

# Rain of Fire

*Get your asbestos umbrella*

**Year:** 1977

**Director:** Alberto de Martino

**Screenplay:** Sergio Donati and Alberto de Martino

**Cast:** Kirk Douglas, Simon Ward, Agostina Belli

One of my favorite cinematic subgenres is "Catholic apocalypse." Give me cool-sounding prophecies, ominous music (preferably with choirs), worried-looking priests, and contrived accidental deaths, and I'm a happy camper.

So I was pleased as punch to see that Lionsgate has dusted off the 1977 Omen ripoff *Holocaust 2000*, repackaged it, and retitled it as *Rain of Fire* (more on this repackaging/retitling later).

Like *The Omen, Rain of Fire* has a slumming respectable star at the center of the apocalyptic shenanigans. *Rain of Fire*'s slumming star is Kirk Douglas and his Square Jaw of Awesomeness™. Kirk plays Robert Caine, an industrialist whose new project is a huge nuclear power plant located in an unnamed Middle Eastern country. At a press conference Caine chitchats with Sarah (Agostina Belli), a photographer. He shows her a nearby cave that has the word "JESUS" carved into the wall, presumably to ward off evil. Even though Sarah spouts some convenient knowledge about the apocalypse, Caine pays her no mind and demolishes the cave with the JESUS carving. Oh, good one, Spartacus.

Caine returns to England where he's greeted by protesters (and if you think their chant "What do our children want to be when they grow up? Alive!" is annoying the first time, wait til you've heard it 100 times!). Things aren't much better at a party thrown to celebrate the launch of the project. Caine's wife (who's a shareholder in his firm) wants to pull the plug, ostensibly because the risk is too great but Caine thinks it all has to do with their son Angel (Simon Ward).

Let me digress for a moment. His son is named Angel. No one normal is named Angel. Moreover, his name is "Angel Caine." Please. Add to this the fact that Angel has a British accent that makes him sound like Legolas (only less butch), looks like an evil kewpie doll, dresses in fashionable 1970s menswear, and lacks the Square Jaw of Awesomeness™. He might as well run around saying, "Hi, I'm Angel Caine and I'll be your Antichrist this evening."

Meanwhile, back at the party, a mysterious scowling bearded man sneaks into the shindig and goes after Caine with a knife. A fight ensues, Angel starts wrestling with the would-be assassin, and in the ensuing struggle Caine's wife gets a fatal stab in the gut. Oops, clumsy! Well, at least with the wife out of the way everything's a go for the building of the power plant. Funny how those things work out.

Everything would be peachy except for the usual Disquieting Things that always show up in these movies. Things like a drawing of a seven-headed dragon appearing in one of the photos Sarah took of Caine, a Mid-East leader opposed to the power plant getting thwacked in the head by a helicopter rotor, and a computer that can recognize the number of the Antichrist (not 666, thankfully, but some square-root thingy). Caine considers this a bunch of hokum and coincidence, and besides, he's got a romance going with Sarah the photographer. (If you think this *affaire de coeur* is happening a bit soon after the gruesome death of Caine's wife, consider that Caine and Sarah start their affair not five minutes after seeing the Mid-East leader get killed.)

Which brings us to the high point of the movie: a nightmare/vision sequence that is pretty cool and totally ridiculous at the same time (much like the rest of the film). Said vision's big payoff would be a lot bigger if it hadn't been blatantly telegraphed just a few scenes earlier. This scene is also notable because Caine spends the whole thing running about naked. I have no objections because even though Kirk was 60 when he made this film, he's in damn fine shape (have I mentioned my latent Elektra complex?) and it's high time we had more gratuitous male nudity in movies.

Where was I? Suffice to say that *Rain of Fire* is cheese, without question. But it's fun cheese. It's even got a few scenes of genuine creepiness (all in medical settings, strangely enough), though there are unintentional laughs, to be sure — you have to love the mid-1970s vision of what a supercomputer would look like.

Kirk Douglas had to know he was just collecting a paycheck for this one, but you can't tell. He and his Square Jaw of Awesomeness™ put in an actual performance and he never seems like he's condescending to the material. As Sarah, Agostina Belli mostly lets her Botticelli beauty do the heavy lifting, but she and Douglas have good chemistry and you want things to work out for their characters. By contrast, Simon Ward is pretty terrible as Angel. He's neither frightening nor compelling and has next to no charisma. You just want Douglas to punch him in his smarmy kewpie doll face.

Direction and story are heavy-handed, to say the least, but you won't mind much. Ennio Morricone's score isn't one of his more original efforts but it does its job and lays on the atmosphere with a trowel.

Some of you out there may know this movie under other names: the aforementioned *Holocaust 2000* or *The Chosen*. For the movie's DVD release Lionsgate has given it a new title and a spiffy new cover that makes it look like one of those *Left Behind* movies. This repackaging is a fine trash cinema tradition and I'm glad to see it's still being done. It makes up for the complete lack of extras save trailers on the DVD and for the flat visual and audio transfer. Oh well, you can't have everything.

# Ravenous

*Looks like meat's back on the menu*

**Year:** 1999

**Director:** Antonia Bird

**Screenplay:** Ted Griffin

**Cast:** Guy Pearce, Robert Carlyle, Jeffrey Jones

I have a soft spot for interesting failures, and *Ravenous* is a prime example.

During the Mexican-American war, Captain John Boyd (Guy Pearce) manages the not-inconsiderable feat of being commended for bravery on the same day he's punished for cowardice. You see, in the heat of battle, Boyd panicked, played dead, and found himself at the bottom of a stack of bloody corpses. After unintentionally swallowing some of the blood, Boyd found himself with a mysterious new strength that allowed him to capture the Mexican fort and assure victory. But his cowardice is known to his superiors, and they send him to the most remote posting possible: a fort high up in the Sierra Nevadas. The fort is manned by a skeleton crew of misfits: a drunkard, a religious fanatic, a loco-weed and peyote enthusiast, and a super-soldier.

Trouble comes knocking one night in the form of Colqhoun (Robert Carlyle), a settler who tells a tale of his party being trapped in a high mountain cave and resorting to cannibalism. Colqhoun says the party's leader, Colonel Ives, has gone mad and may kill the last remaining woman in the party, so Colqhoun has gone for help. The men form a rescue party, only to find themselves trapped and the prey of Colqhoun, who's really the cannibal maniac. Boyd is soon going to have to face up to not just his own cowardice but a certain something that he and Colqhoun have in common. Because the strength that consumption of human flesh gives the eater comes at a great price.

The first half of *Ravenous* is effective if uneven film-making. From the opening credits, which juxtapose a quote from Nietzche with "Eat me" by "Anonymous," there's a peculiar inconsistency to the tone. This continues through the opening credits, which whoosh across the screen in a matter best suited to a comedy, and the film's title appears just as a character vomits. For its first half the film manages its inconsistency more or less effectively, and creates both a sense of overpowering dread while at the same time giving a wink to the more absurd elements of the story.

It's in the second half, when Boyd finds that Colqhoun has taken on the persona of Colonel Ives and is planning to use the fort as his source for victims to prey on, that things fall apart. Boyd and Colqhoun do a lot of facing off and Colqhoun acts as Boyd's shoulder devil, constantly tempting him with the power that cannibalism provides. It all ends in a knock-down, drag-out fight and an ending that was probably intended to be ambiguous but is just frustrating.

It's a shame, because *Ravenous* does have a lot going for it. Carlyle makes Colqhoun one of horror's scarier villains during the scene when he reveals his true nature; it's not surprising that Boyd takes his chances jumping off a cliff rather than go against Colqhoun. Pearce has a much less showy role, but he does well with a difficult role, that of a man who's been rendered almost inert by cowardice and self-loathing. One of his best moments comes at the midpoint when he's confronted with Colqhoun in his Colonel Ives persona and does a cross between fainting dead away and trying to run, with darkly comic results. The mountainous settings are both gorgeous and frighteningly isolated. I'm less fond of the movie's oft-touted score than most others. Half the time it works, albeit in an off-kilter way, but it can then turn on a dime to be jarringly anachronistic or too comical for the scenes it accompanies.

Overall, the film is too much of a mixed bag. It's too gruesome and dark to be successfully comic, too funny to be true horror, and too pretentious in its second half to sustain the thrills of its first. But it is unique, and I'm glad to see a movie that at least tries to do things differently, even if it doesn't always succeed.

## The Reaping

*Plague o' my heart*

**Year:** 2007

**Director:** Stephen Hopkins

**Screenplay:** Carey Hayes and Chad Hayes

**Cast:** Hilary Swank, David Morrissey, Idris Elba, Anna-Sophia Robb

From *The Rapture*, which focuses on losing one's faith, to *The Ninth Configuration,* which takes on the regaining of one's faith, there have been some fascinating genre films about the nature of belief.

*The Reaping* is not one of those movies.

Katherine (Hilary Swank) travels around the world debunking religious miracles, and the movie opens with her finding that the perfectly preserved corpse of a priest is due to toxic vapors from the local industrial plant. We soon learn that Katherine is not a lifelong skeptic — she used to be an ordained minister until she lost her family, calling, and faith in a Big Tragic Event. So when Doug (David Morrisey), a well-spoken fellow, asks for her expert eye on a supposed Biblical plague that's affecting his small bayou town, Katherine is obliging in spite of panicky-yet-vague warnings from her former missionary pal Father Costigan (Stephen Rea, sadly wasted).

Katherine and her assistant Ben (Idris Elba) journey to the small town of Haven where, on the same day a local boy mysteriously dropped dead without any sign of illness or injury, the local river turned blood-red. Katherine's sure it's just pollution or an algae outbreak, but tests show that yes indeed, the water's turned to blood. And faster than you can say "plagues of Egypt" the town's being bombarded with flies, dead livestock, locusts, and more — all of it somehow connected to a young girl (sister to the kid who mysteriously dropped dead).

*The Reaping* is promising for its first half hour or so. The Louisiana bayou location is well-used (though the town's inhabitants are far too cliché'd). The first sight of the river of blood is creepy, as are the scenes of the Katherine and Ben in hip-waders, making their way through the red liquid. Some of the plagues are surprisingly unsettling, such as the flies and the locusts (good use of CGI). Swank's an appealing lead, though I found the character of Ben much more interesting — he debunks bogus miracles not because he's lost his faith but because he still *has* faith.

Unfortunately, the movie descends into mediocrity on all levels. There's far too much reliance on scary! jump! cuts! as well as hand-held camera WobbleVision™ when it's not needed. You'd ask director Stephen Hopkins to hold the camera steady and just tell the story already, but the story is bogged down in pointless "is it a flashback? Is it a hallucination? It's both!" sequences and some bogus-sounding prophecies and ham-handed revelations about the town. By the time events come to hinge on Katherine's return to her faith, the matter seems almost lost in the mass of flashy FX, and the very last scene makes the entire affair almost pointless.

It's a shame, because *The Reaping* has the potential to be an interesting movie. Unfortunately it never makes good on that potential and ends up as just the vehicle for some (nicely-executed, I'll admit) smitings.

# Red Sonja

*Moron the barbarian*

**Year:** 1985

**Director:** Richard Fleischer

**Screenplay:** Clive Exton and George MacDonald Fraser

**Cast:** Arnold Schwarzenegger, Brigitte Nielsen, Sandahl Bergman

I love a fun sword-and-sorcery movie, don't you? Unfortunately you're in trouble if you decide to go with *Red Sonja,* because as promising as it looks, it ends up being too dull to mock and too goofy to take seriously.

The movie opens with our heroine Sonja (Brigitte Nielsen seems to have learned her lines phonetically), sprawled in the dirt outside the burning ruins of her family's home. Then, in one of the more hamfisted backstories ever, a shimmery, glowy figure appears and informs Sonja of how she (Sonja) was propositioned by the local evil queen. When Sonja rebuffed the proposition the evil queen killed Sonja's family, burned her house, and had Sonja raped by a bunch of soldiers. The kicker? Everything the Magical Exposition Fairy is telling Sonja happened to Sonja just, oh, ten minutes earlier!

Sonja seems as puzzled by this bit of awful scripting as we are, but she recovers nicely and goes off to warrior training school. Meanwhile, the evil queen who propositioned Sonja (Sandahl Bergman in an abysmal performance) busts up a temple so she can get this big green glowy ball thingy called the Talisman. Apparently it will give her all kinds of power or something, if it doesn't destroy the world first. (There's always a trade-off, isn't there?) While she's at it the evil queen has most of the temple's priestesses massacred. One, though mortally wounded, escapes, and wouldn't you know it, she happens to be Sonja's sister.

Sonja's sister conveniently runs into Arnold Schwarzenegger — I forget his character's name, so we'll just call him "Not-Conan." He finds Sonja and brings her to her dying sister, and when Sonja heads off to destroy the Talisman (and kick a little evil queen booty) Not-Conan wants to tag along. Sonja's having none of it because she doesn't like men, but Not-Conan follows along anyway and proceeds to show up whenever Sonja gets in over her head, which happens with alarming frequency.

Along the way Sonja meets Short Round. Well, I forget his name but he's some bratty prince whose kingdom was destroyed by the Talisman thingy. Prince Short Round and his Fat Flunky join Sonja and Not-Conan, and after fighting a mechanical critter, together they infiltrate the evil queen's way-too-Freudian castle and there's a big fight in a room with about 10,000 candles. I feel compelled to add that none of this is as interesting as I'm making it sound.

The main problem with *Red Sonja* is that it never finds the right tone. It doesn't have the serious, near-mythic quality that John Milius was able to bring to *Conan the Barbarian*, yet it isn't silly enough to be campy. Except for Schwarzenegger, who seems to be enjoying himself, most everyone else in the cast seems to be going through the motions. This is particularly true for Nielsen, who looks stunning but never seems at home in the role. Acting honors probably have to go to that guy who yells, "I will read the future in your entrails, red woman!" with such gusto. Now **that's** the performance you need for a movie like this.

The story is nothing special and the effects are decent, but what really makes *Red Sonja* interesting is the way it constantly undermines the heroic qualities of its titular character. Every time Sonja gets into a dangerous situation she needs Not-Conan to bail her out. It's not clear whether the moviemakers thought audiences wouldn't buy a heroine who gets the job done by herself, or if they couldn't think of a role for Schwarzenegger except as a *deus ex machina*.

Things get entertainingly wacky when the heroes arrive at the evil queen's palace, which has some really weird Freudian designs to it, as well as a wizard mixing bubbly potions in Erlenmeyer flasks, the aforementioned room with 10,000 candles, and Ennio Morricone's score kicking it all up a notch. *Red Sonja* isn't the nadir of 1980s sword-and-sorcery epics, but it's far from the peak.

# The Ref

*Happy holidays*

**Year:** 1994

**Director:** Jonathan Demme

**Screenplay:** Marie Weiss and Richard LaGravenese

**Cast:** Denis Leary, Kevin Spacey, Judy Davis

I love Christmas, but like most holidays it has the potential for big-time family drama. Few movies demonstrate that better than the underrated comedy *The Ref*.

It's Christmas Eve and catburglar Gus (Denis Leary) is about to make the proverbial last big score. Unfortunately, his plans are spoiled by the combination of a burglar alarm and a Rottweiler. While his not-terribly-competent partner tries to find transportation to get them out of town, Gus needs to find a place to hole up.

Gus decides to take some hostages and gets more than he bargained for when his hostages are Lloyd and Caroline Chasseur (Kevin Spacey and Judy Davis). The Chasseurs have spent their Christmas Eve not at a party or caroling, but in marriage counseling, and they can't have a single conversation that doesn't turn into vicious bickering. Poor Gus is soon wishing he'd taken his chances fleeing from the cops as he endures Lloyd and Caroline sniping at each other and venting all the grievances, petty and otherwise, of their collapsing marriage.

Things only get worse when it's revealed that relatives, including the Chasseurs' son (who we first meet blackmailing the head of his military academy) and Lloyd's horrible mother, are about to arrive for dinner. Gus's only hope to stall things long enough to get away is to pose as the Chasseur's marriage counselor, something that goes both worse than and better than one could expect.

*The Ref* is an interesting comedy; it's dark and the humor is often vicious, yet it neatly sidesteps the "humiliation humor" so prevalent in comedies nowadays. The screenplay takes the time to show Gus, Lloyd, and Caroline as three-dimensional yet flawed people. It helps that the three actors are all equally talented when it comes to dialogue heavy with dark sarcasm, and that there's moments of real pain beneath their cynical exteriors, from Gus's regrets at how his life has gone to the Chasseurs' laments for the loss of their once-solid marriage.

Leary gets top billing, and he's excellent throughout, particularly when he does his many slow burns at dealing with his situation and the people making it so difficult. But the show really belongs to Spacey and Davis, who are never less then entertaining no matter how insulting they are toward each other. Yet though their bickering is the best thing about the movie, it's also clear that the Chasseurs were once deeply in love with each other and are still able, if not always willing, to join forces (the early scene when they both yell "Fuck you!" at their marriage counselor is a highlight of the film). The movie also captures well the stifling nature of families and of the small, wealthy New England town where the film takes place, where resentments can fester for years before exploding in unexpected ways.

It's an extremely quotable and surprisingly enjoyable movie that's become part of the regular holiday viewing at my house; if nothing else, it's a tart antidote to the usual holiday treacle.

# The Reflecting Skin

*Innocence can be hell*

**Year:** 1990

**Director:** Philip Ridley

**Screenplay:** Philip Ridley

**Cast:** Viggo Mortensen, Lindsay Duncan, Jeremy Cooper

Let me start this review with a brief comparison: If David Lynch had directed a movie adaptation of one of Ray Bradbury's darker stories, it would be *The Reflecting Skin*. And if you, like me, think this sounds like a little slice of heaven, then by all means see this movie now.

For those of you needing a little more detail, here goes. It's the early 1950s, in an isolated corner of the American Midwest, and eight-year-old Seth (Jeremy Cooper) is having a less-than-idyllic childhood. His family owns a decrepit gas station that gets very few customers. His mother is bitter, constantly on the brink of hysterical tears, and abusive to Seth, punishing him harshly for minor infractions (in one very upsetting scene, she forces him to drink water until he's close to vomiting). His father is a distant, vague man who spends all his time reading pulp magazines and novels. It's one of these that sets Seth's imagination in motion, and he starts to fantasize that the odd Englishwoman (Lindsay Duncan) who lives nearby is a vampire. (It's hard to blame Seth for thinking that the woman is not normal, since she claims to be 200 years old, and says her name is Dolphin Blue.) Seth's brother Cameron (Viggo Mortensen) is off in the military, stationed somewhere in the Pacific.

This is Seth's everyday world — running about the beautiful, empty fields with his friends, exploding frogs (don't ask), and spinning flights of fancy. But when children are abducted and turn up dead, and ugly family secrets come to light, Seth's dreamlike existence turns nightmarish. Soon Cameron returns, and you could be forgiven for hoping that Aragorn will restore some normalcy to things. But Seth's brother is quiet and seems to be damaged in several ways by what he's seen and done in the military. Cameron soon begins an affair with Dolphin, which terrifies Seth as he's sure Dolphin has vampiric designs on his brother.

There probably isn't an adult who hasn't longed for a return to childhood. But Ridley's astonishing film will make you reconsider this. Granted, few peoples' childhoods are as messed up as young Seth's, but what Ridley conveys very well is how the world feels to a child when he's caught up in life situations he has no way of understanding. Conversations are oblique, with hidden meanings clear to adult viewers of the movie but incomprehensible to a child. The surroundings are beautiful, but too vast and isolated to be comforting (Ridley emphasizes this with scenes showing characters alone in vast wheat fields that are fertile but somehow ominous, or against a sky that's brilliantly, harshly blue) — for all the open space, the surroundings often feel claustrophobic. And situations that could inspire empathy from an adult only add to Seth's confusion (such as when he sees Cameron and Dolphin making love). As Dolphin says at one point, "Innocence can be hell."

This theme brings further comparisons to Bradbury, for though Bradbury often wrote about children, the young people in his stories were not always likable innocents (think of the children in "The Veldt" who sacrifice their parents to lions rather than give up their interactive nursery, or the schoolchildren in "Let's Play Poison" who kill their teacher). Our introduction to Seth is when he and his friends are tormenting a frog; later, he and a friend sneak into Dolphin's house while she's away and trash her bedroom. Seth's innocence often veers into amorality, though the surreal proceedings call into question just what he's witnessing, what's imagined, and how much responsibility he bears for the events that unfold.

Ridley's direction is visually stunning, particularly in the outdoor scenes. His one failing lies in the direction of some of the actors. For the most part performances are fine, occasionally better than fine (Lindsay Duncan is eerie and heartbreaking as the eccentric, lonely Dolphin Blue). However, some of the supporting performances (in particular the father of Seth's murdered playmate, and the weird, one-eyed sheriff) are ham-fisted and break the eerie mood of the film, pushing it into the freak-show territory of David Lynch's *Wild at Heart*.

These minor flaws aside, it's a beautiful if often horrific film that will linger long in your memory.

# The Replacement Killers

*High sizzle-to-steak ratio*

**Year:** 1998

**Director:** Antoine Fuqua

**Screenplay:** Ken Sanzel

**Cast:** Chow Yun-Fat, Mira Sorvino, Michael Rooker, Jurgen Prochnow

For those of you (and I'm one of them) who like action movies to be brainless, but not insulting, there's the oft-overlooked *The Replacement Killers*. It's not terribly original or intelligent, but it's got definite style, and gives you plenty of opportunity to groove on its star, the one and only Chow Yun-Fat.

Chow plays John Lee, ostensibly one of the best hit men ever. I say "ostensibly" because one would think an awesome hit man would skulk in the shadows, not draw attention to himself, and possibly even make the killings look accidental. Nope, not this hit man. In the opening scene, Lee saunters into a crowded techno dance club, puts a bullet on the table in front of a skanky drug lord, and then whips out the guns and kills a bunch of people. This scene is crucial to your enjoyment of the movie. If you say, "That's stupid," then you should turn off the movie and watch something else. If you say, "That's awesome," then settle in and enjoy the ride.

Lee works for crime lord Mr. Wei, who we know is uber-evil because he has a huge, gorgeous house and his assistant is Jurgen Prochnow. When a cop (Michael Rooker, playing a nice guy for a change) is forced to kill Wei's douchebag son, Wei gives Lee a mission...to kill not the cop, but the cop's son. Lee can't do it, and now needs to flee Wei's wrath and get to China, where his family lives and will be killed by Wei if Lee can't get to them. Needing papers in a hurry, Lee turns to forger Meg Coburn (Mira Sorvino). Soon Lee and Meg are on the run from Wei's goons, and have to stop two more hit men (the "replacement killers" of the title) who've been hired to kill the cop's son.

Along with its obvious emphasis on style over substance, *The Replacement Killers* is an odd film in many ways. It has an almost comic-book feel with lengthy passages free from dialogue, and with almost no backstory provided for most of its characters. Odder still, the titular replacement killers don't show up until well after the halfway point, and I'd have trouble even remembering them if one weren't played by Danny Trejo. I strongly suspect studio interference, and wonder what was left on the cutting room floor.

That aside, the movie is enjoyable on its own terms. Though he's no John Woo, director Antoine Fuqua, best known at the time for the "Gangster's Paradise" video, ladles up big helpings of well-lit, showy action. He's aided and abetted by solid actors: Chow Yun-Fat lights up the screen every time he's on it, and he has good chemistry with Sorvino (though one wonders if their relationship was ever meant to progress beyond the bicker-our-way-from-enemies-to-friends arc that's in the final film). Rooker hasn't enough to do, but it's refreshing to see him play a good guy. And Jurgen Prochnow is coolly evil as Wei's enforcer.

It's not the most original action film you've ever seen, but it's 80 minutes of entertainment and has Chow Yun-Fat being a badass.

# Repulsion

*Thank God I'm pretty*

**Year:** 1965

**Director:** Roman Polanski

**Screenplay:** Roman Polanski and Gerard Brach

**Cast:** Catherine Deneuve, Ian Hendry, Yvonne Furneaux

Roman Polanski's first English-language film opens with a close-up of a woman's eye, which looks everywhere but does not seem to see anything. When the credits are over we see that the eye belongs to Carol (Catherine Deneuve), a young Belgian woman who's working at a London beauty spa. It's soon clear that this fuguelike state is not that unusual for Carol. In fact, underneath her beauty and her placid nature, Carol has some very serious disturbance going on.

Primarily, Carol's issues stem from men, and her reaction to them. She resents it when her sister's married lover leaves his toothbrush in the girls' apartment; at night the couple's noisy lovemaking keeps Carol awake. And while Carol ostensibly has a boyfriend, or at least a suitor, she doesn't seem to like him much. In fact, when he kisses her she flees and runs into her apartment to rinse out her mouth. Up to now Carol's madness has been overlooked — or denied — by those around her. But when her sister and boyfriend leave on a vacation and Carol's left alone in her drab apartment, her madness spirals out of control, with fatal consequences.

Without a doubt, *Repulsion* isn't as startling as it was back in 1965. Yet it's still remarkably effective, and its influence can still be felt today (primarily in the work of David Lynch — watch Lynch's use of texture and sound, and the way he can make an ordinary room look terrifying, and you can't doubt that *Repulsion* must have made an impact on Lynch). Polanski uses the limited effects technology and what appears to be a minimal budget to his advantage: at one point Carol touches the wall in her apartment and leaves a handprint, as if the wall had turned to soft clay. It's so simple, and yet impressive on both a visual level and a tactile one. And while most horror movies ask the audience to identify with the victims, in *Repulsion*, moments like the soft walls ask the viewer to identify with Carol and her insanity.

Polanski makes effective use of sound as well. There's very little music throughout the film. For much of the time, the only sounds are those of Carol's apartment — the distant sound of other tenants, the flies buzzing around spoiling food (and corpses). There are scares from the loud sounds of the cracks that appear without warning in the walls, but more disturbing is the dead silence that accompanies Carol's hallucinations that men are coming into the apartment and raping her.

*Repulsion*'s story is, like its visuals, deceptively simple. The screenplay provides just enough detail to generate questions that linger about the nature of Carol's madness. One hallmark of good fiction is that the reader wonders about the characters — usually, what happened to them after the story ended. That's not the case in *Repulsion*, but what the viewer may wonder about is what brought Carol to this state.

The movie drops hints but never outright says what the origin of Carol's madness is. A photograph, present throughout the film but never shown in close-up until the end, may hold the key. But even that leaves much for the viewer to ponder. There are signs throughout that Carol's troubles are rooted to childhood trauma: when intruders real or imaginary come after her, she hides under blankets or under the bed; when her madness leads to murder she conceals the bodies clumsily — one in a full bathtub, one under a tipped-over sofa — the way a child would. Other unanswered questions abound: where are Carol's parents or family aside from her sister, and why does Carol's sister react with such vehemence to her boyfriend's suggestion that Carol see a psychiatrist? No one sees signs of Carol's trouble until it's too late; ironically, the one person who gets even a hint of her feelings is her would-be suitor, who reacts to a drunken male friend's teasing kiss the way Carol reacted to his own kiss. But he never makes the connection.

If you want to see how repressed trauma, denial, and isolation add up to a tale of ordinary madness, watch *Repulsion*.

---

# Requiem for a Vampire

*Ennui*

**Year:** 1971

**Director:** Jean Rollin

**Screenplay:** Jean Rollin

**Cast:** Marie-Pierre Castel, Mireille Dargent, Dominique

---

I don't think you could call Jean Rollin a good film-maker, but he certainly is a distinctive one. I'd only seen one of his films, *Demoniacs*, yet when I saw the trailer for *Requiem for a Vampire* on a *42ⁿᵈ Street Forever* compilation (under the charming and *tres* subtle title of *Caged Virgins*), I thought, "Gee, that looks a lot like that kinda dull, kinda interesting French horror film I saw a while back." Sure enough, both were directed by Jean Rollin.

*Requiem for a Vampire* opens, literally, with a bang. Two young women (dressed as clowns) and their getaway driver are fleeing from a pursuing car, and all the while gunfire is exchanged. The driver is fatally shot but the girls manage to throw off their pursuers; they then douse the driver's corpse and the car with gasoline, set it on fire, and then set off across the countryside. Dressed as clowns. Yeah, I know it's French and all that, but still.

Incidentally, this opening scene occurs exactly as I've described it. There's no context for any of this. Just some girls dressed as clowns running away from some people. The girls (whose names we never learn, by the way) amble along, change out of their clown gear, steal a motorbike, drive until it runs out of gas, steal some food, and take a nap in a cemetery. Oh, and one of the girls nearly gets buried alive. Right about the time you're wondering if anything is going to actually happen, the movie kicks it up a notch when the girls discover a seemingly abandoned chateau, go inside, and get naked together in the chateau's bedroom.

However, the fun and games are interrupted when the girls hear a noise downstairs and investigate, finding a rotting corpse, a skeleton band, vampires whose fang placement varies from shot to shot, and a trio of thugs who help out the vampires and grope anything female along the way. The girls are told they are to become vampires, until the lead vampire emerges from his crypt and has other ideas.

With its striking cinematography (all the more so for being achieved on what's obviously a minimal budget), lovely use of locations, and its repetitive, almost fetishistic use of certain images (in particular the nearly mute, doe-eyed girls), *Requiem for a Vampire* feels less like a movie and more like a filmed dream, presumably Rollin's dream. However, this means it's often about as interesting as hearing someone recount their long, involved dream. You find yourself letting the movie wash over you while you nod and say, "huh" at the more oddball aspects. While he certainly has a way with lightly surreal imagery, Rollin hasn't David Lynch's gift for translating the feel of a dream to the screen.

The result is a film that's too dull to create excitement yet too intriguing in its oddball way to be an outright snoozer. It's worth a peek if you're in search of something different (though be forewarned there's a scene of the thugs groping/molesting/raping several captive women that's not only unpleasant but goes on far too long). But it's probably safe to say that if you've seen one of Rollin's movies, you've seen them all. This isn't necessarily a bad thing — his movies are different from anything else you'll see — but they're just not all that good.

# Romeo is Bleeding

*Sympathy for Mr. Fuckup*

**Year:** 1993

**Director:** Peter Medak

**Screenplay:** Hilary Henkin

**Cast:** Gary Oldman, Lena Olin, Juliette Lewis, Annabella Sciorra, Roy Scheider

There's a peculiar *schadenfreude* to be found in stories of weak-willed men who bring about their own destruction. Those who like such stories should seek out *Romeo is Bleeding*, a neglected little gem from the early 1990s.

New York detective Jack Grimaldi (Gary Oldman) is doing a very risky balancing act. Dissatisfied with his income, he's been betraying mobsters who are supposed to be under police protection to rival gangsters in exchange for money. The money is ostensibly to provide a better life for the wife Natalie (Annabella Sciorra) he professes to love, while he carries on a string of affairs — his latest mistress is the supremely annoying Sheri (supremely annoying Juliette Lewis). But Jack manages to keep it all together, somehow. Until he meets Mona.

Ah, Mona. Played by Lena Olin, she's probably one of the most memorable villainesses to grace the screen in ages — she's what they used to call a *femme fatale*. Mona Demarkov is a Russian gangster who, within seconds of meeting Jack, lures him with her offer of money and the promise of sex. The money-hungry, lust-addled Jack succumbs with little resistance, only to find that Mona is far more clever and ruthless than he is. And soon Jack finds himself ordered by mob boss Don Falcone (miscast Roy Scheider) to kill Mona or suffer grave consequences. But Mona won't be easily caught or killed.

It's hard to say why *Romeo is Bleeding* isn't better known today. Perhaps audiences, not yet primed by *Pulp Fiction*, weren't ready for its blend of brutal violence and ghoulish humor. But while not without its flaws (a slow beginning, too much screen time for the Juliette Lewis character), it's a fun thriller with mostly good performances (look for Will Patton, James Cromwell, and Ron Perlman in minor roles), strong characterization, and stylish but not flashy direction by Peter Medak (director of my favorite underrated horror film, *The Changeling*).

What makes *Romeo is Bleeding* enjoyable also constitutes the movie's major flaw — Jack simply isn't very sympathetic and he deserves what he gets. It's enjoyable to watch him (literally) dig himself in deeper and get worked over by Mona (who takes a savage joy in her work that would not be seen again until Famke Janssen appeared in *Goldeneye*). But at the end, when he's realizing what his actions have cost him, his sadness doesn't resonate with the viewer. He's brought all this on himself and should have known better. He gets the audience's pity but not its sympathy.

But that doesn't matter much. It may be Jack's story but the show belongs to Mona. She's a truly fascinating character, not just because of her viciousness and her beauty (both considerable), but because of her intelligence. She understands the lure of money, sex, and power and uses those to her gain at every opportunity. Two key scenes help the viewer understand Mona. The first is when she escapes from federal agents by stealing a cop's gun. The cop isn't injured physically but the psychological blow is huge, as he repeatedly wails that Mona took his gun, pointed his own gun at him. By taking the cop's gun she's symbolically emasculated him and she knows it. The other scene is a haunting one in which Mona reminisces about her first time. She becomes sentimental and even sheds a tear, and it's not until the end of the speech that it's clear she's talking not about her first lover but about the first man she murdered. Olin does this scene — every scene — justice and the result is a truly memorable villainess, a *belle dame sans merci*.

# Ronin

*Spy vs. spy*

**Year:** 1998

**Director:** John Frankenheimer

**Screenplay:** J. D. Zeik and David Mamet (as Richard Weisz)

**Cast:** Robert De Niro, Jean Reno, Sean Bean, Natasha McElhone

I bet if you took a poll of people my age, whose formative years were the 1970s and 1980s, you'd find that some of us are strangely nostalgic for the Cold War. Sure, we had the threat of nuclear annihilation hanging over our heads, but things were much simpler then. We knew who the enemy was, and there was much less uncertainty about the world.

One can imagine how the front-line soldiers in the Cold War must have felt when the Iron Curtain fell and the world's alliances and conflicts changed so dramatically. *Ronin* is the word for a masterless samurai, and that perfectly describes the characters in John Frankenheimer's suspense film.

We meet the first of our masterless samurai at a café in Paris. Sam (a restrained and subtle Robert De Niro) is supposed to meet someone at the café, but he takes his time about it — giving the layout a once-over, finding an exit route should one be needed. We soon meet other former agents: driver Larry (Skipp Sudduth), resourceful Vincent (ever-awesome Jean Reno), weapons man Spence (Sean Bean), and tech guy Gregor (Stellan Skarsgard). They've been hired by Irish radicals (Natasha McElhone and Jonathan Pryce) to steal a case from a bunch of Europeans. Along the way we'll learn that most everyone on the team is more (or in one case, less) than they seem to be; that loyalty is cheap in this new world; and that there's nothing better than a great car chase when it's well done.

*Ronin* is that rarest of breeds — a smart thriller. The opening scene of Sam's arrival at the café sets the tone. The movie takes its time to show us these characters, their situations, and how they react. There are plenty of characters but the movie never feels crowded with them, and the combination of script and actors give each character, even the most minor ones, a chance to let us see what they're about — to a point. In the end most of the people in this world are as enigmatic as the case everyone wants. We never learn the contents of the case, and we never learn quite as much about the former agents as we think we do. In the end, we're in the same boat as the agents — they are given a job, and whether it comes from government masters or a radical group doesn't really matter. Theirs is not to question, but to get the job done.

Which is a nice, realistic touch, and one of many reasons why, though it may be just as much of a fantasy as James Bond movies, *Ronin* feels more down-to-earth. The cars aren't fancy sports vehicles with all the gadgets. Sam's character shows up with literally nothing but his weapon and the clothes on his back and, when asked why he's taking the job, bluntly says, "I need the money." When things go south, there's no one to call in to clean things up.

Of course, what *Ronin* is most famous for is its car chases, and all praise you've heard is very justifiable. There are three, with each one offering successively greater thrills. What makes these chases all the more thrilling is that they are not CGI, that the actors are doing much of the driving, and the chases are necessary to the plot. They never feel extraneous.

Be prepared to be thrilled, but be prepared to use your brain a bit, too.

# The Room

*Mary Sue: The Movie*

**Year:** 2003

**Director:** Tommy Wiseau

**Screenplay:** Tommy Wiseau

**Cast:** Tommy Wiseau, Greg Sestero, Juliette Danielle

It's both very fitting and quite unfair that Ed Wood Jr. is considered the worst movie director of all time. His movies are by no means the worst out there; if you doubt me, compare them to the works of, say, Coleman Francis, and you'll see that Wood's no Stanley Kubrick, but he's far from the worst. And yet the dubious honor of worst director is appropriate for Wood because of his signature style — the odd dialogue, endearingly ramshackle set design — and because of his sincerity. Wood had stories he wanted to tell, and a deep love for the movies. It's this sincerity that sets Wood apart and makes his movies memorable, when much worse film-makers are forgotten.

If any director today could inherit Wood's "worst director" title, it would be Tommy Wiseau. Wiseau has made only one film, 2003's *The Room*, but he definitely qualifies. Technology has changed and *The Room* uses bad greenscreen instead of *Plan 9*'s cardboard sets, but *The Room* has all the awkwardness, ineptitude, and sincerity associated with Wood's films.

Set in San Francisco (and should you ever forget the setting for the story, Wiseau will refresh your memory many, many times), *The Room* tells the story of a love triangle between Johnny

(Tommy Wiseau), his fiancée Lisa (Juliette Danielle), and Johnny's best friend Mark (Greg Sestero). Johnny is a rising young … something … involved in banking … somehow (the film is very vague about its characters' occupations). He's devoted to Lisa and calls her his princess; he demonstrates his love by bringing her roses and ostensibly sexy red dresses. Unfortunately for him, Lisa is no longer in love with Johnny. More out of boredom than anything else, she instigates an affair with Mark, who puts up infinitesimal resistance to Lisa's charms despite being Johnny's "best friend" (and should you ever forget that, various characters reiterate Mark's "best friend" status throughout the movie).

There's also a small circle of friends and family: Lisa's shrewish, materialistic mother Claudette, who constantly pushes Lisa to marry Johnny so he can provide for her; Denny, a strange man-child whom Johnny has quasi-adopted and is putting through college despite Denny's ill-defined drug problem; Mike and Michelle, who inexplicably and randomly barge into Johnny's house to have goofy sex on his sofa; and Peter, a psychologist who specializes in advice about relationships and in breaking the fourth wall.

The basic premise of *The Room*, though slight, isn't the source of its problems. Love triangles are as old as humanity, and the fallout of failed relationships is never confined to the people directly involved. What makes *The Room* so spectacularly, entertainingly awful is every aspect of its execution.

Let's start with the screenplay. Written by Wiseau, it has a strange feeling to the dialogue and characterization, as if the Ro-Man alien from *Robot Monster* had decided to make a movie about relationships. Most obviously, there's the dialogue, which is idiosyncratic at best with lines like "Leave your stupid comments in your pocket" and "Anyway, how is your sex life?"

Less obvious and even more odd is the film's perception of relationships, whether they're between friends or lovers. Male buddies toss the football around (usually from a distance of 3 to 7 feet) and complain about women — occasionally they do both at the same time. Women tidy up around the house and complain about men. Men are good and loyal, except when they aren't, but when they aren't, that's all the women's fault anyway.

This leads us to the characters, which are particularly crucial to a movie like this one when the plot is so threadbare. The only characterization Wiseau has spent any time on is Mary Sue, I mean Johnny, and every other character only exists to establish Johnny as the heroic and tragically wronged boyfriend. Wiseau tries hard — too hard — to make Johnny someone the audience will care about. He brings his fiancée sexy red dresses! He's getting a promotion soon! He's the favorite customer of the lady at the flower shop! He's putting Denny through college! He's Mark's best friend! You get the idea.

The problem is that none of this makes Johnny come across as an actual character. He's there to be wonderful to everyone, and everyone else is there to betray him. Nowhere is this more true than in his relationship with Lisa, whose boredom with and contempt for Johnny are so glaringly obvious, and whose hostility is so extreme (by movie's end she's telling people Johnny beats her, and spreading false information that the couple is expecting) that rather than feel sympathy for Johnny's treatment at the hands of this harpy, the audience wonders how dumb he had to be to fall for her in the first place.

These are fatal flaws that not even good actors could salvage, and *The Room*'s thespians are far from good actors. With one glorious exception they range from mediocre to inept. But luckily we have Wiseau on hand to take us into Bad Acting Nirvana. Filling the screen with what can only be described as anti-charisma, Wiseau's strange accent, oddball line readings, interesting physical presence, and affectless laugh give everything a train-wreck fascination. What makes it all the more delirious is that this is no phoning-it-in performance. Wiseau puts it all out there, particularly in the "You are tearing me apart, Lisa!" scene, his obvious Oscar Bait moment.

I could go on for pages, but let me just list the other glories of the film: the excruciating sex scenes (Four of them! Four!); the way characters barge into a scene, deliver their lines, say, "I gotta go" and then leave; the shots of San Francisco used not to establish place, but because Wiseau couldn't figure out how to show time passing; the random appearance and disappearance of characters with no introduction; the odd set design that seems cobbled together from an afternoon at Pier One and includes framed photos of spoons; and more. So much more.

Though the film is available on DVD, for a truly amazing experience one must go to a midnight showing of *The Room*, particularly in the Los Angeles area. The movie has become a latter-day *Rocky Horror Picture Show*, drawing regulars who scream in horror at the sex scenes, yell out "Because you're a woman!" to complement the film's more misogynistic moments, count the times someone says Mark is Johnny's best friend, hurl plastic spoons at the screen when the spoon art appears, and toss the football around. With a good crowd it's one of the more hilarious ways to spend an evening.

And yet I sometimes feel guilty laughing at *The Room*, because despite his ineptness in every aspect, Wiseau was truly sincere and serious. The story is clearly something dear to his heart, something he felt compelled to dramatize and share with the world. He's chosen to embrace the derision heaped on the film, even showing up at midnight screenings and claiming that the film was always intended to be a dark comedy. The film's a double-edged sword for the creative among us: we can see what Wiseau was trying to do and how he failed; yet we also know in our hearts that there but for the grace of God go we. We too might have a story we wanted to tell, and failed as badly as Wiseau did.

And with that realization, we can only say, "Oh hai" and move on.

# Rosencrantz and Guildenstern Are Dead

*Nobodies*

**Year:** 1990

**Director:** Tom Stoppard

**Screenplay:** Tom Stoppard, based on his play

**Cast:** Tim Roth, Gary Oldman, Richard Dreyfuss

Occasionally, when I'm in a metaphysical mood, I wonder about characters in books. I know that the characters are all just figments of the writer's imagination, but what if they aren't? What if they have some sort of life off the page?

Taking this idea to hilarious heights is *Rosencrantz and Guildenstern Are Dead*, adapted by Tom Stoppard from his play. We're introduced to our titular duo (played to perfection by Gary Oldman and Tim Roth) who are journeying by horseback. But to where are they journeying, and why? Well, they're not too sure. It seems they were sent for, but can't recall anything before that, nor are they clear on what they're supposed to be doing. They meet up with a group of players, whose leader (Richard Dreyfuss, devouring the scenery with style and gusto) discusses the nature of theater in general and tragedy in particular, namely that "blood is compulsory."

With little segue Rosencrantz and Guildenstern find themselves as characters in *Hamlet*. They do their best to address the questions other characters put to them and to find out why Hamlet is mad, but this is difficult as R&G aren't even clear on their own names. Despite their best efforts, R&G will soon find out the hard way that, as the lead tragedian says, "everyone who is marked for death... dies."

I can think of few better movies for lovers of wordplay; in addition to the bits of Shakespeare that pop up whenever R&G interact with the characters in *Hamlet,* there are delightful scenes in which R&G discuss the nature of their predicament or get philosophical. One reason it all works so well is because of the chemistry between Oldman and Roth — their comic timing and interactions are a joy, making scenes like the "questions" game so memorable. Yet the movie's delights aren't all verbal. Oldman's character is established as the less bright of the two, yet he's always making interesting discoveries about physics that are demonstrated in amusing ways. Another nonverbal sequence, my favorite in the film, is when the tragedians perform for the castle's servants — we soon realize that the play is a pantomime version of *Hamlet.*

Like most play adaptations, the movie feels a bit stagy, but that artificiality only adds to the feeling that these characters are just that — characters. Likewise, a working knowledge of *Hamlet* isn't necessary to enjoy the film. Those familiar with Shakespeare's play might get more of the references, but those unfamiliar with it will identify more with R&G as they try to figure out what is going on and what their role in it is.

# Roxanne

*Love letters*

**Year:** 1987

**Director:** Fred Schipesi

**Screenplay:** Steve Martin, based on *Cyrano de Bergerac* by Edmond Rostand

**Cast:** Steve Martin, Daryl Hannah, Rick Rossovich, Shelley Duvall

It can be difficult to find a genuinely sweet movie. Not sappy, not saccharine. Just sweet. Fortunately there's *Roxanne*, a romantic comedy that should leave you smiling.

In a gorgeous skiing town we're introduced to Fire Chief C. D. Bales (Steve Martin, who also wrote the screenplay). The movie follows Bales as he journeys through town to visit a friend, wisely letting us observe Bales' wit and *joie de vivre* before we see his nose. It's a ridiculously long, pointy nose, of Pinocchio-esque proportions. Some drunk skiers make fun of Bales' nose, and we discover that he's also quite a fighter. The nose is the bane of Bales' existence — he considers himself horribly ugly because of it (though Martin is quite handsome, graceful, and charming in the role). This becomes a crucial matter as Bales meets and becomes smitten with Roxanne (ethereal Daryl Hannah) an astronomer in town for research.

We soon see that Bales and Roxanne are a good match for each other — for one thing, they're the two smartest people in town — but she's drawn to another newcomer, handsome firefighter Chris (Rick Rossovich). Chris is good-hearted but not the sharpest knife in the drawer, and he's also paralyzed by shyness when Roxanne so much as looks at him. We soon have the inevitable comedies of errors and identities, but not to worry. True love will win out for all.

*Roxanne* is a particularly refreshing movie these days, when so many comedies rely on vulgarity and mean-spiritedness. Aside from a few insults hurled at Bales and his nose (from obvious louts who don't count) the movie doesn't have a mean bone in its body. The whole thing is such an enjoyable experience, from the gorgeous setting (Nelson, British Columbia) to the repartee between Roxanne and Bales. Though there's a love triangle, the parties involved are all good people. We want Roxanne and Bales to be together because we can see what they don't — that they are meant for each other. But Chris isn't a bad guy — he's charming, honest, sincere, and good at his job — he's just not the right person for Roxanne.

One particularly nice part about the movie is the townspeople, who have just the right amount of eccentricity to keep things lively: a pack of gossipy older women, the mayor (scene-stealing Fred Willard) with the not-so-brilliant idea of "Oktoberfest in July," Bales' friend Dixie (Shelley Duvall), and the inept members of Bales' fire department.

It's nothing earth-shaking. It's like a glass of ginger beer on a summer day. It's just a pure pleasure to watch. And that can be so hard to come by these days.

# Salò, or The 120 Days of Sodom

*Eat shit and die*

**Year:** 1975

**Director:** Pier Paolo Pasolini

**Screenplay:** Pier Paolo Pasolini and Sergio Citti, based on *The 120 Days of Sodom* by the Marquis de Sade

**Cast:** Paolo Bonacelli, Giorgio Cataldi, Umberto Quintavalle, Aldo Valletti

One of the more famous "endurance test" movies, *Salò* is no mere exploitation film. It's serious, and has a statement to make, but whether these qualities are worth the rough sledding of the film itself is debatable.

Pier Paolo Pasolini's film takes de Sade's *120 Days of Sodom* to World War II Italy. Four fascists — the President, the Bishop, the Duke, and the Magistrate — enter into a pact to satisfy their lust for power and their most base desires. After sealing the pact by marrying each other's daughters, the fascists and their thugs kidnap nine young men and nine young women to be their captive playthings at a remote mansion. The captives are forbidden to have any religious practices, and disobedience is punishable by loss of a limb or by death. The fascists have brought along four prostitutes: one provides piano accompaniment (and begins to look more and more distraught as the days go on and the emotional, sexual, and physical cruelty the men dole out becomes worse); the others gleefully recount increasingly vile tales of perversion, which the fascists use for inspiration.

It's difficult to pin down what makes *Salò* so disturbing after all these years. Though it's famous for its scenes of coprophagia (look it up ... or on second thought, don't) and bloodshed, there's a much more subtle scene early on that lets the viewers know what they're in for. As the four fascists search for their perfect victims, they reject one beautiful girl because she is missing a tooth. But another girl, who's naked, and sobbing because she just witnessed the death of her mother (who was trying to stop the girl from being kidnapped), is clearly what the four men are looking for. Their looks of delight at her humiliation and misery will give you chills.

What may be most unsettling about the film is its peculiarly detached quality. It doesn't leer at or take pleasure in the tortures, but merely sits back and records what's happening. We're given ample information about what's to come (the film is divided into four sections: the Antechamber to Hell, the Circle of Obsessions, the Circle of Shit, and the Circle of Blood), but this only gives the viewer time to dread what's about to unfold. And there is no music or other cue to prepare yourself for the nastiness. Terrible things can happen at any moment. Even the fascists' daughters aren't safe (in fact, they're singled out for some of the nastier humiliations, which makes you wonder what happened to the fascists' wives). This detachedness is most horrifying in the movie's sequence of torture and murder, which the audience sees only through the eyes of the fascists, who coldly observe the proceedings from a balcony, with binoculars — the lack of sound and the quick glimpses of violence are somehow worse than if the cameras had been down in the thick of things.

One of the film's problems may also be its saving grace: there is practically no characterization. We learn nothing about the characters as the film progresses, and this goes for the oppressors as well as the oppressed. While this prevents the viewer from making a connection to the characters, this may not entirely be a bad thing — it's difficult enough to watch ciphers being beaten, whipped, forced to act like dogs, made to eat shit, raped, tortured, and murdered. If these things were happening to characters we knew and cared about, the film would be even more unbearable than it already is.

Yet as much as a reprieve as this is, at the end of the film one is left wondering just what point Pasolini was trying to make. The film isn't gleeful exploitation in the *Ilsa* vein, yet its statements aren't terribly profound, nor will they come as much of a surprise to most viewers. Fascism is bad. Yes, that's true. Power corrupts, and absolute power corrupts absolutely. Indeed. There is such a thing as being too kinky. Glad to hear that. Going along with an oppressive regime may buy you time, but that's all. Again, a worthy point but Pasolini may have been preaching to the choir.

Adding to this sense of "what's the point?" is that the film's progression is so methodical and inevitable. At the beginning, viewers may have hope that the Allies will arrive and save the day (throughout the film the sounds of bombers and battle are heard), yet the mansion remains untouched and no help arrives. Any hope that the captives can rebel is snuffed out in the final chapter, when they rat each other out for a chance at survival. It's clear from the beginning that as the fascists play out their desires, it will take ever-greater levels of violence and humiliation to bring them satisfaction. And at the end, the torch is passed on to the next generation, as two young guards are so inured to the horrors that they pass the time by dancing.

*Salò* is probably the most problematic film I've ever seen, and as such it's impossible for me to simply say yes or no as to whether or not someone should see it. It lacks the entertaining qualities of other controversial films, and perhaps that is the best point to take away from the film. That in reality, violence and oppression **aren't** entertaining. They're just ugly and cruel.

## Scanners

*I've got a headache THIS big...*

**Year:** 1982

**Director:** David Cronenberg

**Screenplay:** David Cronenberg

**Cast:** Michael Ironside, Stephen Lack, Patrick McGoohan, Jennifer O'Neill

I'm not sure if *Scanners* is the ultimate example of a "good idea, not-so-good execution" but it's definitely in the top ten. It's a movie with some interesting ideas and several memorable, if not notorious, special effects set pieces, but it's hampered by a muffled screenplay and a very uneven cast.

*Scanners* opens at a wonderfully dated mall, which has that tacky-but-grim aesthetic so common to the late 1970s, aided and abetted by Mark Irwin's cinematography. Homeless guy Cameron Vale (Stephen Lack brings spooky eyes and not much else to the party) is stealing food off trays in the food court when he psychically overhears a woman thinking disparaging thoughts about him. He proceeds to induce a seizure in the woman, and then he's chased, tranquilized, and captured by some guys in suits.

At a pharmaceutical company run by Dr. Paul Ruth (Patrick McGoohan), Vale soon learns that he's a scanner — one of two-hundred-some people born with telepathic abilities, thanks to an experimental drug their mothers took during pregnancy. Most of the scanners have a very difficult time dealing with their lives, as hearing the thoughts of normal people becomes too overwhelming to bear. Scanners are divided into two groups: good ones who are trying to live their lives as best they can, and bad ones seeking to use their powers to usurp power from normal people. Vale gets chosen to infiltrate the bad scanners, who are led by Daryl Revok (Michael Ironside), a charismatic type with the power to do fun things like make heads explode (this sequence is the movie's claim to fame, and it's still stunning all these years later). Helping the

254

good scanners is Kim Obrist (Jennifer O'Neill), who offers refuge to scanners and seeks to help them through psychic communication with other scanners. Vale and Revok eventually meet, and let's just say that things get ugly.

Director David Cronenberg gives *Scanners* an interesting setup, but nothing seems to really click. There's a cold, detached feeling to the proceedings, probably because none of the "good" characters are very compelling. A painter who had never acted before, Lack has remarkably spooky eyes, but has zero charisma and his wooden line readings become grating before too long. O'Neill's luminous beauty does the heavy lifting for her, but she's hampered by the screenplay, which never goes into much depth about her role in the scanner war and what her techniques do to help the troubled scanners. McGoohan's performance is odd, conveying intelligence and a mixture of arrogance and regret with his face and voice, yet his body language implies that, in the parlance of our times, he gives zero fucks (perhaps he just wanted filming to be over with). So audience attention, if not its sympathy, goes to Michael Ironside, whose charisma and Jack Nicholson-esque looks let him steal every scene he's in.

Likewise, the story is not compelling. The idea of the scanners and the ways their powers affect them is interesting, as is the origin of the scanners — though they're never mentioned, the specter of Thalidomide-related birth defects hangs over the proceedings and gives the film a queasy resonance, particularly if you're a woman of childbearing age. Yet despite the spectacular demonstration of Revok's powers, we never feel that there's anything at stake in the scanner battle. It comes off as siblings bickering more than anything else.

Saving things are the aforementioned 1970s malaise aesthetic, and some truly remarkable special effects sequences. The one with the head, of course, is what people who haven't even seen the movie remember about it, but there are plenty of other highlights as well. It all culminates in an epic duel between Vale and Revok, and what could have been a sequence of two guys making silly faces at each other becomes a showcase for the twists the body can be put through, and feels very real because of (not in spite of) the practical effects of the day.

It's not what it could have been, but it's certainly worth a watch.

# Seconds

*Give me one more chance*

**Year:** 1966

**Director:** John Frankenheimer

**Screenplay:** Lewis John Carlino, based on the novel by David Ely

**Cast:** Rock Hudson, John Randolph, Salome Jens

Is there a person who doesn't wonder what would happen if they could get a second chance at life, and walk on the road not taken? I doubt it. Those thoughts strike all of us, and the next time they strike you, consider watching *Seconds*.

Banker Arthur Hamilton (John Randolph) lives a life of upper middle-class ennui and quiet desperation. His only child has grown up and married, he and his wife barely communicate and have lost all passion for each other, and he seems to have no life beyond work and his daily commute. Then a friend who is supposedly dead calls Hamilton and tells him about a mysterious company that can give Hamilton a chance at a new life. Hamilton pays the hefty fee and the company fakes his death, then through extensive plastic surgery that includes altering his fingerprints and vocal cords gives him a new appearance. Now played by Rock Hudson, Hamilton has become Antiochus "Tony" Wilson, a painter living in California. At first Tony has trouble settling into his new life, but starts to adjust after he meets a beatnik woman, Nora (Salome Jens), who has also forsaken her old life. But it's not enough.

*Seconds* is a frightening film, but its terrors are not of the jump-cut ooga-booga variety. What makes the film so unsettling is that Arthur Hamilton's life could be any person's life — surface pleasantness with dissatisfaction, frustration, and sadness lurking beneath. Worse, Tony Wilson's life is no better. He's unable to enjoy his new identity, and keeps going back to his old life to find out where he went wrong (something the company that gave him his second chance will not tolerate).

There's a strong feeling of paranoia throughout the film, generated largely by James Wong Howe's remarkable cinematography and Jerry Goldsmith's score. Even in the normal, workaday scenes that open the film we feel that something is not quite right — this off-kilter feeling mirrors Hamilton's own dissatisfaction with his life. The paranoia intensifies as Tony tries to reconcile his new and old identities and finds himself spied on by the company.

Even stronger than the paranoia is the film's sense of loss. Hamilton has lost his chance at happiness both in his old life and in his new one, and in the end, he loses everything. Worst of all, the film implies that Hamilton never really had the chance to be happy at all — a man who's dull and boring in his first life will be dull and boring in his second as well.

None of this would work if not for the performances, which are note-perfect across the board. Randolph and Hudson turn in remarkable work: Randolph's performance is quieter, more understated — in a lengthy scene with no cuts he perfectly describes (while actually saying very little) the drab existence his life has become. Hudson's performance, while more showy with a drunken breakdown and a horrifying scene in which he struggles vainly for his life, is equally good as Randolph's. The actors have a certain facial resemblance (particularly around the eyes) and Hudson studied Randolph's vocal mannerisms and inflections — as a result what could have been a ludicrous premise (a la John Woo's *Face/Off*) is completely believable.

The supporting cast turn in excellent work as well, particularly Salome Jens as Nora, and future Grandpa Walton Will Geer as the seemingly benevolent, possibly mad head of the company. (It's worth noting that he hasn't taken advantage of his own company's services.)

At times the stylistic excesses of the film are a bit much — remarkable as Howe's camerawork is, it does call attention to itself. But those are minor flaws in a remarkable but thoroughly depressing film.

# Intermission: Double Bills

Planning a night in? Why not mix and match some of the movies covered in this book? It's a great way to see how different movie-makers tackle similar themes and stories.

### *Art house in disguise:* Under the Skin and Valhalla Rising
Both films are easily classified in the science fiction or action genres, respectively... and both belong at the local art house as well.

### *Guys, grief, and ghosts:* The Changeling and White Noise 2: The Light
There's nothing like a little bereavement (particularly the kind you get when your family is wiped out before your eyes) to get you in touch with the supernatural.

### *The devil inside:* The Devils and Witchfinder General
These movies, based on historical events, shed light on particularly ugly parts of history and human nature.

### *Worst childhoods ever:* The Reflecting Skin and Tideland
Both have an empty Midwestern setting that's very striking, and some of the most fucked-up childhoods ever shown on a movie screen.

### *Bad flashbacks:* Performance and Zabriskie Point
Some of the most insufferable excesses of the 1960s star in these movies, which prove that yesterday's "groovy" is today's "boring."

### *Women in trouble:* Repulsion and Twin Peaks: Fire Walk With Me
Both feature young blond women with serious issues regarding sexuality. The contrast in how the characters and the films address those issues is interesting.

### *Nature's revenge — Australian style:* The Last Wave and Long Weekend
Nature strikes back in that sublimely creepy way that only comes from Australia. The double bill is also good for a contrast of apocalypses global and personal.

### *Crazy sincerity:* The Room and Miami Connection
Two movies that are batshit crazy, completely sincere, and utterly hilarious.

### Musicals for people who hate musicals: **All That Jazz** and **Pennies From Heaven**

Both are fairly dark and quite meta. Keep *Singin' In The Rain* on hand for a chaser afterward.

### Lives of quiet desperation: **Glengarry Glen Ross** and **Seconds**

Proof that escape from a horrible job or banal life can be very difficult.

### Ripping off The Most Dangerous Game again: **Surviving the Game** and **Turkey Shoot**

Because no one said originality was essential for cinematic pleasure.

### Spy games: **Ronin** and **Tinker, Tailor, Soldier, Spy**

One is full of action, one is slow and meditative, yet they are both excellent takes on the spy movie genre.

### Rock and roll all night: **Pink Floyd: The Wall** and **Yellow Submarine**

The yin and yang of rock and roll movies: one is nightmare fuel, the other is candy-colored fun.

### Short stories: **Creepshow** and **Tales From the Crypt**

Omnibus movies of short horror tales, for when your attention span is lacking.

# The Sentinel

*Motel hell*

**Year:** 1977

**Director:** Michael Winner

**Screenplay:** Michael Winner, based on the novel by Jeffrey Konvitz

**Cast:** Cristina Raines, Chris Sarandon, Burgess Meredith

I'm as bored with the recent wave of horror remakes as anyone, but if there was a film that actually needed to be remade, it's *The Sentinel*. As it stands, the film has an interesting premise but is done in by a screenplay in need of another draft, heavy-handed direction, a weak lead performance, and a denouement that's downright tasteless (and not in a good way).

*The Sentinel* opens in Italy where a bunch of religious leaders wearing very distinctive rings meet and look concerned. Then we're off to New York City where model Allison (Cristina Raines) is nervous about committing to her lawyer boyfriend Michael (Chris Sarandon and his ridiculous mustache). Needing time apart, Allison looks for an affordable apartment, but is interrupted by the death of her father. Allison goes to the funeral and it's soon clear that her relationship with dear departed Dad wasn't all that great — a helpful flashback shows her come home from Catholic school to discover her dad in a naked, cake-eating (?) orgy with two hefty prostitutes, an experience that so shattered young Allison that she immediately ran to the bathroom and cut her wrists. Um, OK.

Anyway, Allison returns to the Big Apple and scores a sweet deal on an apartment. It's fully furnished, is insanely gorgeous, and just never mind that blind priest (John Carradine) who lives in the top-floor apartment and spends all his time staring out the window. Allison gets settled in but is soon plagued by headaches and fainting spells, by creepy noises from upstairs, by annoying neighbor Mr. Chasen (scenery-chewing Burgess Meredith), and by the lesbians downstairs (Sylvia Miles and Beverly D'Angelo) one of whom makes a coffee date **really** awkward by masturbating in front of Allison (it's like a coffee commercial gone horribly wrong: "We've replaced this lesbian's coffee with Folgers crystals. Let's see what happens!"). Sounds like a typical New York apartment to me, but nope, there's supernatural shenanigans afoot!

There is no one single huge problem with *The Sentinel* — lots of little problems kill the film. For a 1970s film it's aged relatively well save for the fashions. What's more annoying is the score, which switches between "Look! Spooky stuff is happening!" and schmaltziness that threatens to turn into a ballad (something with a title like "Don't Look Away From Love") but thankfully never does. The cast is extremely odd, a mix of old, familiar faces (Ava Gardner, Burgess Meredith, Eli Wallach, Jose Ferrer) and young ones (Jeff Goldblum, Christopher Walken, and a blink-and-you'll-miss-him Tom Berenger) — many of whom literally have nothing to do (Walken gets about three lines). The bulk of the acting is left up to Raines and Sarandon, neither of whom have the chops or charisma to make much of their underwritten roles. Raines in particular is weak — she's pretty and screams well but simply isn't compelling as Allison.

Director Michael Winner, best known for the *Death Wish* movies, has an adept way with cheap shocks (i.e., the flashback naked cake orgy). But his direction is heavy-handed at best and lacks visual style and subtlety. Worse, it crosses the line into outright exploitation when a host of damned souls show up, portrayed by people with extreme physical deformities. Yuck.

The screenplay is interesting enough to make me seek out the source novel, but has some plot threads that go nowhere. More frustratingly, there are crucial questions that arise by the movie's end. Is Allison's fate redemption or damnation? What exactly happens if she does not accept her fate? If she's redeemed, where is the transcendence that should accompany this? And what does the real estate agent make of all this?

It's a perfect example of good-premise/bad-execution. Bring on the remake, I say.

# The Serpent and the Rainbow

*The voodoo that you do so well*

**Year:** 1987

**Director:** Wes Craven

**Screenplay:** Richard Maxwell and A. R. Simoun, inspired by the book by Wade Davis

**Cast:** Bill Pullman, Cathy Tyson, Paul Winfield, Zakes Mokae

Wes Craven is — oh, how shall I put this? — an uneven film-maker. He's had the occasional flash of brilliance, some total crap, and everything in between. Yet it seems he's not known for his most interesting films, one of which is the voodoo-horror *The Serpent And The Rainbow*.

The story begins in Haiti in the late 1970s, when a man is declared dead at a local hospital. But when he's buried (without embalming, and I'm not sure if this is plot convenience or just the way things were done in Haiti), as his sister weeps loudly and calls the man's name, we see a tear trickle down his face … and then the grave gets filled in. Not good.

Jump forward seven years, and pharmaceutical researcher Dennis Alan (a young Bill Pullman, skinny and floppy-haired) is visiting a shaman in the Amazon to get some local concoction. The shaman insists that Dennis drink some; he obliges and has a nice little vision sequence in which he learns that his spirit animal is a jaguar. Yes, this will become relevant later on, as will the mysterious, evil-looking guy who appears in the vision.

(Am I the only one who doesn't want to know what their spirit animal is? I'm worried that it would be something really mundane, like a hamster, or just plain goofy, like a frilled lizard.)

Anyway, no sooner is he back from the Amazon then Dennis gets another assignment — he's to go to Haiti and look into reports of a drug that turns people into zombies. Seems the gentleman who was buried in the movie's opening segment has been seen, alive and not-so-well.

Despite Haiti being a less-than-fun place in the last days of the Baby Doc Duvalier regime, Dennis arrives there and meets a smokin' hot lady doctor (Cathy Tyson) who's trying to help the zombie man. She takes him around Haiti and along with a local wheeler-dealer (Paul Winfield, who doesn't have enough screen time) they introduce Dennis to the positive side of voodoo in Haiti. Unfortunately Dennis also runs into Peytraud (Zakes Mokae in a scary, captivating performance) who not only is the head of the local secret police, but a voodoo sorcerer as well. Soon Dennis is in way over his head, both in the regular world and in the supernatural one.

It's far from a perfect film, but *The Serpent and the Rainbow* is both creepy and entertaining. There's a perfect blend of the real (zombies are created with a drug, with the subsequent behavior attributable to physical and mental trauma) and the supernatural (the magical properties of voodoo). The horrors take a little while in coming, but it's all for the best as the movie sets up the scene and the players. Once they do come, Craven uses the blend of real and supernatural to let loose with a number of dream and hallucination scenes. And there's a good old-fashioned interrogation scene that shows almost nothing, but the implications … let's just say the menfolk in particular won't enjoy this part.

The film also makes a nice parallel between the oppressed people of Haiti and the captured souls of those who've been zombified; the use of voodoo never feels exploitative (for a contrast see the same year's Santeria horror film *The Believers* — on second thought, don't see it).

That said, there are certainly flaws. Bill Pullman is his usual likable-but-wooden self, and only really takes charge on screen when he's screaming, being buried alive, or recovering from zombie drugs. His weak voice-over narration doesn't help. Cathy Tyson's beauty makes up for a weak performance, but thankfully we have Paul Winfield and Zakes Mokae on hand. The latter gives an excellent performance, genuinely frightening as a man who will use all his considerable power (both as head of the secret police and as a voodoo sorcerer) to torture and enslave. It's not about material gain; at one point a torture victim asks what he wants: "I want to hear you scream."

It's an entertaining yarn with just the right amount of chills that are well executed, a decent story and even a bit of subtext if that's your cup of tea.

# Seven

*Hate the sinner, hate the sin*

**Year:** 1996

**Director:** David Fincher

**Screenwriter:** Andrew Kevin Walker

**Cast:** Morgan Freeman, Brad Pitt, Gwyneth Paltrow, Kevin Spacey

It's been imitated so much and has been such a major influence on films and TV shows, that it's hard to remember just how shocking *Seven* was when it was in theaters. And it's so well made, on every level, that the films that have succeeded it have never quite emulated it, and it's lost none of its power.

In a hellish, rain-drenched, unnamed city, Detective William Somerset (Morgan Freeman) is taking on yet another murder investigation even though he's mere days from retirement. Much to his chagrin, he's joined at the crime scene by David Mills (Brad Pitt, proving that he can act), a young detective who's slated to be Somerset's replacement. Mills and Somerset don't get along, but they've soon got other things to worry about. A grotesquely fat man is murdered — bound to a chair and forced at gunpoint to eat until his stomach ruptures — and the word "gluttony" is found at the scene. When a lawyer is killed by having to carve a pound of his own flesh away, and the word "greed" is at the scene, Mills and Somerset know they have a special type of killer on their hands.

*Seven* is one of those films I can't watch often because of how well made it is. We know we're not in for a happy time from the opening scene, which introduces us to the horrible city the movie takes place in, and to Somerset and his refusal to let the depravity he sees every day ruin him. Somewhere around the third murder, it becomes clear that this film is not going to have a traditional ending with a climactic showdown in which evil is thwarted. There's a sense of inevitable doom and despair that suffuses the film. Every person in it seems to be trapped, whether it's the victims who were unlucky enough to be chosen by the killer to suffer for humanity's sins, or Somerset trapped by his refusal to give in to complete cynicism, or Mills trapped by the ambition that led him to actually seek out a detective job in this city. And though he sets everything in motion, serial killer John Doe is no less trapped by his poisonous obsessions and agenda.

Many films have attempted to re-create the claustrophobic, filthy setting and atmosphere of *Seven*, with varying success. Still others have attempted to put their own spin on its "creative kills" story. But though Andrew Kevin Walker's screenplay is gruesomely effective, the story is not *Seven*'s strongest point — tales of maniacs who kill people in interesting ways have been around for centuries, and one could argue that at times *Seven* is *The Abominable Doctor Phibes* dressed in grungy procedural drag (not that there's anything wrong with that).

What elevates *Seven* is the uniformly excellent acting. I suspect in some hipster circles it's no longer cool to like Morgan Freeman, but he's wonderful here, his best moment a quiet one when he expresses more with one word (a simple "No") than many actors can in pages of dialogue. Brad Pitt is a revelation to those of us who had written him off as just another pretty face; his Mills is brash and not always the brightest light in the harbor, but he's always sympathetic. Also sympathetic is Gwyneth Paltrow as Mills' wife Tracy, all radiance and fragile hope. And we cannot forget Kevin Spacey as John Doe; he's chillingly creepy, almost preternatural in his soulless serenity (after my initial viewing of *Seven* it was years before I could stop feeling creeped out by Spacey and watch him in other films). Director David Fincher puts it all together with deft artistry, an eye for detail (those air freshener trees!), and surprising restraint — its greatest horrors are in the aftermaths and implications.

It's an ordeal, but a rewarding one.

# Shark Attack 3: Megalodon

*Oh when the shark bites*

**Director:** David Worth

**Screenplay:** Scott Devine and William Hooke

**Cast:** John Barrowman, Jenny McShane

I'm a huge fan of the movie *Jaws*, so I find it rather endearing that nearly three decades after its release people are still ripping it off. It's also amusing that the more special effects technologies have evolved, the worse the ripoffs look and the better the original film looks.

*Shark Attack 3: Megalodon* opens with an underwater crew fixing a communications cable. Faster than you can say "Purina Shark Chow" the crew meet a grisly end. Then it's off to "Mexico" (the movie's credits are full of Bulgarian names so if this was really filmed in Mexico I'll eat my hat) where the local beach resort just happens to be nearby one of those communication cables. Resort employee Ben (future *Doctor Who* and *Torchwood* star John Barrowman, looking slightly embarrassed) finds a big shark's tooth embedded in the cable. Shortly thereafter, beachgoers start getting munched by a 15-foot shark.

I know, I was disappointed at first. Because thanks to my kid's *Walking With Dinosaurs* videos, I know that a megalodon was a prehistoric shark with a 10-foot-wide mouth. A 15-foot shark just isn't going to cut it, even if it does eat a parasailor. But not to worry! See, that 15-foot shark was just a baby. Mama shows up, courtesy of some really bad CGI, and then the fun really begins.

*Shark Attack 3: Megalodon* isn't a good movie by any stretch of the imagination. The characters are clichéd, the acting is bad, the story is stupid, and the special effects are laughable. And I giggled my way through the whole thing. It's clear no one involved had any pretensions toward doing anything but doing a *Jaws* ripoff with a **really big** shark. One that eats jet-skiers and speedboats whole. There's your whole reason for watching it, right there. (Well, that and some hilariously off-color ad-libbing from Barrowman.)

# Shoot 'Em Up

*Click bang what a hang*

**Year:** 2007

**Director:** Michael Davis

**Screenplay:** Michael Davis

**Cast:** Clive Owen, Paul Giamatti, Monica Bellucci

*Shoot 'Em Up* is the best cartoon I've seen in years.

I don't mean "cartoon" as in "animated movie." *Shoot 'Em Up* is a live-action movie that takes all the absurdity, violence, and humor of the old-school Warner Brothers cartoons to the logical extreme and then some.

We meet our hero (Clive Owen, pure badass charisma), Mr. Smith, in extreme close-up. It's a perfect Sergio Leone moment … until Smith starts noisily eating a carrot. As Smith sits at a bus stop, a heavily pregnant woman, obviously in the throes of labor and clearly terrified, goes by, followed closely by a skanky hit man. Before the hit man can kill the woman, Smith kills the hit man, then helps the woman deliver the baby. More hit men arrive, led by Mr. Hertz (a delightfully hideous Paul Giamatti), and soon the mother is dead and Smith has charge of the baby. When Smith's conscience and Hertz's pursuit make abandoning the baby an unviable option, Smith enlists the help of a lactating prostitute (Monica Bellucci lends some nice va-voom to the shenanigans) to act as caretaker and wet nurse while he tries to find out why a huge parade of hit men want the baby dead.

It can be difficult as hell to mix comedy with genres such as action or horror. For every *Slither* or *Return of the Living Dead* there are a dozen or more miserable failures. *Shoot 'Em Up* nearly always finds the right balance (such as the aforementioned opening shot), and doesn't wear out its running jokes (Owen's carrot-munching, Giamatti being pestered by his wife via cell phone). Writer/director Michael Davis keeps things moving right along, always tossing in just enough story to keep things rolling — the plot maneuvers won't stand up to intense scrutiny, but like Quentin Tarantino's movies, *Shoot 'Em Up* lives in its own little cartoon world and plays by its own rules. It's a world where death-by-carrot can and does happen.

The cartoon comparison is apt, for the movie is essentially Bugs Bunny vs. Elmer Fudd. The references are obvious (Owen says, "What's up, doc?" at one point, Giamatti calls him a "wascally wabbit") and subtle (Giamatti's cell phone ringtone is "Ride of the Valkyries," familiar to many as the "kill the wabbit" song). Owen and Giamatti's dialogue exchanges often have a "duck season/rabbit season" feel to them. All that's missing is a scene in which Giamatti has his face blackened by a shotgun backfire and for Owen to dress in drag.

Nearly everything works as it should. Mr. Smith is essentially a redux of Owen's role from *Sin City*, but he's great so who cares. Giamatti is obviously having the time of his life as a clever but utterly nasty man — his intelligence makes his character a formidable foe, and his unremarkable appearance is the film's most realistic touch (real-life hit men — the successful ones, at least — blend into the woodwork). Bellucci doesn't have much acting to do, but she's lovely to look at and provides the closest thing the movie has to a moral character. My only complaint is that some of the action is filmed too closely, so it's difficult to tell sometimes exactly what's going on. You get the general idea though ("mayhem ensues").

Those looking for logic, adherence to the laws of the physics, warm 'n' fuzzy characters, and good taste should go see a different movie. But for those who want a damn good time with lots of guns, explosions, and humor, *Shoot 'Em Up* will satisfy and then some.

# Sideways

*Spill the wine, take that girl*

**Year:** 2004

**Director:** Alexander Payne

**Screenplay:** Jim Taylor and Alexander Payne, based on the novel by Rex Pickett

**Cast:** Paul Giamatti, Thomas Haden Church, Virginia Madsen, Sandra Oh

I've never much cared for chick flicks, but I'm often drawn to stories that show the friendships between men. Movies that intelligently portray such relationships aren't as common as one would hope for — too often they're exercises in juvenile excess, or depicting a romantic triangle, or putting the context into an action/adventure story. But for those who want to see a realistic story about the friendship of two ordinary guys — warts-and-all — you could do far worse than to watch *Sideways*.

Miles (a wonderful Paul Giamatti) is a schlumpy English teacher, whose novel is one publisher's rejection away from complete failure. He still hasn't been able get over his ex-wife, let alone move on into another relationship. The one thing Miles seems to enjoy in life is wine. He also enjoys, though to a much lesser degree than he realizes, the company of his friend Jack (Thomas Haden Church). Jack's a past-his-prime TV actor who never made it big, and is now engaged to a girl from a well-to-do family. *Sideways* follows Miles and Jack as they road-trip up to California's central coast wine country to end Jack's bachelor days in style, with wine tasting and golf. But things will get complicated as the boys meet up with Maya (luminously beautiful Virginia Madsen), who loves wine and possibly Miles as well, and Stephanie (Sandra Oh) a sexy, spirited wine-pourer who makes Jack reconsider the marriage he's supposed to commit to.

As a writer, one of the things I appreciate most about good characterization is that it allows people to have flaws. And all four of the main characters in this movie are flawed: Miles and Jack both spend much of the movie telling lies; Miles is probably an alcoholic, and definitely neurotic; Jack uses sexual conquests to bolster his ego now that his career is on the wane; Stephanie foists care of her young daughter onto her mother; and even Maya can be seen as flawed, for though her attraction to Miles is genuine, there seems to be a bit of "settling" involved, and more than a bit of re-routed maternal instincts.

But none of that matters, because these characters are so recognizably real. Even if you don't directly identify with the characters, you know people like them. And despite the mood of quiet melancholy that suffuses much of the film, it's an optimistic movie at its heart — at the end we feel that those who deserve a chance to have things work out for them will get it. Kudos go not just to the screenplay and direction but to the actors, whose chemistry is completely believable. We never doubt that Miles and Jack are old friends, even as we see the friendship becoming strained not just by the events of the road trip but because of their differing personalities and approaches to life. We see the friendship between Maya and Stephanie as well, and the ways that it parallels the relationship between Miles and Jack (Maya disapproves of Stephanie's care of her daughter much in the way Miles disapproves of Jack's womanizing). These well-depicted relationships extend beyond the central quartet, as Miles' brief scene with his mother hints at years of family dysfunction, or as Jack's fiancée rolls her eyes at him and we know their marriage won't last long.

It's a lovely film in terms of its look and its storytelling. Director Alexander Payne takes us all through the central California coastal wine area, with sun-washed vineyards and foggy beaches. There's a sensuousness to the film as it lingers on glasses full of wine. Yet it's a very funny film as well, thanks largely to Giamatti's dry wit and Haden Church's frat-boy enthusiasm.

I don't often watch DVD commentaries, as I just don't have the time, but highly, **highly** recommend the *Sideways* commentary: Giamatti and Haden Church are an absolute delight through the whole thing, offering insightful and often hilarious comments on the making of the movie and on the characterizations. It's one of those rare commentaries you'll want to watch as often as you watch the movie itself.

# The Sign of the Cross

*That old-time religion*

**Year:** 1932

**Director:** Cecil B. DeMille

**Screenplay:** Waldemar Young and Sidney Buchman, based on the play by Wilson Barrett

**Cast:** Frederic March, Elissa Landi, Charles Laughton, Claudette Colbert

Dressing up scandalous fare in sanctimonious attire is a tradition that's probably as old as entertainment itself. And if you'd like a nifty example of this practice, then treat yourself to Cecil B. DeMille's epic *The Sign of the Cross*.

Rome is on fire, and Emperor Nero (Charles Laughton, looking suitably debauched) is watching the flames and playing the lyre. That is, until he learns that the populace is holding him responsible for the blaze. Nero decides to blame the Christians, and puts out a large reward for anyone who turns a Christian over to the authorities. As the Christians try to practice their faith without getting caught, young Christian Mercia (Elissa Landi) catches the eye of Prefect Marcus (Frederic March) who is yearned after by Nero's seductive wife Poppea (Claudette Colbert).

Up to the two-third mark, *The Sign of the Cross* is decent melodrama as Marcus fends off the vampy Poppea while trying to woo Mercia, who's torn between love for Marcus and devotion to her religion. It's in the last third that the movie goes into overdrive and also sheds all pretense as to the kind of movie DeMille really wanted to make.

The appetizer is a scene at Marcus' home when, annoyed because Mercia won't drop all that silly religious nonsense and hop into bed with him, he asks his good friend Ancaria, the most "talented" woman in Rome (if you know what I mean), to seduce Mercia with her song and dance about the naked moon. That's enough to raise eyebrows, but when the film really goes nuts is with its Coliseum scene, which is a cavalcade of wackiness that includes a battle between dwarfs in blackface and "Amazon" women, decapitation, lions and tigers noshing on Christians, gladiator fights, and, most notoriously, ladies who are naked save for strategically placed garlands of flowers, tied down and menaced by packs of crocodiles or by a gorilla. Most of the weird shit happens off screen, of course, but the whole sequence is still plenty messed up. Adding to the fun are the reaction shots of the spectators, which vary from appalled to enthusiastic to unsettlingly bored. It all ends tied up in a nice religious bow with most of the Christians more or less willingly accepting their martyrdom, and with Marcus's eleventh-hour and wholly unconvincing conversion to Christianity.

It's all impossible to take seriously, but plenty of fun. DeMille wisely throws in just enough decadence into the film's first two-thirds to keep things going, whether it's Nero camping it up or Poppea lolling around decadently and bathing in milk. It helps that Laughton and Colbert are clearly having a grand time. Less fortunate are March and Landi as the star-crossed couple. Landi comes off surprisingly well, though she always looks as if she jumped straight from a Busby Berkeley film into this one. March has the most thankless role, as his Marcus seems to be more in love with the idea of Mercia than the actual woman, which makes his conversion and willingness to be sacrificed along with her a matter of the screenwriters' convenience rather than something that's actually in character.

But in the end, none of that matters, because after the movie's over you won't be thinking about Marcus and Mercia and Christianity, but what that gorilla was going to do to that naked lady.

# The Silent Scream

*A quiet kind of murder*

**Year:** 1980

**Director:** Denny Harris

**Screenplay:** Ken Wheat, Jim Wheat, and Wallace C. Bennett

**Cast:** Barbara Steele, Rebecca Balding, Steve Doubet

For a horror fan, I'm actually fairly unschooled in the slasher film subgenre. The problem is that during the subgenre's late 70s/early 80s heyday, I was too young to see the films by myself and my folks weren't about to take me (heck, even now my mom won't read my reviews because horror movies aren't her cup of tea).

*The Silent Scream* is one of those movies I missed, though I vividly recall the TV ads. It took me 30 years but I've finally seen it, and while it's not a great film it's a fairly nifty slasher that puts a spin on some of the subgenre's clichés.

School's about to start at a California college, and students Scotty (Rebecca Balding), Jack (Steve Doubet), Doris (Juli Andelman) and Douchebag (not really the character's name, but you'll be calling him that too, trust me) are left out in the cold thanks to a housing shortage. They all end up at one of those creepy-yet-beautiful Victorian homes, which is owned by reclusive Mrs. Engels (Yvonne DeCarlo) and her nerdy son Mason. Despite Mrs. Engel's proclivity for mysterious silence and staring, and Mason's predilection to spy on the guests and watch movies with rape scenes on his TV, things are going well for the four students until one ends up stabbed to death on the nearby beach.

There's no motive, suspect, or evidence, as local detectives (played by Cameron Mitchell and, in a nice dramatic turn, comic actor Avery Schreiber) admit. But over the next 24 hours things will get ugly for the remaining three students and some ghosts from the Engels' family's past will make their presence known.

*The Silent Scream* isn't notable for its number of kills (low) or their explicitness (tame by today's standards). It stands out from cliché'd slasher fare in more subtle ways. The students don't have a great deal of characterization but they're believable and (with the exception of Douchebag) likable; they're also not dumb as posts. (The screenplay wisely takes the first killing outside the house and then has events happen quickly, so that the characters have a reason besides plot convenience to stay in the house.) The coastal California setting is a nice change from the typical Centerville, USA locale. The stalkings are suspenseful and the attacks are sudden — indeed the victims don't have time to scream. And it's refreshing to see characters not get punished for having a healthy sex life.

The most captivating thing about *The Silent Scream*, though, is the presence of 1960s horror icon Barbara Steele. As a mysterious member of the Engels family, she says not a word yet commands the screen every time she's on it. She's a hypnotic presence, taking a fairly routine film a notch higher.

The film has flaws, to be sure, but those are mostly outweighed by the positive assets. For example, aside from an ill-advised credits sequence that had me hopelessly confused for a while, the scenes with the detectives are story filler that is nonetheless enhanced by Mitchell and Schreiber, who have a genuine chemistry in their performances.

It's a better-than-average film that's handicapped by the conventions of the subgenre, but has enough good qualities to make it worth a watch.

# Silver Bullet

*The guy gets wolf-ier*

**Year:** 1985

**Director:** Daniel Attias

**Screenplay:** Stephen King, from his *Cycle of the Werewolf* novella

**Cast:** Gary Busey, Everett McGill, Corey Haim, Megan Follows

*Silver Bullet* is far from the best Stephen King adaptation, and it's certainly not one of the more well-known ones, but it captures the feel of King's work in a way that few other adaptations have done. This would seem to be a given, as the screenplay was written by King from his *Cycle of the Werewolf* novella, but compare *Silver Bullet* to the disastrous *Maximum Overdrive*, and you'll see that just because King's adapting his own work doesn't mean it will be worth a watch.

The narrator is a grown-up Jane Coslaw (Megan Follows), telling us of dark times in the small town of her girlhood. A beast is terrorizing the town of Tarker's Mills, and while the first death is written off as a freak accident, soon it becomes obvious that someone or something sinister is out for blood. Jane's younger brother Marty (Corey Haim), who's confined to a wheelchair, uncovers the truth — that the killer is a werewolf, and that the killings are getting more brutal because as the moon gets more full, "the guy gets wolf-ier."

271

It's lines like that, along with the small-town atmosphere and the Coslaw family dynamic (equal parts affection and dysfunction) that give *Silver Bullet* such a King feel. The story could definitely be stronger, but there is plenty of entertainment to be found along the way. It's always fun to watch small towns implode when their "everything's fine" facades are ripped away. The relationship between Jane and Marty is well done, particularly with showing Jane's love for and resentment of her handicapped brother. Stealing every scene is Gary Busey as the kids' alcoholic uncle, who does responsible things like giving a little kid a mini-car/wheelchair that can reach speeds of 60 miles per hour.

Aside from a nicely suspenseful scene when Jane goes door-to-door through her neighborhood, hoping to identify the person who's the werewolf, *Silver Bullet* is not remotely scary. In fact, its "scary" scenes are the least effective moments in the film, thanks to poor staging and direction, and some truly dire werewolf effects. If I hadn't read IMDB and seen that Rick Baker and Rob Bottin were involved (though seemingly in minor capacities) I wouldn't have believed it. The scenes are **that** bad.

King once self-deprecatingly described his work as the literary equivalent of a Big Mac, and while he is often much better than that (and sometimes far worse), that perfectly describes *Silver Bullet*. It's a silly B movie that's entertaining as heck, and like a Big Mac, if you're in the right mood for it, it will satisfy.

# Slither

*Meteor shit*

**Year:** 2006

**Director:** James Gunn

**Screenplay:** James Gunn

**Cast:** Nathan Fillion, Elizabeth Banks, Michael Rooker, Gregg Henry

I always love it when previously obscure film-makers hit the big time, and their early films get rediscovered. One of my favorite pop culture moments is when Peter Jackson accepted the Oscar for *The Lord of the Rings: The Return of the King* and gave a shout-out to his early, gory efforts *Bad Taste* and *Meet the Feebles*. I'm hoping something similar happens now with James Gunn, who's now famous for directing *Guardians of the Galaxy*, but whose early effort *Slither* deserves some long-overdue love.

A meteor crashes in the woods outside the small town of Wheelsy, a place so boring that cops kill time by using their radar guns on birds, and where the biggest social event is a party to kick off the start of deer hunting season. The meteor is discovered by local rich guy Grant Grant (played by Michael Rooker, and no, the character's name is not a typo). Grant's on his way back from the bar, where he's taken refuge after being rebuffed in bed by his schoolteacher wife Starla (Elizabeth Banks). Grant makes the supremely unwise decision of poking a gooey mass that came out of the meteor (seriously, dude — if there's one thing that B movies have taught us, it's that no good comes from poking at a meteor or anything that comes out of a meteor), and something nasty and sharp shoots out of the goo and implants itself in Grant.

Soon Grant is stocking up on meat, sprouting weird phallus/tentacle things from his midsection, and generally not looking at all well. Soon the town is overrun with slug creatures and townspeople who've been turned into zombies by the slug creatures, and it's up to local lawman Bill Pardy (Nathan Fillion) to try to save the day.

The line between horror and humor is a difficult one to walk, but *Slither* manages it with aplomb. On the horror side we have some impressively gory and slimy effects, and a willingness to off characters who are usually spared (such as pets and kids). On the humor side we have the great comic chemistry between all the players, with MVP award going to Gregg Henry as the wonderfully profane mayor, a man who can't say a sentence without swearing or being crass, and whose self-centered tirade about being denied a Mr. Pibb in the midst of zombie/slug chaos is worth the price of a rental.

Henry steals every scene with his dialogue, but the other actors all bring the fun. Rooker's Grant Grant is a nice change for those of us who still think of him as the lead from *Henry: Portrait of a Serial Killer*. Grant's not a bad guy, just a bit insecure in his marriage and possessive of his wife, and even when he's been taken over by an alien he tries to be a good husband to Starla. Banks takes what could have been a typical damsel-in-distress role and puts real fire into Starla, portraying her as someone who's realistic about the situation yet still cares about her husband no matter how monstrous he's become. Fillion makes Bill Pardy one of his more memorable if understated characters, portraying Pardy as a genuinely nice guy — the sort of fellow who, when talking to a woman who's so full of slug parasites she's the size of a bus, takes off his hat because that's what you do when you talk to a lady. It's also refreshing that Pardy is neither incompetent nor super-competent; he gets things done but also drops things at crucial moments, has trouble unlocking his car in a crisis situation, and gets beat up by a zombie deer (don't ask).

It's not perfect. Some of the effects (the aforementioned zombie deer) don't work, and the "impregnation" scene when Grant uses his phallus/tentacle things to fill a woman with slugs has a queasy rape vibe. Fortunately, the movie has enough thrills and laughs (as well as fun references for horror fans) to more than make up for the shortcomings. Watch it next time you can't decide if you'd rather be scared or have a laugh.

# Slugs

***Bring the salt***

**Year:** 1988

**Director:** Juan Piquer Simon

**Screenplay:** Jose Escriva, Ron Gantman, and Juan Piquer Simon, based on the novel by Shaun Hutson

**Cast:** Michael Garfield, Kim Terry, Philip MacHale, Santiago Alvarez

With so many animals out there in the world, many of which have the capability to mess you up big time if they really wanted to, you have to wonder just what possessed the makers of *Slugs* to choose, well, slugs as the star of their nature-strikes-back movie. Sure, they're kind of icky, but if you can't outrun a slug frankly I think you deserve to get oozed upon or whatever a slug can actually do to you.

Thank goodness for artistic license! Because the slugs in *Slugs* (or *Slugs: The Movie* as the opening credits helpfully point out, no doubt to distinguish it from *Slugs! The Musical* or *Slugs on Normandy Beach: The Untold Story of D-Day*) don't just ooch slowly along and nibble holes in your lettuce. No, they can do much, much more.

Our first glimpse into the heretofore unknown capabilities of slugs comes in the opening scene, when a young man out fishing is pulled under the water and then messily devoured by something we don't see (presumably because even in a film as ridiculous as this one, a slug capable of such a feat would be pushing it). We then segue into the opening credits, where we learn that this movie is based on a book. I for one was relieved to see this, as I'd hate to think I'd spent my Friday night indulging in art that was without literary merit.

Director Juan Piquer Simon wastes no time in giving the audience what it's looking for: slug attacks, followed by the usual clichés of a nature-run-amok movie. These include but are not limited to: a local authority figure, in this case a health inspector who figures out what's going but is thwarted by local politicians; outside interests who must remain ignorant of the menace for the town's economic well-being; a scientist who knows a lot about the marauding beastie; a local guy who dies in what's supposed to be heroic self-sacrifice but comes off as a clumsy fuck-up; and a climactic showdown followed by one of those "The end! Or is it?" endings.

What makes *Slugs* special as far as nature-goes-bananas movies goes are the little details. Exteriors at least were shot in New York, but the cast has a lot of Spanish names in it and the portrayals of small-town American life are a bit off-kilter, to say the least. This may account for the clunky dialogue and wooden sound, as if everyone had their script run through BabelFish and then all the actors dubbed. This is particularly distracting with the scientist character, who looks like the love child of Pee-Wee Herman and Dario Argento, and speaks with an Austin Powers accent. There's a surprising amount of sex in the film as well, including a scene with two naked lovers becoming Slug Chow. The soundtrack is weirdly inappropriate, ranging from what sounds like an out-take from a TV cop show to the "Love American Style" music over the final scene. But perhaps one of the oddest things about the film is that with one exception there isn't a single likable character, nor has there been any attempt to make the characters likable — everyone is mean, selfish, or drunk, in particular the sheriff who's an asshole to everyone for no reason I can fathom. The one remotely likable character, the sanitation expert, is undermined by the actor's distracting resemblance to President Clinton, and by the fact that the actress who's cast as his wife seems to be a good fifteen years older than him, making for some really uncomfortable Oedipal moments.

*Slugs* also doesn't stint on the slugs, and the sheer volume of them does give the film an ooky feel. It doesn't stint on the gore either, as we see numerous examples of people half-devoured by slugs, not to mention the spectacularly messy demise of one unlucky bastard who ate part of a slug in his salad (don't ask). None of this makes the movie good per se, but it does add up to an entertaining time.

The movie is also very educational. Among the things I learned from watching *Slugs:*

- The ideal ladies' apparel for a fishing trip is a pink t-shirt and bikini panties.
- It's perfectly OK to call your English teacher "The Wicked Bitch of the North" — in fact, she likes to be called that.
- If you are hiding from a guy who's trying to rape you, the slug-infested sewer may not be your best choice of refuge.
- People can easily outrun electricity.
- Cheap, plentiful, and easily accessible weapons against slugs, such as salt, should be brought up once and never mentioned again.
- If a slug is biting your hand, the sensible thing to do is hack your hand off with a hatchet.
- Spilling common gardening chemicals will cause your greenhouse to blow up.
- Massive numbers of slugs can magically appear, and then disappear once they're done noshing on you.
- If local bigwigs need to know about the slug menace, for heaven's sake don't be reasonable or bring along any proof. Try barging into offices, yelling a lot, and then yelling louder. Then stomp out in a huff when no one believes you.
- If slugs can't find any humans to eat, they'll settle for hamsters.
- If your solution to the slug menace ends up exploding half the town, it's OK, no one will mind.
- If a slug ends up chopped up in your salad, tell everyone it's an anchovy.

It's 90 minutes of gross, somewhat sleazy fun and rampant clichés. Really, how can you go wrong?

## Snakes on a Plane

*Truth in advertising*

**Year:** 2006

**Director:** David R. Ellis

**Screenplay:** John Heffernan and Sebastian Gutierrez

**Cast:** Samuel L. Jackson, King Cobra, Black Mamba, Diamondback Rattlesnake, a bunch of other motherfucking snakes

Subtle as an icepick in the forehead, *Snakes on a Plane* should serve for generations as an example of truth in advertising. There are snakes. A lot of them. On a plane.

Oh, first there's some pesky plot to get through. In beautiful Hawaii, a local surfer dude (Nathan Phillips) witnesses the murder of a Los Angeles prosecutor by a badass criminal Eddie Kim (Byron Lawson, channeling Bruce Lee). Surfer Dude has to fly from Hawaii to L.A. so he can testify, and making sure he gets there safely is FBI agent Neville Flynn (Samuel L. Jackson, absolutely wonderful). Eddie, apparently never one to take the easy route, decides to whack Surfer Dude via a bunch of poisonous snakes on the plane.

Further complicating matters, the snakes have been made extra cranky with a pheromone circulating in the plane's air. So instead of lying around snoozing as snakes usually do (trust me, I once had a snake as a pet and they're not the liveliest critters), these snakes are all set and ready for action, biting anything and anyone they can find, and showing a remarkable affinity for peoples' more vulnerable bits.

*Snakes on a Plane* is perhaps the perfect B movie. Just enough plot for the movie not to be incoherent, not enough to slow things down. The actors all find the right note: aware that they're in a completely absurd movie, yet never winking to the camera or descending into camp. Jackson is perfect — aside from his now famous line, he plays the role straight, and is always calm, capable, charismatic, and a badass when he needs to be. He's a guy you want on your side. The effects are fun — most of the snakes are obvious CGI (hint: if a snake is just calmly slithering about, it's real; if it's hissing, growling, or leaping wildly, it's CGI) but that didn't keep the audience I saw it with from screaming, jumping, and hiding their eyes. (I'm not afraid of snakes and kept remarking, "Why are you screaming? That's a king snake! They eat mice!" For my money, the nastiest business was the bit with the high heeled shoe — ouch.)

I was delighted that the movie did not wimp out and gave us lots of gory and wince-inducing snake attacks, not to mention some cheap-thrill nudity. No half measures here.

A disaster movie isn't about a big budget or convincing special effects. It's about hitting the right tone, and parading just the right number of clichés. The instant we see the *Snakes on a Plane* passengers, we know that most of them will be Snake Chow. We have the ready-to-retire flight attendant going for one last flight, the couple on their honeymoon, the young kids flying alone for the first time, the preening celebrity, the asshole businessman, and so on. All we were missing was the young girl flying to L.A. for a kidney transplant.

I suspect it's a movie like *Rocky Horror* or *Heavy Metal*, that doesn't hold up well in a home viewing environment. See it with a crowd. You won't even have to be intoxicated to have a good time. Honest.

# Something Wicked This Way Comes

*Dark carnival*

**Year:** 1983

**Director:** Jack Clayton

**Screenplay:** Ray Bradbury, based on his novel

**Cast:** Jason Robards, Jonathan Pryce, Pam Grier

It's a tricky business, adapting a book into a movie. And trickier still with a writer like Ray Bradbury, whose strengths — atmosphere, language, description — don't always translate smoothly from the printed page to the silver screen. The adaptation of Bradbury's novel *Something Wicked This Way Comes* is intriguing because much of what shouldn't work in the movie does — but there are enough flaws to make the film an interesting failure.

Though I'm a fan of Bradbury's, *Something Wicked...* is not my favorite work of his. Bradbury's a far better short story writer than a novelist — a sprinter rather than a marathon runner — and in *Something Wicked* his ornate descriptions and atmospheric ramblings often get in the way of the story proper. Still, Bradbury's screenplay gets to the core of the story — what price people will pay for the things they want most.

The story opens in Green Town, Illinois, a quiet rural town. It's a peaceful place where visitors seldom come, especially in the fall. But this October a carnival comes to town. Dark's Pandemonium Carnival captures the interest of young Will Halloway (Vidal Peterson); his father Charles (Jason Robards), the town librarian; Will's best friend Jim Nightshade (Shawn Carson); and many of the townsfolk. Mr. Dark himself (Jonathan Pryce) is a suave and sinister figure first glimpsed casting leaflets advertising the carnival into the blustery air of the town's main street.

Will and Jim already know something is strange about this carnival. They sneaked out of bed when they heard its train arriving, only to find the carnival itself set up in a matter of seconds. The carnival in daylight is even more sinister: all the rides and attractions seem to be run by one man, Mr. Cooger. There's the mirror maze that casts a powerful spell on those who enter it. And there's a mysterious woman (Pam Grier) linked to the disappearances of people who've been to the carnival. Will and Jim soon find themselves pursued by the carnival folk, and enlist the help of Will's father.

*Something Wicked...* is at its most chilling in its depiction of those who are tempted by what the carnival offers. The carnival gives people their dearest wish, but the price paid for that wish is very high. What's more, these are wishes that any of us would have — for love, sex, money, beauty, youth, second chances. It brings the horror close to home.

While the concept is realized very well, the execution often falters. The special effects of the time were limited, but what is truly annoying is Disney's insistence on jazzing things up unnecessarily. People don't simply walk into the mirror maze — their entrance is accompanied by a gaudy flash of light. Ooh! Shiny! Likewise, a scene involving lots of tarantulas adds nothing to the story and was clearly inserted at a later date (the child actors are older in this scene than in the rest of the film) to add some ooga-booga.

Also problematical is the setting. While there's a lovely October feel to the surroundings, the town's main street always looks like a soundstage, not like a place where real people live.

Probably the most crucial flaw is in the casting. What works does so very well — so well that it makes what doesn't work that much more obvious. The children who play Will and Jim aren't terrible actors, but they seem to be in a vacuum — never interacting with the adult actors even when they share the scene. Worse, they have no chemistry with each other. If the narrator didn't tell us they were best friends — indeed, blood brothers — we'd never know it. (Plus Peterson has a distracting resemblance to the kid from *A Christmas Story* — I half expected him to ask for a Red Ryder BB gun with a compass in the stock and this thing which tells time.)

Pam Grier isn't charismatic enough for her role as the Dust Witch/Most Beautiful Woman in the World, but she does a good job and the casting is sufficiently intriguing for me not to dock points.

The film's saving graces are Jason Robards and Jonathan Pryce. Robards gives a wonderful portrayal of a man who's feeling the weight of years and the accompanying regrets, along with doubts about his worth as a father. Pryce is magnificent, seductive and frightening at the same time. One of Bradbury's greatest idiosyncrasies is that his characters do not speak English — they speak Bradbury. In the film's best scene, set in the library, Robards and Pryce have a standoff that lets them find the rhythms of Bradbury's language and turn what could have been a dull scene into something magnificent. It's worth the price of a rental to hear Pryce say:

"We are the Autumn People. Your torments call us like dogs in the night. And we do feed, and feed well. To stuff ourselves on other people's torments. And butter our plain bread with delicious pain ... Funerals, marriages, lost loves, lonely beds — that is our diet. We suck that misery and find it sweet."

Unfortunately this scene is so powerful that everything following it smacks of anticlimax.

Reservations aside, I recommend the film to Bradbury fans — while far from perfect, it's an interesting translation of the book.

# Somewhere in Time

*O call back yesterday*

**Year:** 1980

**Director:** Jeannot Szwarc

**Screenplay:** Richard Matheson, based on his novel *Bid Time Return*

**Cast:** Christopher Reeve, Jane Seymour, Christopher Plummer

This may come as a surprise to some of you, but I do have a fairly strong sentimental streak. Under the right circumstances, I'm all for a story of true love, soul mates, and passion that can't be constrained by pesky things like time or mortality.

It's 1972, and young playwright Richard Collier (Christopher Reeve) is at a party with his friends, celebrating his play's debut. In the midst of the celebrations an elegant old woman comes up to Collier, gives him a gold pocket watch, and says, "Come back to me." She departs without further explanation, leaving a puzzled Collier behind.

Some years later, Collier is a success with many produced plays, but is unhappy. On a whim he drives to Mackinac Island and decides to stay a night in its gorgeous Grand Hotel. While idling through the hotel's room of historical artifacts, he sees a photograph of a beautiful woman (Jane

Seymour), and is instantly in love. It turns out the photo was taken in 1912, the woman was an actress, Elise McKenna — the very woman who gave him the watch the night of his first play's debut (and who died that same night).

Collier gathers all the information he can find about Elise, but it's not enough. He consults with a professor from his university days who has theories about self-hypnosis as a means to time travel. Collier throws all his efforts into this, and finds himself in 1912, and ready to woo Elise. But her control-freak manager (Christopher Plummer) has other ideas...

*Somewhere in Time* is unabashedly sentimental, and not the slightest bit realistic. And that's perfectly fine. There is a fairy-tale quality to the film that lets us take in stride things like the sheer implausibility of time travel (let alone the method of time travel), and the instant and enduring love of Richard and Elise, who spend barely 24 hours together before knowing they are soul mates for eternity. A good deal of the film's success can be attributed to the casting of Reeve and Seymour, who have chemistry even when one of them is only represented by a photograph. It helps greatly that both actors were, at the time, arguably two of the most beautiful human beings on the planet, so it seems not just right but inevitable that they should be together. Reeve, always an underrated actor, is particularly strong throughout, from his initial fixation with the photograph, to his Clark Kent-esque bumbling as he maneuvers to meet Elise, and finally his crushing grief when things go awry. Seymour gets less to do, but is particularly endearing in her scenes when she realizes she's in love for the first (and only) time in her life.

Director Jeannot Szwarc lays on the idyllic atmosphere a little too heavily in the 1912 scenes, but overall does a good job with the story. If there's a weak link it's the screenplay, which is odd as it was adapted by Richard Matheson from his own novel. The screenplay gives us very little information about its two principal characters; in fact, we learn more about Elise's manager than we do about Richard or Elise. It's thanks mostly to the charisma of and chemistry between Reeve and Seymour (aided by the swooning orchestral theme by John Barry) that the film succeeds.

It's no masterpiece, but its appeal is undeniable, especially if you have a sentimental streak. If you can make it to the end credits without getting misty-eyed, you're made of sterner stuff than I am.

# Sorcerer

*The nitro on the truck goes boom boom boom!*

**Year:** 1977

**Director:** William Friedkin

**Screenplay:** Walon Green, based on the novel by Georges Arnaud

**Cast:** Roy Scheider, Bruno Cremer, Amidou, Francisco Rabal

In a remote part of South America, an oil rig has recently been blown up by political dissidents, causing a fire that burns unceasingly. It's cost several workers their lives and is costing an American oil company a great deal of money. The only way to stop the fire is to dynamite the source, and the only dynamite available is (a) so old and poorly maintained that it is leaking nitroglycerine and (b) 200-plus miles away over inhospitable terrain. Someone needs to drive it all that way — who would be desperate or crazy enough to take on such a job?

Someone's always desperate enough. In fact, we have four someones. Four men who've fled to this part of the world to escape their pasts, only to find the present unendurable. Scanlon (Roy Scheider) is wanted by the mob after a church robbery he was part of goes awry. Manzon (Bruno Cremer) is a Parisian banker fleeing the collapse of his business. Nilo (Francisco Rabal) is an enigmatic hit man, presumably on the run after his latest mission. And Kassem (Amidou) is a PLO bomber trying to escape Israeli intelligence. These four men are willing to transport a very dangerous cargo over mountain roads, jungle swamps, and the world's most rickety bridge.

William Friedkin's remake of H. G. Clouzot's *The Wages of Fear* is a nail-biting bit of work. It's also the rare film that demands a functioning brain on the part of its audience. It begins with a lengthy prologue that shows how the four men came to the godforsaken corner of the world, and does so without a lot of help for the audience. We're shown, but not told, and Friedkin takes a big gamble by having the most accessible backstory (Scanlon's is the only one set in America and not subtitled) come last. We then get a glimpse of life in South America, and it's a place of squalor and desperation, heat and filth. Small wonder these men take on what's essentially a suicide mission.

The drive to the oil rig is one of the most suspenseful things I've seen in a long time, as the drivers creep along at agonizingly slow speeds (less than ten miles per hour!) lest they jostle the dynamite and set the nitroglycerine off. Along the way there's the aforementioned bridge, a downed tree, and other dangers both expected and unexpected. Even the weather is a threat as the men peer through rainswept windshields. Not even the trucks the men drive can be relied on (the vehicles' animal-like growls and roars do a great deal to ratchet up the tension).

Technically *Sorcerer* is an impressive work. The cinematography has a gritty, almost documentary feel to it. Tangerine Dream's electronic score is an odd choice but works well, lending an almost otherworldly feel to the proceedings. The atmosphere throughout is palpable, from the squalid desperation of the South America town to the isolated jungles and mountain roads. As the journey wears on the men seem more and more beaten down by fear and the elements.

And yet, for all the trouble Friedkin has gone to in portraying these men and what brought them to this dangerous task, he generates little empathy for them. It's difficult to feel too sorry for them, save for Marzon who, business corruption aside, seems a decent sort at heart. The others? One's a hit man we learn little about, one's a terrorist. And even an awesome actor like Roy Scheider can't make us care for his character (his band of thieves steals from a church! While a wedding's going on! And shoot a priest!). The audience's sympathies are generated by the actors, not the characters, which is a shame because an already tense movie could have been even more so had we an emotional investment in the characters' fates.

Fate wasn't kind to *Sorcerer* back in 1977 — audience preconceptions of the film didn't jibe with what they saw (thanks to the enigmatic title and to Friedkin's previous film being *The Exorcist*), and then it got overshadowed by some space opera you might have heard of. *Star* something. *Wars,* I think. Something like that. The movie deserves a look, especially if you're interested in an action/suspense movie that does not insult your intelligence.

# Spirits of the Dead

*For the love of God, Montresor!*

**Year:** 1968

**Director:** Roger Vadim, Louis Malle, Federico Fellini

**Screenplay:** Roger Vadim and Pascal Cousin (*Metzengerstein*); Louis Malle and Clement Biddle Wood (*William Wilson*); Federico Fellini and Bernardino Zapponi (*Toby Dammit*)

**Cast:** Jane Fonda, Peter Fonda, Alain Delon, Brigitte Bardot, Terence Stamp

Certain movies are so much a product of their eras that they should be put in time capsules. That is certainly true of *Spirits of the Dead*: an anthology film of three short stories by Edgar Allan Poe, directed by Roger Vadim, Louis Malle, and Federico Fellini — yep, it could only have happened in 1968.

It's been my experience that anthology movies tend to start off with their weakest story, and *Spirits of the Dead* is no exception. Vadim's entry, *Metzengerstein*, tells of the rivalry between two European nobles. Countess Frederica (Jane Fonda) is a libertine who spends her time hosting orgies where most of the participants are fully clothed. We're informed by the narrator that she's a depraved hedonist on a level with Caligula, but her main crimes seem to be sartorial. Anyway, one day Frederica meets her neighbor and rival, another nobleman whose name I forget and it isn't important anyway. He's a cold and stand-offish guy but Frederica is apparently tired of everyone throwing themselves at her because this becomes a real turn-on. I have to add that there's a nice attempt at stunt casting here, as Nobleman Whatsisname is played by Peter Fonda. This is meant to be oh-so-daring but really isn't, as the two have maybe five minutes of screen time together, tops, and no chemistry whatsoever.

Frederica gets miffed when Whatsisname spurns her advances, and has her lackey burn Whatsisname's stables. Unfortunately Whatsisname runs into the stables to save his favorite horse, and perishes in the blaze. Oops! Frederica mopes a bit but soon cheers up when a mysterious black horse shows up. The horse can only be tamed by Frederica and soon she loses all interest in orgies and spends all her time riding the horse, taking it on picnics, playing tag with it. I'm not making this up. It all ends in a way that's supposed to be surreal and dreamlike but feels more like the film ran out of budget.

Smack in the middle in both order and quality is Louis Malle's entry, *William Wilson*. Alain Delon plays the title character, whom we're introduced to as he runs frantically through the streets, taking refuge in a church to confess his life to a priest. Turns out Wilson has been a nasty little sadist all his life, tormenting schoolmates, unlucky peasants, and Brigitte Bardot. Yet he's pursued and his torments halted by a person who also goes by the name "William Wilson" (though I'm sure some of the people being tormented wish that the other William Wilson had shown up a bit sooner). It's well put together, though you'll see the ending coming a mile away. The film's highlight is a card game between Delon and Bardot, with the stakes rising until they're far greater than mere loss of money.

Saving the best for last is Federico Fellini, with his segment *Toby Dammit, or Never Bet the Devil Your Head*. Terence Stamp plays the eponymous Dammit, an English actor in an alcohol-fuelled free fall. He's been invited to Rome to be in a Spaghetti Western that's a parable for the life of Christ, and from the moment his plane lands in Rome he's in a phantasmagoric world. Photographers swoop in like vultures, the airport is lit and designed to resemble Hell, and there's a creepy little girl who wants to play ball.

Things don't get much better for Dammit as the day goes on. After a curiously hostile TV interview complete with canned applause and laughter, he's a guest at a combination of a fashion show and Italy's version of the Oscars, "The Golden She-Wolf Awards." Surrounded by a cavalcade of Eurotrash grotesques, and unable to kill the pain with booze any more, Dammit flees and drives madly through the streets until he meets his fate.

The problem with adapting Poe's stories to the screen is that movies, for the most part, are plot-driven, and Poe's stories often have very little that actually happens in them. Poe's strengths are in the oddball imagination of his stories, the feverish ravings of the narrators, and the attention to details. Successful Poe adaptations, such as Roger Corman's *Masque of the Red Death*, are able to invent plot that can support Poe's fever-dream imagery.

For the most part *Spirits of the Dead* fails in this regard. The *Metzengerstein* segment, while keeping Poe's basic story idea about rival nobles and a spooky horse, instead turns into a showcase for Fonda gadding about in some very sexy albeit anachronistic costumes. It's eye candy, to be sure, but not enough for a half-hour story. *William Wilson* hews closer to its source material, but all the same lacks a bit of tension. Its best scene is the lengthy card duel between Delon and Bardot, with Delon's goal of making Bardot submit to his creepy desires.

Given this, it's probably best that Fellini appeared to use Poe as a very loose inspiration, and went instead with a character study in the Dante-esque place that is his Rome. Fellini, like David Lynch, has a peculiar gift for making his films seem not like movies but like something coaxed out of your subconscious. As a result, in every movie of his I've seen, there's a strange tension, the feeling you get when trying to wake up from a bad dream (this feeling got so intense when I watched *Fellini Satyricon* that I had to bail halfway through the film). Fellini wisely chose Terence Stamp as his central character. Stamp's Toby Dammit is a dissolute wreck yet also a lost soul; he's a man who's coming apart at the seams and knows it. We know it too, the instant we see him, looking like a fallen angel and with tears hiding behind his drunken sarcasm. He's terrified of the creepy figure that stalks him, yet seems somehow relieved too. It's an affecting performance, and even if the rest of Fellini's segment were not a mini-masterpiece, Stamp's acting would make it worth watching.

The movie as a whole is too uneven to make it much more than a curiosity piece, but it's worth renting for Fellini's sequence (and to giggle at parts of Vadim's).

# Stanley

*Why'd it have to be snakes?*

**Year:** 1972

**Director:** William Grefe

**Screenplay:** Gary Crutcher

**Cast:** Chris Robinson, Alex Rocco, Steve Alaimo

Most of us have some cinematic scene we saw at an early age that made us aware of the beauty and majesty of the medium. For some, it may have been the moment in *The Wizard of Oz* when the cinematography changed from black-and-white to color. For others, it may have been some sweeping Cinemascope moment or a Sergio Leone gunfight.

For me, one of those moments was in the schlocky horror film *Stanley*, when a snake lured two poachers to their deaths in a pool of quicksand. Eight-year-old me saw that scene on the local TV channel's Saturday Creature Feature and thought, "Wow!"

I'm not proud of this.

So you can imagine how delighted I am that *Stanley* is finally available on a nice DVD (previously it had only been available on a cheap compilation set, and in a censored-for-TV cut no less). Not only is the snake-and-quicksand scene just as cool as I remembered, but the whole movie is loads of fun.

Vietnam vet and Native American Tim (Chris Robinson in a surprisingly decent performance) is having a hard time adjusting to post-war life. He refuses to live on the reservation, suffers from bad headaches, and is embittered toward the local businessman Thompkins (Alex Rocco, probably wondering how he went from being in *The Godfather* to this in the same year) who Tim rightly suspects of having had a hand in the "hunting accident" death of Tim's father. Tim's only friends are the snakes he collects for a medical facility (their venom is used to create antivenin), and one in particular — Stanley, a rattlesnake that Tim talks to, snuggles with at night, and frequently wears around his neck. Hey, if it works for Tim I'm not going to judge.

But Tim's idyllic world in the Everglades is disrupted when the loathsome Thompkins, who makes his living by selling snakeskin belts and other animal products, sends two loathsome poachers (Mark Harris and Steve "Wild Rebels" Alaimo) to trap Tim's snakes, and even dispatches a loathsome psycho named Psycho (Paul Avery) to kill Tim. As if all that weren't bad enough, the local over-the-hill stripper who uses Tim's snakes in her act is persuaded by her loathsome manager to start biting the heads off snakes as well as shimmying with them (apparently operating under the dubious principle that geeking + stripping = box office gold!). I'm not making any of this up.

So of course it's time for Tim, Stanley, and the rest of the snakes to start wreaking sweet vengeance.

Those of you who are afraid of snakes will find plenty to give you the willies — this being 1972, all the snakes you see are real. As mentioned earlier, Tim spends most of the movie with at least one snake draped around his neck, and he also talks to the snakes, takes them to bed with him, and feeds them mice for dinner (saying grace beforehand of course).

Even those who aren't afraid of snakes (like me) will find plenty to enjoy here, for director William Grefe and screenwriter Gary Crutcher have populated the movie with one of the most loathsome set of characters ever. Thompkins is a vain, arrogant bastard who relishes killing animals to make a living and isn't above ogling his own daughter (who's loathsome in her own way). The poachers likewise kill for fun rather than sport, and Psycho deserves to die just for his wardrobe (the early 1970s fashions are more horrifying than any of the snaky shenanigans). The Everglades locations are lovely, though it's depressing to speculate that much of it is probably condominiums today. The cast has lots of fun with their cartoonishly evil characters, and Robinson gets a nod for making you root for Tim and his snakes to triumph.

The DVD makes the earlier, public-domain release completely superfluous, as it reinstates the footage cut for TV broadcast and includes a fine set of extras. The featurette is well worth watching, if only to get a glimpse into early-1970s down-and-dirty low-budget film-making and to learn how the snake scenes were filmed.

# Street Kings

*By the book*

**Year:** 2008

**Director:** David Ayer

**Screenplay:** James Ellroy, Kurt Wimmer, and Jamie Moss

**Cast:** Keanu Reeves, Forest Whitaker, Hugh Laurie

If you're looking for a cop thriller that isn't "good cop vs. bad cop" but "dirty cop vs. really dirty cop vs. evil cop," take a look at *Street Kings*. Its silly title aside, it's a fine, gritty movie based on a story by Mr. Demon Dog himself, James Ellroy (author of *L. A. Confidential* and *The Black Dahlia*, among others).

Vice Detective Tom Ludlow (Keanu Reeves, turning in a relatively strong performance) is good at his job — perhaps a little too good. He takes out the bad guys without much concern for due process, but since the bad guys are so bad, his fellow cops and superiors let it slide. But Ludlow's anger, stress, and drinking are getting the best of him, and he learns that his former partner Washington (Terry Crews), a straight-arrow cop, is ratting Ludlow out to Internal Affairs. Ludlow has to be restrained from seeking revenge against his former partner, and soon Washington is gunned down by a couple of gangbangers. Of course, Washington's murder is not a simple robbery-gone-wrong, and Ludlow soon finds himself able to trust no one as he tries to find out who killed Washington and learns how deep corruption in the department goes.

*Street Kings* isn't startlingly original, especially to those familiar with Ellroy's work (several character types and situations feel like *L. A. Confidential* updated for the 21st century — not that I'm complaining). But the screenplay (co-written by Ellroy, Kurt Wimmer, and Jamie Moss) serves the story well, providing just enough surprises to keep things lively and never becoming overly predictable. Kudos must also go to the actors involved. Keanu Reeves will never be Oscar bait but he's very serious and believable as Ludlow, and holds his own even when he's in a scene with Forest Whitaker, who's creepily charismatic as Ludlow's superior. The most memorable performance is from Hugh Laurie as an Internal Affairs captain — he steals every scene he's in and I'd love to see a movie about this character.

David Ayer's direction is strong and energetic without being overly flashy. He handles all the action scenes well without falling prey to the "let's shake the camera around a lot" syndrome, and a chase scene that goes from the streets to rooftops and ends in an unexpected fashion is a highlight.

While *Street Kings* isn't exactly a feel-good movie — there are few innocents in this world and the shades of gray can get mighty dark — it's entertaining as hell. If you're looking for some old-school cop drama with plenty of action and a couple laughs along the way, you won't go wrong with this movie.

# Suddenly, Last Summer

*Beach blanket murder*

**Year:** 1959

**Director:** Joseph L. Mankiewicz

**Screenplay:** Gore Vidal and Tennessee Williams, based on the play by Tennessee Williams

**Cast:** Elizabeth Taylor, Montgomery Clift, Katharine Hepburn

If you're up for some entertainingly macabre family dysfunction, watch *Suddenly, Last Summer*.

Adapted by Tennessee Williams and Gore Vidal from Williams' play, *Suddenly, Last Summer* opens at a mental institution where young, idealistic Dr. Cukrowicz (Montgomery Clift) is demonstrating the latest in psychiatric neurosurgery (a lobotomy!). The doctor is frustrated, though, by the less-than-optimal facilities of the institution (after all, when stray chunks of plaster fall from the operating room ceiling, it can't be good for the patient). But help comes to the doctor in the unlikely guise of Violet Venable (astonishingly creepy Katharine Hepburn) a wealthy widow whose much-adored son Sebastian died "suddenly, last summer" on a European vacation. Violet offers the doctor and the institution an astonishing sum of money, with one tiny string attached.

You see, Violet's niece Catherine (Elizabeth Taylor) was with Sebastian when he died and has been traumatized ever since. Violet insists her son died in a fall, but Catherine keeps "babbling" (as Violet puts it) otherwise. Violet thinks her niece is quite insane and wants to have the doctor perform a lobotomy on her in exchange for her monetary gift to the institution. Catherine's family are supportive of this (they aren't wealthy and Violet has promised them a great deal of money), but the doctor has qualms, and tries to find out if Catherine is indeed mad, and also what exactly happened when Sebastian met his end.

The movie serves up a veritable banquet of dysfunction, from Violet's far-too-close bond with her late son to Sebastian's manipulation of Catherine's beauty and emotional vulnerability to the willingness of Catherine's family to have her lobotomized so Violet doesn't end their gravy train. Though the movie isn't technically a horror film, it's hard not to be fearful for Catherine as her family betrays her and her only hope is a doctor she doesn't even know.

All this, and the revelation of Sebastian's fate too. Suffice to say it's a doozy, and though the gory details are left unsaid and unshown, the flashback sequence has a fantastic atmosphere of unease that slowly becomes terrifying, all the more so because it takes place on a sun-drenched Spanish beach. (Only Ray Bradbury's story "The Women" rivals this scene for combining a sunny idyll

288

with dread.) And suffice to say that after the big revelation, one person in the film will have lost their mind.

Of course it's an adaptation of a play and is subject to all the expected flaws: overly florid dialogue, acting that's just a tad too much (Catherine's family in particular overdo the "we're yokels, us" bit). But it doesn't feel particularly stage-bound, primarily because of the flashback scene. And the primary actors hit the right notes: Hepburn is chilling, Taylor is lovely and surprisingly vulnerable. Clift seems a bit stiff but I'm not sure whether to attribute that to his acting or to the damage a car accident had left to his face not long before making the movie. Credit must also go to the actor who plays Sebastian in the flashback — his face is never seen, making him something of an enigma for viewers to ponder.

# Super

*Shut up, crime*

**Year:** 2010

**Director:** James Gunn

**Screenplay:** James Gunn

**Cast:** Rainn Wilson, Liv Tyler, Ellen Page, Kevin Bacon

On the surface, *Super* seems like another "ordinary person tries to be a superhero" movie. It is, but it's more than that, with a raucous energy and refusal to play by the rules that's very refreshing.

Short-order cook Frank (Rainn Wilson) has exactly two things in life he can look back on with pride: his marriage to the way-out-of-his-league Sarah (Liv Tyler) and the time when he helped police catch a purse-snatcher (his heroism was limited to pointing and saying, "He went that way."). Frank's tenuous happiness comes crashing down when Sarah, a recovering drug addict, falls off the wagon and takes up with local drug dealer Jacques (delightfully skeezy Kevin Bacon). Despondent and broken-hearted, Frank gets a divine vision one night that inspires him to be a crime-fighter as a way of winning back Sarah. With some help from slightly unbalanced comic book store employee Libby (Ellen Page), Frank becomes The Crimson Bolt, armed with a red monkey wrench that he uses to beat down evil-doers.

The story arc is familiar, but along the way director and writer James Gunn throws in a number of deranged and subversive touches, from a silly animated opening credits sequence to a scene of divine inspiration that's fuelled by hentai anime and a cable-access Christian children's TV show.

Likewise, Frank's superhero role is taken up less out of a sense of injustice than a way to lash out at the lifestyle Sarah has abandoned him for, and he and Libby (who becomes his sidekick Boltie) go way overboard in administering brutal payback for minor crimes.

Though obviously made on a low budget, *Super* turns its limitations into assets. The location is an unglamorous part of Shreveport, Louisiana, with no tall buildings to leap in a single bound. Most of the effects are old-school and practical, depicting in gruesome detail just what happens when a person gets their skull caved in by a monkey wrench. The movie's considerable violence is hilarious and appalling at the same time, and in its own way much more honest than the bloodless carnage or off-screen body counts in many action movies.

The acting hits all the right notes across the board. Wilson is perfect as life's whipping boy, and no matter how odd, pathetic, or deranged he gets we're never out of sympathy with him. Indeed, he brings the movie to outright pathos at times, as he desperately prays to regain the happiness he's lost. Tyler spends most of the movie relapsing into drug use, though a flashback portrays her as a fragile woman looking to create a better life for herself, and goes a long way toward explaining why Sarah and Frank got together. Page probably has the flashiest role, as her Libby goes from snarky comic store nerd to off-the-leash sociopath. And kudos go to the numerous people who show up in minor roles. They range from Rob Zombie as the Voice of God (really) to Troma honcho Lloyd Kaufman as a passerby, but the best minor role has to be Nathan Fillion as The Holy Avenger, a superhero on a cut-rate evangelical TV show who helps inspire Frank. Probably the only actor who's not well served is Michael Rooker, whose role as one of the less odious henchmen never gives him enough to do.

It's not perfect. The seams show and the tone shifts wildly from scene to scene. The characters could have done with a bit more fleshing out and not all of the jokes work. But *Super* has an energy about it and a delight in its audacity that's refreshing in this day of cookie-cutter, by-the-numbers movie-making.

# Surviving the Game

*Race for your life, Charlie Brown*

**Year:** 1994

**Director:** Ernest Dickerson

**Screenplay:** Eric Bernt

**Cast:** Ice-T, Rutger Hauer, Charles S. Dutton, Gary Busey

Homeless guy Mason (Ice-T with natty dreads) isn't having a good day. He hasn't found anything in the trash cans worth eating, his dog got hit by a van, and his friend, Drunk Guy Who Occasionally Spouts Wisdom, just died. Some days, it just doesn't pay to crawl out of the dumpster.

Mason thinks his luck is improving when a mission worker (Charles S. Dutton, taking the trouble to act) puts Mason in touch with Burns (paunchy yet somehow still creepy and sorta handsome Rutger Hauer), who runs a wilderness outfit and will take Mason on for a vaguely-described job. But Mason's in for a rude awakening when he finds himself in yet another ripoff of *The Most Dangerous Game*, and has to flee through the picturesque Washington woods to elude a bunch of rich assholes who are jaded enough to think hunting humans is fun.

I don't need to describe the rest of the plot because you know it already. Will Mason prove to be wilier than his pursuers think? Will one of the hunters have a change of heart? Will there be smitings and comeuppance? Will Mason reveal the tragic events that made him homeless? Will a big light appear in the eastern sky tomorrow morning?

What *Surviving the Game* lacks in surprises it makes up for in being a sort of cinematic comfort food. The gorgeous Washington forest serves as a lovely backdrop. The cast is enthusiastic and just oddball enough to lift the movie a cut above the ordinary. Ice-T has limited range as an actor but what he has works well for him here. Hauer lets his icy charm do most of the work but it's enough to save him from embarrassment. Dutton puts in the best performance and consequently ends up being the most loathsome of the hunters. Gary Busey is, well, Gary Busey — 'nuff said. Oscar winner F. Murray Abraham is slumming it here, and it's one of the more surreal sights of the film to see Salieri duking it out with Ice-T. Some other guy shows up as Salieri's wussy son, and That Guy From "Scrubs" is on hand as a somewhat unhinged hunter.

It's the cinematic equivalent of a big bag of potato chips. You'll be entertained for 90 minutes and you won't have to use your brain once.

# Suspiria

*Danse macabre*

**Year:** 1977

**Director:** Dario Argento

**Screenplay:** Dario Argento and Daria Nicolodi

**Cast:** Jessica Harper, Udo Kier, Stefania Cassini

Realism is very overrated. The whole point of art, whether it's a painting, a movie, or a novel, is to take the recognizable and put it through the artist's filter. So what we see is not reality but the artist's reality, and if it's done right it can be a real treat.

Which is a long-winded and pretentious way of saying that *Suspiria* bears about as much resemblance to reality as that dream you had one time (yes, *that* dream). And you won't care.

It's the proverbial dark and stormy night when ballerina Suzy Bannion (the ever-amazing Jessica Harper) arrives in Germany to take up residence at a famous dance school. But when Suzy arrives, she rings the doorbell only to hear a frantic voice telling her to go away. With no other option, Suzy takes a cab to a hotel, and on the way sees another student fleeing the school. This student, Pat, has left the school for unknown reasons, but we can infer that there's something unnatural going on when she's murdered by a mysterious killer.

Things continue to get curiouser and curiouser. The teachers are creepy, most of her fellow students strangely hostile, and Suzy suffers a fainting spell during her first dance practice. Suzy starts to wonder where the teachers disappear to every night, what became of the student she saw fleeing that first night, and what some mysterious words she overheard that night mean. Soon she and fellow student Sara (Stefania Cassini) start investigating, and uncover dark secrets about the school.

*Suspiria* is a triumph of style over substance. Its plot is nothing to speak of and the characterizations practically nonexistent — Suzy's strength of character comes more from Harper's performance than anything the screenplay has given her, and nearly every other character is a victim, monster, or mean girl. Yet none of that matters because, like Suzy when she leaves the airport, we've arrived in a dream world. Director Dario Argento's dream world, to be specific. It's a world that's bathed in hues of red, blue, and green; a world where killers materialize out of thin air and demons flap on the wind; a world accompanied by the world's loudest soundtrack. You either accept it in the way you do the half-logical events of a dream, or you turn it off.

It's a frightening movie in the way that dreams are frightening, because we don't know what's coming next. Scenes of schoolgirl bickering are followed by a shower of maggots from the school's attic level. And there's a masterful sequence of suspense when a student is pursued through the school by a razor-wielding assailant, a sequence that ends in the way you least expect.

*Suspiria* is the best of the Argento films that I've seen, not just because of its singular visual style and its nightmare logic. Two other elements that give the film its power are Jessica Harper's performance as Suzy, and the eerie score by Goblin. Harper has always been an underrated actress, one that Hollywood never seemed to find the right niche for. Her Suzy has a porcelain doll's beauty and seeming fragility, yet she never lets anything about the school intimidate her, and once she makes up her mind to find out what is going on nothing — not the threats from the witches who run the school or the placating logic of a psychiatrist (Udo Kier in a non-creepy performance for a change) — can stop her.

Also unstoppable is Goblin's score, possibly one of the loudest and most over-the-top for a horror film. From childlike bells to clattering drums, with raspy cries of "Witch!" it's one of the most memorable you'll hear, and so effective that I can't listen to the soundtrack if I'm in the house alone. Now that's what I call music.

So if you like your unreality served up with style and no small amount of gruesomeness, by all means watch *Suspiria*.

# Tales from the Crypt

*One from the vaults*

**Year:** 1972

**Director:** Freddie Francis

**Screenplay:** Milton Subotsky, based on comic book stories by Johnny Craig, Al Feldstein, and Bill Gaines

**Cast:** Ralph Richardson, Peter Cushing, Joan Collins, Ian Hendry

Horror is a surprisingly conservative genre — often, its stories focus on the dire consequences of straying outside of societal or moral norms. Nowhere is this idea more obvious than in the E.C.

comics of the 1950s. In *Tales from the Crypt, The Vault of Horror,* and *The Haunt of Fear,* though the innocent suffered, it was the guilty — whether they were adulterers, murderers, or just downright bastards — who met the gruesome comeuppances that made the comics notorious.

It's overshadowed now by the latter-day show and movies with the annoying Cryptkeeper puppet, but this 1972 feature by England's Amicus studios adapts five E. C. stories with a fair amount of success. Despite the obvious low budget, the movie succeeds thanks to the power of the stories chosen for adaptation, some good (even great) acting, and director Freddie Francis' eye for atmosphere.

The film opens with a group of sightseers visiting catacombs where persecuted monks once hid. A group of five people become separated, then are locked into a room where a sinister fellow (Sir Ralph Richardson, all piercing eyes and hypnotic voice) in monk's robes and hood sits on a skull-shaped throne. He then tells the five visitors stories of what he claims is their future (or is it?).

"All Through The House" is the first, and unfortunately the weakest of the tales. A trophy wife (Joan Collins) chooses Christmas Eve as the night to bash in her husband's head with a fireplace poker. She's done this to get his insurance money payoff, but I suspect the God-awful décor in her house is what's driven her to murder. Joan's hands are already full with making her husband's murder look like an accident and keeping her kid from finding out what's happened, but it turns out there's a homicidal maniac prowling about, disguised as Santa Claus. Don't you hate it when that happens?

In "Reflection of Fear," family man Ian Hendry tells his wife and kids he's going on a business trip and doesn't know when he'll be back. Ten points if you guess that "business trip" is really "running away with my hot young lover" and "doesn't know when he'll be back" means "never, and it's been nice knowing you." Ian and his honey get into a wreck on their way to their new love nest, but Ian soon recovers, and seems to be fine … or is he?

"Poetic Justice" is the tale that comes closes to horror, though not for its grisly denouement (which its villain richly deserves, and then some). Kindly old widower Grimsdike (Peter Cushing, in a heartbreaking performance) just wants to live out his twilight years in the house he once shared with his wife. He's happy there with his pet dogs, and he makes toys for the local kids who come to visit him. Unfortunately a neighbor covets Grimsdike's property and starts harassing the poor old man, taking away all the simple joys of his life until Grimsdike's driven to suicide. But a minor thing like death has never stopped anyone in the E.C. universe from enjoying a little well-deserved revenge.

"Wish You Were Here" offers a take on the idea of being careful what you wish for. A wealthy couple learn that oops, they're not as wealthy as they thought and will have to sell off "all our lovely things" to avoid bankruptcy. (The "lovely things" look like what you'd find at grandma's church rummage sale.) Among the prize possessions is a jade statuette that offers the user three wishes. Even though the husband has read "The Monkey's Paw" and warns against using such wishes, the wife goes ahead anyway. Things work out even worse than they usually do in these situations.

The last tale is possibly my favorite, as it's a pure revenge story. "Blind Alleys" is the tale of a retired military major who takes over management of a home for elderly blind men. The major's contemptuous attitude toward his charges is bad enough, but soon he's feeding the men substandard food, turning off the heat, and refusing to call doctors when the men are ill — all the while pampering himself with fine foods and even giving blankets that should go to the men to his German shepherd. When one of the men dies, the others take it on themselves to show the major that justice is blind, and give him a gruesome fate.

It all ends back at the crypt, with a twist that can be guessed a mile away but is still satisfying.

Having read most of these stories in their original comic form, I can attest that for the most part the movie-makers have done a good job adapting them for the screen. It's not a perfect adaptation — "All Through the House" is too short and doesn't sustain its tension, while "Wish You Were Here" doesn't work as comeuppance (the protagonists aren't portrayed as particularly bad people) or as pure horror (they're not particularly nice either). But for the most part the spirit of the E.C. tales is alive and well, demonstrating that if you step outside the bounds — whether you're a murderess, adulterer, covetous bastard, or just plain cruel — sooner or later you'll get what's coming to you.

# The Texas Chainsaw Massacre 2

*What a carve-up!*

**Year:** 1986

**Director:** Tobe Hooper

**Screenplay:** Tobe Hooper and L. M. "Kit" Carson

**Cast:** Dennis Hopper, Caroline Williams, Bill Moseley, Jim Siedow

It's one thing to remember a movie you've seen. It's another to remember all the details of when you saw that movie.

I saw *The Texas Chainsaw Massacre 2* at a midnight show; the venue was a gorgeous old theater in my college town, Columbia, Missouri (go Mizzou!). I plopped into my seat next to my then-boyfriend (hi Charlie, wherever you are!), scarfed down a bucket of popcorn roughly the size of my head, and waited for the show. Mind you, I'd seen plenty of gory movies at that time in my life, and had heard that the first *Texas Chainsaw* movie (which I hadn't seen) was low on blood and high on suggestion, and since I'd seen *Night of the Living Dead* a few weeks earlier and had only been mildly freaked out, I figured this wouldn't be so bad.

I was wrong.

I'm not sure at precisely which point I snatched my popcorn bucket from the floor in case I needed it as a barf receptacle. It was either when a man twitched convulsively as he was beaten in the head with a hammer, or when a person had their face skinned off and said face was put onto another person. Afterward my then-boyfriend, a nice Christian boy from The Bootheel, could only say, "Oh my Lord," in a shaken voice.

OK, not the most pleasant night at the movies, but one I certainly didn't forget!

Considering that it took the better part of a week to get some the images from this movie out of my head, you can forgive me for taking nearly 20 years to rewatch the film. The impetus for a rewatch was seeing cast members Caroline Williams, Bill Moseley, and Bill Johnson at the 2009 Fangoria Weekend of Horrors in L.A. and being floored at how nice they were and at what a fun time they all claimed to have had while making the film. So I decided to take the plunge and revisit *Texas Chainsaw 2*. My verdict? It's a flawed, far-from-perfect film that gets one thing wrong for every two things it gets right, yet puts a kind of insanity and fearlessness on screen the likes of which I've never seen since.

*Texas Chainsaw 2* opens, as did its predecessor, with a lengthy expository crawl and voice-over. This time we're informed that Sally, the lone survivor of the first film, told a tale of insanity and murder to the police (including the memorable phrase "hacked up for barbecue") before lapsing into catatonia. The culprits were never caught, and despite denials from law enforcement officials, tales persisted of mysterious disappearances attributed to the chainsaw-wielding clan.

Deep in the heart of Texas, ranger Lefty Enright (get it?), who's the uncle of catatonic Sally and her late, unlamented brother Franklin from the first film, has been searching all this time for the clan. It's soon clear that Lefty departed South Eccentric long ago and is currently residing well within the town limits of Outer Batshitinsania, and the fact that he's played by Dennis Hopper doesn't give us hope that he'll be the story's voice of reason. Lefty knows he's close when two obnoxious yuppies die in what authorities call a car crash; Lefty sees the strange gashes in the car and on the bodies, which could only have come from a chainsaw. Proof comes from local DJ Stretch (Caroline Williams, in a fantastic and shamefully underrated performance) who was taking a call from the yuppies when they were attacked and has the attack on tape. Stretch wants to cover real news instead of chili cook-offs. Lefty wants to use Stretch as bait to bring the

Sawyer clan (get it?) out of hiding. At Lefty's request Stretch plays the recording of the chainsaw attack on her broadcast, and that night she and her long-suffering boss L. G. (the late Lou Perryman) get two unexpected and very unpleasant visitors named Chop Top (Bill Moseley) and Leatherface (Bill Johnson).

It seems the Sawyer clan are close by — they've set up a lair in an abandoned "Texas Battle Land" theme park (which looks like it was incredibly creepy **before** the Sawyers took it over). They've expanded their barbecue business and are into catering and winning the aforementioned chili cook-offs. Soon L. G. is mostly dead and Stretch is trapped in the lair where she's alternately menaced by Chop Top and the cook (Jim Siedow, the only cast member to return from the original film) and given a dubious sort of protection by Leatherface, who's smitten with her. Meanwhile Lefty, armed with multiple chainsaws, is literally bringing the house down.

The line between humor and horror can be a fine one, and *Texas Chainsaw 2* doesn't so much walk that line as erase it. Unlike its grim, serious predecessor, it offers plenty of opportunities for the audience to laugh: at the Sawyer gang's banter and messed-up family dynamic, at the satirical touches brought to the story by Tobe Hooper and screenwriter L. M. "Kit" Carson (the cannibal family runs a thriving business that's supported by the very people they prey on); at the way Grandpa Sawyer can't even hold a hammer long enough to hit someone. But it doesn't neglect the horror either, thanks to Tom Savini's incredibly graphic effects, a thoroughly uncomfortable scene that explores the phallic implications of a chainsaw blade, and watching a character's sanity erode until they're as crazy as the film's villains. And yet the blend of humor and horror never works as well as it could — the humor often isn't strong enough, and the gruesomeness and insanity tip the balance. We can laugh as Stretch gives Chop Top a brief (very brief) tour of the radio station, but we can't laugh as she's subjected to repeated torments and gradually loses her mind.

Most people aren't likely to watch *Texas Chainsaw 2* for the acting but for the most part it's quite good. Williams is a powerhouse and perhaps too good for the movie. Moseley has one of horror cinema's great entrances as Chop Top — menacing, repulsive, and funny at the same time (though he never gets another scene that quite equals this one). Bill Johnson puts a new spin on Leatherface that makes him the one halfway sympathetic person of the clan; you get the feeling he'd be not a bad sort if he'd had a better family. Jim Siedow makes his cook just sane enough to pass for normal (in Texas anyway) yet it's plain he's as crazy as the others (and also very tired of putting up with Leatherface's and Chop Top's antics). Oddly enough the only acting misstep is Hopper, who is unusually subdued and often seems to be going through the motions.

Acting aside, the film's greatest strengths are its oddball dialogue ("Dog will hunt!"), its sheer audacity (you'll lose count of the "I can't believe what I'm watching" moments), and its truly amazing attention to detail. The cannibal lair is the ultimate nightmare funhouse, full of grotesque caches of bodies, labyrinthine tunnels, collapsing floors, and the family's insane approach to interior decorating. (This last is particularly chilling when you realize that the items have all been scavenged from the clan's victims.)

There are still too many weaknesses to make the film entirely successful. The humor/horror intersection most often creates neither laughter nor scares but a sort of queasy discomfort. Some choppy editing near the end makes the action unclear at times (and Hopper's stunt double is very obvious). While the movie gets props for including Oingo Boingo's "No One Lives Forever," the score is a weird pipe-organ concoction that's supposed to sound like music from a deranged circus but more often sounds like a cat walking on a calliope.

*Texas Chainsaw Massacre 2* is unlike any other movie, and though this will freak out the purists, I found it more memorable in its own way than its more famous predecessor.

# The 13th Warrior

*Vikings vs. GWAR*

**Year:** 1999

**Director:** John McTiernan

**Screenplay:** William Wisher and Warren Lewis, based on the novel *Eaters of the Dead* by Michael Crichton

**Cast:** Antonio Banderas, Vladimir Kulich, Dennis Storhoi, Omar Sharif

Some movies you watch with your brain turned on. Some you watch with your brain turned off.

I can think of few better examples of the latter than *The 13th Warrior*. It's a tremendously entertaining film, as long as you don't think about it a lot. And by "a lot" I mean "at all."

It's medieval times, and we start off with our hero Ahmed Ibn Fahdlan (Antonio Banderas) who has a happy life as a poet in some vague Middle Eastern locale. Unfortunately for him, he makes goo-goo eyes at the wrong woman, and her husband asks the Caliph to send Ahmed on a diplomatic mission to faraway lands, effectively banishing him. Ahmed's caravan is about to be attacked by Tartars, who get spooked off by the presence of a Viking ship. Ahmed hangs around with the Vikings for an evening, and then, through some rather implausible plot turns, gets roped into being the last and thirteenth of a group of warriors who need to protect a Northern king from a mysterious evil that arrives in the mist.

Aside from being the thirteenth warrior, Ahmed is pretty much the fifth wheel for quite a while, until he learns to speak Viking, gains a certain amount of respect from the Vikings, and then has to fight the beasties. I'm not sure if it's a spoiler to say that the whole beastie-fighting bit is *Beowulf* — I'm an English major and I didn't get the connection til the third viewing or so. In my defense, I was somewhat distracted by things like a 10th-century Viking wearing a Spanish conquistador helmet.

Plagued by poor test screenings, re-shoots, and production problems, with the end result being a fairly notorious flop at the box-office, *The 13th Warrior* is better than it has any right to be. Helping matters is that the movie plays everything seriously, without camping it up or acknowledging how ridiculous things get, but is never humorless. Big kudos for this go to Banderas, and to the primary Viking characters Buliwyf (Vladimir Kulich) and especially Herger (Dennis Storhoi) — there's a nice chemistry between them. The conversations between Ahmed and Herger are particularly funny, and help to keep things moving. A highlight is when Ahmed complains that he can't lift the huge Viking sword he's been given, and Herger cheerfully advises him to "grow stronger!" I hereby demand a spin-off TV series in which Ahmed and Herger team up to solve mysteries.

Also of interest is the bond of mutual respect that grows between Ahmed and the Vikings. He may not have the battle skills that they do, but they come to respect his intelligence. He in turn realizes that they are not the mere savages he originally believes them to be.

Nothing about it should work, but just enough of it does to make it extremely entertaining. Take, for example, the sequence in which Ahmed learns to speak Viking. It's a montage of him sitting around the fire with the Vikings, at first not understanding a word they say; then slowly the words begin to make sense. It's notable that his first conversation in the Vikings' language is to defend the honor of his mother and to call the Viking who insulted her "a pig-eating son of a whore." When asked how he learned their language, he replies, "I listened!" It makes absolutely no sense for Ahmed to have learned the language this way, but it's done so nicely and in such an entertaining way that it seems petty to grouse about it. Just as it seems petty to grouse about the mix-and-match armor the Vikings wear, or that we don't really care about the Viking hall that's besieged by beasties, or that Ahmed and his Viking girlfriend aren't that compelling, or that whole plot points (such as the prince's plotting against Buliwyf) are dropped and never heard from again, or that we never learn the names of any of the Vikings (for ages I thought of Buliwyf as "the Viking who looks like David Gilmour" and other Vikings were "the one who looks like Gregg Allman" and "the one who looks like Jurgen Prochnow" and "the one with the Celtic-Maori tattoos" and "the one who looks like Nigel Tufnel").

I could go on, but I won't. Because while you have all this you also have genuinely exciting battle scenes, funny Viking banter, decapitations galore, and a very interesting take on the Beowulf myth, particularly on the nature of the monster. The whole thing is just loads of fun, really. So don't question it. Just go with it, and enjoy.

## Tideland

*Down the rabbit hole*

**Year:** 2006

**Director:** Terry Gilliam

**Screenplay:** Terry Gilliam and Tony Grisoni, based on the novel by Mitch Cullin

**Cast:** Jodelle Ferland, Jeff Bridges, Janet McTeer

One of the trickier things about art — whether it's painting, writing, or moviemaking — is for the artist to ensure that the message he or she intends to make is the message people take away. When that connection doesn't happen, it's disappointing for everyone.

A case in point is Terry Gilliam's much-maligned *Tideland*, which was savaged by many critics and audiences but has a small contingent of supporters. I'm a longtime fan of Gilliam and really wanted to champion this movie. But while it's not the unmitigated disaster its detractors claim it is, neither is it a success. It's an interesting failure, and the reason for its failure is not its stylistic excess or controversial subject matter, but because the movie Gilliam wanted to make doesn't synch with what's on the screen.

The *Tideland* DVD opens with a brief, black-and-white introduction by Gilliam in which he suggests how to watch the movie (with an open mind, through the eyes of a child). It's a gutsy maneuver, not least because he comes across as almost daring people to not like the movie and suggesting that if the viewer doesn't like it, it's the viewer's fault. I respect Gilliam's audacity but it's a misguided tactic — a finished work needs to stand on its own and should not need an introduction to tell the audience how to feel about it.

*Tideland* tells of young Jeliza-Rose (Jodelle Ferland). She's the daughter of has-been rock star and heroin addict Noah (Jeff Bridges, a gone-to-seed Lebowski) and bloated harpy Queen Gunhild (Jennifer Tilly makes Courtney Love look like Grace Kelly). Jeliza-Rose's life consists of prepping her father's fixes for him and looking after her mother, who alternately slaps Jeliza-Rose and then smothers her with affection. When her mother overdoses, Jeliza-Rose and her father flee to an abandoned farmhouse adrift in empty fields. Noah promptly overdoses and sits rotting in the easy chair for days on end, leaving Jeliza-Rose to explore the house and nearby fields, talk to the collection of doll heads that are her only friends, and read *Alice in Wonderland*.

Eventually Jeliza-Rose takes a peek at her only neighbors: Dell (Janet McTeer) a black-clad, veiled woman whose hobby is taxidermy, and Dell's brother Dickens (Brendan Fletcher), a brain-damaged epileptic.

There isn't much technically wrong with *Tideland*. The cinematography is gorgeous, if too prone to tilts and spins, and contrasts the loveliness of the fields with the filth and squalor of the abandoned farmhouse. The acting is mostly fine (Tilly's the exception, but fortunately she's not in the film for long), and if the characters are annoying or repulsive at times it comes across as the way they're conceived, not the actors' performances. The only technical misstep is the score, which feels like it came from another film.

The subject matter of *Tideland* and the situations Jeliza-Rose encounters are what many dislike about the film, and it's not hard to see why. Even in the beginning of the film, nothing is good for the girl as she endures her parents' passive neglect. Later, she's on her own with a corpse for company and only an ant-riddled jar of peanut butter for sustenance. Things don't improve much when she meets Dell and Dickens, both of whom are just as unbalanced and unfit to look after a young child as Jeliza-Rose's parents (things get particularly uncomfortable when Jeliza-Rose and the much older Dickens start playing "silly kisser" games). It's no wonder that Jeliza-Rose takes refuge in unreality, and it's here where the film fails.

It's clear not just from his introduction but from the repeated references to *Alice in Wonderland* that Gilliam means for Jeliza-Rose's fantasies to be an escape measure for survival. But her fantasies aren't escapist — they are heightened, funhouse-mirror versions of her reality. The talking doll heads don't become imaginary friends — they are just blinking, creepy doll heads. Likewise, the few fantasy sequences all showcase the same syringes, corpses, and abusive adults that plague Jeliza-Rose in reality. Compare this to the fantasy sequences of Jonathan Pryce's character in *Brazil* — even the darkest ones gave the character a chance for escape.

None of this would matter if the escapism serves Jeliza-Rose well. Gilliam believes that it does but I can't agree. Throughout, Jeliza-Rose seems so unaffected that her plight inspires pity rather than sympathy. (The one time she has an emotional reaction — when she tries to get comfort from Dell and is rebuffed — is heartbreaking, but it's an isolated moment.) At the end of the film, Jeliza-Rose encounters a scene of human pain and misery and has no reaction to it. She makes contact with another person, but this seems to be less a re-establishment of human bonds than to hide from Dell (who has turned against Jeliza-Rose). What is supposed to be uplifting is troubling. Just as the story has no arc — things happen and it ends abruptly — Jeliza-Rose herself has very little character arc. Her experiences haven't changed her, and she may have less empathy and humanity at the end than at the start. Again, this would be fine if it was the story Gilliam was trying so hard to tell. In the film's haunting last image, there's light in Jeliza-Rose's eyes, but it looks not so much like transcendence as it does madness.

Because of the disconnect between what it wants to do and what it does, *Tideland* isn't a successful film. And yet I thought about it for days afterward, which is more than I can say for many movies these days, and I would like to watch it again some time with the commentary by Gilliam and co-screenwriter Tony Grisoni, to understand their choices when making the film.

I admire Terry Gilliam tremendously, and few films have affected me as deeply as *Brazil* and *The Fisher King*. I respect his failures, such as *Fear and Loathing in Las Vegas* and even *Tideland*. I want him to make a great movie again. Here's hoping that he does.

# Tinker, Tailor, Soldier, Spy

*The tangled webs we weave*

**Year:** 2011

**Director:** Tomas Alfredson

**Screenplay:** Bridget O'Connor and Peter Straughan, based on the novel by John Le Carre

**Cast:** Gary Oldman, John Hurt, Mark Strong, Colin Firth, Benedict Cumberbatch

I love a good James Bond movie as much as the next person, but I think it's safe to say that when it comes to depicting the world of espionage, Bond films are hardly realistic. Of course, the fantasy they present is part of their charm. For a far more realistic look at the world of spies and secrets, look no further than Tomas Alfredson's remarkable adaptation of John Le Carre's classic novel *Tinker, Tailor, Soldier, Spy*.

It's the early 1970s, and a British spy on an assignment in Hungary has been betrayed and shot. The ensuing fallout leads to the forced retirement of intelligence agency head Control (a wonderfully ravaged-looking John Hurt) and his best spy, George Smiley (Gary Oldman, whose performance I'll rave more about in a moment). Control had been of the belief that a Russian mole had worked his way into the highest levels of British intelligence; this was dismissed as paranoia. But a year after the scandal, information surfaces showing that Control was right. During that time Control has died, so it's up to Smiley to come out of his uneasy retirement and ferret out the mole — a task that must be kept secret as the mole is one of the agency's four top-ranking leaders, men who have the power of life and death.

The good news is that there is no one better suited for this task than Smiley, precisely because he is the complete antithesis of a James Bond. In late middle age, he's graying, bespectacled, paunchy, and quiet — the sort of man you would never notice if you saw him walking down the street. Even when he's in conversation with people he fades into the background, and this gives him his power, for by providing silence he coaxes others to spill their secrets. He seems to be a pushover, and while he's been forced into retirement and cuckolded by his wife, he has the tenacity and intelligence to find out secrets. He also has a master spy's cold-bloodedness, as he's willing to exploit others' weaknesses for the greater good.

This wouldn't seem to be a role well suited for Gary Oldman, particularly if one recalls his more over-the-top characters from *Leon* or *True Romance*. But it's a masterpiece of subtle acting. At one point in the film there's a reference to a code name of "Reptile" and that often sums up Smiley's character and Oldman's performance. Sitting still, saying little, not seeming to blink quite often enough, Smiley (and Oldman) exhibit a reptile's perseverance and patience. Yet he's not completely closed off, and Oldman lets Smiley's humanity shine through in several key scenes, most notably in a flashback when he discovers his wife's infidelity, and late in the movie when Smiley finally takes up a gun and Oldman conveys the seriousness of the matter and Smiley's deep loathing of such measures.

But there's much more to the film than Oldman's performance. The screenplay has done a fine job adapting Le Carre's novel. This holds true not just in condensing a complex, at times labyrinthine work into a two-hour film, but restructuring the story arc to suit a visual medium of storytelling. Some have complained of the film being hard to follow. Admittedly it is much easier to take in if you've read the book, but you should read the book anyway. In a way, the movie asks you to be something of a spy like Smiley, as you absorb details and make connections rather than having things pointed out to you. (I find it refreshing that the movie doesn't ask you to leave your brain back at the concession stand.)

Director Tomas Alfredson, best known for making vampires interesting again with *Let The Right One In*, has put together an astounding cast of primarily British actors, even to the smallest roles, and everyone shines: Toby Jones, Colin Firth, and Ciaran Hinds as some of the top intelligence men; Tom Hardy as a field agent who gets proof of the Russian mole; Benedict Cumberbatch as an agent Smiley recruits to help find the mole; Mark Strong as a man with an unexpected connection to the proceedings; and Kathy Burke as a former intelligence worker who in a single scene helps dramatize the human cost of the manipulations and machinations we've seen.

Almost as much of a character is the film's period setting. In the early 1970s so much of the technology we take for granted these days was undreamt of. Espionage in this time involves not digital information and satellite images but rotary dial phones, boxes and boxes of paper files, wiretaps, typewriters, and so on. It's an analog fetishist's dream. Likewise the sets and fashions are perfect capsules of the time without overdoing it; if nothing else, you come away feeling that England at this time was a truly dreary place, gray and comfortless. It's as if the 1960s were a fun party and now the country is suffering a bad hangover. Even the inside of the intelligence agency is drab, with even the most powerful men conducting business in dingy cubbyholes.

*Tinker, Tailor, Soldier, Spy* is a gripping story masterfully told on every level.

---

# Tron

### *Nightmare in neon*

**Year:** 1982

**Director:** Steve Lisberger

**Screenplay:** Steve Lisberger

**Cast:** Jeff Bridges, David Warner, Bruce Boxleitner

---

*Tron* is a curiosity — it's got some interesting concepts that are poorly executed, and manages to be both way ahead of its time and dated at the same time.

Hotshot computer programmer Flynn (my imaginary boyfriend Jeff Bridges) has been trying to hack into the computer system of his former employer, searching for proof that honcho Dillinger (David Warner, a fine villain as always) has stolen Flynn's idea for the Space Paranoids arcade game and made a fortune off it. Unfortunately the Master Control Program has other ideas. It zaps Flynn into the computer where Flynn finds himself put into gladiatorial matches (if gladiators used neon Frisbees) with other "programs" who look like the users that created them. Flynn now has to defeat Master Control to keep it from destroying not just himself, but the programs of his friends, especially the program Tron, created by his friend Alan (Bruce Boxleitner).

The concept of *Tron* is a bit silly but the cast plays it straight-faced. And speaking as a quasi-Luddite who thinks electricity is magic and has no clue how her computer actually works, I don't find the concept of anthropomorphized programs all that far out. (Personally I have a harder time believing that a computer nerd would look like Jeff Bridges.) The computer animation is dated but quaint and a bit endearing. And while I can't buy into Frisbees as weapons, the light cycle race is genuinely stylish and interesting, the best sequence in the film.

But there are real problems with *Tron*, and I'll get my personal issues out of the way first — the neon! Oh, the neon! It's garish and gaudy, and if I wanted to see that much neon I'd go to Las Vegas. The discordant score by Wendy Carlos! And the song by Journey! Agh! My eyes! My ears!

OK, that's off my chest. I feel better now.

The more serious problem with *Tron* is that more than any other movie I've seen, including ones based on actual video games, it **feels** like a video game. The characters, whether they're in the real world or in the computer, are paper-thin and we have no reason to care about what happens to them. Flynn's quest to find proof of the theft of his ideas is a hook to get him into the computer world and not much else, and it doesn't help that Bridges plays Flynn as a smarmy jerk. Basically both story and characters just serve to move things along to the next fight, chase, or special effects moment. Also not helping are gaping holes in the story — neat-looking "grid bugs" make an appearance and then are completely forgotten. There is also some extremely silly dialogue, such as "Who does he calculate he is?" that just doesn't work.

I recall some "Walt Disney is rolling in his grave" reviews of *Tron* when it was released, and its box-office floppage must have pleased those reviewers, but it's not hard to see why this movie does have a devoted audience. Despite its poor performance, it's also been a very influential film — the ancestor of *The Matrix*, definitely. If only there wasn't so much damned neon…

# Tron: Legacy

*Eye candy*

**Year:** 2011

**Director:** Joseph Kosinski

**Screenplay:** Edward Kitsis and Adam Horowitz

**Cast:** Jeff Bridges, Garrett Hedlund, Bruce Boxleitner, Olivia Wilde

I'm on the record about not caring much for the original *Tron*. I watched the sequel with trepidation, and while it's essentially the same movie as its predecessor, with many of the same flaws, it gets enough right to be a marked improvement.

Things start in the mid-1980s, where a not-entirely-believable CGI version of young Jeff Bridges reprises his role as computer wiz Kevin Flynn. Flynn is telling his son Sam about the world inside computers, and how he's made a computer version of himself to make that world perfect. Faster than you can say "hubris," Kevin goes into the computer world and never comes out, leaving Sam to grow up into an underachiever with Daddy issues.

The night that Sam Flynn (Garrett Hedlund) breaks into his father's company, Encom, and steals the latest operating system so he can distribute it for free, he gets a message from his dad's old chum Alan (Bruce Boxleitner, returning from the original). Alan claims to have gotten a page from the long-vanished Kevin, coming from the old Flynn arcade. (Nice bit of 1980s nostalgia when Sam fires up all the old arcade games, including the one time Journey's "Separate Ways" has not made me wish I was deaf.) Soon enough Sam gets zorched into the computer world, where he finds that his dad's plans for a perfect world went just a wee bit awry. Sam and Kevin team up with a new type of program called an "iso" (Olivia Wilde), and along the way they meet Ziggy Stardust (don't ask).

What *Tron: Legacy* has going for it is the benefit of modern movie technology — as eye candy goes, it's the best I've seen in quite some time. The computer world has been very successfully updated, though the jury is still out on whether light-cycles should be able to curve or have right-angles only. Except for the ill-advised scenes in the "real" world, the CGI version of young Jeff Bridges works well — in the computer world his plastic-looking skin texture and bobble-headedness come off as sinister rather than silly. And kudos must go to Daft Punk's excellent score, which works so perfectly that you can simply groove on it while you say, "Ooooh, shiny!" at the visuals.

Which is good, because *Tron: Legacy* suffers from much of the same story problems as its predecessor. The biggest problem is that we have no reason to care about what goes on. Yes, it's sad that Sam lost his father at such a young age but neither the script nor Hedlund (who seems to have been cast for his ability to wear black skintight latex) give the character any weight. Similarly, the two main plot threads — to stop Kevin's computer alter ego Clu and to get the "iso" program to safety — don't resonate because there's no reason to care about this in the "real" world. We're told of the importance and Kevin insists that the "iso" program can change everything, but what reason do we have to believe him? And would that change be good, considering how his attempts to make a perfect computer world turned out? As in the original movie, the "games" sections are the highlight, yet they do nothing for the plot.

Fortunately, aside from Hedlund the actors are game and give it their all. Bridges gives a fine performance as the weary, older Flynn who's achieved a Lebowski-ish Zen attitude to cope with being trapped in the computer world. Olivia Wilde does her best with a role that's more a MacGuffin than an actual character, and Michael Sheen has a ton of fun with his brief but memorable scene as that Ziggy Stardust guy.

Recommended if you're a fan of the original, or simply in need of some good eye candy.

# The Truman Show

*What's on TV?*

**Year:** 1998

**Director:** Peter Weir

**Screenplay:** Andrew Niccol

**Cast:** Jim Carrey, Laura Linney, Ed Harris, Natascha McElhone

Being someone who watches very little TV, I find it a bit odd that one of my favorite films from the 1990s not only is about TV, but predicted with a fair amount of accuracy the direction that TV would take in the coming years.

Truman Burbank (Jim Carrey breaks successfully from his goony funny-man roles) lives an ordinary life in a small seaside town. Every day he goes to work, then comes home to his wife Meryl (Laura Linney); sometimes he gets together with his best friend Marlon, and sometimes he pines for a girl he was smitten with, who vanished. It's a very comfortable life, but Truman yearns for adventure. But every time he attempts to break out of his rut, something stops him. It's almost as if he's being kept prisoner...

And in a way he is, because Truman is actually the unknowing star of a reality TV show. He lives in what is essentially a huge soundstage, where cameras follow him every moment and every other person — including his best friend, his mother, and his wife — are all actors. Truman's been ignorant of this for most of his life, but one day when a camera falls out of the "sky," Truman realizes that his life is not what he thought it was.

*The Truman Show* seems to be underappreciated, probably for several reasons. Some audiences may have been expecting a typical Jim Carrey comedy, while  others felt that Carrey wasn't dramatic enough for the role. The humor is much more subtle than that found in many comedies (my favorite recurring joke is the way Truman's friend Marlon holds out a beer with the label facing the camera every time he enters a scene, for the maximum product placement). But a cynical part of me wonders if many people don't see the awfulness of Truman's situation — how he's been robbed of every opportunity to live a normal life — because hey, he's on TV, and everyone wants to be on TV, right?

It's a film that's sunny on the outside, but dark as hell when you think about it. Because not only has Truman been exploited for his whole life, but so have all the actors who've had to pretend to be his family and friends, 24 hours a day and 7 days a week (indeed, for the actress who plays Truman's "wife" this amounts to something like prostitution). The show of Truman's life so captivates its viewers that they ignore their real-life responsibilities, but as soon as it's over they say, "What else is on?" and change the channel.

In lesser hands the story and concept could have been fumbled, but thankfully we have Peter Weir on hand to lend his usual humanity and subtlety to the proceedings. He gets excellent performances from his entire cast, particularly Laura Linney as Truman's "wife" Meryl, who hits just the right notes of false sincerity and repressed hysteria. Carrey's performance at times seems to still have a bit too much of his manic comic energy, but that can be seen as Truman starting to snap after years of being trapped; he's heartbreaking in a moment when he asks Meryl why she wants to have a child with him when "you can't stand me."

If there's a fault with *The Truman Show*, it's that the logistics of the reality show don't stand up to much scrutiny (it's hard to believe that product placement would be sufficient to pay for the astronomical cost of the show's production; it's also hard to believe that people would be enthralled for decades on end by a very ordinary life). But it's worth buying into the conceit to see Truman try to break out of his cage.

# Turkey Shoot

*Dog will hunt!*

**Year:** 1982

**Director:** Brian Trenchard-Smith

**Screenplay:** Jon George, Neill Hicks

**Cast:** Steve Railsback, Olivia Hussey, Michael Craig

There are times when I give lack of originality a pass, and the best example of this is when a movie decides to rip off *The Most Dangerous Game* yet again. Its central conceit of hunting humans has been done many, many times, yet there's enough life in the premise that its execution is nearly always entertaining at least and captivating when done very well (one could certainly argue that *The Hunger Games* novel is one such case).

Falling a bit lower on the spectrum is *Turkey Shoot,* an "Ozploitation" movie that combines the human hunt with a dystopian society. Some time in the near future, society's unrest is at a boiling point for reasons that are never explained. Society's deviants, which can include anyone from murderers, prostitutes, and revolutionaries to people who happened to be in the wrong place at the wrong time, are rounded up, drugged, and then taken to re-education and behavior modification prison camps. Things are grim at one camp in particular, where overseer Thatcher (Michael Craig) likes to liven things up by setting a few prisoners loose, telling them they can have their freedom if they survive until sundown. The prisoners are given a head start of a couple hours, and then the hunters go after them.

This time the prisoners include Paul (Steve Railsback), a revolutionary/pirate radio broadcaster who's run afoul of the government before, and Chris (Olivia Hussey), a doe-eyed waif arrested for questioning police brutality. Both have had their fair share of problems already (such as torture and attempted rape) and figure they don't have much to lose. Unfortunately, the hunters pursuing them and the other prisoners are a vicious, decadent bunch that include an ambiguously gay hunter who drives around in a mini-bulldozer equipped with a machine gun, and also has a pet werewolf along. I'm not kidding.

*Turkey Shoot* doesn't quite hit the right notes that make it an overlooked classic, but as trash entertainment goes, it's effective. The Australian locations help out a great deal; most of nature in Australia wants to kill you anyway, so the audience is already on edge watching the poor prisoners slog through mangrove swamps or fight their way through shrubbery or clamber over waterfalls. The hunters are all thoroughly evil in a cartoonish, Snidely Whiplash way, and occasional lurid bits like the pet werewolf or the Joan Collins-esque female hunter with a crossbow fetish help keep things lively. Where the movie fails is in some pacing issues in the first half, and an almost complete lack of character development. Of all the prisoners, only Paul and Chris get an explanation of why they've been sent to the camp, and their backstory is so minimal it tells the audience virtually nothing.

The movie has a reputation for being graphically violent, and while it's not overly gory by today's standards, the violence has a realistic, nasty tone that's certainly effective. Probably the most upsetting scene is when a young female prisoner is beaten to death by a guard using only his bare fists. This scene along with one in which a hunted prisoner has a toe amputated to make running more difficult, help bolster the film's reputation for mayhem in a way the numerous gun battles or death-by-machete incidents can't.

A little more backstory and attention to the characters would have gone a long way, but as it stands, *Turkey Shoot* is 90 minutes of cheap exploitation thrills, Australian style. Alternate titles are *Escape 2000* and *Blood Camp Thatcher*.

# Twin Peaks: Fire Walk With Me

*Questions in a world of blue*

**Year:** 1992

**Director:** David Lynch

**Screenplay:** David Lynch and Robert Engels

**Cast:** Sheryl Lee, Ray Wise, Moira Kelly, Kyle MacLachlan

When asked about the plot of his film *Inland Empire*, David Lynch's answer was that it was about "a woman in trouble." The truth is that this summary could have served for many of his other films: think of the murdered femme fatale of *Lost Highway*, the beautiful and bruised nightclub singer in *Blue Velvet*, and the various women of *Mulholland Drive* in all their roles and guises.

But perhaps nowhere does the description apply more than to Laura Palmer in *Twin Peaks: Fire Walk With Me*. Laura's murder set the TV show of *Twin Peaks* in motion, as investigation into the murder of the small-town homecoming queen unearthed secrets of all kinds, from mundane criminality to supernatural evil. *Fire Walk With Me* is a prequel to the show, depicting the hellish last week of Laura's life.

The movie opens not with Laura and the town of Twin Peaks, however, but with another murder and another small town. The murder is that of Teresa Banks, a young woman who was killed a year before Laura and whose killer left a similar clue (a letter of newsprint under a fingernail). The town is Deer Meadow, and it's the dark mirror of Twin Peaks, with characters who are similar to those we know from Twin Peaks, but given a nasty edge. Two FBI men come to investigate: calm and collected Chet Desmond (singer Chris Isaak) and hapless Stanley (Kiefer Sutherland). Yet nothing comes of their investigation, and the killer goes on his way.

We then return to Twin Peaks, where it's approximately a week before Laura's murder, and we soon get a glimpse into Laura's life. Much of it we know about from the show: her cocaine addiction, dating both football player Bobby and wussy biker James. But there's a darkness on display here that for the most part was only hinted at in the TV show. Laura prostitutes herself to get money for drugs, but there's no handsome brothel like One-Eyed Jacks here — she has to pick up men at the local roadhouse. But the most horrifying aspects of the film are the depiction of the abuse and terror she suffers routinely from Bob, the evil spirit that inhabits her father. It's bad enough that her father/Bob has been, as she puts it: "having me since I was twelve." Now

Bob wants to possess her: "I want to taste with your mouth," he says. Laura feels corrupted by this, and indeed, Bob may be getting a foothold into her spirit. All the anesthesia of drugs and the attempts to be a good person can't save her.

Critically reviled on its release, *Twin Peaks: Fire Walk With Me* is without question a flawed film. Its structure is strange to say the least, with its detour into the murder of Teresa Banks. The section showing Laura's life is captivating, largely due to the astonishing performances of Ray Wise as father Leland, Frank Silva as the terrifying Bob, and most of all Sheryl Lee as Laura. Wise is quietly horrifying, especially in a scene at the dinner table when he berates and humiliates Laura; then in the next scene the evil influence recedes and we see a man remorseful for the hurt he's caused his beloved daughter.

But it's Laura's story, and none of it would work if not for Sheryl Lee. Freed from being seen only in dream scenes and flashbacks, she gives Laura a depth of character she never received in the TV show. We understand Laura's conflict — her sexual abuse has robbed her of innocence, and her promiscuity is a way of reasserting control over her sexuality (the movie would make an interesting double bill with *Repulsion*, a story of another blonde with sexual abuse issues). She feels corrupted by what's happened to her, and fears that her corruption is contagious — she seems to be proven right when her best friend, good girl Donna (Moira Kelly), puts on Laura's jacket and begins acting like her. Deep down she senses that none of her escape mechanisms will work for much longer, and feels abandoned by God. Lee makes it all work, and it's a shame that the film fared so poorly at the box office and with critics, as she never got the recognition she deserved.

It's not hard to see why the film didn't do well. It has too much darkness and not enough of the doughnuts-cherry-pie-and-damn-good-coffee that made the TV show so endearing. Lynch doesn't have TV network restrictions on his surrealism and Moebius-loop approach to narration (a good thing, in my opinion, but others didn't agree). Though much of the show's cast appears, few make more than token appearances (some get less than a minute). Though captivating, the film's opening section with the Teresa Banks murder and scenes at the FBI occasionally feel like lots of people wanted to be in the film, and Lynch had to scramble to accommodate them in the screenplay.

What remains, though, is the heart of the story — a woman in trouble. Lynch takes us down her tormented road, immersing us in hellish image and sound. And when the trouble is taken away, the moment of peace is transcendent.

# Under Siege

*"Die Hard" on a boat*

**Year:** 1992

**Director:** Andrew Davis

**Screenplay:** J. F. Lawton

**Cast:** Steven Seagal, Tommy Lee Jones, Gary Busey

You young whippersnappers out there may not believe it, but there was a time when Steven Seagal was not a complete joke. Back in ye olden days, his movies actually played in theaters! They didn't go straight to video! No, I'm not making this up — and get off my lawn!

*Under Siege* is the best Steven Seagal movie, which only sounds like I'm damning it with faint praise. Unlike many of his other movies, it doesn't exist just to show off how (allegedly) cool he is or to (God forbid) give him a chance to pontificate a la Billy Jack. *Under Siege* is actually a taut, reasonably intelligent thriller that just happens to have Steven Seagal in it.

The plot is the usual *Die Hard* variation. This time a gaggle of terrorists have taken over a U.S. Navy battleship to get at the ship's nuclear weapons. The terrorists, led by Tommy Lee Jones as a former CIA operative, have gotten on board by posing as a rock band playing at a birthday party for the ship commander. Seagal is Casey, a former SEAL but now the ship's cook, who gets locked in the meat locker by the ship's second-in-command Gary Busey, who's in cahoots with the terrorists. With most of the crew held prisoner, it's up to Casey, a few remaining crew members, and a *Playboy* Playmate (Erika Eleniak) the terrorists brought along as a decoy, to save the day.

The story is nothing that special, but screenwriter J. F. Lawton throws in some fun dialogue and characters. The banter between Jones and Busey is always a treat, and Eleniak not only holds her own acting-wise as her character plausibly rises to the occasion, but has some of the film's funniest moments (my favorite being when she denies knowledge of the terrorists' plot, proclaiming she's an actress: "I did a *Wet and Wild* video!").

In addition to the same deft hand with action that he would show in *The Fugitive*, director Andrew Davis keeps his actors hitting just the right notes. Busey is just hammy enough to keep things lively. Jones seems like a goofball until his eyes go cold and reveal his character as a killing machine with the soul of a pit viper. Seagal only has two expressions — squinting while frowning and squinting while smiling — but is in good shape and delivers his lines reasonably well.

*Under Siege* is also a refreshing thing these days, an action movie that doesn't bludgeon the viewer with crash-bang-boom and herky-jerky camerawork. You can actually tell what's happening! You can hear the dialogue! What a concept!

It's not a cinematic masterpiece, but if you're looking for something that entertains you without insulting your intelligence, and if you don't mind Seagal's squint, *Under Siege* is perfect popcorn fare.

# Under The Skin

*"Species" for smart people*

**Year:** 2014

**Director:** Jonathan Glazer

**Screenplay:** Jonathan Glazer and Walter Campbell, based on the novel by Michel Faber

**Cast:** Scarlett Johansson, Jeremy McWilliams, Lynsey Taylor Mackay

There are few greater — and rarer — delights these days than a movie that not only asks, but demands that you use your brain. *Under The Skin* is one of those movies. Don't be misled by the folks who reduce it to "alien lady seduces guys just like in *Species*." Yes, there's an alien in disguise as a beautiful woman, and she uses her beauty to lure men, but that's just a jumping-off point for the movie as it goes into some uncharted territory.

*Under The Skin* opens with peculiarly hypnotic imagery: what appear to be planets, followed by a point of bright light, then an unsettling close-up of a human eye. We can assume that the eye belongs to Scarlett Johansson, whose unnamed alien strips the clothes off a dying woman with the cold efficiency of a hunter skinning a deer. Garbing herself in the dead woman's clothes and driving a nondescript white van, she gives rides to men, questioning them to find out if they have friends or family. Men with no close attachments get invited back to her place, and I'll let you discover for yourself what happens then.

Adapted from Michel Faber's novel, *Under The Skin* is deeply unsettling throughout, primarily because its primary point of view is from the perspective of its alien protagonist. Director Jonathan Glazer makes clever use of sound, primarily when the alien is driving around, so that everyday noises are distorted and unfamiliar. Likewise, the thick Glaswegian accents of the male victims are nearly incomprehensible to American audiences, and this further increases our identification with the alien's perspective. But these moments are juxtaposed with scenes in which we realize just how detached the alien is from humans. The most devastating of these

313

scenes is one when the alien is witness to a scene of appalling tragedy; her lack of empathy, already chilling, becomes horrifying with the actions she takes (and doesn't take), which escalate the tragic events to a whole new level. (Forgive me for being vague, but devastating as the scene is, I don't want to spoil it.)

Yet operating in the human world takes its toll on the alien and her mission. She starts trying to live a more human-like existence, but this doesn't pan out in the ways we'd expect. (Kudos to Glazer and co-screenwriter Walter Campbell for not relying on the usual tropes of food, sex, or babies to help an alien get in touch with its inner humanity.)

*Under The Skin* could have been a massive misfire, and I'll admit I was skeptical when I heard that the sublimely creepy book was being adapted for film. I was even more skeptical on hearing that Scarlett Johansson was cast, but she is perfect for the role (as it's portrayed in the film — the book's alien protagonist is considerably different in appearance and manner). Johansson has always had a slightly remote quality, and this serves her well. Adding to the sense of otherworldliness are the aforementioned use of sound, as well as the hypnotic score and some surreal visuals that are presented without explanation. It's up to the viewer to put it all together.

The film's one noteworthy flaw is that the turning point of the alien to be more human-like isn't as well-defined as it could be. It arrives a bit out of left field and doesn't quite resonate as strongly as it should. But in a movie this visually, aurally, and thematically interesting as this one, that's a minor enough misstep. If you want to use your mind and have it messed with at the same time, *Under The Skin* is your movie. Be sure to read the novel as well — aside from the basic premise it's quite different from the movie, but very creepy and interesting in its own right.

# The Unseen

*Cannot be unseen*

**Year:** 1980

**Director:** Danny Steinmann

**Screenplay:** Danny Steinmann

**Cast:** Barbara Bach, Sydney Lassick, Stephen Furst

The reasons I choose movies to review are many, and one that's given me limited success is: "They filmed this movie in a place I like/used to live in!" You'd think I'd have learned from watching *Surf Nazis Must Die*, which (a) was filmed in my old residence of San Pedro, California and (b) stunk. But no, I had to rent *The Unseen*, which (a) was partially filmed in one of my favorite towns, Solvang, California, and (b) was not that great. (Better than *Surf Nazis Must Die*, though, and if that isn't damning with faint praise I don't know what is.)

*The Unseen* opens on a strange note: lingering shots of an ominous sunrise, the interior of a house, and so on … and all the while accompanied by some odd, heavy breathing. Just when you start wondering it it's going to be like **that** scene in *Mulholland Drive*, we find out it's some guy lifting weights. A helpful close-up shows that he's had a knee injury, and soon a woman comes in and looks at him. They exchange silent, rather baleful glares and she leaves.

The woman is TV journalist Jennifer (Barbara Bach) and she, along with two other women, is headed to Solvang for a Danish Days festival (if she's smart, she'll get some great pancakes there while she's at it). Unfortunately there is a problem with their hotel reservations and the town is booked solid, so they go in search of a room. They're offered one at the home of Ernest Keller, a local museum proprietor who has a large house out in the country. It's a bit awkward at the Keller house because Mrs. Keller (Lelia Goldoni) is weepy and seems to be teetering on the brink of hysteria, but the trio soon make themselves at home despite the creepy, clanky noises coming from the heating grates in the floor. And if you can't guess there's some thing down in the basement making those noises, you've never seen a horror movie before.

*The Unseen* has a bit going for it, in its first half. It's nice to have there be a logical reason for people to stay at the Old Dark House™. The relationship between Ernest and Mrs. Keller is intriguing even after some details about it have surfaced (you'll recognize character actor Sydney Lassick from *Carrie* and *One Flew Over the Cuckoo's Nest*, among others). And while the body count of the movie isn't high, there being so few characters, the first couple deaths are unsettling. The movie does for heating grates what *It* did for storm drains.

Unfortunately, the movie falls apart completely in its last third. Much of this is due to Barbara Bach as Jennifer. The character is almost a cipher (we don't even learn her name for nearly half an hour) and the one bit of character development she's given makes her completely unappealing. Bach is pretty but not nearly a strong enough actress to overcome the paper-thin character, and she spends a good chunk of the movie incapacitated from what looks like a very minor injury, cowering, and gibbering incoherently with fear. Add to this the fact that the "unseen" beast is far less terrifying than one of the other characters, and in fact is almost pitiable rather than an object of fear. It's not his fault that he is the way he is.

It's not a complete waste of time but it's not very scary or interesting either.

# Valhalla Rising

*They call him One Eye*

**Year:** 2010

**Director:** Nicolas Winding Refn

**Screenplay:** Nicolas Winding Refn and Roy Jacobsen

**Cast:** Mads Mikkelsen, Maarten Stevenson, Ewan Stewart

I'd read several negative reviews of *Valhalla Rising* online, and I'm actually rather glad. Because I was able to find out ahead of time what it is **not** — a rollicking loot-and-pillage Viking tale. It has Vikings, but if you go into it expecting the usual battles-and-horned-helmets fare, you'll be disappointed.

What you will find is a bleak, violent, strangely beautiful, and often enigmatic film, with interesting explorations on what fear, deprivation, and the unfamiliar can do to people.

The movie starts somewhere in coastal Northern Europe, sometime in the Middle Ages. Christianity is prevalent but there are still bands of pagans about and religious tensions are high. None of that matters much at first to the silent warrior chained to a post in the middle of a field. He's the captive of a group of pagans, and every so often he's pitted against another warrior in fight-to-the-death battles using only bare hands and any handy rocks. When the nameless, one-eyed warrior isn't in a brutal fight, he's kept in a cage. After escaping his captors, the warrior, christened One Eye by a slave boy who accompanies him, meets up with a band of Viking Christians. The Vikings, having run out of pagan villages to sack and slaughter in the name of religion, are headed off to Jerusalem to join the Crusades and think One Eye (whose reputation has preceded him) would make a dandy Crusader.

But the Vikings' ship is soon adrift without wind for its sails, lost in a thick mist. The ship drifts aimlessly and the men start turning on each other or committing suicide by drinking seawater. Eventually the ship arrives in a strange land that is most certainly not Jerusalem, and which seems to be deserted … until unseen attackers start picking off the surviving Vikings, who wonder if they've ended up in Hell.

*Valhalla Rising* is unlike any movie I've seen in quite a long time, and easier to define by what it isn't rather than what it is. It's artsy with its title cards for the various sections of the story, red-tinged segments that may be One Eye's glimpses of the future, and minimal dialogue, yet it never feels like an art film, probably because it takes place entirely outdoors. The events get less explanation as the story goes on, but the unanswered questions are enigmatic rather than frustrating. Refreshingly, it avoids black-and-white characterizations — life is nasty whether you're a pagan, Christian, or something else altogether.

The Scottish locations are alternately bleak and beautiful, but always brutal. (Even the most gorgeous surroundings will do you no good if you're equipped for battle rather than hunting and have no way to hunt game and don't know what plants are edible.) The cinematography is excellent and makes the low-budget movie look fantastic. The music is strange, a sort of artsy techno-metal, but suits the movie's look and its creeping sense of dread.

The acting is all fine — most of all, the actors look the part, rather than like Hollywood people with some dirt smudged on their faces and their hair mussed. Best of all is Mads Mikkelsen as the enigmatic One Eye, who tells us both everything and nothing about his character in an entirely wordless performance. No matter what brutality he may take part in, it's impossible to look away from him whenever he's on screen.

*Valhalla Rising* is definitely not a film for everyone, but if you're in the right mood it can be a fascinating experience.

# The Valley of Gwangi

*I'm a little dinosaur*

**Year:** 1969

**Director:** Jim O'Connolly

**Screenplay:** William Bast

**Cast:** James Franciscus, Gila Golan

I'll be the first to admit that I had a pretty nifty childhood. But I wouldn't be an American if I couldn't find something in it to bitch about, so here goes. I regret not seeing *The Valley of Gwangi* when I was a kid (it ranks just below never getting one of those Snoopy snow-cone machines for Christmas).

Because if I'd seen it as a kid, it would have been the greatest movie ever. How could it not be? It has cowboys vs. dinosaurs. I repeat: **cowboys vs. dinosaurs.** The only thing that could possibly be more awesome would be armored knights on horseback vs. dinosaurs, or Nazis vs. dinosaurs. Yeah.

(Pause to get all misty-eyed.)

317

Where was I? Oh yes — well, the problem is that I'm not a kid any more and after seeing *The Valley of Gwangi* for the first time I'm forced to conclude that it has quite a few flaws (none of them the dinosaurs' fault, I want to be absolutely clear on this).

In turn-of-the-twentieth-century Mexico, smarmy cad Tuck Kirby (James Franciscus, all peroxide hair and impossibly white, even teeth) drops in on a Wild West show that's come to town. Turns out he used to be part of the show, and the show's star T. J. (Gila Golan, possibly dubbed) used to be his girlfriend. Tuck has heard the show isn't doing so well and wants to know if T.J. wants to join him in whatever money-making scheme he's got going now. Ah, but T.J. has a new attraction that she's sure will make the Wild West show the talk of the boonies: a miniature horse about the size of a housecat. She's got a point. It really is the cutest thing.

What T.J. doesn't know is that the teeny horse is a living fossil — a prehistoric ancestor of modern horses, named eohippus (even its name is cute!). Tuck does know this, however, thanks to a lucky chance encounter with the local paleontologist, and soon T.J., Tuck, the paleontologist and a few others are all fighting for the chance to make a quick buck off the eohippus.

There's a problem, though. The eohippus comes from a remote valley that the local gypsies say is cursed by a terrible demon named Gwangi. (Don't question the presence of gypsies in Mexico — we're already dealing with cowboys vs. dinosaurs, so just roll with it.) So naturally everyone ends up at the remote valley and find not just cute, teeny horses, but some other prehistoric animals.

Right about now is when the fun kicks in (and considering how unlikable **all** the human characters are, you'd be forgiven for skipping to the dinos). The cowboys soon find themselves beset by pteranodons, a styracosaurus, and an allosaurus (this last one is the creature the gypsies call "gwangi"). Before long the cowboys decide to forget eohippus — the allosaurus/gwangi would make an even better addition to their Wild West show! (This scheme didn't work in any version of *King Kong*, and it doesn't work here.)

*The Valley of Gwangi* is both entertaining as hell and strangely depressing. Once the movie gets to the valley, it's great. The dinosaurs are a bit dated (particularly in their coloring) but as always Ray Harryhausen is up to the job; the scene in which the cowboys lasso the enraged allosaurus is a masterpiece of stop-motion animation. One can't help but feel a certain childlike joy at seeing these creatures.

At the same time, one can't help seeing the movie through a grownup's eyes, and that means understanding that nearly every character in the film thinks of nothing but their own benefit — this even goes for the paleontologist, who's less interested in living prehistoric animals than in the glory the discovery will bring him. Likewise, you see the callousness with which the cowboys treat the valley and its inhabitants, and the spectacle that poor gwangi (who was perfectly happy eating other dinosaurs and having grudge matches with styracosaurus) is made into.

Flaws aside, it's a fun, unjustly overlooked movie that's essential for anyone who loves dinosaurs in general and stop-motion animation in particular.

Oh, and it's pronounced GWAHN-jee. Learn from my example — don't go around saying GWANG-gee or you'll lose your street cred with cinephiles.

## The Visitor

*WTF?*

**Year:** 1979

**Director:** Giulio Paradisi

**Screenplay:** Giulio Paradisi, Ovidio G. Assontis, Lou Comici, and Robert Mundy

**Cast:** Lance Henriksen, Joanne Nail, John Huston, Paige Conner, Franco Nero

Are you ready for a movie that's part science fiction, part horror, and all crazy? Then you're in luck, because *The Visitor* is now on Blu-Ray.

Some movies take a while to let their freak flag fly, but *The Visitor* is not one of those movies. It opens with a barren landscape, above which a strange-colored sky roils with clouds. Then John Huston shows up, looking a bit like Obi-Wan Kenobi, and stares pensively off into the distance while another figure, robed in black, approaches. Then there's a snowstorm. Then we see that the black-robed figure is a little blonde girl. Then we go to some sort of room in a fancy house where a gentleman I can only describe as Outer Space Jesus (Franco Nero) tells a bunch of bald kids who look like mini-Hare Krishnas about some evil sorcerer-type dude who once knocked up a bunch of Earth women and made them capable of producing children with immense powers for good or evil. Then John Huston shows up again and says he's found one of those kids. Said kid is Katy Collins, whose mom Barbara (Joanne Nail) is dating basketball team owner Raymond (Lance Henriksen all young and baby-faced); Katy's first demonstration of her powers is to make a basketball explode.

And all this is in the movie's first ten minutes, folks.

*The Visitor* doesn't sustain this pitch of craziness for its entirety, which is probably a good thing as that could get exhausting. But suffice to say that it has plenty of weirdness to keep you entertained. It says something about the film that its plot — shadowy cabal wants more kids with Katy's power to use for evil purposes while forces of good want to stop the cabal and save Katy — is the most mundane thing about it.

No, what makes *The Visitor* twenty pounds of bonkers in a ten-pound bag are all the incidental moments along the way. These include but are not limited to: the aforementioned exploding basketball scene, telekinetically induced mayhem at an ice skating rink, the scene when Katy's mom is shot in the spine at Katy's birthday party, more scenes of breaking glass and mirrors than you can shake a stick at, delightfully hideous 1970s fashions and architecture, John Huston conducting a light show, bird attacks, not one but two utterly pointless scenes of Katy doing gymnastics, a bizarre murder attempt using piano wire and a wheelchair stair lift, a mode of transportation that might be a truck or might be a spaceship, and a score that at times sounds like the theme from *Shaft* crossed with "Thus Spake Zarathustra." You'll spend much of the movie scratching your head and saying, "Wait, what?"

To their credit, the somewhat bizarre cast brings the fun as much as they're able to. Huston is surprisingly dignified and never condescends to the ridiculous material. Henriksen doesn't have a whole lot to do, but it's always fun seeing him on screen. Joanne Nail is not the least bit convincing as a paraplegic once she's wheelchair-bound — she's at her best in the movie's last third when the craziness gets to her and she's in hysterics most of the time. Paige Conner as Katy is fairly good when she's being a smug menace but less so when she goes into "kid who cusses so we know she's evil" mode. Glenn Ford shows up to be cannon fodder. Utterly wasted are Shelley Winters as a housekeeper who does almost nothing except sing "Shortnin' Bread" and a dubbed Sam Peckinpah as a doctor. I still don't know what Franco Nero is doing in the film other than to provide exposition, but his scenes greatly add to the overall fever-dream feel of the movie.

It's not a good movie by any stretch of the imagination, but it is entertaining and very "different." Watch it next time you need some surreal shit in your mind.

# WALL-E

*Robot carnival*

**Year:** 2008

**Director:** Andrew Stanton

**Screenplay:** Andrew Stanton and Jim Reardon

**Cast:** Ben Burtt (voice), Elissa Knight (voice)

*WALL-E* is a fairy tale.

It may not seem like one, at first. It's set in the future, when the Earth is a trash-smothered world abandoned by all its inhabitants save for one small robot: a Waste Allocation Load Lifter Earth class (WALL-E). For the past 700 years this robot has been doing his job: compacting trash into cubes, which he artfully stacks in skyscraper-high towers. In the meantime, he's been collecting the bits and pieces of junk that strike his fancy: Christmas lights, silverware, a Rubik's cube, and a VHS tape of the movie *Hello, Dolly!* All the other robots have long since run down, so WALL-E's only friend is a (quite cute) cockroach.

This has been WALL-E's routine for centuries, but everything changes when he finds something he's never seen before — a plant, whose vibrant green is a shock in the brown and gray landscape. Soon afterward a spaceship deposits probe robot EVE. WALL-E and EVE begin a tentative friendship that's on its way to courtship when EVE sees the plant. It turns out her mission is to find evidence of plant life on Earth, and when she returns to the spaceship, WALL-E tags along. The journey takes WALL-E to a space cruiser where humanity waits for Earth to become habitable again (a wait that was supposed to only take 5 years but has taken 7 centuries). The arrival of the plant and WALL-E will mean some changes for the remaining humans and for the robots that have done all the humans' labor for them.

Pixar's ninth movie may not be my favorite of their films (that honor goes to *Ratatouille*), but it's quite possibly one of their best. The opening sequence alone is worth admission. Not since Terry Gilliam's *Brazil* (which *WALL-E* resembles in many ways) has ugliness been made so beautiful. And yet the beauty doesn't detract from the grimness of this world with its piles and piles of trash, filthy brown skies, and even an orbit that's crammed full of junk. WALL-E's cheerfulness can't disguise the longing he feels for companionship, and when EVE arrives, despite her willingness to shoot at anything that moves, he soon makes overtures of friendship that reach the sleek, all-business EVE.

WALL-E's personality is infectious as he reaches the *Axiom,* the space cruiser where humanity has been awaiting rehabilitation of their planet. In contrast to the desolate Earth, everything on the *Axiom* is in motion. Everything, that is, save for the humans themselves: waited on hand-and-foot by robots, glued to TVs and computer chat screens, their complacency (and the long-term effects of living in space) have made them Weeble-like creatures incapable of getting up should one tumble from his hovering chair. It's WALL-E's presence that jolts an important few of these people out of their daze and gets them to **do** things — like actually enter the spaceship's pool, or to notice the insanely beautiful starscape, or to find out what life on Earth used to be like.

It's weighty and at times fairly dark stuff for a children's movie. But what makes the movie so special is WALL-E himself, for he's not just a drone. Although all he's known is the worst of humanity — left on an abandoned planet to help clean up the consequences of human carelessness — he's become imbued with the best qualities of humankind. He sees the wonder in small things, and he hasn't let his surroundings make him bitter. He touches every life he comes in contact with, for the better.

None of it would work were it not for the heartbreakingly beautiful animation, the voice acting by Ben Burtt and Elissa Knight (who carry the first half of the movie using little more than their names as dialogue), a story that's satirical and sentimental by turns, and the clever direction by Andrew Stanton.

It's a fairy tale. It's a redemption story. It's *The Lorax* for the new millennium. It's *Brazil* with a happy ending.

# War of the Gargantuas

*Brotherly brawl*

**Year:** 1970

**Director:** Ishiro Honda

**Screenplay:** Ishiro Honda and Takeshi Kimura

**Cast:** Russ Tamblyn, Kumi Mizuno, Kenji Sahara

Oh, how I miss Saturday afternoons when I was a kid, when you could turn on the TV and be almost guaranteed that a Japanese monster movie was playing on at least one channel.

Yet somehow, during those years, I never saw *War of the Gargantuas* in its entirety. But I've now remedied that situation and have to say that while it's far from classic kaiju, it breaks the mold in some interesting ways.

It's a dark and stormy night, and a fishing vessel comes under attack. Not from a gargantua, as the title would have you believe, but from a giant octopus. This is rather an effective scene, all the more so because the octopus seems to be sadistically toying with the poor soul who's just trying to steer the boat, grabbing him with tentacles and putting the squeeze on him. But suddenly the octopus is dragged away and killed by a giant, green, hairy, apelike creature. *Gargantua ex machina!* Or not. Because once the gargantua has vanquished the octopus, he promptly sinks the fishing boat.

This is just the first of several attacks by the not-so-jolly green giant. At first his attacks are confined to seaports and fishing villages, but he soon branches out to an attack on an airport (a bloodless but strangely grisly scene, as the gargantua stuffs people in his mouth and spits out their shredded clothes). So the people of Japan turn to the world's most laid-back scientist, Dr. Stuart (Russ Tamblyn phones it in) and his assistant Akemi (Kumi Mizuno). They had captured a baby gargantua some years ago, but it escaped (Tamblyn delivers this line with total unconcern, as if losing a rare and possibly dangerous creature was up there with misplacing your Starbucks treat receipt). Could there be two gargantuas? Could a big battle be in the offing? Especially one with lots of destruction of model buildings?

While *War of the Gargantuas* does stick close to the formula, but there are some things to set it apart from the usual. First, the gargantuas are not the usual reptilian creatures but apelike ones, and as such they are more human in their movements, body language, and expressions. There's a bit of genuine pathos when the brown or "good" gargantua tries to protect his cranky green relative, and when those efforts come to naught. Also, the military's big weapon, an elaborate laser, actually is semi-effective for a change, causing visible harm to the green gargantua.

But there are the usual clichés as well, some welcome and some not. Tamblyn's performance is truly terrible, not just because he is obviously just collecting his paycheck, but because it makes his character look pathologically unconcerned with the goings-on. More horrifying than any of the gargantua predations is the musical number "The Words Get Stuck In My Throat" which unfortunately should be titled "The Song Gets Stuck In Your Head." And I won't spoil the ending, but an eensy-weensy bit more thought might have gone into it. Just saying.

Though flawed, it's a fun treat for those of us looking to recapture those lazy Saturday afternoons of monster movies.

# Watership Down

*Rabbit, run*

**Year:** 1978

**Director:** Martin Rosen

**Screenplay:** Martin Rosen, based on the novel by Richard Adams

**Cast:** John Hurt (voice), Richard Briers (voice), Zero Mostel (voice)

The beauty of the story archetypes of heroic quests and journeys is that they are universal. All it takes is a little imagination and they can even apply to non-human characters, as *Watership Down* so ably demonstrates.

A rabbit warren in the English countryside is peaceful and prosperous, but under threat from men who want to develop the land. One of the rabbits, Fiver, who has the gift of precognition, gets a vision of the grassy fields covered in blood. Persuaded by Fiver's vision, his sensible brother Hazel reaches out to some of the other rabbits to find out if any want to leave in search of a safe place. His band of pilgrims soon consists of a number of rabbits, most notably fighter Bigwig and clever Blackberry.

After some trials and tribulations, the rabbits find their safe place on top of a hill (the titular Watership Down). But soon it becomes clear that the new warren is doomed unless they can find some female rabbits to join. Hazel and his friends make an expedition to an overcrowded, totalitarian warren to escape with some of the does. And when that warren's leader, the fearsome General Woundwort, comes seeking revenge, it's time for some real heroics.

*Watership Down* has the reputation (undeserved, in my opinion) of being one of the more traumatic animated films out there. Certainly it doesn't paint a rosy picture of rabbit life. As the opening creation myth explains, rabbits have so many enemies that they simply refer to them collectively as "the Thousand" and spend so much time fleeing from danger that "stop running" is a euphemism for death. Cats, dogs, badgers, hawks, and rats are just a few of the predators our intrepid bunnies face. But the worst threat comes from man, as amply demonstrated in the surreal, impressionistic sequence in which we learn what happened to the rabbits' old warren (men blocked the holes and killed the rabbits with poison gas).

It sounds grim but isn't really, for Hazel, Bigwig, and the rest are sympathetic characters, clever and resourceful. There are definitely moments of joy to be found in the film, from the lovely countryside to the peace of a warren untroubled by men or other enemies, or the endearing friendship the rabbits form with a gull named Keharr (voiced by a scene-stealing Zero Mostel). The film also does a good job of immersing us in the rabbits' world and culture, trusting the audience to use context and understand the occasional bits of rabbit-language (though one of my favorite moments from the book, when Bigwig essentially tells Woundwort to eat shit and die, was left out).

My main quibbles with the film lie in the adaptation, which is good but could have been better. Then again, bear in mind that I have re-read the book many times, and when my vintage paperback finally fell to pieces a couple years ago I cried. So I had high expectations for the film, which aren't quite met. Director and screenwriter Martin Rosen shortchanges the characters, both in terms of number and characterization, so while we get a good feel for Hazel, Fiver, and Bigwig, less prominent characters like Dandelion the storyteller and Blackberry the innovator have reduced screen time and the story suffers for it. Likewise, the animators run out of ways to show different rabbits in the film's latter half, leading to the rabbits from the totalitarian warren having blue eyes to distinguish them from the "good" rabbits.

These quibbles aside, it's still an affecting film and a memorable story. The animation is limited by today's standards but suits the film well, particularly with its watercolor-inspired images of the English countryside. And while it's not as traumatic as it's been hyped to be, it still may not be the right film for young children. (I saw it at age 10 and suffered no ill effects except for

324

psychological maladjustment and blurred vision, so there.)

---

# What Have You Done to Solange?

*Ouch*

**Year:** 1972

**Director:** Massimo Dallamano

**Screenplay:** Massimo Dallamano and Bruno di Geronimo

**Cast:** Fabio Testi, Karin Baal, Christina Galbo, Camille Keaton

---

I'm not sure what it is about giallo movies that makes me turn to them in times of stress. Maybe it's because they don't seem to take place in our reality, and that quality is somehow soothing (this would explain why I watched *Suspiria* the night of 9/11 — don't ask, it just seemed right at the time).

So after a yucko week I went to a friend's house and popped in *What Have You Done to Solange?* Much to my surprise, while not without flaws it's a well-plotted, smart (but still sleazy) giallo that exists as more than just an excuse for flashy set pieces.

*What Have You Done to Solange?* opens with two lovers sharing an idyllic afternoon in a rowboat. As Henry (Fabio Testi) starts coaxing Elizabeth (Christina Galbo) toward third base, Elizabeth gets a quick glimpse of something happening on the riverbank: a man in black, a frightened girl, the flash of a knife. Henry thinks Elizabeth is just making it up to distract him from getting into her knickers, but alas, she's no longer in the mood and asks him to take her back to school.

School being St. Dollybird's School for Incredibly Hot Girls. Elizabeth's a student there. As for Henry, he's a teacher; his subjects are Italian and gym. Yes, gym. Nice work if you can get it! It's heavily implied that Henry's dalliance with Elizabeth isn't the first time he's been in this somewhat unprofessional, um, position, and it's earned him the enmity of his academic colleagues and much bitterness from his buttoned-up, frosty wife Frau Blucher (Karin Baal).

Well, it turns out that Elizabeth wasn't imagining things. Henry hears a news report of a girl found murdered on the riverbank in an especially gruesome way. (Suffice to say that the ladies should avoid this movie if they've got a gynecological visit in the near future.) Henry goes to scope out the scene, where he manages to both drop his pen *and* end up in an incriminating photo (good one, Henry). His attempts to keep his relationship with Elizabeth secret only make the police, who aren't the dolts we usually see in these movies, even more suspicious. Soon more girls are murdered, both Henry and Frau Blucher are doing some amateur sleuthing, and some ugly secrets emerge about the murder victims and their relationship to a girl named Solange (*I Spit On Your Grave*'s Camille Keaton).

*What Have You Done to Solange?* is a rare bird — it's intelligent trash. The film-makers didn't just dream the story up as a way to show inventive ways to kill people, but put thought into the characters of the victims, murderer, and others. The relationships between the characters are interesting — if not always plausible, especially with Henry and Frau Blucher ("Next on *Oprah*, how being a suspect in a hideous murder spree helped save one man's marriage."). The killings are nasty but not explicit — aftermath shots and descriptions (and in one case, an X-ray image) bring the nastiness home. And both the reason for and the method of the killings are logical, given the killer's motivations.

Yet the movie doesn't ignore its trashy side — rather, it revels in it. There are two (count 'em, **two**) wholly gratuitous shower scenes that offer up a bounty of young female nudity. Not to mention lascivious professors, sleazy photographers, and mean slutty girls.

It's not perfect — Henry's not a very compelling character, and the locale seems to be a very Italian section of London. But the flaws actually work in the film's favor, lightening what could have been — and at times is — a relatively grim affair.

# Whisper

*Careful, he might hear you*

**Year:** 2007

**Director:** Stewart Hendler

**Screenplay:** Christopher Borrelli

**Cast:** Michael Rooker, Blake Woodruff, Josh Holloway, Sarah Wayne Callies

Certain areas of life are made a whole lot easier by low expectations. It's like that old joke about pessimists often being pleasantly surprised. When you don't expect much from a movie, it can please you simply by not being awful.

A case in point is *Whisper*, which tells of a kidnapping that goes wrong in an unexpected way. The crooks are ringleader Sidney (Michael Rooker in an all-too-brief appearance), annoying whiner Vince (Joel Edgerton), decent-guy-who-just-wants-to-open-a-diner-and-go-straight Max

(Josh Holloway), and Max's wife Roxanne (Sarah Wayne Callies). Their plan is to kidnap David (Blake Woodruff), the only child of a very wealthy family and make the ransom their proverbial last big score.

The kidnapping goes without a hitch, but the kidnappers soon discover that David isn't an ordinary kid. He's literally a hellion who can command wolves, cause unfortunate "accidents" to happen to people, and can put thoughts in peoples' heads and turn them against each other. Throw in an isolated winter setting, medical complications, and some long-buried secrets, and the kidnappers start wishing they'd tried another way to make some money.

*Whisper* is basically a mashup of *The Omen* and *The Ransom of Red Chief*, and for what it is, it's fairly entertaining. The death scenes are mostly bloodless but well-executed (particularly the scene on the frozen lake) with some red herrings thrown in. The adult actors acquit themselves well, though Rooker isn't in the movie nearly enough for my taste. The snowbound isolation of the kidnappers' hideout sets the mood nicely.

As David, Woodruff isn't bad but he's so obviously a Cliché'd Creepy Kid from the start that you wonder why the other characters don't get spooked and abandon the kidnapping plan right away. More subtlety and mystery about David's true nature would have been nice, and made for a more suspenseful film. But it's clear from the start what is going to happen, and the only suspense is figuring out how it's going to happen. Fortunately the plot plays out in ways that are just unexpected enough to keep things interesting.

Aside from a somewhat bogus ending that screams of studio/test audience interference, *Whisper* is a reasonably entertaining movie that's ideal for when you don't feel like using your brain very much.

# White Noise 2: The Light

*He thought there was Serenity in the light and ... oh, never mind*

**Year:** 2007

**Director:** Patrick Lussier

**Screenplay:** Matt Venne

**Cast:** Nathan Fillion, Katee Sackhoff

Full disclosure time — I've never seen the first *White Noise* film, and I only rented this one because it stars my beloved Nathan Fillion, who complimented me on my hat when I met him at a convention. But for a direct-to-DVD sequel to a movie I've never seen and haven't heard much good about, *White Noise 2: The Light* is better than it has a right to be.

Abe Dale (Nathan Fillion is the movie's saving grace) has a wonderfully happy life with his loving wife and young son. So of course, tragedy looms. Before the opening credits Abe's wife and son are murdered by a random lunatic. Abe is distraught and grieving, and worse still, he doesn't have my phone number. If he did, I could invite him over and aim to misbehave. I mean, I could make him some cinnamon toast and give him consoling hugs. Lots of consoling hugs. *Oh mais oui.*

Where was I? Anyway, Abe can't handle the grief, so he downs several bottles of pills and a quart of booze. Unfortunately, he neglected to read chapter four of *Suicide for Dummies*, in which they tell you not to leave your suicide note on your answering machine in case well-meaning friends hear it and try to change your plans. Abe gets rushed to the hospital where he flatlines, has the whole light-at-the-end-of-the-tunnel experience, and is just about to have a happy reunion with his wife and kid when the doctors zap him with the paddles and resuscitate him. Thanks a lot, doc!

Once Abe recovers he finds that he's hearing all sorts of audio/visual distortions on electronic devices, and even more worrisome, starts seeing a white light around people who are soon to die. You'd think, after finding out first-hand about the afterlife, Abe would be reconciled to the whole mortality thing, but instead he starts trying to save those marked for death, and opens up a big spooky can of worms in the process. So much for being a Good Samaritan.

The main problem with *White Noise 2* is that it can't decide what it wants to be. Is it a spooky yet poignant film about mortality, like *Jacob's Ladder*? Or is it a ripoff of *The Ring*? Unfortunately the film's most successful moments are in the former category but it spends way too much time in the latter, with lots of "Boo! Gotcha!" scares with mangled ghosts showing up randomly and TVs going all static-y. The special effects have a surprising amount of good stunt work, but far too much overdone CGI (i.e. the tunnel of light scene, which should be serene but has too much extraneous spookiness). Likewise, the screenplay is strong in places, with some plot twists that are actually surprising, but a tacked-on "stinger" ending almost ruins the whole thing. The film-makers would have done well to emulate *Jacob's Ladder* or perhaps *The Changeling*, and left the *Ring* business alone.

Luckily we have Nathan Fillion on hand to give it his all and more or less save the film. He gets to run the full emotional spectrum from happiness to despair, from confusion and terror to bittersweet resignation. He does a great job with the role and he's fairly well served by the screenplay, which presents Abe as a good-hearted and intelligent man. It's too bad the role and performance weren't in a stronger movie. (And as a *Firefly* fan I did appreciate the reference to Captain Reynolds, clumsy as it was.)

The rest of the cast is fine, with *Battlestar Galactica*'s Katee Sackhoff as a nurse who befriends Abe. Her character's a shade too cheery considering the downbeat goings-on of the movie, but she and Fillion have good chemistry and their relationship is believable.

The extras are quite fun, including two featurettes about the film with Fillion being his incredibly charming and funny self (anyone who's seen his other behind-the-scenes features or his convention appearances will know exactly what I'm talking about). There's also a documentary on near-death experiences with survivors testifying about the experience.

*White Noise 2* isn't the movie it could have been, but it's better than I expected.

# Witchfinder General

*Much of Madness, and more of Sin*

**Year:** 1968

**Director:** Michael Reeves

**Screenplay:** Tom Baker and Michael Reeves, based on the novel by Ronald Bassett

**Cast:** Vincent Price, Ian Ogilvy, Hilary Dwyer, Robert Russell

"Historical horror" may not be an official subgenre, but I'm certainly a fan of it. The past holds plenty of scary stuff, and mankind's cruelty is more frightening than any ghost or ghoul. Case in point is *Witchfinder General*, a film notable not just for its portrayal of historical horrors, but for showcasing Vincent Price's best genre performance, and for being one of the most relentlessly downbeat films ever.

It's the 1640s and England is being torn apart by civil war. With war has come a breakdown in order and justice, leaving whole swaths of the country vulnerable to ruthless sorts like witchfinder Matthew Hopkins (Price). Accompanied by his repulsive assistant John Stearne (Robert Russell), Hopkins travels from village to village, singling out those accused of witchcraft, torturing them, killing them, and then collecting a nice fee from the local magistrate.

One day Hopkins' work takes him to a village where the local Catholic priest has been accused of demonic practices. Hopkins and Stearne waste no time in torturing the priest, only to be interrupted by Sarah (Hilary Dwyer), the priest's adopted niece. In a desperate attempt to save her uncle from further torment and execution, Sarah submits to Hopkins' sexual advances. However, after Stearne rapes Sarah, Hopkins sees her as soiled goods and has the priest executed anyway. Sarah's fiancée Marshall (Ian Ogilvy) finds out what happened and swears vengeance — and things go from bad to worse.

The horrors of *Witchfinder General* are many, starting from its opening scene when a woman is dragged, screaming, through town to a gallows. It's clear that she's doomed, and will die as unpleasantly as possible (when she faints from sheer terror, she's revived with a bucket of cold water so she can be hanged seconds later). We never learn who the woman is or why she was convicted of witchcraft, and the worst part is that those details don't matter — in this society, anyone can be accused, tortured, convicted, and executed on the flimsiest of grounds. It's a cruel irony when Hopkins speaks of "due process," for his victims are doomed from the moment they are accused: if they protest the charges or somehow manage to survive the ordeals they're put through as part of interrogation, it's because the Devil helped them.

Price expertly gives a face to the evil not just of Hopkins himself but of the social, religious, and political climate that made witch hunts possible. Putting aside the hamminess that crept into many of his genre performances, Price portrays Hopkins as coldly arrogant and intelligent, a man who cleverly uses religion to satisfy his lust for money, power, and women. Whether he actually believe in witches or has any religious faith at all is beside the point. His overriding emotion seems to be contempt: for the superstitious villagers who accuse their friends and neighbors of witchcraft; for the women he can't have except through extortion and rape; for his assistant Stearne and the blatant, casual sadism Stearne employs in their witch-hunting partnership (one of the more subtle joys of the film is watching Hopkins and Stearne seethe with mutual resentment of each other).

But it's not just Price's show, and the other actors all acquit themselves well. Russell is wonderfully loathsome as the thuggish Stearne — your skin crawls every time he's on screen. Ogilvy has the most difficult role: at first glance he's the heroic soldier bent on justice for his fiancée, but by the movie's end he's become so consumed by his need for revenge that he's gone off the deep end. Dwyer has what at first appears to be a simple damsel-in-distress role, but she clearly portrays her resolve to save her uncle and her dismay at the revenge-obsessed Marshall. She's probably the only character who truly understands that justice hasn't been meted out at the movie's end.

The movie may be familiar to Americans under the title *The Conqueror Worm*, which comes from a poem by Edgar Allan Poe. It was retitled when acquired by American-International Pictures, to make audiences think it was one of their Poe-inspired films, and an intro and close with Price narrating part of the poem were added. (These additions are available on the *Vincent Price Collection* Blu-Ray set.)

# Wizards

*Peace out*

**Year:** 1977

**Director:** Ralph Bakshi

**Screenplay:** Ralph Bakshi

**Cast:** Bob Holt (voice), Jesse Welles (voice), Richard Romanus (voice)

I believe it was Tolstoy who said that all happy families were alike, but that every unhappy family was unhappy in its own way. A similar thing can be said of movies. Good movies are just that — good. Consequently they're difficult to review, and that is why I review so many movies of questionable quality.

Bad movies, on the other hand, come in many varieties, from the painful to the merely boring. And then there are what I call Perfect Storm bad movies — films in which lunacy, sincerity, and ineptitude come together. *Wizards* is one of those films.

(Now, I know the "ineptitude" point is going to get me some flak from the Ralph Bakshi acolytes, but trust me — watch *Wizards* when you are sober and no longer 15 years old. You'll see what I mean.)

*Wizards* is one of those films that was both ahead of its time and incredibly dated the moment it hit screens in 1977 (it didn't help that its brief moment of box-office glory was stolen the very next week by *Star Wars*). This is apparent from its first frames, which use a cheesy futuristic typeface and have Tangerine Dream knockoff music. Lengthy voiceover tells us how the world was destroyed by nuclear war, and after many thousands of years Earth is finally being restored. In the "bad" lands are what's left of humanity, mostly reduced to mutants and monsters. The "good" lands are populated by fairies and elves, which are supposed to be beautiful and awesome but for the most part end up being twee and annoying.

One day two wizards are born: the cuddlesome and good one is Avatar, and the creepy-looking bad one is Blackwolf. Maybe if their mother had given them names a little less stereotypical things might have worked out differently. Anyway, years pass. Avatar is now an older dude who seems to have gotten a bit lazy and mostly likes to hang around with zaftig fairy princess Eleanor. Meanwhile, Blackwolf has gone full-throttle evil and we know this because he has red eyes and parts of his arms are raw bone, as if he'd been spending some vacation time in the *Men Behind The Sun* prison camp. For years Blackwolf has been leading armies of demons and mutants in an effort to take over the good fairy-and-elf lands, but with no success. But now he's uncovered a secret weapon — something that will both inspire his troops and demoralize the elven warriors. What could this weapon be? Ordinarily I wouldn't spoil it since it's the jaw-dropping peak/nadir of the film, but here goes: it's stock footage of Hitler and Third Reich propaganda.

And this is just the backstory, folks.

The plot itself gets in motion when an assassin named Necron 99 kills a fairyland president who just happens to be Eleanor's father. This gets Avatar off his ass and he takes Eleanor and an elf warrior named Weehawk to go after Blackwolf. They're guided by the assassin, who's undergone a personality transformation thanks to … um, I'm not really sure. Magic? Brain damage? Plot convenience? Anyway, Necron 99 is now renamed Peace (you may have gathered that subtlety is not this movie's strong point). And off they go to stop Blackwolf and his army.

The really vexing thing about *Wizards* is that it's best known for the things that are its biggest flaws. For an animated film, there's surprisingly little animation in it. Lengthy chunks of the film are told using still drawings with voiceover by an uncredited (and quite good) Susan Tyrrell, and Blackwolf's army is largely depicted by rotoscoped footage from live action films, primarily Sergei Eisenstein's *Alexander Nevsky*. The animation itself is repetitive, cheap-looking, and ugly even when it's supposed to be depicting the peaceful fairy-and-elf lands. Which is a shame because when taken as individual images, some of Bakshi's creations are quite striking (a prime example is the famous poster with Peace on his two-legged steed). Moreover, some of the backgrounds in Blackwolf's land are captivating — post-nuclear industrial wreckage with a M. C. Escher twist.

But even if the animation were stronger and more consistent, it wouldn't change the fact that the story of *Wizards* is trite and hamfisted. Entire plot threads and characters, such as the other assassins and Blackwolf's queen, are brought up and then discarded. The use of Nazi imagery as an example of ultimate evil is understandable, yet this aspect of the film is so heavy-handed that the whole thing ends up being almost offensive. Similarly unsubtle is the "nature and magic is good, technology is evil" theme repeatedly brought home in the film, though it gets a nice subversive touch in a cynical ending that says sometimes you need to fight fire with fire.

*Wizards* isn't a good movie, and yet it's so out there, so crazy that it sticks in the mind afterward. You may not like it, but you have to admit there's nothing else out there quite like it. This may seem like a backhanded compliment, but in an age when so many bad films vanish from memory the moment you leave the theater, it's not so bad.

# Wolfen

*It's a dog-eat-dog world*

**Year:** 1981

**Director:** Michael Wadleigh

**Screenplay:** Michael Wadleigh and David Eyre, based on the novel by Whitley Strieber

**Cast:** Albert Finney, Gregory Hines, Edward James Olmos

Remember Spaghetti-Os? When you were a kid you just loved them, and weren't they the tastiest damn thing? You could eat them every week!

Then you got older and tried Spaghetti-Os again, and realized they weren't all that great. Kind of lousy, in fact.

Watching *Wolfen* is a bit like that. I first saw it on cable when I was 12 or so and thought it pretty neat. But rewatching it a number of years later shows it to be a movie with a few good ideas that's sabotaged by a sluggish pace and a too-great sense of its own importance.

Based on a novel by Whitley "I got anal probed by aliens" Strieber, *Wolfen* opens in a derelict section of the South Bronx that makes Beirut look like a great place to raise your kids up, where the billionaire head of a big corporation is taking part in a ground-breaking ceremony for an urban renewal project. The billionaire grins for the cameras and the press, and all the while some other eyes with cool heat-vision effects are watching him too.

That night the billionaire, his coke-sniffing wife, and their bodyguard stop to lollygag around Battery Park when they're slaughtered by an unseen attacker. The next morning the police chief calls in retired detective Dewey Wilson (Albert Finney) to investigate. Suspecting terrorism, Dewey first teams up with terrorism expert Rebecca Neff (Diane Venora); but the case soon takes a different turn when coroner's assistant Whittington (Gregory Hines) figures out that the wounds don't look like they were caused by anything human.

*Wolfen*'s director, Michael Wadleigh (best known for directing *Woodstock*), said he wanted to create a thinking-person's horror film, and that should tell you all you need to know. Like John Frankenheimer with *Prophecy,* Wadleigh doesn't know how to make a horror film actually scary. He's too busy making points about society and "who is the real savage" and all that. When he tries to make things scary, it doesn't always work. The point-of-view shots that are arguably *Wolfen*'s best-remembered feature, are not only wearying after a while, but they drain all the suspense out of things. When you see a lone wino standing in an empty lot, and the killer-cam starts racing toward the wino, it's not hard to figure out what's going to happen, but much harder to care, or even be interested.

Because the audience has a pretty good clue from the beginning what's going on, the terrorism subplot only serves to drag things out unnecessarily. Also contributing to the film's sluggish pace is the acting. Albert Finney spends the film looking rumpled, cranky, and sleepy, like Winnie-the-Pooh roused from hibernation. He's also a complete cipher — we learn nothing about why he retired, nor why he's the right man for the job. Diane Venora has nothing to do except provide a dubious love interest for Finney. Gregory Hines has fun as the coroner, but his performance seems to be coming from another, more enjoyable movie. Edward James Olmos livens up the screen, though, as a Native American who's initially a suspect in the case. Future Francis Dolarhyde Tom Noonan shows up briefly as a nerdy zoologist but doesn't do much.

*Wolfen* isn't a complete loss. Its central idea is interesting. The wolves wait too long to make their appearance, but they are beautiful animals. The New York locations are good, though I hope the South Bronx has gotten fixed up a bit since. There's some effective gore, including one of cinema's better decapitation scenes, though the scenes are so quick that if you glance at your popcorn bucket you might miss them.

# Xtro

*Icky*

**Year:** 1983

**Director:** Harry Bromley Davenport

**Screenplay:** Harry Bromley Davenport, Iain Cassie, Michel Parry, Robert Smith

**Cast:** Philip Sayer, Bernice Stegers, Maryam d'Abo

Some movies are very much a product of their time and place, and *Xtro* is an excellent example of this. Made in the early 1980s, when aliens were still quite the thing thanks to *Alien* (and its many ripoffs) and *E.T.*, it also overuses the era's favorite practical special effects and boasts a synthesizer score that couldn't be more 80s if it tried. Does it hold up today? Not really, because what had shock value back then doesn't now, and shock value is pretty much all *Xtro* has going for it.

We're at a cottage somewhere in the English countryside where dad Sam and son Tony are playing with the family dog. The suddenly the sky goes dark and Sam is taken away by a spaceship. Three years later, Tony is still having nightmares about his father's abduction. Tony's mother Rachel insists that Sam just ran out on the family, and she's taken up with a new fellow, Joe.

Then another spaceship arrives and leaves behind a weird crab-human creature. Said creature promptly kills two people, then impregnates a woman who then has the world's fastest pregnancy (about two minutes, tops) and gives birth to the (fully grown!) Sam. Sam heads home and the movie then vacillates between kitchen-sink drama as Sam, Rachel, and Joe try to sort out the awkward domestic situation, and increasingly bizarre and icky manifestations of Sam's alien powers, along with his turning Tony into an alien as well.

You've most likely gathered that *Xtro* isn't a terribly logical film. It has a very "throw it at the wall and see what sticks" approach, tossing in things like: toys that can be made large and usually deadly, a black panther materializing out of nowhere, a weird fixation on women being forced to breed aliens in various ways, and a clown. It's not nearly as interesting as it sounds, and the unlikable characters don't help. Neither does the "I just got a new keyboard! I wonder what this button does?" synthesizer score. The effects are decent for the time, although there's far too much of the "skin puffing up" visual that was popular at the time, and if you feel like you haven't seen enough slimy things in the movies these days, *Xtro* will give you all the slime you need, and then some.

Despite the occasionally interesting visual (the crab-human alien, especially), *Xtro* just doesn't work. It's a curiosity piece, primarily for those of us who saw its admittedly grabbing VHS cover art on the video store shelves back in the day, and wondered what the hell all that was about.

# Yellow Submarine

*The love you make*

**Year:** 1968

**Director:** George Dunning

**Screenplay:** Lee Minoff, Al Brodax, Jack Mendelsohn, and Erich Segal

**Cast:** Paul Angelis (voice), John Clive (voice), Dick Emery (voice), Geoffrey Hughes (voice), The Beatles

The list of films that could have gone disastrously wrong but ended up as classics is a long one. Somewhere in the upper echelons of this list is *Yellow Submarine*. Though made for the most part without the direct participation of its ostensible stars, the Beatles, and featuring a storyline that's thin to say the least, it succeeds through a combination of inventiveness, fun, and the undeniable power of the music.

In faraway Pepperland, the inhabitants spend their time enjoying life and reveling in beauty, primarily the beauty of music. But on the outskirts of Pepperland dwell the Blue Meanies, who despise happiness in general and music in particular. They launch an attack on Pepperland with missiles that destroy anything beautiful and cause the people become drab and pale. Most crucially, music is silenced. It's up to Captain Fred to voyage in the Yellow Submarine to get help, which he does, from four guys named John, Paul, George, and Ringo.

The wonderful thing about *Yellow Submarine* is that it never troubles to explain anything. Pepperland and the Blue Meanies are presented without any sort of backstory or mythology. It's simply understood that Pepperland is a happy place, and the Meanies don't like it. Likewise, when Fred meets the Beatles (you see what I did there?) we take it for granted that they are the ones to help. And as the submarine makes its journey to Pepperland, it passes through the Seas of Time, Science, Monsters, and Holes; as the characters meet up with the Nowhere Man; as the story stops to give us another beautifully animated song, we go along with it. It's a ride, and a fun one.

That's really what the film is about: fun. It's got a childlike inventiveness and enthusiasm for its central conceit of what would happen if the Beatles went on an adventure. They could run into some monsters! Yeah, that would be great! And the Meanies' ultimate weapon is a giant flying glove! How cool is that! And don't get me started on the house where the Beatles live — it's a kid's fantasy of the Coolest House Ever. Yet the movie's got a grownup wit to it, particularly in the dialogue between the band members, and in the Blue Meanie leader's rants.

The movie truly shines in its visualization of the songs. All have something to offer, but the highlight has to be "Eleanor Rigby" — this sequence is probably one of best marriages of animation with music, perfectly capturing the song's melancholy.

If there's one flaw with the film, it's that the Beatles themselves don't provide the voices for their animated characters. Fortunately, the voice actors do a reasonable job of impersonation, and most crucially, the screenwriters captured the public personalities of the band members nicely — snarky John, good-hearted lunk Ringo, mystical George, and gentlemanly Paul. The original characters fare well too, particularly the leader of the Blue Meanies and his second-in-command Max, and the not-quite-as-brilliant-as-he-thinks Nowhere Man.

It's a feast for the eyes, the ears, and the mind. If you haven't seen it yet, you owe it to yourself to watch it.

# The Yellow Wallpaper

*Either this wallpaper goes or I do*

**Year:** 2012

**Director:** Logan Thomas

**Screenplay:** Logan Thomas and Aric Cushing, based on the short story by Charlotte Perkins Gilman

**Cast:** Juliet Landau, Aric Cushing, Dale Dickey, Veronica Cartwright

One of my favorite pieces of horror fiction is "The Yellow Wallpaper," a short story published in 1892 by Charlotte Perkins Gilman. It's the journal entries of a woman whose physician husband has rented a house for the summer, and has confined the woman to an upstairs room. The isolation is supposed to help the woman recover from "nervous depression — a slight hysterical tendency" (in fact, the woman may be suffering from post-partum depression, as there are references to a baby the woman is unable to take care of). She's forbidden to read or have visitors, as her patronizing husband deems those things too stimulating; she has nothing to do but sit in her room for hours on end. The room is covered in a particularly unattractive yellow wallpaper, and with nothing else to do, the woman obsesses over the wallpaper, becoming more and more mentally unstable.

What makes the short story so effective is its ambiguity — is it a ghost story, or a tale of ordinary madness? However, this ambiguity, coupled with the fact that it takes place entirely in the narrator's mind, makes the story not the best choice for a film adaptation. Perhaps someone like David Lynch, who can make horror out of the most mundane surroundings, could turn it into a powerful short film.

Unfortunately, the makers of *The Yellow Wallpaper* decided to use the story's title and a few small bits of the story, and then make their own story. Which could be forgiven, if the proceedings were compelling. But aside from scattered moments of effectiveness and Juliet Landau's performance, there's little to recommend the film.

The film opens with a married couple, Charlotte and John (Juliet Landau and Aric Cushing) and Charlotte's sister Jennie (Dale Dickey), seeking a new home after theirs burned down, causing the death of Charlotte and John's child Sarah. Apparently the news that a home was available for rent came to the couple while the ashes of their home were literally still warm, is available for an extremely low price, is fairly isolated, and so on. In short, everything about this house screams, "BAD SHIT WILL HAPPEN HERE" but the trio miss all the obvious signs and move in anyway.

The sequence that follows is actually rather effective, focused less on supernatural shenanigans and more on the family's attempts to cope with the loss of literally everything: their daughter, their house, their possessions. Indeed, they have nothing but the clothes on their backs and have to make do with old clothes they find in the attic. John and Charlotte are driven away from each other by their grief (and by guilt as well), and Jennie finds herself with no purpose in life now that there's no child to help care for. But then things start going bump in the night and the emotional drama gives way to drawn-out scenes of things skulking around the house, creepy townspeople, the bad history of the house, and more, until it all ends in a wholly unsatisfying way.

There are saving graces: The always underrated Juliet Landau turns in a nice performance, giving Charlotte's character nuance and depth, particularly in her scenes shortly after moving into the house. Unfortunately she's not on screen nearly enough to save the film. Likewise, the aforementioned scenes of the family struggling to put its life back together. I was particularly taken with a scene in which Charlotte and Jennie have to host a flock of gossipy, superficial local women who've come to visit, and are visibly uncomfortable with the situation as they're still in shock from the fire and the death of Charlotte's child.

Sadly, far too much time goes to John's character. He's already an unpleasant character, brusque and dismissive of the women, and Aric Cushing's performance is probably the film's greatest failing, a one-note affair that makes his scenes a chore to watch. Add to this numerous scenes so dark as to be incomprehensible, subplots that go nowhere, heavy-handed music, and some truly bizarre scenery (what's with the weird desert surroundings?). There's little tie-in to the short story — save for some scenes in a yellow wallpapered room where Charlotte spends an inordinate amount of time (we're told this, not shown it), and a reference to Charlotte writing the title story, but there's no resonance between that and the rest of the film's events — it feels tacked on.

It's a shame, because in the right hands the story could make an excellent short film, one in which Landau's performance wouldn't have gone to waste. I give the film-makers props for at least trying to bring a story that today's horror fans may not have heard of to the screen, but they didn't go about it in the right way.

# Zabriskie Point

*Fall down, go boom*

**Year:** 1970

**Director:** Michelangelo Antonioni

**Screenplay:** Michelangelo Antonioni, Franco Rossetti, Sam Shepard, Tonino Guerra, Clare Peploe

**Cast:** Mark Frechette, Daria Halprin, Rod Taylor

Pop culture intersections are such a strange thing. Aside from some art cinema enthusiasts and a few relics from the 1960s, probably the group of people most interested in the DVD release of *Zabriskie Point* are Pink Floyd fans rabid for the songs the band wrote for the movie's soundtrack. It's a bit similar to the way the video for Metallica's "One" got metalheads interested in the movie *Johnny Got His Gun.*

Well, the wait is over! *Zabriskie Point* is now on DVD and while watching it may not be the stupidest thing I've ever done in pursuit of Perfect Floyd Fandom, it's in the top fucking five.

*Zabriskie Point* opens with a lengthy scene at a student meeting where lots of talk about the revolution happens, along with loads of bickering about who is a more authentic revolutionary. The scene goes on and on, made all the more painful because it's clear that Antonioni hired non-actors, presumably for authenticity.

I must insert a caveat here — the DVD I rented was defective and we had to skip a bit. It was kind of a shame because I think we might have missed some police beating up students (not that I condone violence, but at least something would have been happening). Anyway, we rejoin the movie at the police station where students are getting hassled by the pigs, who won't give injured people medical attention, write down a history professor's occupation as "clerk," and when a student jokingly gives his name as "Karl Marx" they write it down as "Carl Marks." See, not only are they fascists, they're stupid too! How delightfully amusing! Boy, do I feel superior now!

The student who gave the "Karl Marx" name is Mark (Mark Frechette), who is 100 percent personality-free. Mark and his room-mate/fellow revolutionary Sonny Bono (not really, it just looks like him) have a very vague confrontation with the police that may result in Mark killing a policeman. To be honest, it's hard to tell if what we're seeing is ambiguity or bad film-making. At any rate, Mark's on the lam now and decides to do the only sensible thing — he steals a small plane and flies out to the desert.

Said desert is where he meets our heroine, Daria (Daria Halprin). (Have you noticed that the character names are the same as the actors' real names? That's not an accident.) Daria works for an Evil Capitalist (Rod Taylor) and is driving to his mansion in Phoenix for some sort of meeting, I think. (Details may have been in that portion of the film I had to skip.) Daria drives on (and on and on) through the desert and after an encounter with some sexually aggressive 11-year-olds (thereby increasing the movie's Squick Factor), finds herself repeatedly buzzed by Mark in his stolen plane. She writes a message for him (that we never see) in the sand and he buzzes her again. Daria realizes that Mark is a douchebag, or a fun guy, which in this movie amounts to the same thing; he lands the plane and the two of them gad about the desert for a while, exchanging the occasional bit of revolutionary/philosophical banter. They finally get to the titular Zabriskie Point and commence the second-most notorious scene of the movie: the Death Valley orgy (a bunch of other hippies appear out of nowhere for a big group sex scene and promptly disappear once the lovin' is over).

Want to see how boring and wholly lacking in eroticism an orgy scene can be? Watch this movie. (Not to mention physically uncomfortable — they're rolling around in the sand and don't even have a blanket or anything. Ow.)

After the sandy frolic, Mark and Daria get some paint from a desert-dwelling hermit (because Lord knows desert-dwelling hermits always have buckets of day-glo paint laying around). They paint the plane with revolutionary slogans and crude pictures of breasts, then Mark flies the plane back to Los Angeles. Of course a boatload of cops are waiting for him and as he lands the plane they shoot him.

At this point I was desperately hoping the movie would be over, but no, we have to follow the grief-stricken (I think — her emoting leaves something to be desired) Daria to Evil Capitalist's house. Daria wanders all forlorn past the pool where establishment women jabber meaninglessly, then hugs a fountain. Really. Then the disc went defective again and I had to skip to the film's most notorious scene: Shit Blows Up.

Daria, having fled the lair of the Evil Capitalist, stands staring up at the mountaintop house. She imagines it blowing up. From several angles. Repeatedly. Then she imagines the trappings of capitalist society blowing up in slow motion: a refrigerator, a TV set, racks of clothes, shelves of books, and so on. It's all done in super slow-motion so as you watch the refrigerator blow up you can see steaks and cucumbers falling slooooooowly through the air. Wheeee. Jump cut back to Daria, who smiles at her destructive fantasy, then drives off into the sunset and the movie finally ends.

Those of you who want a detailed analysis of why this movie sucks, read on. For those with limited time to read, I'll answer your most burning questions:

**Q: Does the Floyd music kick ass?**

**A:** What you hear of it does. There's a tiny snippet of a country-ish song. More compelling is the weird opening number "Heart Beat, Pig Meat" over the opening credits. The final number, set during the big blow-up, is a reworked version of "Careful With That Axe Eugene" titled "Come In Number 51, Your Time is Up." The song kicks all kinds of ass but it's honestly not worth slogging through the film. The soundtrack (complete with unused Floyd tracks) is available on Amazon or downloadable on iTunes. Go ahead and get it, Roger would want you to.

**Q: Is that explosion scene as cool as I've heard?**

**A:** Sadly, no. It's impressive at first (remember, this was before CGI so it's a real explosion) but then it just drags on and on and on. It's as if Michael Bay had directed *Koyaanisqatsi*. Not helping matters is the fact that Antonioni completely bungled the meshing of music with the timing of the explosions.

**Q: Does the chick who can't act show her boobs?**

**A:** Yes, but only briefly and they're all covered with dirt so it's not a terribly sexy sight.

All right, now for the more detailed analysis, although there are so many things wrong with this movie it's hard to know where to begin.

There's no story to speak of. Revolutionary stuff happens, Mark steals a plane, harasses Daria, they hook up, he gets killed in a stupid way, and she imagines stuff blowing up. That's it. And every scene in the film is stretched out as long as possible. Watch Daria drive on and on through the desert! Watch Mark buzz her over and over and over again! Watch obnoxious students prattle endlessly about their revolutionary street cred. You'll find yourself screaming, "**Do** something!" more than once, I guarantee it.

I'm not going to come down too hard on Mark Frechette and Daria Halprin — yes, they can't act and were picked solely to give the revolution a pretty face, but not even good actors could pull off the atrocious dialogue (which took five — yes, that's right, **five** — writers to concoct). Frechette went to jail on a bank robbery charge a few years after the film and ended up dead with a barbell on his neck; Halprin was briefly married to Dennis Hopper. So things didn't work out too well for either of them.

Probably the most obnoxious part of the film is Antonioni's direction. The camerawork is pretty, but it's overwhelmed by pretentious direction (check out the framing he uses for Evil Capitalist, always shot from below at odd angles with the American flag billowing in the breeze behind him. Yes, we get it.) Just as subtle is the kids-good/adults-bad and the revolutionaries-good/cops-bad imagery. Look at the commercial for the desert development that uses mannequins instead of real people. Look at the fat, ugly Midwesterners who scarf down ice cream while they fail to appreciate the desert's beauty. And the worst part is that this is all deadly serious. It may look like that Monty Python parody skit "Le Fromage Grande" but sadly, it's not.

The most fun one can have watching this movie is imagining the reaction of the suits at MGM. Clearly hoping to have another *Easy Rider* on their hands, instead they watched the film receive scathing reviews and tank horribly at the box office.

# Finale: And the Award Goes to...

Now it's time to hand out some awards to the movies covered in this book.

**Worst Song**
"Friends" — *Miami Connection*
Honorable Mentions: "Little Child" in *The Naked Kiss* and "The Words Get Stuck In My Throat" in *War of the Gargantuas*

**Best Title**
*Nude For Satan*
Honorable Mention: *Master of the Flying Guillotine*

**Worst Ending**
*Fist of the North Star*
Honorable Mentions: *The Gates of Hell, Zabriskie Point*

**Best Sequel That Has Almost Nothing To Do With The Original Film**
*The Curse of the Cat People*

**Worst Demises**
Curb stomp — *American History X*
Drowned in the bathtub by own dad — *The Changeling*
Pages of book stuffed down throat — *The Cook, The Thief, His Wife, And Her Lover*
Buried up to neck below high tide line — *Creepshow*
Human skull vs. fire hydrant — *King of New York*
Covered in clay and then baked — *The Naked Prey*
Falling into a room full of razor wire — *Suspiria*
Eaten by a bed — *Death Bed: The Bed That Eats*
Knife up the hoohah — *What Have You Done to Solange?*
Impregnated by alien-crab-human monster — *Xtro*
Bitten by rattlesnake while sinking in quicksand — *Stanley*
Head explosion — *Scanners*
Bisected by runaway elevator cable — *Damien: Omen 2*
Stabbed with pitchfork while in huge pot of boiling water — *Mandingo*
Head turned into mass of bugs and snakes — *Halloween III: Season of the Witch*
Raped by giant worm — *Galaxy of Terror*
Burned at stake — *The Devils*
Buried alive — *The Serpent and the Rainbow*

**Worst Deus Ex Machinas**
The volcano — *War of the Gargantuas*
Convenient life rafts — *Poseidon*

**Performances Much Better Than The Movies They're In**
Paula Sheppard — *Alice, Sweet Alice*
Camille Keaton — *I Spit On Your Grave*
Tim Robbins — *Jacob's Ladder*
Caroline Williams — *The Texas Chainsaw Massacre 2*
Nathan Fillion — *White Noise 2: The Light*
Lena Olin — *Romeo is Bleeding*

**Worst Literary Adaptation**
*The Yellow Wallpaper*

**Best Literary Adaptations**
*Jaws*
*L.A. Confidential*
*Tinker, Tailor, Soldier, Spy*

**Worst Choices for "Dinner and a Movie"**
*The Cook, the Thief, His Wife, and Her Lover*
*Salò or The 120 Days of Sodom*
*Matango*
*Meet the Feebles*
*Cannibal Ferox*
*Ravenous*

**Best Candidates for TV Spinoffs in Which the Characters Team Up to Solve Mysteries**
Elvis Presley and John F. Kennedy — *Bubba Ho-Tep*
Django Freeman and King Schultz — *Django Unchained*
Father Dyer and Detective Kinderman — *The Exorcist III*
Sam and Vincent — *Ronin*
Rosencrantz and Guildenstern — *Rosencrantz and Guildenstern Are Dead*
Ahmed and Herger — *The 13th Warrior*

# Don't stop now: 200 more films to watch

So you've made your way through all 200 films in this book. Congratulations! I commend you on your taste (or lack thereof, depending).

And now here are 200 more films I consider worth viewing. Some are good, some are bad, some are in the middle, and some are just plain nuts. Have fun!

**The Abominable Dr. Phibes** (1971): Vincent Price and his beautiful henchwoman kill people in interesting ways.

**The Adventures of Baron Munchausen** (1988): Undisciplined but visually dazzling fable from Terry Gilliam.

**The Adventures of Robin Hood** (1938): Errol Flynn is the most charming, handsome outlaw ever.

**The Adventures of Tintin** (2011): Spot-on movie adaptation of the comics by Hergé.

**Aguirre: The Wrath of God** (1972): Conquistadors led by Klaus Kinski lose their way and their minds in the jungle.

**Airplane!** (1980): This send-up of airport disaster movie is still hilarious decades later.

**Alien** (1979): The original terror-in-space film has lost none of its power over the years.

**Alligator** (1980): Giant alligator lives in the sewer and munches on people. Pretty intelligent for an animal-attack movie.

**Amelie** (2001): Endearing French whimsy.

**American Beauty** (1999): Drama about modern suburbia is good for its first two-thirds, then turns into an episode of *Three's Company*.

**Angel Heart** (1987): Mickey Rourke investigates a singer's disappearance and finds murder, voodoo, and worse.

**Annie Hall** (1987): Woody Allen's comedy about love and relationships is a delight and one of his best films.

**Animal Crackers** (1930): The Marx Brothers unleash their usual brand of anarchy.

**Apocalypse Now** (1979): Vietnam War meets Joseph Conrad's "Heart of Darkness" and they really hit it off.

**Army of Darkness** (1992): Third and funniest of Sam Raimi's Evil Dead films, with Bruce Campbell being hilarious and gorgeous.

**Audition** (1999): A widower tries to find a new lady and things go terribly wrong.

**The Atomic Cafe** (1982): Hilarious and chilling compilation of atomic safety films.

**The Big Lebowski** (1998): What happens when a stoned doofus tries to solve a complicated noir mystery.

**Big Trouble in Little China** (1986): Kurt Russell runs afoul of mystical shenanigans. John Carpenter's most delightful film.

**The Birds** (1963): Animal attack movie a la Hitchcock.

**Birdy** (1984): Story of two friends, one obsessed with birds and flight.

**Black Dynamite** (2009): Hilarious and delightful parody of/homage to 1970s blaxploitation films.

**The Black Stallion** (1979): Adaptation of Farley Mowatt's novel is one of the best and most beautiful children's films ever made.

**Black Swan** (2010): Crazy ballerina psychodrama.

**Blazing Saddles** (1974): Mel Brooks' Western spoof could never be made today.

**Bloodsport** (1988): Jean-Claude Van Damme competes in a fight tournament, unencumbered by plot or characterization.

**Blue Velvet** (1986): David Lynch's peek at the seedy underbelly of suburbia.

**Boiling Point** (1993): Underrated mystery/thriller with Wesley Snipes and Dennis Hopper.

**Das Boot** (1981): Unbearably tense story of the crew of a German U-boat. See the uncut, undubbed version if you can.

**Brazil** (1985): Terry Gilliam's masterpiece is a blackly comical dystopia that looks more relevant with each passing year.

**Bring Me the Head of Alfredo Garcia** (1974): Crazed Sam Peckinpah thriller about the quest to collect a large reward for a severed head. One of cinema's best titles.

**The Brood** (1979): David Cronenberg classic about fractured families and body mutations.

**The Brother From Another Planet** (1984): Low-key, likable film about a mute alien and his interactions with the people he meets.

**Brotherhood of the Wolf** (2001): A savage beast and savage aristocracy prey on peasants. Not much for historical accuracy, but who cares.

**Cabaret** (1973): Musical set in a decadent German nightclub as the Nazis gain power. At times chilling, and always entertaining.

**The Cabin in the Woods** (2012): Marvelous, humorous deconstruction of horror film tropes.

**The Cabinet of Dr. Caligari** (1920): Hugely influential German silent film whose look and feel has been often emulated but never quite duplicated.

**Candyman** (1992): Urban-legend horror adapted from a story by Clive Barker, with remarkable lead performances by Virginia Madsen and Tony Todd.

**Casablanca** (1942): Classic film of romance, intrigue, and wartime sacrifice. If you haven't seen it yet, rectify this situation immediately.

**Cathy's Curse** (1977): One of the worst horror films I have ever seen (and that's saying a lot). Enjoy it with a cocktail or two for guaranteed giggles.

**Un Chien Andalou** (1929): Surreal Luis Bunuel film with its notorious eyeball scene.

**The City of Lost Children** (1995): Oddball French fantasy about a man who cannot dream, and who kidnaps children so he can experience their dreams.

**A Clockwork Orange** (1971): Unsettling Stanley Kubrick adaptation of the Anthony Burgess novel, with an iconic look and a fabulous lead performance by Malcolm McDowell.

**Closet Land** (1991): Alan Rickman and Madeleine Stowe in what is essentially a two-person play that's a metaphor for political oppression.

**Clue** (1985): Adaptation of the board game (yes, that's right); extremely quotable and far more successful than it has any right to be, thanks mostly to a stellar cast headed by Tim Curry.

**Con Air** (1997): Ridiculous and highly entertaining thriller featuring prisoners taking over a plane.

**The Crow** (1994): Brandon Lee's last film; he plays a musician back from the dead to avenge the murder of himself and his fiancée.

**Dark City** (1998): Noir mystery meets "what is reality?" film.

**Dark Star** (1974): Low-budget sci-fi effort from John Carpenter and Dan O'Bannon.

**Daughters of Darkness** (1971): Female vampires seduce their prey; possibly the only film with fades to red rather than to black.

**The Day of the Locust** (1975): Vicious satire of the early days of Hollywood features a hallucinatory scene of riot and mayhem. Based on Nathanael West's novel.

**Days of Wine and Roses** (1962): A couple's descent into alcoholism makes for gripping viewing, particularly if you only know Jack Lemmon from comedies.

**Dead Alive** (1992): Peter Jackson's zombie gorefest is also a sweet romance. Dialogue highlight: "Your mother ate my dog!"

**Dead Ringers** (1988): Jeremy Irons as twin gynecologists who are plenty creepy **before** they become mentally unhinged.

**Deep Red** (1975): Non-supernatural giallo from Dario Argento is intriguing, effective, intelligent, and creepy.

**Dirty Harry** (1971): Tense, effective thriller with Clint Eastwood as a cop trying to stop a Zodiac-like serial killer.

**Dr. Strangelove or: How I Learned to Stop Worrying and Love the Bomb** (1964): Blackly comic satire of Cold War brinksmanship, most famous for Peter Sellers in three roles.

**La Dolce Vita** (1960): Federico Fellini's portrayal of a society bent on the search for empty pleasure.

**Drowning by Numbers** (1988): Strangely playful Peter Greenaway film about three women, all with the same name, who all drown their husbands.

**Ed Wood** (1994): Tim Burton's biopic of Edward D. Wood, Jr., the man some call the worst director of all time.

**The Elephant Man** (1980): David Lynch-directed story of John Merrick is one of the director's most human and beautiful films.

**The Emperor's New Groove** (2000): Delightfully silly Disney film about a South American monarch who's turned into a llama.

**Enter the Dragon** (1973): Bruce Lee film that brought martial arts movies to the consciousness of middle America. Deftly parodied in the "Fistful of Yen" segment in *The Kentucky Fried Movie* (see below).

**Evil Dead 2: Dead by Dawn** (1987): Second film in Sam Raimi's *Evil Dead* series is a deft mix of humor and horror.

**Eyes Without a Face** (1960): Haunting film about a surgeon determined to restore the beauty of his daughter's scarred face.

**A Face in the Crowd** (1957): A radio personality's transformation into a demagogue; has an astonishing lead performance by Andy Griffith, and is more relevant today than ever before.

**Face/Off** (1997): Bonkers John Woo film with John Travolta and Nicolas Cage assuming each other's bodies and identities.

**Fear No Evil** (1981): Ridiculous but somehow compelling story about a teenage Antichrist and the angels in disguise who must defeat him.

**Fearless** (1993): Jeff Bridges survives a horrifying plane crash and loses both his fear of death and his connection to the people in his life.

**The 5,000 Fingers of Dr. T** (1953): Bizarre fantasy written by the one and only Dr. Seuss.

**The Fly** (1986): David Cronenberg's take on what happens when a man and a fly combine their DNA is scary, gory, and surprisingly affecting.

**Fortress** (1992): Excellent B-movie fun with Christopher Lambert trying to escape an inescapable prison and reunite with his wife.

**The French Connection** (1971): Cold and gritty suspense from the 1970s, when they knew how to do this sort of thing and do it well.

**Frenzy** (1972): One of Alfred Hitchcock's last films is definitely his most brutal one, with ghoulish gallows humor and a disturbing rape scene.

**F/X** (1986): A special effects artist is hired to help fake a political assassination, and things go awry.

**The Game** (1997): Story of an asshole rich guy caught up in reality games is like a weird adaptation of *A Christmas Carol.*

**Gladiator** (2000): Russell Crowe up against a decadent Roman emperor. Vastly entertaining if not historically accurate.

**Glen or Glenda?** (1953): Ed Wood's quasi-autobiographical film about transvestites is notable for dime-store surrealism and Bela Lugosi's narration.

**The Gods Must Be Crazy** (1980): A discarded Coke bottle causes discord in a Kalahari Desert tribe, and one of the tribesmen goes on a quest to return it to the gods. Utterly delightful.

**The Golden Voyage of Sinbad** (1973): Enjoyable adventure taken to the next level by some of Ray Harryhausen's best work and by Tom Baker as the lead villain.

**Goldeneye** (1995): The first and best of Pierce Brosnan's outings as James Bond has a post-Cold War setting and Sean Bean dying (again).

**The Good, the Bad, and the Ugly** (1966): Classic Sergio Leone Western.

**The Great Race** (1965): Rivalry between daredevil drivers Tony Curtis and Jack Lemmon turns into slapstick worldwide race.

**The Grifters** (1990): Nasty noir in this adaptation of the novel by the always underrated Jim Thompson.

**Guardians of the Galaxy** (2014): Arguably the funniest of the Marvel movies, guaranteed to get you in touch with your inner twelve-year-old.

**Hannah and Her Sisters** (1986): One of Woody Allen's best, about the lives and relationships of three sisters.

**A Hard Day's Night** (1964): If one needed proof of how effortlessly likable and charming the Beatles were, here it is.

**Harold and Maude** (1971): Love story between a 20-year-old man obsessed with death and an 80-year-old woman obsessed with life.

**The Haunting** (1963): A group investigates a haunted house and get much more than they bargained for. A black-and-white classic with iconic performances and imagery.

**Haxan: Witchcraft Through the Ages** (1922): Silent-era documentary on witchcraft. Some editions feature narration by William S. Burroughs.

**Heavenly Creatures** (1994): Peter Jackson proved he was capable of much more than entertaining gorefests with this story of two adolescent girls and their strange, imaginative bond.

**Heavy Metal** (1981): Half eyeroll-inducing juvenilia, and half excellent setpieces.

**Henry: Portrait of a Serial Killer** (1986): Well-made but deeply disturbing film about a man who's a methodical, casual murderer. With a standout performance by Michael Rooker.

**The Hidden** (1987): Better-than-it-should-be movie about an alien parasite that's being hunted by two policemen.

**The Hitcher** (1986): Rutger Hauer is a maniacal hitcher and C. Thomas Howell is the driver who shouldn't have picked him up. Not as violent as one would think but plenty unsettling.

**The Incredible Melting Man** (1977): Inept movie somehow is still effective through the use of thoroughly disgusting makeup effects.

**Industrial Symphony No. 1** (1990): Concert by David Lynch and Angelo Badalamenti (and featuring Julee Cruise) is an excellent companion to *Twin Peaks* and *Wild at Heart*.

**Inferno** (1978): Sequel to *Suspiria* is disappointing as a whole but has its moments.

**Inglourious Basterds** (2009): Alternate history of World War II as only Quentin Tarantino can do it. The movie that introduced America to the awesomeness that is Christoph Waltz.

**The Iron Giant** (1999): Someday I will make it through this movie without crying ... someday.

**Jason and the Argonauts** (1953): Ray Harryhausen's effects bring the fun in this story from Greek myths. Highlight is the skeleton fight sequence.

**Jennifer** (1978): Ripoff of *Carrie* involves a girl with power over deadly snakes.

**Johnny Got His Gun** (1971): Utterly depressing story of a World War I soldier who's lost his limbs, face, sight, and hearing. The fantasy sequences don't always work but it's still a powerful film, clips of which appeared in Metallica's "One" video.

**The Karate Kid** (1984): Wax on, wax off! Picked-on kid becomes a karate black belt. Nice triumph-of-the-underdog story.

**The Kentucky Fried Movie** (1977): Dated but still funny satire that takes on everything from *Enter the Dragon* to courtroom dramas to TV commercials.

**Kill Bill** (2003): Quentin Tarantino revenge saga.

**The Killer** (1989): John Woo's classic stars Chow Yun Fat as a hired killer trying to make amends.

**Koyaanisqatsi** (1982): The title is a Hopi Indian word for "life out of balance." Scenes of nature are juxtaposed with scenes of civilization, accompanied by Philip Glass' classic score.

**Lawrence of Arabia** (1962): Find in the dictionary next to "magnificent, epic film-making."

**Leon/The Professional** (1994): When Natalie Portman (in her debut) runs afoul of corrupt DEA agents, only assassin-for-hire Jean Reno can save her. Seek out the longer, European cut.

**Let the Right One In** (2008): Story of love and friendship between a bullied boy and a vampire girl.

**License to Kill** (1989): Second and last of Timothy Dalton's underrated turn as James Bond is uneven but has some great scenes and surprisingly nasty violence.

**Liquid Sky** (1982): Aliens prey on pretentious New York fashion/art world junkies. Title is a slang term for heroin. Featuring the amazing song "Me and My Rhythm Box."

**Little Shop of Horrors** (1986): Wonderful musical about carnivorous plants from outer space and sadistic dentists.

**The Lost Weekend** (1945): Writer battles alcoholism. Makes me happy that caffeine is my preference.

**M** (1931): Peter Lorre as a child murderer hunted by both police and criminals.

**The Magic Christian** (1969): Messy but occasionally hilarious satire on wealth starring Peter Sellers and Ringo Starr.

**The Man Who Would Be King** (1975): Michael Caine and Sean Connery as British soldiers out for a bit of glory for themselves.

**The Mangler** (1995): Amusingly terrible Stephen King adaptation with a better-than-the-movie-deserves performance by Ted Levine.

**Manos: The Hands of Fate** (1966): Legendarily terrible movie about a family that meets up with weird cultists; its biggest crime is how deeply boring it is in its non-*Mystery Science Theater 3000* version.

**The Mask** (1994): Jim Carrey gets a mask that turns him into a human cartoon. With lots of homages to Tex Avery's animation.

**Masque of the Red Death** (1964): One of the few Edgar Allan Poe adaptations to get things right, primarily due to Vincent Price's malevolent protagonist and Nicolas Roeg's gorgeous cinematography.

**Maximum Overdrive** (1986): Machines turn on people in Stephen King's directorial debut. First 20 minutes are excellent, then it turns into a colossal mess.

**May** (2002): Angela Bettis is a revelation as a lonely woman who just wants to make a friend.

**Monty Python Live at the Hollywood Bowl** (1982): Concert film of the Pythons is also an excellent sampler of some of their funniest bits.

**Much Ado About Nothing** (2012): Joss Whedon and a bunch of his friends put on a play in Whedon's backyard, and it's one of the best Shakespeare adaptations (of course, it helps when your friends include Amy Acker, Alexis Denisof, Clark Gregg, and Nathan Fillion).

**Mulholland Drive** (2001): David Lynch's story of Hollywood, thwarted love, and fluid identities is captivating, in no small part because of Naomi Watts' astonishing performance.

**The Muppet Christmas Carol** (1992): It has muppets, Michael Caine in an excellent performance, meta references, humor, and ridiculously catchy songs (written by Paul Williams). It's also one of the most faithful adaptations of the story.

**The Music Lovers** (1970): Crazed, unsettling biographical film of Tchaikovsky, done as only Ken Russell can.

**Naked Lunch** (1991): Blend of William S. Burroughs biography and an adaptation of his most famous novel.

**O Lucky Man!** (1973): Uneven but occasionally brilliant social satire by Lindsay Anderson.

**O.C. and Stiggs** (1985): Disjointed comedy is despised by many but I found it funny. Includes music by King Sunny Adé.

**Office Space** (1999): Close-to-home satire of white-collar workplaces will ring true for many people.

**One Flew Over the Cuckoo's Nest** (1975): Classic story of nonconformity set in a mental institution. It's (justifiably) famous for Jack Nicholson's performance but the supporting cast is fantastic as well.

**Orca** (1977): *Jaws* ripoff featuring a killer whale out for revenge against the people who killed his mate. Includes an overqualified cast and a score by Ennio Morricone.

**Orgy of the Dead** (1965): The damned souls of strippers do their routines. Script by Ed Wood Jr. includes the classic line: "Torture! Torture! It pleasures me!"

**Pacific Rim** (2013): A giant monsters vs. giant robots film to delight the young and the young-at-heart.

**Pandora's Box** (1928): Silent film icon Louise Brooks is truly luminous and captivating as Lulu, a woman whose very presence causes men to self-destruct.

**Parents** (1988): Creepy and darkly hilarious horror/satire about the 1950s and cannibalism.

**Peeping Tom** (1960): Terrifying study of obsession, voyeurism, and murder.

**Phantasm** (1979): Low-budget but effective horror tale of mysterious goings-on at the local mortuary. Some nicely surreal imagery.

**Picnic at Hanging Rock** (1975): Unsettling story of the disappearance of some young women at a rock formation in Australia.

**Plan 9 From Outer Space** (1959): The classic so-bad-it's-good film of alien invasion and zombie resurrection.

**Poltergeist** (1982): Effects-heavy tale of demons haunting an ordinary suburban home.

**Prince of Darkness** (1987): Occasionally silly but for the most part quite creepy John Carpenter film. The "transmission" sequences alone will haunt your dreams.

**Quatermass and the Pit** (1967): Underground workmen unearth a spaceship and much more.

**Raising Arizona** (1987): Coen Brothers comedy about an infertile couple who steal a baby.

**The Rapture** (1991): Mimi Rogers is a born-again Christian whose faith is put to the test in unexpected ways when the Apocalypse arrives. The end is quietly devastating.

**Ratatouille** (2007): Tale of a rat who loves to cook is a tribute to foodies and artists everywhere.

**Red Rock West** (1993): Neo-noir featuring a surprisingly subtle Nicolas Cage.

**Repo Man** (1984): A disaffected punk becomes a repo man and runs afoul of aliens and government conspiracy. Soundtrack features Black Flag, Iggy Pop, and others.

**Resurrection** (1980): Affecting tale of a woman who gains the power to heal after a near-death experience.

**Return of the Living Dead** (1985): One of the better blends of humor and horror, as punk rockers battle zombies. Excellent soundtrack including 45 Grave, Roky Erickson, and The Cramps.

**Return to Oz** (1985): Sequel to *The Wizard of Oz* is strange, downright frightening, and much more faithful to the L. Frank Baum books than its more famous predecessor. Will most likely scare the crap out of young kids.

**The Right Stuff** (1983): Enthralling story of the Mercury Seven astronauts.

**The Ring** (2002): Chilling horror tale of a cursed videotape that kills the viewer in seven days after it's watched.

**Robocop** (1987): Brutally violent and wickedly satirical view of a near-future when only cyborgs can stop rampant crime.

**Robot Monster** (1953): Endearingly amateurish tale of alien invasion. Best known as "the one where the monster is a man in a gorilla suit with a diving helmet and antennae on his head."

**Romper Stomper** (1992): A young Russell Crowe stars in this story of Australian white-power skinheads.

**Rumble in the Bronx** (1995): Jackie Chan fights street gangs and corrupt businessmen in the Bronx, which looks a lot like Vancouver.

**Santa Sangre** (1989): Insane Alejandro Jodorowsky film about a young man raised in a circus, scarred by tragedy, who becomes his mother's assistant in murder.

**Serenity** (2005): Even cancellation can't stop the signal, as the *Firefly* crew take on the Alliance.

**Seven Samurai** (1954): Classic by Akira Kurosawa is the tale of samurai who join forces to defend a small village from marauding bandits.

**Shallow Grave** (1994): Three roommates acquire a bag full of drug money, and things go very badly very quickly.

**Shock Corridor** (1963): Sam Fuller drama about a reporter who goes undercover at a mental hospital is even crazier than you'd expect.

**Sid and Nancy** (1986): Alex Cox's film portrays the doomed romance between Sid Vicious and Nancy Spungeon. With an electrifying performance by Gary Oldman as Sid.

**Singin' in the Rain** (1952): Delightful musical set in Hollywood as movies made the transition from silent to sound. Thoroughly enjoyable, even if you don't like musicals.

**Skyfall** (2012): Arguably Daniel Craig's best outing as James Bond has the superspy as a damaged, fallible man.

**Slaughterhouse Five** (1972): Surprisingly successful adaptation of Kurt Vonnegut's novel about a man "unstuck in time."

**Soldier** (1998): Kurt Russell turns in an excellent, underrated performance as a futuristic super-soldier who's not quite as obsolete as his superiors think.

**Some Like it Hot** (1959): Classic comedy about two musicians who witness a gang execution and hide out in an all-female band.

**Splash** (1984): Fun romp about the love between a man and a mermaid, with a scene-stealing John Candy.

**Stalker** (1979): Hypnotic, enigmatic Russian science fiction, directed by Andrei Tarkovsky. Images from this will stay with you for a long time, and it's even more relevant in our post-Chernobyl world.

**The Stunt Man** (1980): A fugitive from justice poses as a stunt man in a film with an increasingly maniacal director.

**Super Infra-Man** (1975): Utterly crazy film about a dragon princess and her army of monsters, who can only be defeated by one super martial arts fighter.

**Tank Girl** (1995): Flawed but entertaining comic-book movie, with a young, brunette Naomi Watts as Jet Girl.

**Tetsuo: The Iron Man** (1989): A salaryman runs over a metal fetishist, and things get weird.

**There Will Be Blood** (2007): Paul Thomas Anderson's epic character study of an oil baron who gains the world and loses his soul.

**The Thing** (1982): John Carpenter's tense movie about a group of Antarctic researchers pitted against a shape-shifting alien; Rob Bottin's effects are still shocking today.

**Thriller: A Cruel Picture** (1973): Story of a mute girl who seeks revenge after being forced into prostitution is half art film, half exploitation trash.

**Titus** (1999): Julie Taymor's highly stylized adaptation of *Titus Andronicus* goes overboard but is always visually interesting.

**Time After Time** (1979): Charming film with H. G. Wells time-traveling to modern San Francisco to pursue Jack the Ripper.

**Total Recall** (1990): Arnold Schwarzenegger gets his ass to Mars. Fun, violent hijinks ensue.

**Tucker and Dale Vs. Evil** (2010): Tyler Labine and Alan Tudyk as two nice backwoods guys mistaken for evil hillbillies by some college kids.

**Unforgiven** (1992): Clint Eastwood Western about the toll revenge takes on everyone.

**Urotsukidoji: Legend of the Overfiend** (1989): If you must watch a tentacle-rape *hentai*, this one is your best bet.

**The Usual Suspects** (1995): Knowing who Keyser Soze is doesn't make this movie any less effective or enjoyable.

**Videodrome** (1983): You know how your mom said too much TV would rot your brain? She was right.

**What Dreams May Come** (1998): Visually stunning film about the afterlife is hampered by an unnecessarily convoluted story and a miscast Robin Williams. Based on the novel by Richard Matheson.

**What Ever Happened to Baby Jane?** (1962): Dark side of Hollywood and sibling rivalry.

**What's Up, Tiger Lily?** (1966): Woody Allen takes an outlandish Japanese spy movie and dubs over it with his own dialogue. Uneven but often amusing.

**When Dinosaurs Ruled the Earth** (1970): It's got cavemen, dinosaurs, and giant crabs. What else could you ask for?

**Who Framed Roger Rabbit?** (1988): Amazing blend of live action and animation in a cartoon/film noir setting.

**The Wicker Man** (1973): Uptight policeman investigates a child's disappearance and runs afoul of neo-pagans. Featuring Christopher Lee's best performance.

**The Wild Bunch** (1969): Brutal, magnificent Sam Peckinpah Western.

**The Witch Who Came from the Sea** (1976): Weird psychodrama about an emotionally damaged woman who kills men with a razor.

**Young Frankenstein** (1974): Mel Brooks' hilarious take on the Frankenstein films is a loving tribute as well as a spoof.

**Zardoz** (1974): Batshit insane futuristic sci-fi/fantasy with Sean Connery in a red diaper, a flying stone head, and Charlotte Rampling being sexy. Worth watching for dialogue like: "The gun is good, the penis is evil."

**Zentropa** (1991): Hypnotic Lars Von Trier film about an American in post-World War II Germany whose involvement with a femme fatale gets him in way over his head in more ways than one.

**Zodiac** (2007): Story of the (fruitless?) hunt for the Zodiac killer. An excellent character study and tale of the toll obsession takes.

Feel free to share your movie recommendations with me! Drop me a line at smitepublications@gmail.com or follow me on Twitter at @Kelly_Cozy

# About the author

Kelly Cozy is a lifelong movie geek, and when she isn't watching movies, cooking, or attending conventions, she writes fiction. Her novels include *The Day After Yesterday, Undertow,* and the *Ashes* suspense series.

She plans on publishing *A Nerd Girl's Guide to Cinema 2* in 2019.

She lives in California with her husband, son, and cats.

**Visit her on Facebook:** Kelly Cozy, Author

**Subscribe to her email newsletter:** kellycozy.blogspot.com/p/subscribe-to.html

www.ingramcontent.com/pod-product-compliance
Lightning Source LLC
LaVergne TN
LVHW061217060426
835508LV00014B/1333